James Mann

ABOUT FACE

James Mann, author of *Beijing Jeep*, is a diplomatic correspondent and foreign affairs columnist for the Washington bureau of the *Los Angeles Times*. He served as the paper's Beijing bureau chief from 1984 to 1987. In the years since then, he has covered all aspects of U.S.–China relations. From 1996 to 1997, he was a guest scholar at the Woodrow Wilson International Center for Scholars. He has won an Asian Pacific Award and the New York Public Library Helen Bernstein Book Award for Excellence in Journalism. He lives in Silver Spring, Maryland.

ALSO BY JAMES MANN

Beijing Jeep

ABOUT FACE

ABOUT FACE

*A History of America's
Curious Relationship with China,
from Nixon to Clinton*

JAMES MANN

VINTAGE BOOKS

A Division of Random House, Inc.

New York

FIRST VINTAGE BOOKS EDITION, FEBRUARY 2000

The Library of Congress has cataloged the Knopf edition as follows:
Mann, James, [date]
About face : a history of America's curious relationship with China, from Nixon to Clinton /
James Mann. — 1st ed.
p. cm.
Includes bibliographical references and index.
ISBN 0-679-45053-X (alk. paper)
1. United States—Foreign relations—China. 2. China—Foreign relations—United States.
3. United States—Foreign relations—1945–1989. 4. United States—Foreign relations—1989–
I. Title.
E183.8.C5M319 1998 98-6285
327.73051—dc21
CIP

Vintage ISBN: 0-679-76861-0

www.vintagebooks.com

Printed in the United States of America
10 9 8 7 6 5 4 3

For Caroline

Contents

A section of photographs follows page 214

ABOUT FACE

Prologue

I N THE GLOOM OF AN empty restaurant, Winston Lord looked and
sounded depressed. He had visited Beijing for nearly 15 years, always as
an honored guest. Now, he was for the first time living in China, and the
country seemed profoundly different from the one Lord first encountered in the days when he played the role of Henry Kissinger's one-man
Rosencrantz and Guildenstern.

It was the beginning of 1986. Lord had arrived a few weeks earlier to
take up his new job as American ambassador to China. He was sitting
over lunch in Maxim's, a new Beijing restaurant opened by the French
fashion designer, Pierre Cardin, as a replica of the Paris original. Maxim's
interior included gilded doors, ornate mirrors, plush carpets, dark wood
furnishings—almost everything but Chinese customers. For that matter,
on this gray, chilly afternoon, there weren't many non-Chinese diners,
either.

Lord had been invited by two American correspondents who wanted
to talk about China, the country they were covering. But the new
ambassador seemed to be having trouble making much of a connection
with his new environs. Outside, the Beijing winter was closing in: The
days were sunless, the air heavy with soft-coal grime. Inside, Lord
returned the conversation again and again, wistfully, to the familiar territory of the America he had just left. The Mets, his favorite baseball team,
had just finished their best season in 16 years, and the team's prospects for
the coming year were bright.

Starting the new job in China was something of an anticlimax for
Lord. He had been one of only three staff aides to accompany Henry
Kissinger on Kissinger's secret mission to Beijing for Richard Nixon in
1971. Just before the Pakistani plane carrying the party had crossed into

Chinese territory, Lord, the youngest member of the group, had rushed to the front of the plane. By doing so, he had been able to brag that he had been the first American official to visit China since the founding of the People's Republic in 1949.

Lord had been present, too, during President Nixon's meeting with Mao Tsetung the following year. Kissinger had furtively brought him along to take notes. Lord was thus the only American in the room with Mao besides Nixon and Kissinger; he occupied a seat that might otherwise have been taken by Secretary of State William Rogers, Kissinger's adversary within the Washington bureaucracy. When the pictures of that historic meeting had been released to the world, Lord's face was cropped out; Kissinger didn't want to remind the secretary of state that he had lost his seat to a 34-year-old functionary. The following year, in a gesture of kindness, Chinese officials had quietly presented Lord with his own, uncropped copy of the picture.

Accompanying Kissinger, Lord had returned to Beijing several times during the Nixon and Ford administrations. Afterward, he worked in New York City as president of the prestigious Council on Foreign Relations, always waiting for a chance to return to government. Even after Ronald Reagan had nominated him as ambassador to China in 1985, he had been forced to wait a little longer. Senator Jesse Helms had held up the vote on Lord's confirmation for several months, until Reagan promised Helms in writing to cut off all American help for the United Nations agency that supported population control in China.

Like most other American officials, Lord had come to know China only on brief visits. American delegations would stop in Beijing for two or three days, with a full itinerary. They were lodged at Diaoyutai, the Chinese state guest house, or in one of the well-guarded downtown hotels for foreigners. They spent their days in meetings with senior Chinese officials and their evenings at banquets. Their trips were a series of rituals. After a couple of days and a bit of sightseeing, they either resolved or smoothed over conflicts with Chinese officials. Finally, the American visitors would hold a press conference at which they would exaggerate the points of agreement and minimize the differences between the United States and China, and then depart for the airport. The China they saw on these brief trips was gracious, orderly, controlled and resolute.

Now, Lord was beginning to deal with day-to-day China, the country that endured before and after the excitement and artificiality of the occasional visits by American presidents and secretaries of state. It was a more frustrating place. The bureaucracy was pervasive. American officials, even the U.S. ambassador, didn't get the sort of treatment reserved for short-term visitors from Washington. Everything moved more slowly. The promises made on the high-level trips weren't always carried out.

Finally, after the waiters at Maxim's had delivered the coffee, the new American ambassador turned the conversation from baseball to China itself. Awkward and formal with strangers, Lord was groping to figure out some way in which he might make this lunch useful to his new assignment.

How can we come into contact with a younger generation in China, the sort of people who might be future leaders of the country? Lord asked the journalists. This was, he said, one of the things he most wanted to do during his time in China, something U.S. officials in Washington also wanted him to do.

A younger generation of Chinese leaders: Lord's question was mundane and yet startling.

In an interview many years later, Lord insisted that if he had been sent to any other country, he would have asked the same question.[1] He believed it was part of the job of an American ambassador to meet people on their way up, in or out of power, and to cultivate them in such a way that the United States could influence the future leadership of the country. It would have been the same in Brazil or Switzerland.

And yet China was not just any other country. Indeed, the relationship the United States had worked out with China's Communist Party leadership had been based on the unstated premise that China was unique, that it would not be subjected to the standards and principles applied to other countries. China was America's partner in fighting the Cold War; the United States secretly shared intelligence with Chinese officials and helped to arm the People's Liberation Army. For America's policymaking elite, China was considered a special relationship. The United States chided countries like South Korea and Taiwan about human rights abuses, but it refrained from similar criticism of China. In Washington, Soviet dissidents were often honored, sent personal messages and welcomed to the White House; Chinese dissidents were all but ignored.

In the decade and a half after Kissinger's secret mission of 1971, America had dealt with China almost exclusively from the top down. The people who counted above all were China's most senior leaders, Mao Tsetung, Chou Enlai and Deng Xiaoping, and their associates in the Defense Ministry and the Ministry of Foreign Affairs. This may have been a narrow base on which to build a relationship with a country of more than a billion people; but it had been crucial in achieving the ultimate American objective, which was China's cooperation with the United States and against the Soviet Union.

In the mid-1980s, at the time of Lord's arrival, China seemed to be changing, and the United States was trying to adapt its policy to suit the times. Deng was beginning to open up parts of the economy to market forces. On the streets of Beijing and Shanghai, Chinese were wearing new clothes with some color and flair. Residents of cities who had once owned only a bicycle were buying new consumer goods: telephones, television sets, refrigerators. The changes even seemed to reach some of the leaders: Deng's carefully selected successors, Communist Party Secretary Hu Yaobang and Premier Zhao Ziyang, were appearing in public in Western suits and ties.

Nevertheless, from the distance of Washington, American officials had trouble grasping exactly what was changing in China and what wasn't. During the mid-1980s, American policy toward China was based on a series of beliefs and assumptions, many of which turned out to be tragically inaccurate.

The first of these assumptions was that China's political system was being opened up and reformed along with its economic system. Deng Xiaoping's record as a political leader, both under Mao Tsetung and on his own, was that of a dedicated Leninist,[2] yet in Washington, this fact was usually overlooked or deemed inconvenient. After visiting Beijing in 1984, President Reagan referred to the country as "so-called Communist China," suggesting that its political structure had somehow been altered.[3] One of America's most widely recognized China scholars, A. Doak Barnett cf the Johns Hopkins University School of Advanced International Studies, proclaimed that the Politburo and its six-member Standing Committee, the institutions through which the Communist Party had ruled the country since 1949, didn't have much influence over policy anymore. "A new generation of leaders now manages policy making in both domestic and foreign affairs," Barnett wrote in the *New York Times*. "Most older leaders have been eased into the background."[4]

The second American assumption was that Deng Xiaoping was steadfastly in control of the changes to which Chinese society was being subjected. In the United States of the 1980s, Deng was often perceived as all-wise, all-powerful and all-knowing. In 1985, after its editor, Henry Grunewald, led a group of corporate advertisers on a visit to China, *Time* proclaimed Deng to be its Man of the Year.

Inside China itself, the picture looked considerably less harmonious. In 1985, the very year *Time* beatified Deng, there had been, for the first time, signs that his economic reform program was in trouble, inciting passions that were difficult to control. Price increases were imposed, then suspended. Citizens were encouraged to buy consumer goods, then told to stop doing so after massive purchases of foreign goods caused China's foreign-currency reserves to drop. Most important, the reforms were stirring a wave of political reactions and counterreactions. Chinese students launched small-scale demonstrations to protest corruption, inflation, privileges for high-ranking officials, and what was called Japanese exploitation of China. Some Communist Party leaders—led by Chen Yun, a party figure with nearly as much seniority as Deng—questioned the wisdom of moving toward a market economy.

The third assumption was that the warm relationship between China and the United States dating back to the Nixon-Kissinger era had become so firmly entrenched that it would and could endure. Chinese leaders might occasionally proclaim their independent foreign policy, but on the whole, it was thought, China was firmly aligned with the United States.

At one point in the late 1980s, Morton I. Abramowitz, head of the State Department's intelligence unit and one of the government's brightest and most respected officials, was asked to testify before Congress about American relations with China in the coming decade. Abramowitz assured Congress that there would be little change. "Political stability in Beijing will continue, and we expect no dramatic shifts in China's domestic or foreign policies for the foreseeable future," he asserted. "We do not anticipate major changes in either the political or the military dimensions of U.S.-China relations." [5]

Within barely a few years, these confident American assumptions would be proved wrong. The elderly Communist leaders whom Barnett had written off as increasingly irrelevant turned out to be powerful enough to force the dismissal of Hu Yaobang and Zhao Ziyang, the two younger party leaders being groomed as Deng's successors. When students and ordinary citizens massed on the streets of Beijing in 1989, Deng called in the army to remove them with terrorizing force, proving to all doubters that he was indeed an orthodox Leninist.

In the aftermath of the Tiananmen demonstrations and the breakup of the Soviet Union, Chinese foreign policy changed to the point where, by the mid-1990s, the United States was being characterized once again, as it had been in the 1950s, as the principal obstacle to the achievement of China's interests and ambitions. China was challenging American foreign policy both in Asia and the Middle East.

By that time, Winston Lord's hopes of transferring the Sino-American relationship of the 1970s to a new generation of Chinese leaders seemed quaintly out of place.

THE RELATIONSHIP between the United States and China established by Nixon, Kissinger and their successors in the Carter and Reagan administrations was, in many ways, the strangest, most extraordinary relationship America has had with any nation in this century. In the midst of America's Cold War ideological struggle against the Soviet Union, the United States formed a close partnership with China, a country whose leadership was no less dedicated to Leninist political principles than the leaders of Moscow. Washington proceeded to support, arm, share intelligence with and nurture the economy of a Chinese government it had previously attempted to overthrow.

It was a relationship beset with contradictions, a strategic marriage of convenience and the classic example of Kissinger's obsession with geopolitics. Two countries with fundamentally different political and economic systems worked together to defeat a third nation, the Soviet Union, perceived as a more immediate threat to themselves. Such an affiliation was hardly without precedent in American history; after all, the United States had joined hands with Stalin's Soviet Union during World War II.

The archives show that in private, some American leaders, particularly Nixon, could be candid about the regime they were dealing with. Talking in the Cabinet room of the White House three weeks before Kissinger's groundbreaking mission, Nixon said he felt Chinese leaders were "more dedicated to Communism than the Soviets," because China was at an earlier, lower stage of development.[6]

Yet in public, American leaders presented their new relationship with China as something different from and greater than their wartime association with Stalin. Washington's Cold War partnership was colored by romance and sentimentalism, a legacy of the American experience in China dating back to the trader ships and the missionaries. Americans wanted to believe, once again, that they were changing China.

There were other contradictions, too. During the 1970s and 1980s, the United States forged a network of societal ties with China far more extensive than with any other Communist nation—indeed, broader even than with Eastern European nations such as Poland, Hungary or Yugoslavia. Chinese students came to America by the tens of thousands, and American tourists visited China in still greater numbers. American companies did far more business in China than with any other Communist country.

Nevertheless, despite this web of contacts, America's governmental links with China were probably more secretive and more narrowly based than those with any other major nation in the world. The real business between Washington and Beijing was carried out by a remarkably small number of people, an elite group of U.S. officials often fearful of what might happen if Congress or the American public learned or thought too much about what the United States was doing with China or about the nature of the Chinese leadership.

For nearly two decades, these contradictions in American policy didn't seem to matter much. But after the tumultuous upheavals from 1989 to 1991, the contradictions became overwhelming. When Chinese rulers were willing to use troops to shoot citizens on the streets of its capital, then America's ties to Beijing could be justified only as geopolitics, not as a means of helping or changing the country. When the Soviet Union no longer posed a threat to China or the United States, then the original, strategic basis for the relationship with China evaporated, too. Small wonder that throughout most of the 1990s, Presidents George Bush and Bill Clinton attempted to come up with a new rationale and framework for American policy toward China. Bush tried, futilely, to preserve the old American relationship with Beijing, while Clinton fumbled in efforts to create something new.

The purpose of this book is to investigate the relationship the United States formed with China in the Nixon era; to examine how those ties developed in the late 1970s and 1980s; and to describe how the Cold War association then unraveled in the aftermath of the Tiananmen Square upheavals of 1989 and the collapse of the Soviet Union. What drove the two countries together? What happened between the leaders of the two countries, and what bargains were struck? Why and how did the relationship change so dramatically after 1989?

I first decided to write this history because, as a newspaper correspondent based in Beijing during the 1980s, I became intrigued by the extraordinarily secretive nature of the associations between the United States and China and by the contradictions raised by the Cold War partnership. Later, working in Washington in the late 1980s and the 1990s, I watched as year by year and sometimes week by week the ties between the two countries eroded and became more contentious. In Washington, China was transformed in the 1990s from a sideshow of American foreign policy, about which few questions were asked, into a preoccupation.

I had several other reasons for undertaking this historical examination. The first is simply that enough time has passed for greater perspective. Several worthy books have been written about the American opening to China, but they were published too early to take into account the Tiananmen Square period and the subsequent upheavals during the Bush and Clinton administrations.[7]

Moreover, many early accounts of the American opening were based, necessarily, on the information provided by U.S. officials themselves, particularly the memoirs of Kissinger, Nixon, Carter and his national security advisor, Zbigniew Brzezinski. However, over the past few years, a wealth of new material has come to light, providing information not included in these memoirs. Some of the other U.S. officials involved have written their own memoirs or are now willing to be interviewed. Documentary material of the period has been declassified, such as, for example, transcripts of some of the top-level meetings and Nixon's own handwritten notes before and during his trip to China in 1972. In addition, using the Freedom of Information Act, I obtained a classified history of U.S.-China relations done for the Central Intelligence Agency by the Rand Corporation; this study summarizes all of the high-level meetings between America and China from 1971 to 1985.[8]

Another reason for writing this book is that it may help to bring up to date the longer history of America's relationship with the world's most populous country. Over the past two centuries, U.S. attitudes to China have fluctuated between attraction and revulsion—such as, in this century, the romance and then disillusionment with Chiang Kai-shek's Nationalist China. In a sense, the quarter-century period from the Nixon opening through the late 1990s represented merely a new, modern-day swing of the cycle.

Yet this most recent swing had its own special qualities, infused with the unique characteristics of the Cold War. Virtually everything that took place in U.S. policy toward China after 1989 flowed directly from what happened during the two previous decades.

The weak hold on American public opinion that bedeviled President Bush in dealing with China was a direct consequence of the secretive, narrowly based, elitist nature of the U.S. relationship with the Chinese leadership worked out by Kissinger and his successors. The broad scope of the conflict between America and China after 1989—over Chinese students, over cultural exchanges, trade and economic ties—was an outgrowth of the extensive web of ties between the two societies over the previous two decades. So, too, the fears in the 1990s that China might become a military superpower were the mirror image of America's eagerness, during the previous two decades, to strengthen China's ability to resist the Soviet Union. Indeed, examining America's relations with China in the 1970s and 1980s provides some perspective on the Cold War itself; China became a crucial part of American strategy toward the Soviet Union.

Understanding America's conflicted dealings with China of the 1990s is impossible without knowing what happened in the last half of the Cold War—from the time of the Nixon administration until the

Tiananmen crackdown. And it is equally impossible to grasp and evaluate America's opening to China in the 1970s without looking at its consequences in the years beyond 1989. Each period is part of the same history; each one sheds light on the other.

The final reason for this book is that it may help illustrate how American foreign policy is made. Decisions about China were often reached in ways and under circumstances that do not conform to civics textbooks. American presidents, the State and Defense Departments, the CIA, Congress, the U.S. embassy in Beijing, economic and trade officials, leading American corporations, organized labor, the Republican and Democratic Parties, the government of Taiwan, Tibetan exiles, human rights groups, right-to-life organizations, Asian business leaders, the former British government in Hong Kong—all played a role, working with and against one another from issue to issue.

Within most administrations, intense infighting erupted among high-level officials and within executive-branch departments over how to deal with China. In theory, decisions should be part of a careful, deliberative process, carried out by the formal structures of the State Department and the White House, arriving at a unified judgment. In practice, the process of dealing with China was intensely personalized. Often, no more than one or two officials within an administration were entrusted to handle dealings with China. Sometimes, not even the secretary of state knew what was happening. The secret CIA study found that leaders in Beijing were often able to exploit or manipulate the differences in Washington, rewarding and flattering China's friends, instilling a sense of obligation, freezing out those U.S. officials who were considered less sympathetic.[9]

China policy demonstrated that Congress doesn't conform to the civics texts, either. In theory, Congress is a passive force on foreign policy, one that merely confirms appointments, enacts legislation, passes budgets and oversees the executive branch. But especially after 1989, Congress's involvement in China policy was far more pervasive. American decisions about Chinese students, grain sales, human rights, arms-control policies, business contracts and transfers of technology were not only influenced but, in some cases, initiated by Congress. In some cases, Congress was merely responding to American public opinion, at times when the executive branch was not. In other instances, individual congressmen, or staff members, were able to wield surprising power on their own initiative.

Ideas about how America should deal with China originated almost haphazardly. The military relationship during the final decade of the Cold War grew out of the work of a single idiosyncratic consultant who attracted the interest of patrons in the Pentagon. The congressional effort during the 1990s to use most-favored-nation benefits as the vehicle for seeking changes in China's human rights practices grew out of the casual meetings of a few Chinese students.

One limitation should be made clear: This book is a history of *American* policy toward China. That task is arduous enough. The book is not and does not attempt to be the full account of relations between America and China, because not nearly so much information is available about the Chinese government as about the American side. For example, I was able to learn, primarily through interviews, about the tensions within the Bush administration in February and June 1989 over dealing with the Chinese dissident Fang Lizhi. There were probably tensions within the Beijing government, too, but China's internal processes remain cloaked in secrecy. I once asked a Chinese ambassador whether I might interview him for this book. He replied with a careful smile, "You want to put me in jail?" Chinese archives are not available to outsiders. We await the work of some astute Chinese researcher who may be able some day to publish, for example, the internal memos that Lin Biao wrote to Mao Tsetung or that Hu Yaobang sent to Deng Xiaoping.

American policy itself was often shrouded in secrecy. The leaders of a new administration usually came to office without knowing much of what had transpired before their arrival. In some instances, such as the Carter and Reagan administrations, U.S. officials found themselves rummaging through old archives, trying to figure out what their predecessors had promised China and what they hadn't. (The Chinese made use of this American foible of changing governments every four or eight years, too: They sometimes told new administrations they had been secretly promised more than they actually had.)

The ultimate goal of this book is to explore, describe and interpret American policy toward China over the past quarter-century, in hopes that we may overcome our collective ignorance and see what has taken place in our very recent past.

CHAPTER ONE

Opening Moves

Aftrer nearly four years of dreaming, scheming and secret diplomacy, Richard Nixon was finally en route to China. On February 18, 1972, stopping in Hawaii on the first leg of his journey across the Pacific, the anxious president tried to relax. He and his wife were housed overnight in the residence of Brigadier General Victor Armstrong, commander of the First Marine Brigade at the Kaneohe Marine Corps Air Station. Although he found the commander's residence to be disappointingly drab, Nixon was too preoccupied to leave it, even for a quick drive around the island. For only five minutes, from 2:35 to 2:40 p.m., Nixon stepped out of doors in the gray, rainy weather to tour the grounds of the commander's residence. Otherwise, he sat inside, talking occasionally with his chief of staff, H. R. Haldeman, and with his national security advisor, Henry Kissinger. He ate breakfast and dinner alone with his wife, and had lunch by himself.[1]

He was contemplating his coming meetings with the leaders of China's Communist government, whom America had shunned for more than two decades. Nixon set down his thoughts. His handwritten notes, which are now declassified and in the National Archives, give new insight into the nature of what Nixon sought and how he viewed the diplomatic initiative that altered the course of the Cold War. Trying to reduce to barest essentials what the American and Chinese governments were trying to obtain from one another, he wrote:

What they want:
1. Build up their world credentials.
2. Taiwan.
3. Get U.S. out of Asia.

What we want:
1. Indochina (?) [2]
2. Communists—to restrain Chicom [Chinese Communist] expansion in Asia.
3. In Future—Reduce threat of a confrontation by Chinese Super Power.

What we both want:
1. Reduce danger of confrontation and conflict.
2. a more stable Asia.
3. a restraint on U.S.S.R.

Kissinger and other U.S. foreign policy and intelligence officials had attempted to give Nixon some insight into the nature of Mao Tsetung, the revolutionary leader and founding father of the People's Republic of China. No American official had met Mao for nearly a quarter-century. In Hawaii, Nixon jotted down this advice, too:

Treat him (as Emperor)
1. Don't quarrell [sic].
2. Don't praise him (too much).
3. Praise the people—art, ancient.
4. Praise poems.
5. Love of country.

Kissinger had even offered Nixon a way to find common cause with Mao, whose personality and experience were seemingly as different from Nixon's as they could possibly be. "RN and Mao, men of the people," Nixon wrote to himself; both he and Mao had had "problems with intellectuals." As an analogy, it was preposterously flimsy. Nixon couldn't begin to rival Mao as a popular figure in his own country. Moreover, despite Nixon's wellspring of resentments against American intellectuals, he had never subjected them to class struggle or forced them to raise pigs in the countryside, much as he might have liked to. Still, Nixon liked Kissinger's comparison so much that he wrote it down not once but twice.

It was not Mao but the underlying strategy of his China trip that dominated Nixon's thinking. Preparing what he would say to Mao and Premier Chou Enlai, Nixon came up with an idea that would have special resonance in China two decades later, after the end of the Cold War:

Your [China's] interests require two superpowers. Would be dangerous if [there was only] one.

Five days later, Nixon once again wrote down some notes to himself as he sat in the Diaoyutai State Guest House in Beijing preparing for private talks with Chou Enlai. His suggestion was that America was willing to make concessions on Taiwan in exchange for China's help in obtaining a peace settlement in Vietnam:

Taiwan = Vietnam = trade off.
1. Your people expect action on Taiwan.
2. Our people expect action on Vietnam.
    Neither can act immediately—But both are inevitable—Let us not embarrass each other.[3]

THE NIXON administration's opening to China has by now come to be taken for granted; it effectively banished from American foreign policy the unreality that had prevailed for the previous two decades, during which the United States pretended that Chiang Kai-shek's Nationalist regime on Taiwan was the legal government for the Chinese mainland.

Yet this shift was merely the starting point in Nixon's and Kissinger's multifaceted, often clandestine diplomacy with Beijing. The opening to China was accompanied by a series of bargains, negotiations and what Nixon privately referred to as a trade-off. Other recently declassified materials show that when the leaders of America and China sat down with one another, they began working together to shape the future of the rest of Asia, including Japan, the two Koreas and India. Indeed, the reality was that Nixon and Kissinger, Mao and Chou were not just reopening ties between America and China but were teaming up to determine the course of events elsewhere on the world's largest continent. They did so amid extraordinary secrecy, pledging that what China and the United States said to one another would not be disclosed to anyone else.

It is worth recalling the several ways in which America's foreign policy had been frozen at the time Nixon took office. In Asia, the United States was stuck with a China policy that obliged it to act as though Chiang and the other losers of the Chinese civil war were someday going to retake the mainland. The United States was enmeshed in a war in Vietnam that was costing up to 15,000 lives a year; Nixon had pledged during his presidential campaign to end the war, but had never made clear how he planned to do that. Moreover, America was locked in a Cold War against the Communist governments of the Soviet Union and China. In 1969, Americans perceived China to be the more threatening and hostile of the two; during the Kennedy and Johnson administrations, American officials sometimes talked about collaborating with the Soviet Union against China.[4]

Nixon's initiative was aimed at breaking all of these shackles and creating a world in which American foreign policy would have greater flexibility. It was also designed to increase Nixon's own political fortunes. In many ways, Nixon succeeded, but not without also making more compromises than he and Kissinger were eager to admit. He obtained some of the help he sought from China on the Vietnam War, but not nearly so much as he wanted; and it was not sufficient to bring about a lasting Vietnam peace settlement. For its part, China managed to win important concessions from the United States concerning Taiwan, yet these did not go far enough to enable it to regain control of the island.

CHINA'S EXPECTATIONS for Richard Nixon at the time he took office in 1969 were best expressed in a protest note it sent to American diplomats less than three weeks after Inauguration Day. With their usual penchant for political vituperation, the Chinese declared that Nixon and his predecessor, Lyndon Johnson, were "jackals of the same lair."[5]

China had no particular reason to believe Nixon would be any different from the Democratic presidents who preceded him. John Kennedy and Lyndon Johnson had occasionally talked about changing American policy toward China but did nothing, in part because of their fear of attack from the political right. Nixon himself had originally been one of the leaders of the conservative wing of his party; in the late 1940s, he depicted the Chinese Communist Party as simply a tool of the Soviet Union.

Since the time of Nixon's opening to China, most of the accounts of his changing views have begun with an article he wrote for *Foreign Affairs* in the fall of 1967, as he was preparing to run for the Republican nomination for president. Nixon himself had instructed his aides to point journalists to this article at the time of his 1972 trip to China. In *Foreign Affairs,* he asserted:

> Any American policy toward Asia must come urgently to grips with the reality of China. . . . Taking the long view, we simply cannot afford to leave China forever outside the family of nations, there to nurture its fantasies, cherish its hates and threaten its neighbors. There is no place on this small planet for a billion of its potentially most able people to live in angry isolation. . . . The world

cannot be safe until China changes. Thus, our aim, to the extent we can influence events, should be to induce change.[6]

Taken by itself, the article may not be as significant as has often been assumed. Nixon did not advocate any new diplomacy toward China. He did not propose U.S. recognition of Beijing or its admission to the United Nations. He maintained that in the short run, America's policy toward China should be one "of firm restraint, of no reward." Above all, the article could be discounted as merely serving the political needs of a presidential candidate who was, at the time, desperate to show that he had developed some fresh ideas since his earlier, unsuccessful race for the presidency.

However, interviews show that there had indeed been a fundamental and important shift in Nixon's thinking about China, one that emerged from and during his travels in Asia in the mid-1960s. The *Foreign Affairs* article was not the beginning of Nixon's transformation. Rather, it was the first written evidence of it.

Nixon had traveled through Asia in 1965 and again in 1967, visiting Southeast Asian countries and Vietnam, talking to foreign leaders and American diplomats. The accounts of U.S. officials who talked with him there are strikingly similar. In the midst of the Vietnam War, Nixon was reexamining some of the assumptions underlying American policy in Asia, including its commitment to Chiang Kai-shek and Taiwan.

In 1965, Roger Sullivan was head of the political section at the American embassy in Singapore when Nixon stopped there for a visit. Sullivan, assigned to serve as Nixon's control officer (the embassy official who makes arrangements for a visiting dignitary), recalls having a long conversation with Nixon in an airport VIP room. "He pretty well spelled out how we could reach a normal relationship with China, and said that was what we ought to do," recalls Sullivan, who later became one of the State Department's leading specialists on China.[7]

During that same trip, Nixon also stopped in Taipei, where he talked in his room at the Grand Hotel with Arthur W. Hummel Jr., deputy chief of mission at the American embassy. To Hummel's considerable surprise, Nixon asserted that Chiang Kai-shek's Nationalist regime would never achieve its dream of returning to the mainland. Therefore, he said, America's relations with the People's Republic of China would have to be improved. "He said that in the hotel room, with all the microphones in it," recalls Hummel, remembering that Taiwan's intelligence service was probably monitoring the conversation and reporting it back to Chiang.[8]

These reminiscences during the 1990s may conceivably have been colored by an awareness of Nixon's opening to Beijing. Yet there is also contemporaneous evidence of Nixon's quiet transformation, written by an American official who had no knowledge of what Nixon would later do. During a visit to India in 1967, Nixon talked with Ambassador Chester Bowles, questioning the underpinnings of American policy and strategy in the Cold War. Bowles quickly cabled back to Secretary of State Dean Rusk the substance of the conversation:

> The one somewhat offbeat concept which seemed to be on [Nixon's] mind involved our relationships with the Soviet Union and China. In his opinion we should "stop falling all over ourselves" to improve our relationships with Russia since this would "make better relationships with China impossible."
>
> On several occasions, he almost suggested that good relationships with China were more important than good relations with the Soviet Union. I disagreed with him strongly on this point, pointing out that the door to Moscow was ajar while the door to Peking was locked and bolted.[9]

While Nixon's evolving views ran contrary to the dogma of the American foreign policy establishment, they hardly qualified as thinking the unthinkable. The Senate Foreign Relations Committee had held hearings in 1966 on the need for a new China policy. During the 1968 campaign, Nixon's rival for the Republican nomination, Nelson Rockefeller, called for more "contact and communication" with China. The Democratic nominee, Hubert Humphrey, proposed "the building of bridges to the people of mainland China" and also advocated a partial lifting of the American trade embargo against China.[10]

Outflanking the Democratic opposition, and getting to China before the Democrats did, became one of the driving forces behind Nixon's initiative to Beijing. Politics and political credit were never far from his mind, and they constituted an even greater part of his secret diplomacy with China than has been realized.

At the same time, Nixon was also willing to take political risks, patiently and carefully nursing along the right wing of the Republican Party at each step. His contribution lay not merely in his recognition of the need for change, but in the political skill with which he developed and executed his new policy.

AT THE OUTSET of the new administration, it was by all accounts Nixon, not Kissinger, who seized the initiative on China. It was one of the subjects on his mind even during the transition period before he arrived in the White House. Vernon Walters, who was then serving as the army attaché at the American embassy in Paris, called on Nixon at the Pierre Hotel in New York City. According to Walters's memoirs, Nixon told him then that "among the various things he hoped to do in office was to manage to open the door to the Chinese Communists. . . . He felt it was not good for the world to have the most populous nation on earth completely without contact with the most powerful nation on earth." [11] In his own memoirs, Nixon says that at the time he interviewed Kissinger for his job as national security advisor, he asked Kissinger to read the *Foreign Affairs* article and spoke to him of the need to reevaluate America's China policy. [12]

In the earliest days of the Nixon White House, Kissinger wasn't thinking about China much, if at all. Alexander Haig, Kissinger's deputy at the National Security Council, recalls one telling episode a few weeks after the new administration took office in which Kissinger came back from a conversation with Nixon and confided, sarcastically, that the president wanted to normalize relations with China:

> [Kissinger] was the picture of a man taken unawares. . . . "Our Leader has taken leave of reality," he intoned in mock despair. "He thinks this is the moment to establish normal relations with Communist China. He has just ordered me to make this flight of fancy come true." He grasped his head in his hands. "China!" [13]

Kissinger himself gives somewhat grudging credit to Nixon in his memoirs: "He had thought up the China initiative (even though I had reached the same conclusion independently)." [14]

THE BEGINNINGS were undramatic. Nixon, before taking office, approved a resumption of the talks with China in Warsaw, the only channel of diplomatic communication between Washington and Beijing. The Warsaw talks had opened in 1955 as the vehicle for obtaining the release of American prisoners who were being held in China; they had occasionally attempted to settle other, larger issues, but without success. In the autumn of 1968, China, responding to an American overture, said it would be willing to resume the talks, probably because of its growing concern about the Soviet Union's invasion of Czechoslovakia that summer. But in the first weeks of Nixon's presidency, the Chinese called off the meeting to protest America's supposed role in the defection of a Chinese diplomat. [15] Officials at the State Department weren't surprised; that was, for China, typical behavior.

On February 1, 1969, Nixon told Kissinger in a written memo: "I think we should give every encouragement to the attitude that this Administration is 'exploring possibilities of raprochement [*sic*] with the Chinese.' " As Kissinger later noted, the memo didn't require him to do anything with China, merely to create an impression of doing so. Nevertheless, prompted by Nixon, Kissinger ordered an internal review of America's policy toward China.[16]

ANATOLY DOBRYNIN, the Soviet ambassador to Washington, wasn't given to the sort of rhetoric that had prompted China to call Nixon and Johnson "jackals of the same lair." Nevertheless, when it came to American policy toward China, Dobrynin, too, clearly believed the new Republican president would carry on the fundamental policies and strategies of the Johnson administration. During his early years in Washington, Dobrynin had come to expect that one of the few subjects on which the United States and the Soviet Union could find common ground was the danger from China.

The Johnson administration's viewpoint was best expressed in its handling of China's development of nuclear weapons. In 1964, in the final weeks before China's first nuclear test, Washington convened a series of top-level talks to decide whether to take unilateral military action to destroy China's nuclear installations. According to a memorandum by National Security Advisor McGeorge Bundy, Johnson met in the Cabinet room of the White House on September 15, 1964, with Bundy, Secretary of State Dean Rusk and Defense Secretary Robert McNamara, and decided against any preemptive strike against the Chinese nuclear facilities. Nevertheless, Bundy's memo continued:

> We believe that there are many possibilities for joint action with the Soviet Government if that Government is interested. . . . We therefore agreed that it would be most desirable for the Secretary of State to explore this matter very privately with Ambassador Dobrynin as soon as possible.[17]

Nothing came of the initiative; the Soviet leadership was, at the time, preoccupied with the internal power struggle that led to the overthrow of Nikita Khrushchev. Nevertheless, it exemplified American policy toward China in the years before Nixon took office. Moscow had been trained by prior experience to believe that in any conflict between the Soviet Union and China, Washington would side with the Soviets. That would prove to be a fundamental misreading of the new Nixon administration.

In March 1969, after the first in a series of border skirmishes broke out between Soviet and Chinese forces along the Ussuri River, Dobrynin raised the subject of the clashes with Kissinger, who repeated the conversation to Nixon, suggesting that the United States might gain in strategic terms from the Sino-Soviet conflict.

Shortly thereafter, the CIA reported another border clash, this one involving armor and artillery. "The results of the battle were apparent to our satellites," recalled former CIA Director Robert M. Gates in his memoirs. "One photo interpreter told us that after the battle, the Chinese side of the [Ussuri] river was so pockmarked by Soviet artillery that it looked like a 'moonscape.'" Afterward, Dobrynin sounded out Kissinger again. The Soviet ambassador "suggested that there was still time for the two superpowers to order events, but they might not have this power much longer," Kissinger later recalled.[18]

Dobrynin, apparently acting on orders from Moscow, thus inadvertently succeeded in attracting Kissinger's attention to China. (In his memoirs, written in 1995 with a quarter-century of hindsight, Dobrynin mourned: "Personally, I believed that we were making a mistake from the start by displaying our anxiety over China to the new administration.")[19] As the Sino-Soviet clashes intensified through the spring and summer, Kissinger became increasingly worried about the possibility that the Soviets would invade, defeat or intimidate China.

In August 1969, at Nixon's summer home in San Clemente, California, Nixon was briefed by Allen S. Whiting, a University of Michigan professor and former State Department intelligence specialist on China. Whiting highlighted the importance of U.S. intelligence reports that the Soviet Union was constructing airfields in Mongolia, redeploying bombers from Eastern Europe to bases in Central Asia and practicing air raids against Chinese targets. There was also a large buildup of Soviet forces in progress near China's borders.

Privately, Kissinger ordered the Defense Department, CIA and State Department to figure out what the United States should do if the Soviet Union attacked China. In public, the Nixon administration, increasingly nervous, sent out word that it was strongly opposed to any Soviet military action against China. Undersecretary of State Elliot Richardson, appearing before the American Political Science Association in New York on September 5, asserted that

> In the case of Communist China, longrun improvement in our relations is in our own national interest. . . . We could not fail to be deeply concerned with an escalation of this quarrel into a massive breach of international peace and security.[20]

By now the United States was, for the first time, beginning to side with China in its conflict with the Soviet Union. The stage was being set for Nixon's China initiative.

Even in these early days, Nixon was fully aware both of how an American overture to China would unsettle the Soviets, and also of the domestic politics involved in changing China policy. The archives of the Nixon administration show that, far more than has been realized, he was coordinating his earliest moves toward Beijing with the leaders of the old China lobby for Chiang Kai-shek, such as Representative Walter Judd of Minnesota and Senator Karl Mundt of South Dakota, and even with representatives of Chiang's Nationalist government. In a memo to Kissinger on September 22, 1969, Nixon wrote:

> I think that while [Soviet Foreign Minister Andrei] Gromyko is in the country would be a very good time to have another subtle move toward China made. I would suggest that when it is convenient you discuss the matter with Mundt and see whether he would be willing to have another move in that direction. On the same subject, I would like for you to see Walter Judd if he calls and asks for an appointment. Also, I want you to call in the Chinese Nationalist Ambassador and give him a little background.[21]

Nixon's memo was written at a time when the United States had not yet communicated once, even indirectly, with the Communist government in Beijing; it is a striking demonstration of how careful he was in cultivating the right wing even as he was beginning to undercut the old China policy it had fostered and was determined to preserve.

At the outset, Nixon and Kissinger were working with and through the State Department on China policy; Richardson's speech was one example of this. On overseas trips, Nixon left messages with other world leaders about his eagerness to talk to Chinese leaders, first with French President Charles DeGaulle in March and then, over the summer, with Pakistani President Yahya Khan and Romanian President Nicolae Ceauşescu. There were no immediate responses.

During the fall of 1969 and the early winter of 1970, the administration made its first serious attempt to establish direct talks with China. Nixon and Kissinger decided to reopen the long-frozen Warsaw talks. In September 1969, they ordered Walter Stoessel, the American ambassador in Poland, to contact his Chinese counterpart and ask for a new meeting.

To Kissinger's mounting irritation, Stoessel took nearly three months. Finally, on December 3, Stoessel saw Chinese Charge d'Affaires Lei Yang and his interpreter in the unlikely setting of a Yugoslav fashion show at Warsaw's Palace of Culture and followed them outside the building after the show. Lei Yang did not even turn around or acknowledge his presence. Speaking in Polish, Stoessel introduced himself to Lei's interpreter as the American ambassador and told him: "I was recently in Washington and saw President Nixon. He told me he would like to have serious, concrete talks with the Chinese." The Chinese interpreter listened, expressionless, and replied: "Good. I will report that." This brief, almost comical exchange was the first direct contact between the two governments since Nixon had come to the White House.[22]

What followed was the little-recognized first step in the Nixon opening to China. On January 20 and February 20, 1970, Stoessel and other State Department officials sat down with Lei Yang and his aides in Warsaw. These extraordinarily significant meetings enabled the United States and China to show one another that they were eager for change in the hostile relationship of the past. The United States made plain to China that it was willing to back away from two decades of policy concerning Taiwan and Chiang Kai-shek's government. At the same time, these Warsaw talks effectively ended the State Department's role in China policy; they paved the way for what became Kissinger's personalized diplomacy.

In January, Stoessel opened the talks by declaring, "It is my government's hope that today will mark a new beginning in our relationship." He offered a series of assurances designed to appeal to Beijing. Despite the ongoing war in Vietnam, he pledged that the Nixon administration's goal was "a reduced American military presence in Southeast Asia, which we recognize is near the southern borders of China."

The most important part of Stoessel's message, which had been carefully worked out with the White House, concerned Taiwan. Since 1949, the United States had steadfastly maintained that Chiang's regime was the legitimate government for all of China. Now, in these secret talks, the United States spoke of a possible settlement between Communists and Nationalists. Stoessel explained that while America would honor its commitments to defend Taiwan, "the United States position in this regard is without prejudice to any future peaceful settlement between your Government and the Government in Taipei." Moreover, Stoessel went on, "it is our hope" to reduce U.S. military deployments and installations on Taiwan "as peace and stability in Asia grow." A link was being drawn between the American presence on Taiwan and the Vietnam War; for the first time, the United States was suggesting that it might withdraw some of its forces from Taiwan in exchange for help in getting out of Vietnam.[23]

Stoessel offered the Chinese another olive branch. The Nixon administration, he said, would consider sending an emissary to Beijing or receiving a Chinese representative in Washington for "more thorough" talks. That seemingly innocuous offer was, at the time, also a startling proposal; for two decades, American and Chinese officials had met rarely, and only in Warsaw or international conferences like Geneva, where John Foster Dulles had famously refused to shake the hand of Chou Enlai.

At another Warsaw session in February, China embraced the Nixon administration's proposal—or, at least, the part of the proposal China liked the most. "If the U.S. Government wishes to send a representative of ministerial rank or a special envoy of the United States President to Peking . . . the Chinese Government will be willing to receive him," Lei told Stoessel. The alternative proposal of talks in Washington was dropped. You come to us, China was saying.

Thus was established for the first time the pattern that would be repeated for decades. China was willing to talk or negotiate, but on its own turf; and America, persuading itself that the setting didn't matter so much, was usually willing to accommodate China's desires.

At the February talks, the Nixon administration also took a small step further by changing the wording concerning Taiwan. A month earlier, Stoessel had said the United States "hoped" to draw down its forces there as tensions in Asia abated; this time, he declared that it was the Nixon administration's "intention" to do so.[24]

By this time, the State Department was becoming nervous about how fast things were moving. Led by Marshall Green, the assistant secretary of state for East Asia, State argued that nothing would come of higher-level talks, except that Taiwan and American allies from Japan to Australia would be unsettled. "The likelihood of success in achieving a genuine improvement in Sino-U.S. relations is small; the probability that the Chinese are interested in talks primarily for their impact on the Soviets is great; and the unsettling and potentially damaging impact on some of our friends and allies and their assessment of our China policy is substantial," the State Department told the White House in one memo.[25]

As a result, the Nixon administration dithered. The Warsaw talks were twice postponed. Preparing for the next meeting, State Department officials went to work drafting new language that could smooth over America's differences with China over Taiwan. As it turned out, however, their efforts were too early: There would be no further Warsaw meetings. On May 1 Nixon ended all prospects for immediate talks with China by sending American troops into Cambodia, an action that the State Department also opposed.

The die was now cast: Henceforth, Nixon and Kissinger would pursue their China policy on their own, clandestinely, treating the State Department as their adversary. They were establishing a pattern that was to be repeated in administration after administration: Dealing with China was special, kept apart from normal diplomatic and institutional processes.

Kissinger had already opened up covert channels to the Chinese through American intelligence, using CIA stations in Pakistan and Romania.[26] Other secret avenues were pursued through the American consulate in Hong Kong, the Pakistani and Romanian ambassadors in Washington, and Norway's ambassador in China, who happened to be a friend of Henry Cabot Lodge. "The feelers were out, a whole series of them," recalls James R. Lilley, then a CIA operative, later American ambassador to China.[27] After the invasion of Cambodia in May 1970, Nixon and Kissinger sent a message to China through another channel: Vernon Walters, the military attaché in Paris, who had already been conducting secret talks with the North Vietnamese. Despite the Cambodian invasion, the Chinese were told, the United States had no aggressive intentions in Indochina. If the Chinese were interested, the issues could be discussed, secretly, with Henry Kissinger.[28]

CHAPTER TWO

The Kissinger and Nixon Trips

O F ALL THE GOVERNMENTS in the world, India and Pakistan know the Chinese best. For them, China is not so much exotic as imposing; it is the unavoidable neighbor on whose huge house one always keeps an eye, whether as ally (in Pakistan's case) or as sometime adversary (for India). Diplomats from the subcontinent serve two, three or more tours of duty in Beijing and can compare it, in ways that Americans cannot, with the China of the 1950s or early 1960s. One of Pakistan's leading China specialists was Sultan Muhammed Khan.

In 1969, Khan returned to Pakistan after his second tour as ambassador to Beijing to assume a new position as foreign secretary. At the time, the situation in China was grim. Domestically, China was in the midst of the Cultural Revolution; abroad, it saw threats virtually all around its periphery.

"At the time, the Chinese were very depressed about Vietnam," Khan remembers. "They were worried about how long it would take for themselves to be involved in a war with the United States."[1] China was also in the midst of turmoil within its top leadership; in the summer of 1970, in a Central Committee meeting at Lushan, Chou Enlai and his allies emerged triumphant over the forces of Defense Minister Lin Biao, who seemed to be opposed to Chou's opening to the United States.

In October 1970, Khan and Pakistani President Yahya Khan (who are not related) traveled to the United States for the 25th anniversary of the founding of the United Nations. On Saturday, October 24, Yahya Khan was attending a White House dinner for more than 30 heads of state and government, when Nixon asked him to stop by the next day. That Sunday, the Pakistani president had one-on-one talks with Nixon. Although he didn't yet tell his foreign secretary, Yahya was given a message from the American president to pass on to Chinese leaders. "It is essential we open negotiations with China," Nixon's message said. "We will send a high-level emissary to Beijing." He also promised that the United States would not enter into a partnership with the Soviet Union against China, thus addressing China's deepest fear.[2]

As it happened, Yahya and his foreign secretary already had a trip planned to Beijing soon after Washington. Within a couple of weeks, the Pakistani president met, again one-on-one, with Chou Enlai in Beijing. Still, he said not a word to Sultan Muhammed Khan about what had been discussed.

As the two men were leaving China, the news broke of the massive cyclone that devastated what was then East Pakistan, the area that would later become the independent nation of Bangladesh. The disaster consumed the time of the Pakistani president for another couple of weeks; he was too busy to play the role of Nixon's and Chou Enlai's messenger.

Finally, Yahya Khan told his foreign secretary of Nixon's offer, and said Chou was willing to go along. "And then he told me to take over," says Sultan Muhammed Khan. "He said there should be only three people involved: myself, the Chinese ambassador in Pakistan, and the Pakistani ambassador in Washington."

Nixon and Kissinger by this time despaired that their latest and highest-level overture to the Chinese seemed to be going nowhere. They had already begun to set the full U.S. bureaucracy in motion on the subject of China. On November 19, Kissinger ordered a series of studies from the State and Defense Departments and the CIA on China policy, addressing such subjects as U.N. membership, Taiwan, and the impact of China on American policy toward the Soviet Union, Japan and Southeast Asia.[3]

These formal studies were eventually used to prepare for the opening to China, but they served other purposes as well. "I think Henry used these [studies] largely as a dodge, to distract people while he was carrying on his secret diplomacy," recalls James Lilley, then a CIA specialist on China. The studies also enabled Kissinger to gain effective control over the State Department's China experts, who began working for the White House out of a special office, where the only secretary was supplied by Kissinger's NSC. One of these China hands, Roger Sullivan, remembers being regularly given assignments at 4 p.m. with orders to get the finished work to the NSC by the end of the day.[4]

On December 9, Pakistan's ambassador to Washington, Agha Hilaly, hand-carried to the White House the reply from China that Nixon and Kissinger had been awaiting through the weeks of frustrating silence. "In order to discuss the subject of the vacation of Chinese territories called

Taiwan, a special envoy of President Nixon's will be most welcome in Peking," the note said. Kissinger was beside himself: "This was not an indirect subtle signal to be disavowed at the first tremors of difficulty. It was an authoritative personal message to Richard Nixon from Chou Enlai." The following month, the Romanians brought in another message, saying Nixon himself would be welcome in China.[5]

While the communication from China represented progress, it was the beginning, not the end, of making arrangements. Employing the Pakistani channel, the Americans and Chinese haggled over the terms for the meeting. Chou Enlai had said the sole purpose of the talks would be to discuss Taiwan, a limitation the Nixon administration could not accept. "We had to explain to the White House that for China, this was only a starting gambit," said Sultan Muhammed Khan.

For its part, China was miffed at the Nixon administration's insistence that the entire visit should be kept secret. The Pakistanis explained to Chinese officials the Nixon administration's reasoning: If word of the visit leaked in advance, the Taiwan lobby in Washington might try to prevent the trip. Each step was time consuming; the Chinese ambassador in Pakistan spoke no English, and thus each secret message had to be translated for him.

AMERICAN POLITICS—that is, making sure the Nixon administration would get the edge over the Democrats on the opening to China, and that China would help Nixon's reelection—became one of the recurring themes of the back-channel diplomacy. In their memoirs, Nixon and Kissinger alluded gingerly to this subject, but the emerging evidence of other memoirs and declassified files shows that politics was a far greater preoccupation than they ever let on.

From the outset of the Nixon administration, the Democrats had been agitating for a change in China policy. In March 1969, Senator Edward M. Kennedy, the presidential rival Nixon feared most, had called for recognition of China at the United Nations and the removal of American troops from Taiwan.[6] Kennedy was merely following the lead of Senate Majority Leader Mike Mansfield, the former history professor who was the Democrats' leading expert on Asia. Mansfield had been trying to visit Beijing since the Johnson administration, arguing that China's help could bring about an end to the Vietnam War. Moreover, the Nixon archives show that Mansfield had been writing his own letters to Chou seeking permission to travel to China, and had been giving copies of the letters to Bryce Harlow, Nixon's congressional liaison.[7]

In April 1971, Chou played American politics almost as brilliantly as Nixon ever had. Early that month, China invited the American team playing at the World Table Tennis Championship in Japan to visit China. The team's trip, quickly dubbed "ping-pong diplomacy," produced extensive U.S. press coverage showing that China was beginning to open itself up to American visitors.

During the ping-pong team's visit, a Chinese official sounded out an American reporter about the possibility of inviting three Democratic presidential contenders (Kennedy and Senators Edward Muskie and George McGovern) to China, along with prominent journalists like James Reston, Walter Lippmann and Walter Cronkite. The reporter mentioned the conversation to an American diplomat in Hong Kong, who passed along word to Washington.[8] Chou was thus hinting that China's next step might be with the Democrats in Congress, not the Republicans in the White House.

At the time, Nixon and Kissinger had not heard from Chou Enlai for months. They had answered the December invitation, but had made clear that an American emissary would not be sent to Beijing for talks that were confined exclusively to the subject of Taiwan.

Finally, in late April, Chou sent word through the Pakistani intermediaries that he was willing to receive a Nixon emissary; he dropped the condition that the talks would be about Taiwan. That cleared away the main obstacle. Nixon and Kissinger were euphoric; Nixon broke open a bottle of Courvoisier to celebrate.

"This is the most important communication that has come to an American president since the end of World War II," Kissinger told Nixon. (Upon some reflection, Kissinger apparently decided this extravagant claim was still too modest; a few weeks later, he told the president that the American opening to China was the country's greatest watershed since the Civil War.)[9] Although Nixon briefly unnerved Kissinger by weighing the possibility of sending some other envoy to China, he quickly settled on his national security advisor.

Yet the problem remained that China might invite Nixon's Democratic rivals, too. Thus, the Pakistanis were enlisted for another delicate bit of diplomacy: The Chinese were specifically told not to invite other American politicians, such as the Democrats. The Nixon White House wanted an exclusive franchise on visits to China.

That message, sent on April 28, 1971, was to be the first in a series over the next several months in which Nixon enlisted China's help for his own political benefit. According to the CIA's secret study of U.S.-China negotiations, Kissinger, during his trip to Beijing in July 1971, told Chou Enlai that Nixon "wants no political visitors" before he himself could visit China the following year. Not long afterward, Nixon and Kissinger returned to the subject of politics once again, this time through the channel to Chinese officials established by Vernon Walters, the U.S. military attaché in Paris. The first Sino-American exchanges must be kept free of partisanship, Walters told Chinese Ambassador Huang Zhen, so as not to inhibit the president's freedom of action. Kissinger himself, at a secret meeting with Chinese officials in Paris a few days later, took things one step further by telling the Chinese regime the American anti-war movement, too, was off-limits; he asked that Chinese leaders not only shun Democratic leaders, but "keep their distance from American left groups." [10]

Thus in the earliest days of the Nixon era was established the pattern that China would follow for decades in dealing with American leaders. American politicians regularly sought permission to visit China. The Beijing leadership could either grant the invitations or hold them in abeyance, depending on which option would be better for China. The handling and scheduling of presidential candidates, ex-presidents, opposition party leaders and out-of-office politicians was to become an important component of China's handling of America.

THE PLANNING and logistics for Kissinger's trip were carried out covertly, with the help of the Pakistanis. The White House announced that Kissinger was leaving on a general tour of Asia. In Pakistan, Khan arranged for a commercial jet to carry Kissinger and a small party of aides to Beijing. Two days before Kissinger's arrival in Pakistan, the plane did a test run to China and picked up Chinese navigators. The Pakistani crew members were told they would be taking President Yahya Khan on a special mission to China. [11]

Nixon and Kissinger still hadn't bothered to tell Secretary of State William Rogers about their dealings with China. Nixon's papers in the National Archives show that in the weeks before the trip, Nixon and his closest aides—Kissinger, Haldeman and Haig—were preoccupied with determining how to handle Rogers. Their problem was made more acute when the secretary vigorously protested that Kissinger shouldn't stop in India and Pakistan because doing so might unsettle the State Department's diplomacy with these two countries.

Nixon solved the problem by telling Rogers a lie. After Kissinger had reached Pakistan, the president confided to Rogers that during his trip, Kissinger had gotten an unexpected, last-minute invitation to China. The invitation had been, of course, anything but sudden.

Feeling what appear to have been some pangs of guilt, Nixon two days later ordered Haig (while Kissinger was still out of the country) to tell Rogers more of the national security advisor's secret diplomacy. Rogers was now informed for the first time that Kissinger had also been holding talks with the North Vietnamese in Paris.[12] He thus discovered that he had been excluded from the most important foreign policy initiatives of the administration in which he was serving.

In a sense, Rogers was not alone. By the time of Kissinger's trip to China, many of America's top leaders and its foreign policy institutions were intriguing against one another—including Nixon and Kissinger themselves.

The president had asked Kissinger to go to some Chinese city other than Beijing, so that Nixon himself could later become the first American official in the Chinese capital. Kissinger dissembled, leaving Nixon with the impression he might stop elsewhere in China, but he never really intended to go anywhere but Beijing.[13] In Pakistan, the American ambassador and CIA station chief had been called home and enlisted for help in planning the trip, but they were told not to tell the State Department or their own embassy. For good measure, the Joint Chiefs of Staff were busy spying on Kissinger, too.

Kissinger arrived in Pakistan on July 8. After an afternoon of talks, he had dinner with Yahya Khan and top aides, complained loudly of a stomachache, and retired, all according to the plan worked out by the CIA station chief. His meetings in Pakistan for the next two days were canceled. Pakistani officials took him to the airport for the flight to China at 4 o'clock the following morning.

At the airport in the pre-dawn darkness, two members of Kissinger's security detail were told that they were about to go with him on a mission to China. Stunned, one of them turned to Dick Smyser, a Kissinger aide, and asked, "Should we take extra guns with us?" Smyser thought for a moment and replied, "Don't worry, you'll be outgunned either way."[14]

A few hours after the plane left, a dummy entourage was brought up to Nathia Gali, a private estate near Pakistan's presidential guest house, where Kissinger was supposed to be recuperating. Sultan Muhammed Khan, the foreign secretary, went along. The chubbiest member of the American security detail was assigned to pretend he was Kissinger, in order to keep up the pretense. "We got there around lunch time. In every room of the guest house, there was a plate of mangoes," recalls Sultan Muhammed Khan. "The man playing Kissinger ate the mangoes, and he really fell ill."[15]

In Beijing, Chinese officials greeted Kissinger and his party with considerable mistrust. Just as State Department officials had feared that a high-level visit would be exploited for propaganda purposes by China's regime, so too Chinese leaders were afraid the Americans were playing games with them. Their suspicions had been heightened by Nixon's and Kissinger's insistence upon total secrecy for the trip. Why were the Americans so ashamed of a visit to China? They had greeted with skepticism the Pakistani explanations that Nixon was worried Chiang Kai-shek's minions in Washington might learn about the trip and try to stop it.

In a memoir, John Holdridge, one of the NSC aides who accompanied Kissinger on the trip, writes that shortly after the plane carrying the Americans landed in Beijing, he was pulled aside by Huang Hua, then China's ambassador to Canada. Huang, later to become foreign minister, asked Holdridge whether Kissinger was going to shake Chou Enlai's hand. The Chinese had never forgotten John Foster Dulles's refusal to touch Chou's hand in Geneva 18 years earlier.[16]

Kissinger had no intention of imitating Dulles; when Chou appeared, he held out his hand. More generally, the Chinese need not have worried about the national security advisor. From the start, Kissinger was utterly captivated and enthralled by Chou Enlai. In Kissinger's memoirs, Chou is portrayed considerably more warmly and positively than Nixon or any other American official. "Urbane, infinitely patient, extraordinarily intelligent, subtle, he moved through our discussions with an easy grace that penetrated to the essence of our new relationship, as if there were no sensible alternative," Kissinger wrote.[17]

The strongest indication of the lingering Chinese mistrust of the Americans was an incident that neither Kissinger nor any of his aides recorded in their memoirs. In the midst of their two days of talks, on the afternoon of July 10, Chou proposed that he and Kissinger tape-record a summary of their discussions. The episode is described in the CIA's history of U.S.-China negotiations.[18]

Chou apparently feared that the Nixon administration might back away in public from what Kissinger was telling him in private. He wanted Kissinger's promises on tape, above all his assurances concerning Taiwan. Chou may well have hoped to use such a tape as ammunition in China's domestic politics: Within the leadership, Lin Biao opposed Chou's opening to the United States, and a tape recording of what Henry Kissinger was saying might have helped bolster Chou's cause.

Kissinger didn't like the idea, and in a half-hour meeting late on his second and final night in Beijing, Chou relented. There was no need for a tape recording, he agreed.

IN HIS MEMOIRS, Kissinger minimized the importance of Taiwan and the concessions he made on his first trip to Beijing. Writing of his opening meeting with Chou Enlai, he asserted, "Taiwan was mentioned only briefly during the first session."[19]

Recently declassified records and memoirs show, however, that Kissinger's account was at best misleading and incomplete. According to the record of the negotiations later prepared for the CIA, during his initial meeting in Beijing with Chou, Kissinger pledged that the United States would not support independence for Taiwan or the Taiwan independence movement, which even then was growing in strength on the island. That new assurance went well beyond promises in Warsaw to draw down American forces on Taiwan and to support a settlement between the governments of Beijing and Taipei.[20] What Kissinger told Chou also contradicted the official position of the U.S. government, announced by the State Department less than three months earlier, that sovereignty over Taiwan was "an unsettled question subject to future international resolution."

In his recent memoir, Holdridge corroborates the CIA study and gives a fuller picture of what actually happened:

> Chou indicated that it was always the Chinese custom to let the guests speak first. Dr. Kissinger began by indulging in rather lengthy pleasantries while I waited impatiently for him to get to the point about Taiwan. He finally said what I had written for him on no two Chinas; no one China, one Taiwan; no independent Taiwan. Chou's response was immediate: "Good," he said, "these talks may now proceed."[21]

In other words, if Taiwan was barely mentioned, this was only because Kissinger gave China the private assurances it sought at the beginning of the first meeting.

Kissinger also promised Chou that American recognition of the Communist government in Beijing could come during Nixon's second term in office, the CIA study indicates. The following afternoon, he appeared to go still further, assuring that normalization could come in the first *two years* after Nixon's reelection. He discussed with Chou the details of China's bid for membership in the United Nations.[22] In a late-night conversation, he pledged to Chou that the United States would not support military action by Taiwan against the mainland.

In short, the discussions of Taiwan on Kissinger's trip were considerably more extensive than Kissinger or Nixon ever wanted to admit. The Nixon administration made many, though not all, of the concessions China had sought.

What Kissinger wanted from the Chinese was help in bringing about an end to the Vietnam War. For that reason, he had brought his National Security Council staff aide on Vietnam, Dick Smyser. But on Vietnam,

Kissinger's results were, at best, mixed. To be sure, the very presence of a high-ranking American official in Beijing would be, by itself, unsettling to the North Vietnamese, raising uncertainty over whether China might abandon its support for Hanoi. But more concrete help from China proved problematical.

Kissinger was seeking China's support for a negotiated settlement to the war, one that would leave the South Vietnamese government of Nguyen Van Thieu with at least some of its power intact. The Chinese response was equivocal. According to the CIA study, Chou held his position by telling Kissinger that the United States should withdraw all its forces from Vietnam.

"Nothing was resolved [on Vietnam]," recalled Smyser in an interview. "Chou Enlai said what we thought he would say, that the Vietnamese were fighting the war and it was up to them."[23] Days after Kissinger's trip, Chou made a secret visit to Hanoi, assuring the North Vietnamese of China's continued support, yet also apparently urging some sort of compromise that would end the fighting.[24] The North Vietnamese rebuffed the overture with such vehemence that, as we shall see, China turned down later requests by Nixon for further help in ending the war.

Looking back at these talks, one can see a rough equivalence between the handling of Taiwan and Vietnam. The United States didn't hand over Taiwan to China, nor did China abandon North Vietnam to the United States. Yet each big power was eliminating the other side's worst fears. The two nations were helping one another to overcome the legacy of the previous decades.

Throughout the Vietnam War, the United States had been afraid that China would enter the conflict in support of Hanoi, just as it had sent its troops across the border in the Korean War. Fear in Washington of Chinese intervention in Vietnam—however unlikely in the midst of the Cultural Revolution—had been a principal factor inhibiting American escalation of the war. Now, by talking directly with China, the Nixon administration was giving itself a freer hand. Over the next 18 months, the United States was able to mine the harbors of Haiphong and launch massive bombing raids over Hanoi without worrying that by doing so, it would prompt China to enter the war. More broadly still, the American fear dating back to the Eisenhower administration had been that the fall of South Vietnam would open the way for Communist victories throughout the other countries in Southeast Asia where Mao Tsetung was trying to export revolution. For U.S. foreign policy, in other words, Kissinger's trip to China marked the true end of the domino theory.

China had its own anxieties. It had worried for two decades that

Chiang Kai-shek's Nationalist forces would try to retake the mainland and, worse yet, that American troops would help or accompany them. By the late 1960s, this prospect may have become increasingly attenuated; still, it was a factor that had to be considered by the military planners in charge of defending China. More generally, China's political leaders had worried that through Taiwan, the United States might try to overthrow the People's Republic of China. With Kissinger's trip, all of these fears were being finally dispelled.

Kissinger and Chou may not have been carving up the world, but in the broadest sense, they were determining the future of East Asia.

The driving force that propelled these discussions forward, of course, was the Soviet Union. China was seeking to defend itself against the Soviet threat along its borders, and the Nixon administration was trying to unsettle Moscow enough to make Soviet leaders more interested in detente with the United States. "We want our China policy to show Moscow that it cannot speak for all communist countries, that it is to their advantage to make agreements with us," Kissinger asserted in a memo to Nixon.

In Beijing, Kissinger gave Chou Enlai a remarkable assurance: The United States would tell China in detail about any understandings it made with the Soviet Union affecting China's interests. Because this was such an extraordinary promise, Chou wanted to see it in writing (if not on a tape recording). Kissinger made certain that Nixon reiterated this pledge in a letter to Chou a few days after Kissinger returned home.

The letter was sent through Vernon Walters in Paris. In Beijing, Kissinger and Chou had decided to dispense with their Pakistani intermediaries and agreed that Paris should be used in the future for direct contacts between the two governments.[25] Within weeks, Kissinger himself broadened the original promise by telling Chinese Ambassador Huang Zhen in Paris that the United States would inform China of any talks it had "with other Socialist countries," thus including not only the Soviets but Eastern Europe and North Vietnam.[26]

Kissinger's willingness to bring China into the secrets of America's diplomacy with Moscow went far beyond anything he and Nixon had given to the Soviet Union. (In fact, the Soviets had asked to be informed about the details of America's talks with China, and had been rebuffed.) Yet these promises were not the end of the benefits the Chinese would receive from the United States. The CIA study confirms that Kissinger was soon offering intelligence information to China about Soviet troop deployments against it. "Extremely sensitive exchanges of information had begun by mutual agreement in late 1971," one U.S. national security aide, Robert McFarlane, later disclosed. Indeed, by some accounts, Kissinger supplied some of this information, including communication intercepts and high-resolution satellite pictures, during his first visit to China in July and on a second trip to Beijing in October.[27]

THE TRANSCRIPTS of the talks between Kissinger and Chou Enlai became an instant collector's item among the highest and mightiest of Washington and Beijing.

In July 1971, Dennis Kux, an American diplomat serving in Islamabad, was assigned the thankless job of serving as Kissinger's embassy control officer and was told to make arrangements for Kissinger's visit to Pakistan. Kux was not informed of the trip to Beijing, and he still didn't know about it when Kissinger reappeared in Pakistan's capital city after two days with his stomach supposedly on the mend. Kux recalls that at one point, a couple of Pakistani servants obligingly tried to pick up Kissinger's bags and briefcases. Kissinger's aide Winston Lord anxiously rushed over, hustled off the Pakistanis and picked up the bags himself.[28]

These efforts at secrecy, however, were not entirely successful. One of the U.S. military assistants on Kissinger's worldwide tour (although not on the side trip to Beijing) was Charles Radford. Officially a stenographer and clerical aide, he was spying on Kissinger and passing on documents for the benefit of Admiral Thomas H. Moorer, chairman of the Joint Chiefs of Staff, who wanted to know about the national security advisor's diplomacy. Radford managed at one point to go through Kissinger's room, suitcase and briefcases, obtaining, among other things, Kissinger's memo to Nixon about his talks with Chou.[29]

Chinese military leaders were no less eager to get their hands on the transcripts. By some Chinese accounts, Lin Biao, China's defense minister and Mao's designated successor, had planned to carry the record of the Kissinger-Chou talks with him to Moscow when his plane crashed in Mongolia in September 1971.[30]

EVEN AFTER Kissinger returned from China to Pakistan and proceeded around the world and back to the United States, his visit to Beijing was kept secret. Kissinger had obtained from Chou the single tangible, political benefit Nixon sought the most: China's willingness to welcome the American president for a visit. What remained was the public announcement. It was time to tell the American public and other governments.

The diplomacy surrounding the announcement was handled in a shoddy fashion. Kissinger was careful with the Soviets, far less so with the Japanese. Dobrynin recalls in his memoirs that he was summoned to the

White House at 9 a.m. on July 15, 1971, and put on a secure phone with Kissinger, who was in California with Nixon. The Soviet ambassador was told that the American president would go on television that evening to announce that Kissinger had just been in China, and that Nixon would visit China by early 1972.

By contrast, Japan, an American ally, was given almost no advance notice. At first, the administration made plans to dispatch Undersecretary of State U. Alexis Johnson to Tokyo to break the news in person to Japanese Prime Minister Eisaku Sato. However, Nixon and Kissinger canceled the trip because they were afraid the news would leak. (They apparently had no such fears about the Soviets and the KGB.)

Finally, the hapless Rogers was assigned to telephone the Japanese ambassador to Washington in the early evening hours, just before Nixon's speech, and let him know about America's secret diplomacy with China.[31] Years later, Kissinger conceded that, though the secrecy was generally necessary, "I believe in retrospect that we could have chosen a more sensitive method" of informing Tokyo.

In domestic politics, Nixon was considerably more careful and skillful. He and his political operatives left nothing to chance. His announcement of the opening to China brought forth what was, for Nixon, a virtually unprecedented outpouring of praise, which White House officials clipped, collected and sent on to the president in astonishment.

Most of the reactions were spontaneous. Yet the archives show that the China initiative, like everything else, was carried out under Nixon's rules and with his usual obsessions. Nixon was keeping up on the politics of the China trip over the phone with Charles Colson, his main political henchman. For three days after Nixon's announcement, Senator Edward Kennedy said nothing at all. Finally, Kennedy released a statement praising the China initiative.

Colson, it turns out, had been actively working to build up pressure on Kennedy. Colson said in a memo to the president,

> We had tipped certain columnists to the fact that he [Kennedy] had issued no statement, and their calls to his office yesterday may well have brought about his rather abrupt change of heart.[32]

In dealing with the right wing, Nixon was, as usual, extremely solicitous. He encouraged Kissinger to call and brief conservative political figures, like Senator Barry Goldwater and California Governor Ronald Reagan. His political master stroke in the months after Kissinger's trip was to persuade Reagan to visit Taipei as Nixon's personal representative to Taiwan's annual October 10 National Day festivities.

"Nixon appealed to him [Reagan] personally and got it done," says Richard Allen, who later was Reagan's national security advisor. "I think he [Reagan] always had some lingering regrets about having been used in that way, but his reasoning was that when the president asked him to do something, he [Reagan] was going to do it for him." [33]

WITHIN MONTHS, Kissinger's trip brought about far-reaching changes in several important aspects of American foreign policy.

In October 1971, the People's Republic of China was admitted to the United Nations, and Chiang Kai-shek's Nationalist government lost its seat. Officially, the United States pushed for a dual-representation formula in which both Beijing and Taipei would be represented. However, the American effort was half-hearted, in part because the Nixon administration was beset by internal divisions.

Kissinger himself didn't support the idea of dual representation, and at the time of the U.N. vote, he was on a second visit to Beijing, preparing for Nixon's trip. United Nations Ambassador George Bush later complained that the timing of Kissinger's trip, dramatizing the growing American relationship with Beijing, cost America a few votes and thus undercut the effort to help preserve Taiwan's seat. Kissinger insisted the U.N. vote came a week earlier than had been expected when he planned his trip, although he had accepted without protest China's proposal for when he should come. In the intensely paranoid milieu of the Nixon White House, Kissinger even privately tried to blame Rogers for the U.N. debacle. "Henry is convinced that Rogers pushed the UN vote for Monday night so as to downgrade Henry's trip and give Henry's trip the blame for the Taiwan loss," H. R. Haldeman wrote in his diary.[34]

The new relationship with China also prompted the Nixon administration to support Pakistan in the India-Pakistan War. Throughout 1971, the United States said as little as possible about atrocities by the Pakistani army in East Pakistan, overriding State Department pleas and protests. At the end of the year, after fighting broke out between Indian and Pakistani forces, Nixon and Kissinger viewed the conflict primarily as a way to demonstrate to China that the United States could be counted on to support China's ally, Pakistan, over a Soviet ally, India.

"In interagency debates, my office was not infrequently accused of an obsession with 'protecting the trip to China,' as if preserving that option were somehow an unworthy endeavor," Kissinger grumbled.[35] The episode was a telling indication of how the China initiative had come to dominate Nixon's and Kissinger's thinking in foreign policy, even about a shooting war in which Beijing was not involved.

The preparations for Nixon's China trip became all-consuming. Nixon and his aides wrangled and plotted over who should accompany him. The debates extended even to Nixon's wife, Pat. "If she goes, then the P [president] doesn't have to go out into the people. If not, he would have to," Haldeman wrote in his diary after one meeting with Nixon and Kissinger. "If she goes, she goes solely as a prop." [36] She went.

In the wake of Kissinger's two trips to Beijing, yet another high-level White House delegation, headed by his deputy Alexander Haig, visited Beijing to work out logistics and communications. Haig told Chou Enlai that Nixon wanted no problems, no incidents, on his trip.

"In view of opposition from the 'left' and 'right' in the U.S. to Nixon's China policy, it is crucial that there be no public embarrassment to the President as a result of his visit to Beijing," Haig warned. [37] Such a request underscored to the Chinese how badly Nixon wanted the trip to succeed and thus how much leverage China had in dealing with him.

ON THE EVE of the trip, Nixon and Kissinger launched a last, unsuccessful foreign policy initiative, one that was kept secret at the time and wasn't mentioned in their memoirs. On February 6, 1972, through their covert diplomatic channel in Paris, they asked China to arrange a meeting with Le Duc Tho, the North Vietnamese negotiator, on Chinese soil during the Nixon visit. If it took place, promised the White House, the situation in Indochina could be discussed "with generosity and justice." From Nixon's perspective, such a meeting would have been a diplomatic coup, one which would have enabled him to show that he was trying to end the Vietnam War and, in the process, to demonstrate to the American public the concrete benefits that could flow from the opening to China.

The effort failed. Chinese officials frostily rejected this White House request. Whatever low-key, amorphous, behind-the-scenes help China was willing to provide for the United States on Vietnam, this request went much too far. Within five days, China replied in Paris that it supported North Vietnam and would not be drawn into Hanoi's negotiations with the United States. [38]

In private, but never in public, Nixon came to recognize that his opening to China would not bring about what had been one of its original objectives: that is, Chinese help for a negotiated peace settlement in Vietnam. The archives show that at the White House on February 15, two days before he departed for China, Nixon jotted down

some handwritten notes of what he planned to tell Chou Enlai about
Vietnam:

> *V. Nam:*
> 1. We are ending our involvement—
> 2. We had hoped you would help—but now it doesn't matter
> 3. We must end it honorably—+ *will.*[39]

NIXON'S VISIT to China from February 21 to 28, 1972, is justifiably
credited with changing the course of history. Yet it most certainly did not
change the way business was conducted in the administration. From the
outset, the visit to China was plagued by the same obsessive secrecy, skul-
duggery, personal bickering and institutional rivalries that beset his
administration in Washington.

At first, Kissinger himself seemed ill at ease to have his boss alongside
him in China. Nixon's presence put Kissinger in a subordinate position.
Until then, virtually everything Chou Enlai knew about Nixon's views
and all Nixon knew about Chou Enlai had been filtered through
Kissinger as intermediary; now the American president and the Chinese
leaders could talk face to face.

When in early pleasantries Chou Enlai praised Kissinger for setting
up Nixon's trip, the president shifted the focus by talking more generally
of the good work of his advance men. That remark "had Henry disturbed
that it would put him down in the eyes of the Chinese," Haldeman
recorded in his diary. "He wanted me to talk to the P [president] about
that." Nixon had hoped to be able to speak at least once with Chou Enlai
alone, without Kissinger or other aides present, as he sometimes did with
other world leaders; but with Kissinger making the arrangements, the
one-on-one session never happened.[40]

Throughout the trip, Kissinger treated Rogers in particular and the
State Department in general as enemy powers. Rogers was kept out of
Nixon's and Kissinger's only meeting with Mao Tsetung; China was
enlisted as the White House's ally in plotting to make sure the State
Department did and knew as little as possible. "They [Chinese officials]
scheduled the meetings and kept the information compartmentalized as
if they had dealt with our strange practices all their lives," marveled
Kissinger. This was a role that both ingratiated the Chinese to the top
American leaders and also, in the process, increased China's bargaining
power; yet Kissinger was convinced that China never tried to exploit its
role as intermediary among the warring Americans.[41]

All of Nixon's and Kissinger's passion for secrecy and loathing of the
State Department were encapsulated in their decision to rely on inter-

preters from the Chinese side. Nixon had brought with him three American interpreters fluent in Chinese: The leading one was Charles W. Freeman Jr., a young Foreign Service officer who was to be involved in diplomacy between China and the United States for the next quarter-century. However, the interpreters worked for the State Department, and because of that, Nixon feared that they would leak—if not to the press, then within the U.S. government.

About an hour before the opening-night banquet in Beijing, White House aide Dwight Chapin summoned Freeman and told him to serve as interpreter for Nixon's toast, which was to be broadcast live throughout the world. Freeman asked for a copy of what Nixon would say. Chapin told him there was no text; Nixon would speak extemporaneously. Freeman said he knew an advance text existed because he had worked on a draft of it and had followed its progress with the speechwriters; it had included a loose, English-language rendition of some poetry by Chairman Mao.

"If you think I'm going to get up and ad lib Chairman Mao back into Chinese you're out of your mind," Freeman said. "Either give me the text, or I'm not doing it." Chapin told him it was a presidential order, but Freeman still refused. Finally, the White House aide took the text out of his pocket and handed it to Chinese officials, who hurriedly began the task of retranslating Mao into his native language. That night, one of them, Ji Chaozhu, served as interpreter for Nixon's toast. The president, meanwhile, glared furiously at Freeman throughout the banquet.[42]

The following day, when the president and Kissinger went to their first private meeting with Chou Enlai, Nixon's handwritten preparatory notes show that the very first subject for discussion was the need for secrecy. He emphasized that among Americans, only he, Nixon, had seen the transcript of Chou's earlier talks with Kissinger, and only Nixon would see what was said in the meeting they were about to hold. "The interpreter is yours," Nixon told the Chinese premier. Americans, he explained, have a problem keeping secrets.[43]

WHAT WAS the purpose of all the secrecy? What private business did Nixon and Kissinger want to conduct?

After more than a quarter-century, the full transcripts of Nixon's conversations in China have still not been made public. However, the general outlines of the talks emerge from the handwritten notes he made both before and during his meetings and from the CIA history of U.S.-China negotiations.

The Soviet Union was, of course, one of the principal subjects. Near the beginning of his first meeting with Chou Enlai on February 22, 1972, the president promised that Kissinger would give a briefing to Chinese officials about what Nixon termed "sensitive info" and that Kissinger would also brief them after U.S. talks with the Soviet Union. The CIA study confirms that the next day, in a three-hour meeting with Vice Foreign Minister Qiao Guanhua, Kissinger told the Chinese about Soviet military deployments against the People's Republic and about the state of negotiations between Washington and Moscow.[44]

Nixon's handwritten notes for his meeting with Chou show that he made a series of points and assurances about the Soviets:

Russia:
1. Maintain balance of power—
2. Restrain their expansion (if our interests are involved)
3. Try to reduce tension between us
4. Not make them irritated at you—
5. Make no deals with them we don't offer to you—
6. Will inform you on all deals[45]

This was a sophisticated presentation, one that went far beyond the simplistic anti-Soviet formulas in which American and Chinese leaders would later indulge. Nixon and Kissinger were attempting both to prepare China for the possibility of Soviet-American agreements on arms control and also to ease lingering Chinese fears that the United States and the Soviet Union would collude against China. They were addressing China's fears of a Soviet invasion by declaring that the United States would, at least within limits, seek to stop Soviet expansion. At the same time, they were giving China an incentive to go along with improvements in Soviet-American relations: The United States would offer China whatever it gave to the Soviets.

The other major powers covered in Nixon's presentation to Chou Enlai were India and Japan. The president was, in effect, outlining how American and Chinese leaders should deal with the countries on China's periphery. On India, Nixon's notes show that his presentation was relatively simple:

India:
1. Will go in tandem
2. We should balance Russia—

In other words, China and the United States should coordinate their policies toward (or against) India. This was the collaboration to which Nixon and Kissinger had been devoting themselves at the time of the

India-Pakistan War the previous year. Such a policy was not likely to please the many American supporters of India, the world's largest democracy, which had enjoyed strong support from the United States in the early years of its existence. It was, once again, an American policy highly favorable to China, which considered India a rival power within Asia.

Japan was the most sensitive subject. Nixon's notes show that in the week before his arrival in Beijing, he carefully prepared what he would say to the Chinese about Japan, which had so brutally invaded and occupied China less than four decades earlier but now was America's ally. Nixon and Kissinger had weighed the nuances of his every word. "Don't say, 'We oppose rearmament of Japan,'" Kissinger instructed the president in one of their prep sessions. "We oppose [a] nuclear Japan."[46]

Nixon and Kissinger's principal objective was to preserve America's bases and troops and its nuclear protection for Japan. The deployments in Japan were to be one of the linchpins of America's continued presence and military power in Asia as the United States drew down its forces from Vietnam and gave Asian allies more responsibility for their own defense. "We have to reassure the Asians that the Nixon Doctrine is not a way for us to get out of Asia but a way for us to stay in," Nixon told British Prime Minister Edward Heath before his China trip.[47]

Nixon and Kissinger were also worried about the return of Okinawa to Japan. The Japanese government had insisted upon the removal of nuclear weapons from Okinawa, although Nixon had obtained assurances that the United States could reintroduce them in an emergency. China's Communist regime had for more than two decades been vehemently opposed to the American presence in Japan. Nixon and Kissinger were seeking Chinese acceptance of, and accommodation to, the American military alliance with Japan.

Nixon realized that the Chinese were particularly worried about the implications of Japan's growing economic power. According to the notes Nixon made as he was preparing for the China trip, Chou Enlai had already told Kissinger that "Japan's feathers have grown on its wings and it is about to take off." He had asked Kissinger, "Can the U.S. control the 'wild horse' of Japan?" China was especially worried that the United States, while withdrawing its own troops from Taiwan, might encourage its Japanese allies to station their forces on the island.

The solution was to work out an understanding with China that the United States would protect Japan but would restrain both its military development and its political influence in Asia. Nixon wrote down to himself in Hawaii as he was en route to China:

Best to provide nuclear shield—
1. To keep Japan from building its own.
2. To have influence for US
   We oppose Japan "stretching out its hands" to Korea, Taiwan,
   Indonesia.[48]

These themes were to form the basis of Nixon's message to Chou
about Japan in their first talks. Nixon's notes for the meeting carry the
message that "our friendship with Japan is *in your* interests—not *against*"
[Nixon's emphasis]. Nixon also raised the specter of "a very great danger" concerning Japan, a danger that he described as "Korea, Taiwan."
That was an allusion to the prospect that Japan, if it were not controlled
by the United States, could regain its once-dominant influence in these
other parts of Northeast Asia.[49]

Seymour Hersh suggested in his book *Price of Power* that Nixon may
have threatened to Chinese leaders that he would let Japan develop
nuclear weapons if they didn't go along with American protection
for Japan. Nixon is said to have told Watergate special prosecutors in
secret testimony in June 1975, "We had these tough negotiations with
China. . . . We told them that if you try to keep us from protecting the
Japanese, we would let them go nuclear. And the Chinese said, 'We don't
want that.' "[50]

However, Hersh found no evidence to corroborate that such a threat
was actually delivered to China; and the recent material that has come to
light, such as Nixon's notes and the record of U.S.-China negotiations
prepared for the CIA, also contains nothing about such a threat. The
chances are that in telling this story to the Watergate special prosecutors,
Nixon was indulging in his proclivity for tough talk and was embellish-
ing what he and Kissinger told the Chinese. Nixon may have been sub-
stituting his own interpretation of the underlying message for what
was actually said. In fact, Nixon and Kissinger were no more eager to
see Japan become a nuclear power than were Mao Tsetung and Chou
Enlai.

NIXON'S HANDWRITTEN notes for the first private session with Chou
show that he referred to Taiwan and Vietnam as "irritants." That was a
curious choice of word, both for Chiang Kai-shek's government, which
the United States had supported for so long, and especially for Vietnam,
where tens of thousands of Americans had already died. Nixon used the
word in trying to explain to Chou how the United States and China
might collaborate in dealing with the other large powers in Asia: the
Soviet Union, India and Japan. It would be easier for Washington and

Beijing to work together if they could smooth over Taiwan and Vietnam by looking at them from the lofty perspective of two giant nations dealing with pygmies. "We can't handle [Taiwan and Vietnam] in way that destroys or weakens our position of leadership," Nixon said.[51]

On Vietnam, Nixon's and Kissinger's expectations had already been dampened by China's refusal to arrange a meeting with Le Duc Tho or to provide other new help toward a peace settlement. "I said that I fully understood the limitations of our talks and that I had no illusions about being able to settle the Indochina war in Peking," wrote Nixon in his memoirs, leaving out the fact that he had reached this conclusion only after the failed secret diplomacy of the previous few weeks.[52]

Notes that Nixon scribbled of what Chou told him at their first session in Beijing show that the Chinese premier offered the American president one significant assurance: Chinese policy toward Vietnam was "different from Korea," Chou said, thus further easing American fears that China might ever send its troops to fight in Vietnam as it had in the Korean War. President Truman had compelled Chinese intervention in Korea "by Seventh Fleet and Yalu," Chou told Nixon. (He was referring to Truman's positioning of the Seventh Fleet in the Taiwan Straits and his decision to send American forces toward the Yalu River along China's border with North Korea.) America had been more careful about China in the Vietnam War than it had been in Korea.

At the same time, Chou once again appealed to Nixon and Kissinger to withdraw from Vietnam, and he found brilliant ways of deflecting their eagerness for Chinese help in bringing about a settlement. Chou played to Nixon's sense of grandeur by saying that French President Charles DeGaulle, whom Nixon revered, had been right to withdraw from Algeria. Chou appealed to the American president's distaste for the Soviet Union by saying that he "should take bold action on Vietnam, or otherwise the Soviet Union benefits [from a protracted war]."

Finally, Chou handled the Vietnam issue by touching Nixon's rawest nerve, his fear and loathing of his Democratic opponents. The Democrats have "put us on [the] spot," the Chinese premier told Nixon, by trying to "come to China to settle Vietnam." Of course, said Chou, that was impossible. These words served as a reminder that Mao and Chou could revoke Nixon's exclusive franchise on China by dealing with the Democrats; they were also an implicit warning to Nixon not to make the same mistake as the Democrats by assuming China would help the United States in reaching a settlement on Vietnam.[53]

TAIWAN WAS a touchier subject than any other. It was the one divisive issue that needed to be addressed not just in the private talks between

Nixon and Chou, but also in the formal communique that was to be issued at the end of the trip. Kissinger had been working on the communique since his October visit to Beijing, and he continued these negotiations during the Nixon trip, usually in exhausting late-night sessions with Vice Foreign Minister Qiao Guanhua after the banquets were over. "After a dinner of Peking duck I'll agree to anything," Kissinger told Qiao during one of their nocturnal get-togethers.[54]

Nixon was able to go further on Taiwan in his private talks than in the public communique—and he did. The notes for his opening presentation to Chou Enlai indicate that he was prepared to give a stronger private commitment to a one-China policy than the communique contains. He also secretly promised to normalize relations with Beijing:

Taiwan:
I reiterate what our policy is:
1. Status is determined—one China, Taiwan is part of China—
2. Won't support Taiwan independence
3. *Try* to restrain Japan—
4. Support peaceful resolution
5. Will seek normalization—

Can we deliver?
1. Reduce troops—yes
2. But if it appears we sold out Taiwan Left egged on by Soviet & Right will make it an issue—
3. Must say we keep our commitments; no secret deals—but I know our interests require normalization and it will occur.[55]

The "no secret deals" wording would later become the basis for Nixon's and Kissinger's public comments and press briefings about the trip. They left out the fine print—that is, the details of Nixon's several private assurances to Chou that Taiwan was part of China, that the United States would not support the independence of Taiwan, would limit Japanese influence there and move toward normalization with China.

So much for the private diplomacy. In the haggling over the formal, public communique, Chinese officials sought to nail down an American commitment to withdraw all U.S. troops from Taiwan, preferably within a fixed time period. Nixon and Kissinger wanted to condition withdrawals upon an end of the war in Vietnam, a linkage that would give China an incentive to help end the conflict. The Americans also hoped for language about a "peaceful settlement" in Taiwan, in a way that would prevent China from trying to retake the island by force. China wanted the United States to say it merely hoped for, but did not insist upon, a peaceful resolution in Taiwan.

At one juncture during these talks, Qiao resorted to a ploy that would, decades later, become the heart of China's negotiating strategy with the United States: He used the American hunger for trade as a lever to try to win concessions in other areas.

China had already been dangling the prospect of business deals in front of the Americans. In Paris, Vernon Walters had earlier been told by Chinese Ambassador Huang Zhen that China would undoubtedly buy American planes for its domestic routes once relations between Washington and Beijing were more normal. Now, on the Nixon trip, the American leaders sought language in the communique about expanding trade between the two countries. In a bargaining session with Kissinger on the morning of February 24, Qiao threatened that if the two governments could not agree on the wording about Taiwan, then China would not commit to expanding trade.[56]

Eventually, the Chinese compromised, giving Nixon and Kissinger some of the qualifying language they were seeking. The trade provision was included in the communique. The United States said that its "ultimate objective" was to withdraw all American forces from Taiwan, and that it would "progressively reduce" these forces "as the tension in the area diminishes"; this promise fell short of what China wanted. The two sides also settled on wording in which the United States "reaffirms its interest in a peaceful settlement of the Taiwan question by the Chinese themselves"; this was less than what the Americans wanted, since China did not itself commit to a peaceful settlement. Over the next quarter-century, the American insistence upon a peaceful settlement on Taiwan would come up again and again in relations between China and the United States, both when Chinese leaders threatened the use of force against Taiwan and especially in 1996 when China fired missiles near the island.[57]

Chinese leaders were willing to make some concessions because, in the larger context, they were obtaining so much of what they wanted from Nixon and Kissinger. They were drawing America into a new relationship that would help China to counteract the threat from the Soviet Union. Nixon and Kissinger had privately given extensive assurances about Taiwan, conceding that it was part of China. The agreed-upon wording of the communique didn't go so far, but it certainly went well beyond the previous U.S. position that Taiwan's status was "undetermined." Ironically, this all-important new formula on Taiwan was essentially borrowed from what State Department officials had drawn up two years earlier in preparing for the talks with the Chinese in Warsaw.[58]

The communique said:

> The United States acknowledges that all Chinese on either side of the Taiwan Strait maintain there is but one China and that Taiwan is part of China. The United States Government does not challenge that position.

EVERYTHING WAS over but the shouting after Kissinger and Qiao wrapped up their talks on the communique. The shouting came from the State Department, which Nixon and Kissinger had assiduously excluded from these negotiations. When State officials were finally shown the proposed communique as Nixon and his party left Beijing for Hangzhou, Rogers, Assistant Secretary Marshall Green and their aides were irate.

They pointed out several difficulties. The communique specifically cited America's treaty commitments to Japan, South Korea and the Philippines, but didn't mention the similar treaty with Taiwan. State officials recalled how Secretary Dean Acheson left South Korea out of a description of America's defense commitments in early 1950, leading to criticism that his omission had inadvertently contributed to the outbreak of the Korean War. After a flurry of last-minute wrangling among the Americans, Nixon instructed Kissinger to reopen the talks, but China refused to allow any mention of the American security commitment to Taiwan. The problem was resolved by eliminating the references to the other treaty commitments, so that Taiwan would not be singled out.

Rogers and Green also pointed out that many native Taiwanese did not agree with the Nationalist government's position that Taiwan was part of China. Therefore, the State Department officials argued, the language in the communique should say merely that "Chinese on either side of the Taiwan Strait," rather than "*all* Chinese," agree on the status of Taiwan. They had no way of knowing, of course, that Nixon and Kissinger had gone much further in private, conceding that Taiwan was part of China and agreeing to oppose independence for the island.

During another three-hour marathon ending at 1:40 a.m. in Hangzhou, Kissinger tried to obtain the wording the State Department wanted, but Chinese officials would not budge. The commitment to one China, issued the next day as the Shanghai Communique, referred to "all Chinese." Thus, the communique did not so much as hint at the existence of the Taiwanese who make up four-fifths of the population of the island.[59]

.   .   .

It had been left to Nixon himself to settle the disagreements in China between his top two foreign policy advisers—one of whom, Kissinger, frequently threatened to quit and the other of whom, Rogers, certainly had cause to do so. The stakes were not small: Nixon knew that any hint of discord over the communique, and particularly over Taiwan, would have been seized upon by his many critics back home. In the end, the president told the secretary he expected him and the whole State Department bureaucracy to support the Shanghai Communique. They did. Word of the intramural disputes didn't leak.

These strains—and, perhaps, the strange environment of China and the long hours—evidently took their toll on Nixon. On the last night there, Haldeman noted in his diary, Nixon "ordered some Mao Tai [*sic*] and had several of those, which he had done at dinner, and had at least half a dozen before and during lunch today." At a banquet in Shanghai that night, Nixon gave his only genuinely extemporaneous toast of the trip. In it, he seemed to go far beyond what had been negotiated by proposing what sounded like a defensive military alliance with China. A startled Kissinger rejoiced that "by that hour, the press was too far gone itself" to notice.[60]

The president wrote down a few notes for what he planned to say to Chou in their final meeting in China. The notes showed that, as usual, secrecy was uppermost in his mind:

> Will be discreet—
>   our discussion about Russ-Japan-India
>   our business only.[61]

Nixon departed from China believing that he would finish the process of establishing diplomatic relations with Beijing during his presidency. His thoughts about diplomatic relations, in the talks with Chou Enlai, are doubly poignant in light of the scandals that were about to unfold. The words are scrawled in the margins of his notes, just above the assurance that "I know our interests require normalization and it will occur":

> *Age:* My life is 10 months or five years
>   —Then done—
>   I have little time + will do it.[62]

When Nixon talked of "my life," he was of course referring to his career. He couldn't seem to envision an existence without politics; he thought that when he left office, either after the 1972 elections (in ten months) or at the end of his second term (in five years), his life would be over. Still less could Nixon have imagined that his life in the White House would come to an end in two years and five months, in the middle of his second term. Nixon's secret promise that he would normalize relations with China during his second term would haunt his two successors in the White House.

IN BOTH style and content, Nixon's and Kissinger's diplomacy guided America's relationship with China for at least a quarter-century.

The Nixon administration devised and articulated the main themes that came to dominate American thinking about China: Close relations with China could help America to deal with the Soviet Union; Washington and Beijing should work together to settle arrangements throughout East Asia; and, meanwhile, the United States should not and would not challenge China's Communist Party leadership.

Later presidents, secretaries of state and national security advisors built upon and sometimes modified the edifice that Nixon and Kissinger had constructed. Rarely did they challenge the fundamentals of Nixon's and Kissinger's China policy or reevaluate the underlying assumptions to see if they still made sense. Indeed, as the years passed, the Nixon-Kissinger approach to China became a new dogma, replacing the old one that had guided America's conduct in the 1950s and 1960s.

Did Nixon achieve his own goals with his China initiative? Did China? One way to judge is to look back, with some historical perspective, at the notes Nixon jotted down in Hawaii on the eve of his trip to Beijing: that is, his analysis of "what they [Chinese leaders] want," "what we want" and "what we both want."

The main thing Nixon said he sought from his opening to China was "Indochina": a way out of the Vietnam War. On this, he was largely, though not entirely, unsuccessful. China was unwilling and unable to bring enough pressure on Hanoi to force it into a coalition government or to bring about a peace settlement that would endure. The American opening to China did manage to undercut some of Hanoi's international support; it gave Nixon a freer hand to escalate the war and the bombing without worrying too much about what Beijing might do in response. Yet this wasn't sufficient for Nixon to get what he wanted. China didn't deliver a Vietnam settlement.

However, on the second of Nixon's goals, "restraining Chicom expansion in Asia," he was more successful. As China's relationship with the United States developed, Chinese leaders stopped supporting the cause of Communist revolution in other Southeast Asian countries such as Malaysia and Indonesia. While Nixon and Kissinger would never have explained it in such negative, pessimistic terms at the time, their opening to China helped to minimize the negative impact elsewhere in Asia of the eventual American defeat in Vietnam.

On the goals Nixon thought the United States and China shared, he succeeded beyond what he could even have hoped or imagined. The two countries did, in fact, reduce the danger of confrontation and bring about a more stable Asia. Their collaboration did serve as a restraint upon the Soviet Union. If the impact of the new partnership upon the Soviets was important to the United States, it was all the more so for China, which saw itself as threatened by a Soviet invasion. The new partnership brought benefits to both China and the United States, although the Chinese probably needed them more urgently than did America.

What else did China want from the Americans? At the top of Nixon's list was the idea that the Chinese sought to "build up their world credentials." In this endeavor, they were stunningly successful. Kissinger's and Nixon's trips opened the way for China's admission to the United Nations. The American diplomacy also prompted other countries, like Japan, to rush to establish new relationships with Beijing. Most importantly, Nixon's initiative conveyed America's acceptance, for the first time, of the outcome of the Chinese civil war and the defeat of Chiang Kai-shek. The United States stopped challenging the Chinese Communist Party's authority to rule the country.

Nixon also calculated, rightly, that through China's opening to the United States, Mao and Chou hoped to get Taiwan. In this regard, the Chinese were partially successful. The Chinese won extremely important commitments from the Americans concerning Taiwan, both in secret assurances and in the Shanghai Communique. The American acceptance (in the communique) and, indeed, its embrace (in Nixon's private talks) of a one-China policy was to govern American conduct from that point onward. The American promise not to support independence for Taiwan became ever more significant when, two decades later, Chiang Kai-shek's old mainland allies lost their control over Taiwan and the independence movement became increasingly powerful. Nevertheless, the American concessions went only so far. China did not regain the island.

NIXON'S AND Kissinger's operating style in dealing with China set the tone for future administrations, too. The two men relied heavily on secrecy. They were often willing to let Chinese leaders set the terms, conditions and setting for negotiations, especially by conducting high-level meetings almost exclusively on China's turf. The Nixonian diplomacy was intensely personalized. It circumvented the ordinary processes of government, allowing Chinese leaders to concentrate on a single top-ranking U.S. official with whom they would do business, an individual like Kissinger who could be cultivated and flattered.

This style had more logic in the very earliest days of the opening to China than it would come to have later on. Some degree of secrecy may have been necessary to get the Nixon diplomacy with China off the ground. Later, the secrecy became nearly an end in itself, leading subsequent administrations into disastrous foreign policy ventures. During the Reagan administration, Robert C. McFarlane believed he was duplicating the Nixon administration's opening to China when he delivered arms to Iran in what became the Iran–Contra scandal.[63] In the Bush administration, secrecy became counterproductive in America's relations with China; the visits of National Security Advisor Brent Scowcroft to Beijing in 1989 were a contributing factor in the Bush White House's loss of public and congressional support for American policy toward China.

So, too, in those earliest days, it may have been excusable for Nixon administration officials to talk with Chinese leaders mostly on Chinese soil. The United States was trying to create a relationship out of nothing. It was easier for Kissinger and Nixon to travel to Beijing than for Chinese leaders to visit Washington, particularly when Chou Enlai, America's principal interlocutor, and Mao himself were in poor health. But the pattern of American pilgrimages to Beijing proved hard to break, contributing to China's sense that the Middle Kingdom was an imperial power dealing with a tributary. Years later, the American willingness and eagerness to do business in Beijing was not only unnecessary, but gave the Chinese a distinct negotiating advantage. After studying China's negotiating tactics, Richard H. Solomon concluded: "Negotiating in the Chinese capital gives the Chinese the opportunity to manage the ambience so as to maximize the sense of gratitude, dependence, awe, and helplessness they evoke in their guests."[64] It was an apt description of the psychology of American officials on visits to Beijing.

Kissinger's personalized diplomacy was questionable from the start. Even Nixon came to marvel at the degree to which Kissinger built up a personal stake in the new relationship with China. Nevertheless, Nixon's and Kissinger's successors either embraced the notions of secrecy and personalized diplomacy or found themselves unable to break the pattern. Over the next decades, American officials who followed Kissinger to Beijing sang many of the same tunes, in the same rhythm and style, as the Meistersinger.

CHAPTER THREE

Tacit Allies

W HEN RICHARD NIXON delivered his opening toast to Chou
Enlai in the Great Hall of the People, among those looking on
was William F. Buckley Jr. He was one of the illustrious journalists (others included Theodore White and Walter Cronkite) whom the White
House had favored with a seat on the trip. Buckley was not nearly so
enthusiastic about the rapprochement with China as were Nixon and
Kissinger. "Watching the face of Chou," the conservative columnist
wrote, "one could not help but reflect that the smile must have been similar on the face of his hero, Stalin, when the boys got together to toast
peace and dignity, and self-determination of all peoples, at Yalta." [1]

On the plane ride home from China, Kissinger observed that Patrick
J. Buchanan, the White House speechwriter and resident conser-
vative, was "morose. . . . He blamed pernicious advisers (meaning me
[Kissinger]) for the president's departure from grace." Back in Washing-
ton, Buchanan threatened to resign because of his anger over the
Shanghai Communique, but finally agreed to stay on. A month later,
Nixon asked Buchanan to draft some talking points for his wife, Pat,
explaining what she should say about China in her public appearances.
Buchanan loyally did as asked, but his memo revealed some of the horror
he had himself felt over Nixon's courtship of the Chinese leadership. He
stressed ideological themes and Communism in ways that Nixon and
Kissinger did not.

Chou Enlai and other leaders, Buchanan wrote,

> are first-generation revolutionaries and True Believers in Commu-
> nism, yet retained some of those characteristics in social encounter
> that we traditionally associate with the Chinese people.

... The children seemed disciplined and orderly; one could see them trooping along, marching, if you will, to and from their schools. The soldiers at the airport seemed a tough and impressive lot. . . .

My strong view is that the First Lady praise the non-Communist aspects of the society, i.e., the incredibly magnificent food put on for the foreign visitors, the tremendous historic wonders there in the Great Wall, Ming Tombs, and Forbidden City and West Lake.[2]

In short, Buchanan seemed to be struggling to reconcile his own political beliefs about Communism with the need to put forth romantic, positive images of his president's visit to Beijing.

Nixon's opening to China shook the very foundations of how Americans viewed the world, and nowhere more so than on the political right. The new relationship with Beijing raised some fundamental and, for many, unsettling questions: Why exactly was America fighting the Cold War? Was the Cold War an ideological struggle, aimed at combating Communism? Or was it fundamentally a geopolitical conflict, aimed at stopping the expansion of the Soviet Union?

For the previous two decades, Americans had been told repeatedly that the Cold War was a national effort, or crusade, against Communism. Not everyone believed in such simple verities; within the foreign policy elite, the justifications for the Cold War often focused on more complicated ideas, like the need to prevent the Soviets from dominating the Eurasian land mass. These strategic explanations, however, would not have been sufficient by themselves to galvanize the American people to assume a new series of international involvements, more extensive than any the United States had assumed in its history. Ideological anti-Communism had provided the extra impetus needed to launch and carry out the Cold War.

Nixon's opening to China forced America to devise new rationales at home for its conduct around the world. If the United States was combating Communism, why did it have such friendly relations with China's Communist leaders? Was individual freedom more important in Europe than in Asia? Was Asian Communism different from European Communism?

Throughout the 1970s and 1980s, American leaders, from presidents on down, struggled to come up with a variety of new explanations for the remarkable disparity between America's conduct toward China and toward the Soviet Union. Nixon and Kissinger sometimes explained the differentiation in personal terms: Chinese leaders, and particularly Chou Enlai, were more likable, less crude, than the Soviets.

"Unlike the Soviets, who ritually insisted that everything they had was the biggest and the best, the Chinese were almost obsessed with self-criticism and with seeking advice on how to improve themselves," wrote Nixon. Even Mao's wife, Jiang Qing, was humbler than Soviet leaders, he concluded.[3]

For Nixon, the philosophical problem presented by Communist China was not so acute as for others. What mattered most for Nixon was simply to show that he was the American leader who could best deal with foreign leaders, including adversaries: In a sense, going to China was merely an extension of Nixon's famous 1959 "kitchen debate" with Khrushchev in Moscow. "He [Nixon] says the main thing for us in China is the P's [president's] position as a big-league operator," Haldeman recorded in his diaries.[4]

For Kissinger, the philosophical questions also were not particularly troubling—indeed, even less so than for Nixon. Although Kissinger occasionally invoked anti-Communism when it suited his purposes, he never concealed the fact that his main interests were geopolitics and the balance of power.

Over the years, Americans less inclined to Kissingerian realpolitik tried to solve philosophical qualms about the China relationship in their own ways. President Carter, a Democrat hesitant to invoke the cause of anti-Communism, came up with his human rights policy as a new rationale for challenging both the Soviet Union and right-wing dictatorships; he then ignored the problem of human rights abuses in China. During his presidency, Ronald Reagan neatly redefined China as not really Communist, a "so-called Communist" country.

It was on the political right, of course, that the cause of anti-Communism had been strongest. Among conservatives, the opening to China led to new cleavages. In the years after Nixon's visit, tensions emerged between, on the one hand, an anti-Communist right that remained hostile to China, and, on the other, an anti-Soviet right eager to court China. For the truth was that if America truly wanted to combat the Soviet Union, China would be a useful partner in that endeavor. That idea was not lost on the Pentagon, whose own preoccupation during this period was to counteract Soviet military power.

Gradually, after 1972 the cause of anti-Communism began to lose some of its steam, and the nature of the Cold War was slowly redefined in a subtle but important fashion: America wasn't fighting Communism in general, but the Soviet Union in particular.

For the remainder of Nixon's tenure and during the presidency of Gerald Ford, what didn't happen between the United States and China seemed at first glance to be more important than what did.

Nixon and Kissinger had promised to normalize diplomatic relations with China after the 1972 elections. They found themselves unable to do so: Nixon was soon beset by Watergate, and after he resigned in 1974, Ford struggled to stave off conservative challenges for the Republican presidential nomination in 1976. To be sure, both sides kept up the appearances; Kissinger made pilgrimages to Beijing at least once a year. Yet normalization of relations, which had seemed so inevitable when Nixon and Chou Enlai were planning the future in Beijing in 1972, remained out of reach.

However, what was happening beneath the surface between America and China in the mid-1970s was more significant than the lack of progress toward normalization. The nature of the partnership was changing, in ways beyond what Nixon and Kissinger had first envisioned.

They had not designed the American opening to China as a joint venture against the Soviet Union. Rather, they had intended to foster better U.S. relations with China as a means of goading the Soviet Union into detente. Over the long run, the opening to China was supposed to make America's ties with the Soviet Union more amicable, not more adversarial. The original idea was to have better relations with both countries. "With conscientious attention to both capitals, we should be able to have our *mao tai* and drink our vodka, too," Kissinger wrote to Nixon in early 1973.[5]

Yet during the years from 1973 to 1976, a series of factors—American politics, the behavior of the Soviet Union and the dynamics of the relationship between Washington and Beijing—came together to create a different sort of partnership. The United States and China began laying the groundwork for an extensive collaboration against the Soviet Union. They began to share ideas and anti-Soviet strategies. The United States started to provide technology to China. Both countries groped slowly toward a partnership in which military and intelligence issues became increasingly prominent.

When American and Chinese officials gave toasts to friendship, they talked increasingly of their common enemy. Recently declassified files of some of Kissinger's early conversations with Deng Xiaoping show that the two men could barely say hello to one another without swapping lines about the Russians.

"I have just recovered from the frost of Vladivostok," Kissinger told

Deng on November 25, 1974, on the night he arrived in China after a visit to the Soviet Far East.

> *Deng:* We hear the present name Vladivostok means "Rule the East."
>
> *Kissinger:* We don't know what it means, but in any case we don't agree with it [laughter]. . . .
>
> *Deng:* This [Soviet attitude] seems an established policy that goes back to Tsarist days.
>
> *Kissinger:* It is a policy of hegemony.
>
> *Deng:* Yes, and it seems it won't be remedied, at least in the Brezhnev generation.[6]

A year later, Kissinger introduced his top Soviet adviser, Helmut Sonnenfeldt, to Deng by informing the Chinese leader: "Mr. Sonnenfeldt once sent me a cable from Moscow after three days there saying, 'The only thing keeping me here is the joy of anticipating my departure, which will be exceeded only by the joy of completing it.' "[7] The Soviet Union was not only the heart and substance of the relationship between American and Chinese officials; it often dominated their small talk as well.

One of the underlying factors was that Kissinger initially was uneasy and unimpressed with Deng Xiaoping, and talking about their shared dislike of the Soviet Union helped forge a bond between the two men. By 1974, with Chou Enlai increasingly ill, Deng became Kissinger's principal interlocutor in dealing with China.

Declassified files show that Kissinger at first seriously underestimated Deng. During the secretary of state's visit to China in November, 1974, he cabled President Ford the patronizing judgment that Deng was "a stocky, tough-looking individual who seems to have gained more self-assurance since my only other meeting with him in New York last April." A couple of days later, Kissinger informed the president that Deng "did liven up considerably and presented the Chinese position competently and somewhat humorously, but he has none of Chou's elegance, flair, breadth or subtlety—though admittedly Chou represents a very high standard."[8]

THE ORIGINS of America's military relationship with China could not have been more modest. On November 28, 1972, a bright, garrulous, undisciplined young China scholar from Columbia University named Michael Pillsbury dropped by the United Nations, where he had briefly worked, to attend a National Day reception given by the government of

Albania. Pillsbury struck up a conversation with Chinese General Zhang Wutan, who had recently been assigned to the United Nations as part of China's new responsibilities on the Security Council.[9]

The talk wandered. Zhang began quizzing Pillsbury about Taiwan, where the American had spent two years as a graduate student. Pillsbury grumbled that the Soviets effectively controlled the U.N. Secretariat. Zhang, laughing, replied, "And the Indians, too."

Zhang invited Pillsbury to visit him at the Chinese mission to the United Nations from time to time. Pillsbury took up the offer, stopping by to talk with Zhang in New York City every few weeks, even flying back regularly to New York after he moved to California in early 1973 to begin work as a China analyst for the Rand Corporation.

At the time, the United States had had virtually no contact with the Chinese People's Liberation Army since the end of China's civil war. The assumption in Washington was that China's army adhered to a doctrine of strict self-reliance. Despite Mao Tsetung's and Chou Enlai's interest in improving relations with the United States, few if any in Washington expected China to seek Western military supplies or technology or, indeed, a military relationship of any kind.

Outward appearances indicate that Pillsbury may have been working with American intelligence agencies from the very start of his relationship with Zhang. If not, he was soon effectively doing so. He wrote long memos about his conversations with the Chinese general and distributed them to the Defense Department, air force intelligence and the CIA. U.S. Defense and intelligence officials began supplying Pillsbury with questions and topics of conversation for his New York meetings.

What emerged was startling. Zhang expressed an interest in American military technology. He also made it plain that within the People's Liberation Army, many military officials did not believe in Mao's strategy of "people's war." Under this military doctrine, China was supposed to be able to overcome a better-armed, more powerful enemy like the Soviet Union by falling back on its territory and relying on its superior numbers. Yet from Pillsbury's conversations, it appeared that some generals like Zhang thought the idea of "people's war" was outdated. They wanted to modernize the People's Liberation Army with advanced weaponry. They also desired to defend China in a "local war" at its borders, rather than by falling back to the interior. That prospect had important military implications for the United States.

Pillsbury's employer, Rand, based in Santa Monica, was a think tank where scholars worked under U.S. government contracts to conduct studies and devise American strategy for the Cold War. For Rand, China was a sideshow. Most of its efforts and personnel were engaged in the study of the Soviet Union; Rand officials often shuttled to consulting work at the Pentagon and sometimes to full-time jobs there. By the mid-1970s, Pillsbury's own mentor from Rand, Andrew Marshall, had taken up residence at the Defense Department's Office of Net Assessment, the unit that studies how long-term trends affect America's military posture. James Schlesinger, the secretary of defense in the late Nixon and early Ford years, was himself a Rand alumnus.

In the fall of 1973, Pillsbury submitted a classified memo suggesting the novel idea that the United States might establish a military relationship with China. Such ties, Pillsbury argued, might strengthen those within the Chinese leadership who supported strong links with the United States. A defense relationship might also prevent rapprochement between China and the Soviet Union, help China defend against a Soviet invasion and give Washington new leverage over Moscow. Not least important, if the United States could induce China to build up its defenses to fight a "local war" along the Sino-Soviet border, the Soviet Union might be required to deploy more of its own troops near China, thus tying down forces that might otherwise be directed against Western Europe.

This was the genesis of the idea of a "China card," the notion that the United States might use China to gain Cold War advantage over the Soviet Union. The concept would eventually come to dominate American thinking about the new relationship with China. Where Nixon and Kissinger had sought to improve American relations with both superpowers, the proponents of the "China card" envisioned siding with China as a means of combating the Soviet Union.

Pillsbury's report, labeled L-32 (Rand's 32nd memo of 1974 to the government), began bouncing around America's national security apparatus. Traditionalists in the uniformed services, such as officials working for the Joint Chiefs of Staff, thought the idea was preposterous. They noted that Mao's China had been a frequent adversary of the United States, and they speculated that it might someday return to its Communist partnership with the Soviet Union. Nevertheless, Marshall, Deputy Assistant Secretary of Defense Morton Abramowitz and Schlesinger himself were intrigued with Pillsbury's idea, and ordered their own government studies of an American military relationship with China.

In the fall of 1975, with the blessing of Rand and the Pentagon, Pillsbury went public. He rewrote his classified memo as an article for the magazine *Foreign Policy,* which was then being edited by Abramowitz's friend Richard Holbrooke. "We should modify the specious policy of 'even-handedness' which now governs exports of advanced defense technology," Pillsbury wrote. "The same restrictions should not apply to both the Soviet Union and China. China is not nearly as large a security threat to us as the Soviet Union." [10]

Pillsbury suggested a series of steps the United States could take to establish a military relationship with China, from an exchange of delegations between the two nations' military academies to outright military sales by the United States and its allies. In order to deflect criticisms that such a relationship might infuriate the Soviet Union or Taiwan, he proposed that the United States sell China only defense equipment, such as a military reconnaissance system or over-the-horizon radar.

Pillsbury's article represented, in effect, the Pentagon's way of preparing the American public for a military relationship with the Chinese army, against which the United States had fought in Korea. Such an idea would have seemed unthinkable five years earlier, when the United States and China were struggling to figure out how even to talk with one another.

Pillsbury's article produced no immediate results. The United States was not yet prepared for military ties with China. But the idea of a "China card" was being explored and was attracting a wider audience in America.

ON FEBRUARY 16, 1973, Kissinger returned to Beijing. Nixon had just been inaugurated for his second term. At the time, Nixon, Kissinger and Chinese leaders believed the Vietnam War had just been concluded with the signing of the Paris peace accords. In this relaxed climate, Kissinger had a series of meetings with Chou and Mao that brought the two countries much closer together than they had been, or indeed would be until the end of the decade.

"The flood gates opened," Kissinger gushed in his private report to Nixon. He noticed, and relished, the symbols of status in Beijing: the fact that his plane was for the first time allowed to taxi right up to the terminal at the Beijing airport and that, in his proud words, "Guards saluted us for the first time as we entered the Great Hall and our Guest House." [11]

Indeed, Kissinger's secret memos to the president during and after this trip are startling in scope and enthusiasm. In one of them, he compared China to Britain as a friend of America:

We are now in the extraordinary situation that, with the exception of the United Kingdom, *the PRC might well be closest to us in its global perceptions.* No other world leaders have the sweep and imagination of Mao and Chou, nor the capacity and will to pursue a long range policy. [12]

In his meetings, Kissinger reaffirmed to Chinese leaders the private assurances made by Nixon the previous year that the United States would not support Taiwan's independence and would discourage Japanese involvement in Taiwan. Kissinger also went further, and in considerably more detail, on Nixon's earlier promise to normalize relations with Beijing. Kissinger told Chou that the United States would be prepared to take steps toward normalization of relations after the 1974 midterm elections and would be ready to establish full diplomatic relations "before mid-1976." This was a promise that would come back to haunt him.[13]

One night at 11:30, on a half-hour's notice, Chou escorted Kissinger for a session with Mao that lasted nearly two hours. Until that juncture, Kissinger had met the Chinese leader only once in Nixon's presence. Kissinger's private report to Nixon on the session overflowed with enthusiasm and admiration for Mao:

> He [Mao] radiates authority and deep wisdom, and Chou—as in your meeting—was deferential. . . . In short, I was even more impressed by the grandeur of the Chairman this time than last. One can easily imagine the power and intelligence of this man in his prime.[14]

The conversation with Mao wandered. Kissinger suggested that the United States and China should coordinate their actions throughout the world. He and Mao also talked about women, with Mao returning repeatedly to this subject. "If you want them, we can give a few of those to you, some tens of thousands," Mao told Kissinger. A few minutes later, he asked, "Do you want our Chinese women? We can give you 10 million."

Kissinger himself imbued these last remarks with deep political significance, believing Mao was indirectly alluding to his problems with his politically active wife, Jiang Qing.[15] There is also a simpler, earthier interpretation. The conversation was late at night, Mao maintained an active curiosity about sex and he knew that at the time of their conversation Kissinger was a bachelor, whose dates with a variety of women from Hollywood to Paris had been widely reported in the press. Mao may have been merely indulging in some boy-talk.

They talked about espionage, too. Mao told Kissinger, apparently with a straight face, that the American delegation wasn't the subject of Chinese spying.

> We don't steal your documents. You can deliberately leave them somewhere and try us out. Nor do we engage in eavesdropping and bugging. There is no use in those small tricks.[16]

Mao opined that the CIA wasn't very good at spying, and that neither was China's intelligence service. "They [Chinese intelligence] didn't know you wanted to come," he told Kissinger, referring to the events leading up to his first secret trip in 1971. That was a dubious assertion, if not an outright lie. Many years later, the Americans would discover that Larry Wu-Tai Chin, a Chinese spy working inside the CIA, had been reporting to Beijing about developments in Washington, including Nixon's and Kissinger's efforts to establish ties with China.

The central topic of Kissinger's conversations with Mao and Chou was the Soviet Union:

> *Dr. Kissinger:* There is a strong community of interest which is operating immediately.
> *Chairman Mao:* Is that so?
> *Dr. Kissinger:* Between China and the United States.
> *Chairman Mao:* What do you mean by community of interest? On Taiwan?
> *Dr. Kissinger:* In relation to other countries that may have intentions.
> *Prime Minister Chou:* You mean the Soviet Union?
> *Dr. Kissinger:* I mean the Soviet Union.[17]

Mao and Chou hardly needed prompting. Indeed, they favored considerably tougher policies against the Soviets than did Nixon and Kissinger. On this trip the Chinese leaders voiced strong suspicions about American and Western European efforts to improve relations with Moscow. "The Chinese see a false detente in the region [Europe] freeing the Russians' Western flank and 'pushing the ill waters of the Soviet Union eastward,'" wrote Kissinger, quoting the words of Chou Enlai.[18]

In other words, China—which by this time faced 45 Soviet divisions along its borders, more than twice as many as it had in 1969—was trying to make sure Moscow didn't succeed in working out some sort of accommodation with the United States and Western Europe, one that would leave the Soviet Union with a freer hand to threaten China. In his blunt fashion, Mao accused Nixon and Kissinger of wanting the Soviet Union to become bogged down in China, so that once the Soviets were worn out, the American leaders could "poke [their] finger at the Soviet back."[19]

Still, Kissinger was not ready to abandon detente. He made plain that the United States intended to try to do business with the Soviet Union, although he couched his language in ways that would be appealing to Chinese leaders. "I said that the nature of our relationship meant that we had to pursue a more complicated policy than the PRC which could oppose the Soviet Union outright on issues," Kissinger reported to Nixon. "Whereas we saw two possibilities, i.e. that the Soviet Union would pursue a peaceful or a menacing course, the Chinese saw only the latter." The differences between the American and Chinese policies toward the Soviet Union were becoming apparent, and they were to become ever more important over the next few years.

Kissinger's trip was not devoted exclusively to strategic abstractions and late-night conversation. One concrete gain was made: China agreed that the two governments should exchange liaison offices in each other's capitals, opening the way for American diplomats to begin working for the first time in Beijing and for Chinese officials to come to Washington. Before, U.S. officials had believed Mao and Chou would allow an American presence of a much lower level, like a trade office, in Beijing, and that China would not open an office of any kind in Washington while Taiwan's Republic of China embassy was still open there. To America's surprise, China's proposal for liaison offices went much further than they had expected.

Summarizing where things stood between the United States and China after his trip, Kissinger wrote to Nixon:

Since [July, 1971] we have progressed faster and further than anyone would have predicted, or the rest of the world realizes. *For in
plain terms, we have now become tacit allies.* [Kissinger's emphasis][20]

Tacit allies: It was an accurate summary of the secret relationship being forged between Washington and Beijing. It was an alliance never formally acknowledged, either to the American people or the rest of the world.

THE LIAISON office in Beijing opened a few months later. It was headed by one of America's most experienced ambassadors, David Bruce, and staffed largely by young Chinese speakers at the State Department. They handled a variety of tasks, both important and mundane, under the watchful eyes of the Chinese, who remained so suspicious of the Americans that they viewed the handful of U.S. Marine guards as an "organized foreign military force."[21]

One of the unpublicized jobs of the liaison office in those early years was to obtain movies from the United States for Mao's wife. A deal was quietly worked out with the help of Jack Valenti of the Motion Picture Association of America. American officials discovered that Jiang Qing had curious tastes: The first American movie she wanted to see was *Day of the Jackal,* a film about political assassination, and she later asked to see *Z,* yet another picture about assassinations. No one ventured to ask Jiang Qing why she was so interested in this particular theme.[22]

The American liaison office included one mysterious figure, an urbane Yale alumnus named James R. Lilley. He was the first U.S. intelligence official in China, the CIA's first station chief in Beijing.

Lilley was an experienced Asia hand who had served for the CIA's directorate of operations, its clandestine service, in Laos, Cambodia, the Philippines, Thailand and Hong Kong. In China, he was what is known in the intelligence trade as a "declared agent," meaning that the United States had formally identified him as an intelligence official, while permitting China to station its own professional spy in Washington. (The arrangement was not entirely reciprocal. China did not give the name of its intelligence official beforehand, but American officials later identified him as a diplomat named Xie Qiemei.)[23]

State Department officials had attempted to block Lilley's assignment, arguing that the presence of the CIA would tarnish the new American presence. But Kissinger had backed the CIA in an intramural turf battle. "Henry actually told them that this deal had been made personally with Chairman Mao," recalled Lilley.[24]

Before Lilley left for China, Kissinger ordered the CIA official to be proper and careful. "His [Kissinger's] point to me was, 'Don't take any separate instructions from CIA which violate mine,'" Lilley said. "Namely, I don't want you carrying out any unilateral activity. You're there as a declared man. Whatever you do has to be passive. You don't go out and recruit [Chinese] people and that sort of thing." In other words, Lilley, like other declared intelligence agents, was supposed to read the papers, collect public reports, talk to diplomats and stick to official interviews.

Lilley may have stretched his mandate nevertheless. A quarter-century later, in testimony before a presidential commission reviewing American intelligence capabilities, he admitted that he had laid down some of the infrastructure for future spying:

> What you did [in Beijing] is to spend painstaking hours going out and finding certain locations that in the future you could use for clandestine operations. . . . We didn't have any agents at the time. I'll tell you, when I came back fifteen years later, in the inventory were certain contributions that I had made fifteen years ago. It took that long. . . . I can't go into this very much, but all I can say is we started a collection technique when I was there which was going on when I came back as ambassador [in 1989], which was again

producing real understanding. But it was the evolvement [*sic*] of fifteen years of collection of a lot of data.[25]

Still, the budding American intelligence relationship with China was more friendly than hostile. In Beijing, Lilley was in a position to keep an eye on Soviet, Eastern European, Vietnamese and North Korean diplomats, and perhaps to try occasionally to recruit them. China had many similar interests.

The most significant American intelligence-sharing with China in the early 1970s was run not by the CIA station chief in Beijing, but directly out of the White House. The transmission of intelligence information about the Soviet Union that Kissinger had initiated in 1971 became regularized and more detailed. In Washington, two of Kissinger's top aides, Winston Lord and Jonathan Howe, worked with the CIA to prepare extensive intelligence briefings for China. According to Robert McFarlane, who replaced Howe in July 1973, the intelligence

involved not only strategic nuclear forces, but also conventional army, navy and air forces positioned on the Chinese border and in ocean areas. In addition, the U.S. would brief the Chinese on the extensive Soviet military aid program to dozens of countries and guerrilla movements around the world, including Vietnam.[26]

During a Kissinger trip to Beijing in 1974, McFarlane carried stacks of notebooks with hundreds of pages of U.S. intelligence information, lugging them into the Great Hall of the People to give Chinese officials briefings so thorough that the process took three full days. On a Kissinger trip in 1975, he repeated the performance.

These American briefings about the Soviet Union provided China with a wealth of new intelligence information. China not only didn't have the capabilities of American intelligence, such as satellites, photoreconnaisance, and other electronic gadgetry; at the outset, the Chinese had barely even known what was technically possible. Now, the United States was giving China an inside look at the intelligence dimensions of the Cold War.

As CHINA saw it, the new ties between Washington and Beijing were thrown into jeopardy by the Watergate scandal and Nixon's resignation. Within the United States, Watergate was widely viewed as a demonstration that American law and institutions work, that their power is more important than that of individuals. While this principle was comforting to many Americans, it was deeply unsettling to Chinese leaders.

Chinese political culture has traditionally been based on the idea that persons count more than institutions. Nixon and Kissinger, far from dispelling this venerable belief in the personalized nature of politics, had actively encouraged and reinforced it. Don't worry, they said, about the official policy pronouncements of the State Department, or our speeches and congressional resolutions; listen to what we are telling you privately.

The tension between the Nixon White House on the one hand and America's formal institutional framework on the other had been at the very heart of the opening to China. Nixon had circumvented the bureaucracy to arrange Kissinger's secret trip. When the State Department declared that Taiwan's status was "undetermined," Kissinger told Chou to ignore the formal position. Most of China's hopes and beliefs about the future of its relationship with the United States were based on secret promises from Nixon and Kissinger. These included, above all, Nixon's private assurances to Chou that Taiwan's status was settled and that the United States would normalize relations with Beijing in Nixon's second term. In letters to Chou and to Mao on March 17, 1973, Nixon had once again spoken of his and the Chinese leaders' "joint determination" to normalize relations.[27] What if all of Nixon's secret assurances to China were invalidated by his resignation?

As soon as Nixon's helicopter lifted off from the White House lawn after his resignation on August 9, 1974, Kissinger immediately went to work assuring the Chinese that nothing would change. That very afternoon, Huang Zhen, the head of China's liaison office in Washington, was summoned to the White House. From 4:50 to 5:20 p.m. on the day of Nixon's departure, Huang spoke with Kissinger, who said that "all previous discussions, understandings and commitments by President Nixon are reconfirmed." It was a remarkably sweeping promise, one that Gerald Ford and Kissinger would eventually find impossible to keep.

Kissinger then walked the Chinese ambassador down the hall for a 15-minute talk with the new president. Hours after he had been sworn in, Ford handed Huang a personal letter to Mao, reconfirming the continuity of American policy toward China; the letter also promised that Kissinger would stay on as secretary of state, that Taiwan policy would remain unchanged and that "no policy has higher priority than accelerating" the process of normalization with China.[28]

China needn't have worried. Ford had no intention of altering the direction or shaking up the personnel of Nixon's foreign policy team, at least not at the outset. Richard Cheney, who served as Ford's White House chief of staff, recalls that on the day the new president took over from Nixon, he appointed a transition team to set up his administration. "The marching orders were to go and view the Office of Management and Budget, and White House domestic operations, and relations between the White House and Cabinet, and report back to me," said Cheney. "But stay out of the national security area."[29]

In short, on foreign policy Ford intended to leave Kissinger with a free hand.

KISSINGER'S PENCHANT for secrecy and his personalized diplomacy with China served his own purposes by augmenting his power. If American relations with Beijing were viewed as clandestine and extremely delicate, then other American officials, from the new president on down, might be persuaded to allow him greater latitude. Indeed, under Ford even more than under Nixon, Kissinger worked assiduously to ensure that nothing and no one should interfere with his own dominance over diplomacy with Beijing.

The records suggest that Kissinger was mildly threatened even by Ford's appointment of George Bush, who had been the Republican National Committee chairman, to replace David Bruce as head of the U.S. liaison office in Beijing. Bush had clashed with Kissinger three years earlier, when he was serving as the U.S. ambassador to the United Nations and was trying unsuccessfully to preserve Taiwan's seat. When Bush dropped by the White House on October 15, 1974, to say good-bye to the president before leaving for Beijing, Kissinger prepared talking points for Ford that, though phrased delicately, effectively asked the new ambassador to steer clear of Kissinger's own high-level, high-profile diplomacy.

> Ambassador Bush probably will not see Mao, and perhaps not Chou, during his initial calls, but he can convey the [presidential] messages through the Foreign Ministry. . . . I am confident that you [Bush] will take in stride some of the frustrations of working and living in Beijing, including the low-key nature of our public posture there.[30]

Kissinger needn't have worried, because Bush was eager to please. In a very brief good-bye session in the Oval Office, he said the "big thing" on his agenda was a trip to China by Kissinger. Bush also had other interests in mind, ones that went beyond his diplomatic assignment. "If there is anything I can do to help you politically as '76 approaches, just let me know," Bush told the president, according to a now-declassified transcript.[31]

Indeed, although Bush would in later years make much of his work as head of the U.S. liaison office and speak sentimentally of his stay in

China, the reality is that within a remarkably short time in Beijing, he was maneuvering to come home. After arriving in the fall of 1974, Bush returned to Washington over Christmas to be inaugurated as president of the prestigious Alfalfa Club. He was also hospitalized in Washington with a serious stomach ailment and did not return to Beijing for several weeks.[32] On March 20, 1975, barely five months after Bush first landed in Beijing, White House Counselor Jack Marsh was given a memo by his deputy Russ Rourke:

> It's my impression and partial understanding that George Bush has probably had enough of egg rolls and Peking by now (and has probably gotten over his lost VP opportunity). He's one hell of a Presidential surrogate, and would be an outstanding spokesman for the White House between now and November '76. Don't you think he would make an outstanding candidate for Secretary of Commerce or a similar post sometime during the next six months?[33]

Nevertheless, while biding his time and waiting for another job in Washington, Bush stayed in Beijing long enough to take part in some of Kissinger's most acrimonious high-level diplomacy with China.

BY 1975, China had waited more than three years for the full normalization of relations that Nixon had promised. Chinese leaders and Kissinger wanted to work out a deal that could be completed during Ford's trip to Beijing at the end of that year. In Washington, Kissinger's aides spent part of the spring and early summer preparing the details of how the United States would establish diplomatic relations with the People's Republic. By the end of May 1975, the United States had withdrawn its F-4 squadrons, the last of its combat aircraft, from Taiwan, a step aimed at paving the way for normalization with China.[34]

Yet Ford was no more able to achieve this goal than Nixon had been after the onset of Watergate. The new president was blocked by events overseas and their consequences in American domestic politics. In the spring of 1975, the Vietnam War came to its conclusion with the frantic, chaotic flight of American and South Vietnamese officials from the country. Kissinger's pursuit of detente and arms control with the Soviet Union was under attack in both parties.

Ford and his political advisers grew increasingly worried that he was vulnerable to an attack from the political right in the 1976 presidential primaries. California Governor Ronald Reagan was already preparing to run against Ford, who realized he would need at least some support from conservative Republicans in order to win his party's nomination. Establishing diplomatic relations with China was too politically risky.

Among those who warned Ford not to move ahead too precipitously in breaking relations with Taiwan was George Bush. The head of the U.S. liaison office in Beijing had hopes of winning a spot on the Republican ticket in 1976. Declassified files show that on May 23, 1995, barely a month after the fall of Saigon, Bush sent Ford a secret memo outside the normal State Department or National Security Council channels. Its contents represented "sheer politics," Bush said; the advice could be shared only with Kissinger and no one else in the foreign policy apparatus.

"Your own personal interests dictate that serious thought be given to what is possible from a purely political standpoint," Bush told Ford. "Answers to the Taiwan question that may have been possible before the collapse in Cambodia and Viet Nam [*sic*] may no longer be any answers at all." Bush warned that Taiwan was an explosive issue, and he urged that "thought be given as to how to keep this issue from building into a major weapon for your opponents be they Republican or Democrat."[35]

The secretary of state quickly got the message. He was already brooding about losing influence within the Ford administration. The declassified archives show that during a meeting on July 6, 1975, Kissinger's own aides, Winston Lord and Richard Solomon, pressed hard for him to move ahead toward establishment of diplomatic ties with Beijing. Kissinger turned them down. "For political reasons it's just impossible for the US to go for normalization before '76," he told Lord. "If there's any one thing that will trigger a conservative reaction to Ford, that's it."

Kissinger worried aloud that others within the Ford administration, such as White House Chief of Staff Donald Rumsfeld, were gaining influence and that he was losing it. Pressed by his aides to follow through on the promised normalization with China, Kissinger told them, "I'll try to raise it with the President, but I know the answer. Those guys over there [at the White House] won't even take on Panama right now." That was a reference to the need for a new treaty governing the Panama Canal, another issue that Ford decided to leave to his successor.[36]

The Chinese were not informed of the decision for several months. Finally, on September 28, 1975, during a meeting at the United Nations in New York, Kissinger told Chinese Foreign Minister Qiao Guanhua that normalization could not be completed during Ford's visit to China later that year, though perhaps some intermediate steps might be possible.[37]

Chinese leaders were furious. They apparently were convinced that Kissinger and other American leaders had been taking advantage of

China, both within Asia and in pursuit of detente with the Soviet Union. They also felt that China had done some favors for the Americans. Earlier that year, China had dampened the ambitions of its North Korean allies to capitalize on the American collapse in Saigon. "When Kim Il Sung came to China about the time of the fall of Vietnam, he was saying to the Chinese, 'This is the time to hit the United States,'" said James Lilley. "And the Chinese wouldn't have any part of it."[38]

Ford, like Nixon before him, had failed to follow through on the promise of diplomatic relations. That set the stage for the most contentious series of exchanges between China and the United States of the entire Nixon-Ford era.[39]

In October 1975, Kissinger flew to Beijing to prepare the way for Ford's trip in December. White House files show that he expected to be able to work out the language of a communique, just as he had for Nixon in 1972. "On my China trip, I would propose negotiating the communique of your trip, so you don't have to do it," he told Ford in the Oval Office.[40]

But China wanted the real thing, a full normalization of relations, not another airy proclamation about how much the two governments liked and cooperated with one another. By this time, Chou Enlai was dying of cancer, and Deng was under attack from the left-wing faction of Communist Party leaders later dubbed the "Gang of Four"; he was in no position to be conciliatory, particularly to Americans who were not following through on their secret promises. It was Deng's behavior during this era that prompted Kissinger to say at one point that Deng was a "nasty little man."

In Beijing in the fall of 1975, Kissinger was rebuffed. On the first day of his trip, he laid out a proposal for a communique. Deng and other Chinese officials said nothing about it. Instead, the secretary of state was smothered with empty hospitality; one afternoon, he and his delegation were taken on a long picnic in the Western Hills outside Beijing to see the leaves, taking up time that Kissinger had hoped would be used in negotiations. When he asked repeatedly about his proposed communique, he was told it was still being translated. He was granted another audience with Mao, but the Chinese leader told Kissinger sarcastically that America was trying to "leap at Moscow by way of China's shoulders, but China's shoulders are now useless."

Finally, at midnight on the final day of Kissinger's trip, Qiao, the Chinese foreign minister, rejected the proposed communique and suggested a toughly worded Chinese version that Kissinger termed "completely unacceptable." It would have advertised to the world the many differences between America and China.[41]

After Kissinger returned to Washington, some of Ford's political advisers recommended that the president cancel his planned visit. One of them, Robert Hartmann, warned the president in a private memo that at the very time when Reagan was challenging him from the political right,

> you will be on TV nightly smiling at Chinese Communists and making toasts to Chairman Mao ("the murderer of millions") in Peking. . . . Far beyond the Chinese aspect of it, there is undoubtedly a very broad concern in this country about any form of detente or the doing of any kind of business with the Communist world—witness the grain deals [with the Soviet Union].

Although Kissinger himself gave Ford the option of canceling his trip, the president decided to go ahead without a communique. "I think to cancel it would be a disaster, both internationally and with the left and right," Ford said in one Oval Office strategy session.[42]

Ford's visit to China turned out to be largely a charade, orchestrated to conceal the disagreements between the two governments. Kissinger, who only six weeks earlier had insisted privately to Chinese officials that a presidential visit should end with a communique, reversed course and told American reporters not to make too much of the fact that there was none. At the opening banquet, Deng made plain China's unhappiness with America's too-conciliatory policy toward the Soviet Union. "Rhetoric about detente cannot cover up the stark reality of the growing danger of war," Deng said.[43]

Ford held out to Chinese leaders the prospect that he would normalize relations with Beijing after the next presidential election, but the Chinese had heard the line too many times to be impressed.

The American president was escorted to the obligatory audience with Mao, who was so frail that his interpreters often were unsure what he was saying. Mao told Ford, "God has sent me an invitation," an allusion to the fact that he expected to die soon. Ford may not have understood the Chinese leader; at the end of the session, groping for something to say, he cheerily told Mao: "I hope you get your invitation soon!" For years, this remark was passed on privately among Kissinger's top aides as a sign of how far things had fallen when Ford replaced Nixon.[44]

Soon after Ford returned to Washington, in a clear demonstration of their disenchantment with the American president, Chinese leaders invited Nixon himself to Beijing. From Ford's point of view, the timing could not possibly have been worse: Nixon made his trip in late February 1976, at the beginning of the presidential primaries, thus attracting sev-

eral days of news coverage that served to remind the American public of
how Ford had pardoned Nixon. Although years later Nixon would be
regarded in the United States as something of an elder statesman, in 1976
he was decidedly in public disgrace; China was, in fact, the first overseas
trip since his resignation. So cool was the State Department to the visit
that one of the American diplomats working in Beijing informed Nixon
he would be welcome to come see the U.S. liaison office that had been
set up as part of his opening to China—but only in private, without any
press coverage. Nixon declined the invitation.[45]

On February 26, 1976, the lead story in the *New York Times* reported
that Ford had narrowly defeated Reagan in the New Hampshire primary.
The front-page picture, however, was of Nixon in Tiananmen Square. It
was to be the first of many times in which China opened its arms to out-
of-office or opposition leaders from the United States in order to register
its unhappiness with American policies of the moment.[46]

During the 1976 elections, Kissinger played the China issue both
ways. Records show that he told American conservatives that no commitment had been made to normalize relations with China; privately he
reassured Beijing it would get what it wanted after the presidential
campaign had ended. In one noteworthy episode, Senator Barry
Goldwater, Taiwan's staunchest supporter in Washington, wrote a private
letter to Kissinger on May 28, 1976, saying he had heard news reports
that the administration might recognize China after the elections. Goldwater threatened to withdraw his earlier endorsement of Ford over
Reagan:

> I would like to have immediate verification or non verification of
> this [story], because it will strongly affect whether or not I will sup-
> port the President. It doesn't make any sense to me to forego [*sic*]
> our friends on Taiwan, and I don't intend to stay quiet about it, so
> please within twenty-four hours let me know what the truth is and
> I mean the truth.[47]

Faced with this ultimatum, Kissinger responded with less than the
whole truth. In his mind, private assurances to Chinese leaders didn't
count. A notation on the letter from White House counselor Jack Marsh
says, "Henry called the Senator this afternoon. Says he turned him off."
Goldwater immediately informed others that Kissinger had assuaged his
fears about a post-election normalization. The following day, records
show, an anxious Huang Zhen, the head of China's liaison office in
Washington, visited Kissinger to ask what on earth he had told Gold-

water. Kissinger calmed Huang down, too, letting him know that nothing had changed in the administration's plans for normalization.[48] It was a classic illustration of how Kissinger sometimes gave contradictory accounts to opposing sides of an issue, telling each party what he or she wanted to hear.

THERE WAS an underside to this apparent stalemate over normalization. As Kissinger found himself unable to deliver on the old Nixon promise of diplomatic relations with Beijing, he began to search for other ways to keep China happy. In 1975 and 1976, he turned to the fields of military, intelligence and technology cooperation as one way to advance America's relations with China.

The steps were small ones, but they began to move the United States down a new path. The idea of playing a "China card" against the Soviet Union, at first the novel idea of Pillsbury and a few patrons in the Pentagon, was becoming an important element in mainstream American policy toward Beijing.

Lilley, the first CIA station chief in Beijing, had returned to Washington in early 1975. While still in China a few months earlier, he had been publicly identified as an intelligence official in a magazine article by CIA critic John Marks and in a subsequent newspaper column by Jack Anderson. Although this fact was hardly news to the Chinese government, it was a revelation to some other governments dealing with Lilley.

Lilley felt that after these stories were published, his two-decade-long career in the CIA's Directorate of Operations had reached its end. "I was getting sort of tired of that stuff, anyway, because it loses its flavor after a while," he explained in an interview. "It's pretty dreary stuff, especially if you're doing passive kind of work."[49]

Back in Washington, Lilley took a position as the national intelligence officer in charge of U.S. government analyses of China and the rest of East Asia. One of the studies he directed was of whether China might import Western military technology. It was the first examination by the U.S. intelligence community of the issues raised by Pillsbury. The report suggested that U.S. military ties with Beijing could help strengthen those Chinese leaders who favored strong links with the West, and that these links could help improve American relations with China at a time when normalization was impossible.[50]

The intelligence report was delivered to the White House just before Kissinger's October 1975 visit to China. In Beijing, Kissinger for the first time proposed the establishment of intelligence ties between the United States and China—that is, a regular relationship of the sort that went well beyond the occasional American briefings on Soviet troop deployments. "We made the first proposal to the Chinese for real intelligence cooperation [on Kissinger's trip]," said Lilley. "They [administration officials] were looking for ways for cooperation other than normalization, because the Chinese were being very difficult." [51]

Kissinger also first proposed the idea of military cooperation on this same trip. A transcript of part of his conversation with Mao shows that he told the Chinese leader, "We have tried to suggest to you that we are prepared to advise or help in some of these [defense] problems." [52]

At this early stage, the Americans were taking the initiative. This was not a case of China coaxing the United States to turn over military technology, as happened in later years. In fact, China was cool to Kissinger's proposal, at least at the top levels of its leadership, when it seemed as though the military cooperation was being offered as a consolation prize instead of formal diplomatic relations. "As for military aspects, we should not discuss that now," Mao told Kissinger on October 21, 1975. "Such matters should wait until the war breaks out before we consider them." Lilley says China similarly rebuffed the first suggestions of an intelligence relationship. [53]

Still, the administration persisted in these endeavors. During a midnight meeting on Ford's trip to China six weeks later, Kissinger told Chinese Foreign Minister Qiao Guanhua that the United States was prepared to buy Chinese petroleum and to sell what Kissinger called "equipment of a special nature" to China. He was, in effect, proposing that China could use its oil to buy American technology.

During Ford's trip, he and Kissinger also took an even more significant step in the direction of military cooperation. They gave their final authorization for a $200 million deal in which China would buy Spey jet engines from Britain's Rolls-Royce. These engines were used in British F-4 Phantom jets, and it was plain that China's aim was to install them in Chinese fighter bombers, too. One part of the deal called for Britain to help China set up a factory so that it could build its own Spey engines in the future. It was the first time China had been permitted to buy military-related technology from the West.

The American role in the arrangement was hidden, but crucial. Ordinarily, any such sale would have had to go to what was known as COCOM: a committee, composed of NATO countries and Japan, that restricted high-technology sales to Communist countries. However, the Ford administration allowed the British to proceed without asking for the approval of America and its allies.

The Rolls-Royce deal illustrated, once again, how Kissinger worked secretly to undermine the formal processes of the U.S. government on China policy. Although officials in the State and Defense Departments were opposed to the sale of the engines to China, the White House had known about it for two years, dating back to Nixon's tenure in the White House. At one point, Nixon informed Prime Minister Edward Heath that he planned to announce America's opposition to the deal. Nixon told the British leader simply to ignore his public statements.[54]

IN POLITICAL terms, the year 1976 was a watershed for the Chinese leadership and for America as well. Chou Enlai died in January and then Mao himself died the following September. In the United States, Ford overcame Reagan's challenge for the Republican nomination, but then lost to his Democratic challenger, Jimmy Carter, in November.

In both countries, larger political forces were also at work. In China, Mao's death led to the arrest of Jiang Qing and the Gang of Four. Those arrests removed from power the Chinese leaders who were most strongly opposed to ties with the United States; they also opened the way for the return to power of Deng Xiaoping and other leaders who were committed to modernizing China with the aid of Western technology and education.

In the United States, the 1976 election demonstrated that the conservative wings of both political parties were still divided over American policy toward China. The anti-Communist right, represented by Republicans like Reagan, Goldwater, Buckley and Buchanan, were still determinedly opposed to the normalization of relations with China, particularly if it would require cutting off ties with Taiwan. However, anti-Soviet sentiments had much wider appeal, and a growing number of conservatives were attracted to the idea of forming a stronger relationship with China, or using a "China card," to counteract the Soviets. When Senator Henry M. Jackson, the Democrats' leading opponent of detente with the Soviet Union, called for normalization of relations with China. Buckley's *National Review* accused Jackson of moral blindness about China: "The People's Republic, in fact, is a far more totalitarian state than the Soviet Union, against whose repressive policies the Senator has made it his trademark to thunder."[55]

Throughout 1976, Kissinger and other American officials tried to curry favor with those who might emerge as China's new leaders. When Mao died, Ford immediately sent a condolence note to Jiang Qing. "Dear Madame Mao," he wrote on September 9, 1976, "Mrs. Ford joins me in extending to you our deepest sympathy."[56] Despite Ford's best wishes, Jiang Qing was destined to spend most of the rest of her life in prison.

Technology had become, by this time, the biggest favor the United States could bestow. A few weeks after Mao's death, the Ford administration approved the sale of the first two American computers to China. The Cyber 72 computers, made by Control Data, were supposed to be for oil exploration and seismological research, but they also had military applications. Kissinger won approval for the computers on October 12, 1976, less than a week after the arrests of the Gang of Four. The sale was aimed at helping those individuals within the Chinese leadership, eventually to be led by Deng, who favored modernizing China through strong ties with the United States.

To maintain appearances that it was not siding too much with Beijing over Moscow, the Ford White House also cleared the way for the sale of a similar computer to the Soviet Union. Nevertheless, the Soviets already possessed other computers, and the Chinese did not; the sale was, in that sense, far more helpful to China. Gradually, the United States was putting itself into position to provide China with the sort of technology that could be put to military use.[57]

AFTER CARTER won the November election, China confronted the first genuine transition of power over U.S. foreign policy since the Nixon-Kissinger opening to China five years earlier. The prospect made Chinese officials nervous. On December 21, 1976, Huang Zhen, still the head of China's liaison office in Washington, called upon Kissinger.

Huang grilled the secretary of state about what President-elect Carter, whom Kissinger had just seen in Plains, Georgia, might do in China policy. The ambassador also asked about Kissinger's plans to write his memoirs. Above all, Huang had one overriding concern: secrecy. Recently declassified documents show that at the December meeting, Huang sought "reassurances that PRC-related documents of the Nixon-Ford period will not be disclosed."[58]

China didn't want the new administration to make public the substance of the conversations between Nixon and Kissinger on the one hand, and Mao and Chou on the other. It didn't want Congress or the American public to know about the extent of cooperation between the two countries, or the secret understandings that had been reached on issues like Taiwan. Kissinger assuaged the Chinese fears. Some of those conversations were not made public for decades, and others have not been released at this writing.

By early January 1977, the transition to a new Democratic administration was well advanced. Kissinger introduced Secretary of State Cyrus Vance and Huang Zhen to one another. The Chinese ambassador lost no time putting Vance on the defensive, complaining that one of President-elect Carter's statements had seemed to imply a degree of support for Taiwan.

This time, unlike the beginning of the Ford presidency, the transfer of control over American foreign policy was genuine. Kissinger was departing, to be replaced by a Democratic administration that had criticized him. A new era was coming for the United States and China.

CHAPTER FOUR

Carter and Recognition

ONE DAY IN THE EARLY summer of 1977, the small coterie of American diplomats working at the U.S. liaison office in Beijing was summoned to the room they called "the tank." This is the embassy's inner sanctum, a secure area specially designed to protect against Chinese bugging and eavesdropping. The purpose of the session was for the diplomats to meet their new boss, Leonard Woodcock, the former head of the United Auto Workers, whom President Carter had named to head the liaison office.

The new ambassador lost no time getting down to business. "You may wonder what I'm doing here," he told the gathered Americans. "I was the head of one of America's leading labor unions, and we helped deliver Michigan and several other states to President Carter during the campaign last year. He asked me what I wanted, and I said I wanted to be an ambassador.

"You may think I'm a dilettante, but I'm not," Woodcock continued. "I've read everything I can about China, including the transcripts of the Warsaw talks, the Paris talks [between Vernon Walters and Chinese Ambassador Huang Zhen], and Secretary of State Kissinger's talks with the Chinese.

"And let me say one thing. Never again shall we embarrass ourselves before a foreign nation the way Henry Kissinger did with the Chinese." [1]

Woodcock's little speech captured perfectly the attitude of several successor administrations toward the nature of the relationship that Nixon and, especially, Henry Kissinger had established with Beijing. For a quarter-century afterward, new arrivals in the White House snickered privately and sometimes publicly that Kissinger had been overly charmed by Chinese leaders and had been too eager to please his hosts.

If anything, Woodcock had been somewhat less critical of the previous administration than was Carter himself. Before dispatching one of his top advisers to Beijing, the president gave instructions that "we should not ass-kiss them [the Chinese] the way Nixon and Kissinger did."[2]

In the same fashion as Carter, Presidents Reagan and Clinton also came to the White House determined to change the direction or style of American policy toward China. Indeed, in the two decades after Kissinger's departure from office, the only American president who sought to maintain the status quo on China policy was George Bush— and he, ironically, found himself the least able to do so.

Nevertheless, altering the Nixon-Kissinger approach proved not so easy to accomplish. Indeed, most of Nixon's successors found themselves perpetuating not only the China policies set down in the early 1970s, but also, more surprisingly, much of the style and the texture of the Nixon-Kissinger era.

Despite Carter's and Woodcock's protestations that they would do business with China in a different way, they soon fell into many of the same patterns as their predecessors. Where Nixon and Kissinger conducted secret diplomacy, so did Carter, to the point where his own secretary of state, Cyrus Vance, regretfully acknowledged in his memoirs the extent to which the administration's China policy had been kept hidden from Congress.[3]

Just as Kissinger had conducted intensely personalized diplomacy with Beijing, so did Carter's national security advisor, Zbigniew Brzezinski. Just as the Nixon administration had allowed China policy to be plagued by nasty skirmishing between the National Security Council and the State Department, so did the Carter administration. Such problems were easy for Chinese leaders to exploit in their negotiations.

What accounted for the remarkable longevity of the Kissingerian approach to China? Kissinger left office in 1976 and, indeed, had been weakened by intense criticism during his last two years as secretary of state. Yet even while out of office, he exerted a powerful hold over American policy toward China well into the 1990s.

One factor was the role of personnel. Few thought of Kissinger in this way, but he was, in effect, a godfather, the leader of a small cadre of men serving under him who were to guide American policy toward China for the next quarter-century. Among those working under Kissinger at the National Security Council and the State Department were two future secretaries of state (Alexander Haig and Lawrence Eagleburger); three national security advisors (Brent Scowcroft, Robert McFarlane and Anthony Lake); and one ambassador to China (Winston Lord).

These top-level jobs were only the beginning of the story. Other key positions down through the American foreign policy bureaucracy were also occupied by Kissinger alumni. For example, during the 16-year period from 1981 to 1996, the job of assistant secretary of state for East Asia, the official responsible for directing America's day-to-day transactions with China, was occupied three times by former Kissinger aides: John Holdridge (1981–82), Richard Solomon (1989–92) and Lord (1993–96).

In some cases, Kissinger's influence on his former aides was simple and direct: He could pick up the telephone and offer his views. In other cases, it was more subtle. Even those former Kissinger aides who broke with their former mentor, such as Lake and Lord, shared many of his underlying assumptions—including the ideas that China was of surpassing strategic importance to the United States and that the Shanghai Communique negotiated by Nixon should be the foundation of future American policy toward China. Moreover, the mystique about visits to China fostered by the Kissinger and Nixon trips of 1971–72 set a style that successors often imitated, either deliberately or unconsciously.

Carter appointed far fewer Kissinger alumni to high-level posts than other presidents. Yet in its behavior toward China, his administration demonstrated some of the other factors that helped perpetuate Kissinger's approach and many of his policies.

One was that there were strong though often hidden constituencies in Washington in favor of close ties with China. Many in the Pentagon and in the U.S. intelligence community were interested in obtaining China's help in combating the Soviet Union. While new presidents might arrive committed to altering American policy toward China, sooner or later they encountered pressures from within Washington to keep following along the same path as their predecessors. The American courtship of China became so closely linked to the larger dynamics of the Cold War that no new president could change it in any fundamental way.

Another factor was that China liked and often insisted upon doing business with America in the fashion that it had with Nixon and Kissinger. Chinese leaders preferred to deal with a single, high-level American official, an interlocutor who could be courted, flattered and praised for his wisdom, in the fashion of Kissinger. Such an official (Brzezinski, Haig) would in turn often become a forceful advocate in Washington for policies that served China's interests.

Indeed, China tried to make it difficult, if not impossible, for American officials to conduct business in any other way. Whenever America sent an emissary to Beijing whose style was more impersonal, institutional or lawyerly, such as Carter's secretary of state, Cyrus Vance, or, many years later, President Clinton's secretary of state, Warren Christopher, Chinese leaders treated him badly. Getting along with Beijing seemed to require an acknowledgment that China was unique and should be treated differently from all other countries.

Unfortunately, the approach of treating China as unique had drawbacks. It reinforced Chinese leaders' sense that they deserved special treatment, that the American policies on issues like arms control and human rights that applied to other countries didn't apply to China. Moreover, says Roger Sullivan, who worked on China policy in both the Nixon and Carter administrations, "We gave them [Chinese leaders] the impression we wanted the relationship so badly that we could be bluffed." [4]

During his four years in the White House, Carter succeeded in accomplishing what his two predecessors had promised but failed to do: He completed the job of establishing diplomatic relations with China. Yet the fashion in which he did so perpetuated both the secrecy and the mystique about China that had been fostered by Nixon and Kissinger.

To his credit, Carter also broadened the social basis of the relationship between the United States and China. He opened the way for China to send its scholars to the United States (and, to a much lesser extent, for America to direct students to China). This was a far-reaching step, one that would, in later years, exert a significant if unanticipated influence on the relations between the United States and China.

Despite these accomplishments, Carter's policy was, in many respects, a disappointment. The administration was responsible for giving a military, anti-Soviet cast to America's relationship with China, creating ties in which the interests of the Pentagon and the CIA became all-important. By the time diplomatic relations were finally established, American and Chinese leaders spent much of their time talking about coordinating actions against the Soviet Union, and about arms sales, technology transfers and intelligence sharing. Questions about the long-term implications of these policies—about what might happen to America and China if the anti-Soviet basis of their friendship collapsed—were swept aside.

So, too, were human rights questions in China largely ignored, even though Carter himself had been the driving force behind American human rights policies elsewhere in the world. The Carter administration was the first to be confronted with questions about how to respond to the pleas of ordinary Chinese for freedom of speech and democracy; it was during Carter's tenure, in 1978–79, that the Democracy Wall movement spread across Chinese cities. The Carter administration failed this important test. It proceeded to look the other way as dissidents like Wei Jingsheng were arrested and jailed. In so doing, Carter undercut the moral basis for his human rights policy and established the double standard, perpetuated through the 1980s, in which the United States gave the strongest possible support to dissidents in the Soviet Union while refusing to give comparable help to critics of the regime in China.

CARTER TOOK office intending to establish diplomatic relations with China.

The month before he was sworn in, Kissinger flew to Carter's home in Plains, Georgia, to brief him on the secret China diplomacy of the Nixon and Ford administrations. During the transition period, Carter also read for the first time the transcripts of the Nixon-Kissinger conversations with Mao Tsetung and Chou Enlai. In February 1977, during an initial meeting at the White House with Chinese Ambassador Huang Zhen, Carter paid obeisance to Nixon's Shanghai Communique and talked of his hopes for recognizing the People's Republic of China. The new president also informed Huang he hoped to normalize U.S. relations with Vietnam. "We think this is good," Huang answered amicably, although Vietnam would later became a sensitive issue between Washington and Beijing.[5]

China was not at the top of the new administration's list of priorities. When they first took office, Carter and Vance were eager to pursue detente and a new arms control agreement with the Soviet Union. Moreover, during his first year in the White House, Carter was trying to win Senate approval to return the Panama Canal to Panama, and he realized that establishing diplomatic relations with China would infuriate conservative senators, such as Barry Goldwater, whose votes he needed on the Panama Canal treaties.[6]

In August 1977, Vance visited Beijing, offering to establish diplomatic relations but, at the same time, proposing terms that the Chinese viewed as less than what Nixon, Ford and Kissinger had promised. Vance later acknowledged that, with the Panama Canal treaties pending, the administration deliberately gave China its "maximum position" in the negotiations over normalization, expecting, correctly, that China would reject the Americans' first offer.[7]

The main issue in dispute was what sort of ties the United States would have with Taiwan after it recognized the Beijing regime as China's government. Over the previous four years, Chinese leaders had repeatedly listed three conditions the United States would have to meet for the establishment of relations: to cut off diplomatic links with Taiwan's government, end its defense treaty with Taiwan and remove all U.S. military personnel and installations from the island. This approach was commonly termed the "Japanese formula," because Japan, which had hurriedly established relations with Beijing after the initial shock of the Nixon trip, had cut off all diplomatic relations with Taiwan and had carried out its business on the island through representatives who had no official or government status. The United States, however, couldn't simply replicate the "Japanese model" for establishing relations with China, because it had too much at stake. Japan, after all, didn't have defense links or a defense treaty with Taiwan.

The Carter administration was divided. Some officials, led by Anthony Lake, the State Department's director of policy planning, argued that the United States ought to try to preserve an official consulate in Taiwan, because otherwise, the legal status of America's relationship with Taiwan would be too complicated. Others in the administration, including the National Security Council and some of the State Department's China hands, countered that such an approach wouldn't work. The United States ought to cut off all official ties with Taiwan, they said.[8]

Vance decided to try for a Taiwan consulate. On his 1977 trip, he told Chinese leaders that the Carter administration wanted to maintain U.S. government personnel on Taiwan, even if they weren't working in an embassy. The Chinese, irritated, pointed out that this offer was less than they had been promised by Nixon and Kissinger. Indeed, declassified archives show that in February 1973, Kissinger told Chinese leaders "that we would be prepared to move after the 1974 elections toward something like the Japanese solution with respect to diplomatic relations."[9] Ford, too, had spoken of the Japanese formula for normalization, meaning a cutoff in ties with Taiwan, during his visit to Beijing in 1975.[10]

As a result, Deng Xiaoping angrily rejected Vance's offer. In a long meeting on the afternoon of August 24, Deng branded the Carter administration's terms for normalization as a "retreat" from what Ford had promised two years earlier. The new American proposal, Deng said, amounted to having a "flagless embassy" on Taiwan.[11] With this issue unresolved, Washington and Beijing weren't ready to establish relations. The delay was not especially disappointing to Carter administration officials, preoccupied as they were with the Panama Canal and other controversies.

China responded by letting the Carter administration know of its displeasure in the customary ways. It gave lavish treatment to representatives of the administration's domestic political opposition—in this case members of the Republican Party. In the fall of 1977, former Ambassador George Bush was welcomed to China, along with an entourage that included Lilley and Bush's close friend James A. Baker III. The fact that Bush had just been CIA director, and that Lilley had been a senior official at the CIA, served as an added reminder of China's interests in intelligence and strategic issues.

According to Lilley, Bush told Chinese Ambassador Huang Zhen before this trip that he would soon be a Republican presidential candidate. "He said, 'I'm running for president in '80. You're the first to know,' " recalls Lilley. "Of course, they weren't [the first], but he told them that, and they felt very flattered." Bush and his party were granted an audience with Deng Xiaoping. They were also among the first Western observers permitted to visit Tibet since it had been occupied by Chinese troops more than a quarter-century earlier. Upon his return, Bush wrote an article for *Newsweek* in which he passed along to the American public, without judgment, China's own viewpoint about its supposedly benevolent rule in Tibet:

> Religion is not encouraged, and the Dalai Lama, who now lives in India, is the subject of constant attack for the lavish splendor of his former life-style and his callous attitude toward the people. . . . The Chinese seemed justifiably proud of economic achievements.[12]

BY THE spring of 1978, the Carter administration had become more enthusiastic about establishing relations with Beijing. The politics in Washington were shifting. The Senate was in the process of ratifying the Panama Canal treaties, and now Carter wanted to proceed with another, still more contentious issue: SALT II, a new arms control treaty with the Soviet Union. He would need Senate approval for this treaty, too.

This time, Carter calculated that normalization with China could indirectly help rather than hurt him in the Senate, because it was a cause that appealed to the anti-Soviet sentiments of some conservative senators. "Some of the senators known to be doubtful about a SALT II treaty with the Soviet Union had expressed the hope that we would develop better relations with China," he later explained. Once again, China was treated as a sideshow, an outgrowth of other, more pressing foreign policy issues.[13]

Carter's White House had its own forceful advocate for viewing China in anti-Soviet terms in the person of National Security Advisor Zbigniew Brzezinski. Brzezinski, a Polish émigré, made no effort to hide the fact that he thought of American policy toward China as extremely useful in what he saw as the worldwide struggle between Washington and Moscow:

> The Soviet dimension [of China policy] was one of those considerations of which it is sometimes said, "Think of it at all times but speak of it never." I, for one, thought of it a great deal, even though

MARCH

9

TUESDAY

At the beginning of "Treehouse of Horror XII" (CABF19), who are Homer and Marge dressed as for Halloween?

a. Fred and Ginger
b. Fred and Ethel
c. Fred and Wilma
d. Fred and Daphne

Answer: c

I knew that publicly one had to make pious noises to the effect that U.S.-Chinese normalization had nothing to do with U.S.-Soviet rivalry.[14]

Brzezinski's views ran directly contrary to those of Vance, who warned repeatedly against the dangers of trying to use China against the Soviet Union:

The Chinese must . . . be made to understand that we do not perceive our relations with them as one-dimensional (i.e., vis-à-vis the USSR). . . . Right now, the U.S. has a closer relationship with each Communist superpower than either has with the other. We must continue to maintain that fragile equilibrium.[15]

In the earliest days of his administration, Carter sided with Vance. As time went on, however, the president shifted increasingly toward his national security advisor's view of the world.

In the last months of 1977, Brzezinski had quietly urged Carter to let him travel to China. Through Michel Oksenberg, his specialist on China at the NSC, Brzezinski had let Chinese officials in Washington know he would like to visit Beijing; the Chinese, never slow to detect possible divisions within an administration, had taken the hint. Vance told Carter he was opposed to the trip, on grounds that the president and secretary of state should be the main spokesmen for the administration on foreign policy and also that Brzezinski's trip would undercut the American position about conditions for normalizing relations with China. Yet by Brzezinski's account, he pestered and badgered the president for months to let him go to China, and he persuaded Vice President Walter Mondale and Defense Secretary Harold Brown to lobby for him.[16]

In March 1978, Carter decided to unleash Brzezinski. He apparently convinced himself the move was a balanced one: The national security advisor would be sent to Beijing, while Vance would visit Moscow. In fact, however, it turned out to be the decisive step in the administration's development of a China policy based overwhelmingly on Sino-American collaboration against the Soviet Union.

IN TAKING office, Carter had insisted his administration would treat China in a less reverential fashion than had Kissinger. But by the time Brzezinski landed in Beijing on May 20, 1978, he was clearly trying to follow the path of his famous predecessor. Brzezinski, like some national security advisors to follow (McFarlane in Tehran, Scowcroft in Beijing) believed he was on a Kissingerian mission.

Like Kissinger, Brzezinski viewed himself as an academic and a strategist, more knowledgeable and less bureaucratic in style than the secretary of state. Like Kissinger, he believed Chinese leaders recognized his superior wisdom and vision. Indeed, Brzezinski's memoirs show that his identification with Kissinger was still more intensely personal:

> I could not help but think of the strange coincidence that the Sino-American relationship was being forged in the course of a single decade by two U.S. officials who were of immigrant birth and who approached this task with relatively little knowledge of or special sentiment for China, but with larger strategic concerns in mind.[17]

Brzezinski arrived in Beijing laden with gifts. After a series of Cabinet-level meetings in Washington, the administration had secretly decided to open the way for China to obtain Western arms, military equipment and technology. Brzezinski informed Chinese officials that Washington would allow China to obtain American technology that could not be sold to the Soviet Union, and which had previously been withheld from China. One of the items authorized, for example, was Landsat infrared scanning equipment, which China had previously been denied.[18]

The United States remained unwilling to provide China with its own arms or weapons systems. However, Brzezinski offered China something nearly as good. He indicated that the Carter administration would help China to buy arms from America's Western European allies and would not raise objections within the Western alliance if European governments wanted to transfer advanced technology to China.

The Carter administration was thus aiding China's armed forces, but secretly, without direct American involvement. The best description of what Brzezinski did was provided three years later by then Secretary of State Alexander Haig. According to this account, "Zbig told the Chinese the U.S. would see that they got weapons, and asked them for a list of what they want(ed). The Chinese, in response to the U.S. initiative . . . provided a list of 47 items. Zbig then went through Western Europe with the list, saying, 'We can't sell right now, but you do it.' "[19]

It was a clever solution. For the remainder of the Carter administration, senior U.S. officials would be able to assert, truthfully, that the United States did not sell arms to China. Yet the administration's action opened the way for China to obtain advanced weaponry from elsewhere. It also set the stage for the next step: A few years later, the United States would be able to justify arms sales to China by arguing that Beijing was already obtaining these arms from other countries, and that America merely wanted to be able to supply the same sorts of weapons systems the Europeans were already selling.

Brzezinski offered China other blandishments. His delegation included the first representative of the Pentagon to visit China: Morton Abramowitz, the deputy assistant secretary of defense for international security. Abramowitz, who had for years promoted a military relationship with China, briefed Chinese officials on Soviet troop deployments along the Sino-Soviet border. His briefing was considerably more detailed than any given to China in the past, and included actual reconnaissance photographs of the Soviet installations.[20]

Brzezinski also brought along one of the administration's leading experts on the Soviet Union, Samuel Huntington, to give Chinese officials a detailed briefing on what was called Presidential Review Memorandum 10, the administration's analysis of the strategic balance between the superpowers. Another top NSC official, Benjamin Huberman, held out the prospect of exchanges in science and technology, including joint intelligence gathering against the Soviet Union. It was an important first step toward an intelligence deal that would be consummated before the end of the year.

In case the Chinese still didn't get the message, Brzezinski used his moments of tourism in Beijing to joke about the possibilities for America and China to team up in the Cold War. Climbing the Great Wall with Chinese officials, he joked, "If we get to the top first, you go in and oppose the Russians in Ethiopia."[21]

Like Nixon's visit to China in 1972, Brzezinski's trip was plagued by internal bickering among the Americans, again the product of the intense rivalries between the State Department and the National Security Council. As the ten-member American delegation had left Washington, Ambassador Leonard Woodcock received an urgent cable instructing him to go to Tokyo and join Brzezinski's party there as it flew into Beijing. The baffled ambassador thought he was being summoned for his advice or help on some urgent policy problem.

In Tokyo, Woodcock discovered the reason for the summons: Richard Holbrooke, the assistant secretary of state for East Asia, was irate that Brzezinski planned to bring only two other American officials— neither of them Holbrooke—into his session with Deng Xiaoping. Holbrooke wanted Woodcock to cable or call the president to get him into the meeting. Woodcock demurred, saying he would himself be in the session with Deng and would tell Holbrooke everything that was said. Holbrooke remained out in the cold. Brzezinski's NSC team wasn't entirely high-minded, either; as the trip proceeded, members of the delegation boasted that they were getting more time with Chinese leaders than had Vance's State Department team the previous year.[22]

Brzezinski's main assignment was to tell the Chinese leadership the Carter administration had decided to proceed with the establishment of diplomatic relations. In Carter's written instructions for the trip, which Brzezinski and Oksenberg had drafted, the president said, "You should state that the United States has made up its mind on these issues [of normalizing with China]."[23] Carter did not want to leave Chinese leaders with the sense of ambiguity about America's intentions that they had been given during Vance's visit.

Chinese leaders handled Brzezinski brilliantly. On the opening day of talks, the national security advisor told Chinese Foreign Minister Huang Hua:

> At the outset I would like to express to you our determination to move forward on the process of normalization. I can say on behalf of President Carter that the United States has made up its mind on this issue.

Later in the same conversation, Brzezinski repeated again, "As I said when I began, the U.S. has made up its mind on this issue."

The following day, however, Deng Xiaoping, then China's vice premier, acted as though he hadn't heard Brzezinski's message yet.

> *Deng:* The question now remains how to make up one's mind [on normalization]. . . .
>   I think that is about all on this question. We are looking forward to the day when President Carter makes up his mind. Let's now shift the subject.
> *Brzezinski:* I have told you before, President Carter *has* made up his mind.[24]

By this time, the national security advisor seemed to be overly eager, if not desperate. One scholar, working on a contract for the U.S. intelligence community, later concluded that the handling of Brzezinski was an excellent illustration of a Chinese negotiating stratagem he called "Show Us That You Care." The episode illustrated "how the Chinese can hold off an interlocutor to entice him to accommodate to their position," he wrote.[25]

Brzezinski ritually repeated the secret promises about Taiwan that

Nixon had first given to Chou Enlai in 1972: The United States agreed Taiwan was part of China, wouldn't support independence for the island, would prevent Japan from taking America's place on Taiwan and would support any peaceful settlement of the island's status.

To the Chinese, this may have seemed like a rerun of an old show. What followed was new, however. Brzezinski announced that the United States was now ready to meet China's conditions for establishing diplomatic ties, including the withdrawal of any official U.S. government presence on Taiwan. There would be no American consulate on the island. For the first time, America was telling China both that it was ready for formal diplomatic relations and that it would meet China's terms.

This was, however, to be the beginning, not the end, of negotiations. Important issues remained to be resolved. The Carter administration hoped to obtain a commitment from China that it would not use force against the island. It also wanted to preserve the right to sell arms to Taiwan. Brzezinski suggested to Chinese officials that the two countries start negotiations within a month on how to finish the task of formally recognizing one another.

Brzezinski's trip broke the long stalemate over diplomatic relations with China. It also turned the national security advisor into a determined supporter of the Chinese regime. On May 26, 1978, Carter noted in his diary that Brzezinski had returned from China to Washington. "He was overwhelmed [with the Chinese]," Carter observed. "I told him he had been seduced."

ADMINISTRATION OFFICIALS set a target date of December 15, 1978, for finishing and announcing the deal for recognition of China. The State Department had previously suggested that the months immediately after the November congressional elections would be the best possible time. The administration was planning to finish a new SALT treaty with the Soviet Union and bring it to the Senate by the spring of 1979; Carter and his aides hoped to complete normalization with China before moving forward with the arms control treaty, because it would be politically impossible to fight congressional battles over both SALT and recognition of China at the same time. Everyone realized that by late 1979 the next presidential campaign would be in full swing, and therefore it would be too late to take on an issue as potentially touchy and time-consuming as China. The end of 1978, then, was the "window" for recognition of Beijing.

Woodcock was assigned to conduct the detailed negotiations in Beijing. They were to be pursued in the strictest secrecy. "I don't trust (1) Congress (2) White House (3) State, or (4) Defense to keep a secret,"

Carter scrawled on one memo. Only a handful of administration officials knew about Woodcock's talks.[26]

One other foreign policy issue had to be resolved. Throughout this period, and continuing into the early fall of 1978, the Carter administration had also been moving toward normalization of relations with Vietnam. It had conducted a series of talks with the Hanoi government, which only three years earlier had completed its victory in the Vietnam War. With the war over, however, the historic enmity between Vietnam and China had once again burst into the open. Vietnam had expelled ethnic Chinese from its borders, and the two countries were at odds over China's support for the Khmer Rouge regime in Cambodia.

Would the United States normalize relations with both China and Vietnam? At the State Department, Vance and Holbrooke were eager to recognize both Communist governments. At a meeting with Vietnamese officials in New York City on September 27, 1978, Holbrooke reached an agreement in principle for normalization of relations after the Vietnamese government agreed to drop its requests for American reparations or financial aid.

China made clear it didn't like the idea. At a tense meeting in New York a few days later, Chinese Foreign Minister Huang Hua angrily told Vance the United States should think twice about normalizing with Vietnam at a time when the Soviet Union was trying to establish military bases there. At the NSC, Brzezinski had branded Vietnam as a "Soviet proxy," overriding protests by the State Department that this claim wasn't true. Now he and Oksenberg, the driving forces behind the creation of an anti-Soviet partnership with China, argued strongly against establishing relations with Vietnam. "This in my judgment could prejudice our efforts with the Chinese," Brzezinski wrote the president.

Carter sided with Brzezinski. At a meeting with Brzezinski and Woodcock in the Oval Office on October 11, he decided to postpone normalization with Vietnam until after America finished the process of recognizing China. Vietnam proceeded to enter into an alliance with the Soviet Union. It was to be another 17 years before Vietnam would obtain the diplomatic relationship with the United States that it nearly obtained in 1978.

WOODCOCK, MEANWHILE, plowed forward with his talks in Beijing on the final details of normalization. In addition, Brzezinski began a last intensive round of talks with China's Ambassador Chai Zemin, head of the liaison office in Washington. He was evidently willing to seize upon any sign, however cosmetic, that China was becoming more like the United States. When Chai one day showed up at the White House in a brown suit and bright tie instead of his usual Mao jacket, Brzezinski noted in his journal: "A total sartorial transformation, symptomatic of the ideological transformation of contemporary China."[27]

Since the earliest days of the Nixon opening, the United States had been trying to get China to say it was committed to a peaceful outcome on Taiwan, but China had consistently refused. The Carter administration tried but again failed to obtain such a commitment. Instead, the two governments worked out a deal in which, at the time of normalization, the United States would call for a peaceful resolution of Taiwan's future, and China would not dispute or challenge the American position.

The last, most important issue in the negotiations was American arms sales to Taiwan. The administration had told China the United States would end its defense agreement with Taiwan over a one-year period rather than abrogating the pact immediately, as China had initially wanted. Carter also agreed to suspend any new arms sales during that period, but insisted upon the right to sell arms to Taiwan afterward.

In the last hours of the negotiations, Carter and Brzezinski instructed Woodcock to go back to Deng and remind him that, even though the United States would not provide arms during 1979, it would resume these sales the following year. Woodcock thought the reminder was unnecessary, but carried through with the White House instructions. He was subjected to a furious lecture from Deng, who said China could never agree to these arms sales. Nevertheless, the talks were near to completion, and neither Deng nor Carter wanted any delay. They decided to put aside this dispute and finish the deal.[28]

It was, by this time, mid-December. They decided to move quickly. The two countries agreed to establish diplomatic relations on January 1, 1979; they also decided that Deng should visit the United States later that month. The Chinese leaders were in a hurry; they were, at the time, secretly moving toward a military strike against Vietnam, and wanted to solidify their relationship with the United States beforehand.

The Carter White House had reasons not to waste any time, either. In their own accounts, Brzezinski and Oksenberg have explained that they were afraid news of the agreement on normalization would leak, in a way that might let congressional supporters of Taiwan seize the initiative.[29] However, there was another reason for the rush to announce normalization, one that Brzezinski especially kept in mind: the desire to show that the Carter administration's relations with China took precedence over those with the Soviet Union. To do that, they needed to upstage and undercut the work of Cyrus Vance.

Vance was preparing to meet Soviet Foreign Minister Andrei Gromyko in Geneva in late December 1978 to try to complete the final details of a new arms-limitation treaty. The administration had considered inviting Soviet leader Leonid Brezhnev to Washington in January 1979 to consummate this deal. The Chinese had been anxiously asking Brzezinski and other American officials about the plans for a possible Carter summit with Brezhnev.[30] An agreement on normalization between Washington and Beijing and the announcement of a Deng visit would help ensure that any Soviet-American summit would be delayed.

Vance left for the Middle East in mid-December, believing that normalization with China would not be completed until after his talks with Gromyko on SALT. While the secretary of state was out of town, Brzezinski struck quickly. The final details for normalization with China were settled on December 13, and, using a fear of leaks as justification, Brzezinski persuaded Carter that the deal on China should be announced on December 15—a few days before Vance's talks on a new SALT treaty and a possible Brezhnev summit. The secretary of state was in Jerusalem when the crucial decisions on China were made; like Nixon's Secretary of State William Rogers before him, he was unaware of what was happening. Vance later acknowledged:

> The news came as a shock. At a critical moment, Brzezinski had blacked [Deputy Secretary of State Warren] Christopher and Holbrooke out of the decision making for about six hours, and they had been unable to inform me of what was taking place.

In Geneva a week later, Vance could not complete the arms-control agreement he had been seeking. Gromyko was furious over the timing of the China announcement. When Vance tried to work out a compromise on the SALT details, it was rejected in Washington; over an open phone line, audible to Soviet officials, Brzezinski instructed Vance to take a tough line. As a result, the Carter-Brezhnev summit was postponed.[31]

By that time, the Carter administration had launched upon its new course. On December 15, Carter announced the agreement on the establishment of diplomatic relations between the United States and China. Because of Brzezinski's efforts throughout the previous months, it was to be a relationship based overwhelmingly on shared opposition to the Soviet Union. That was not necessarily the best way to establish ties with China over the long term.

WHILE VANCE had been kept in the dark about the White House's drive toward normalization for a few crucial hours, Congress had been blacked out for most of the year. Earlier in 1978, Senator Bob Dole won approval of a resolution calling upon the administration to consult with the Senate before it made any deal affecting the American defense treaty with Taiwan. Before Vance left for the Middle East, he and Christopher argued strongly that the administration should start to talk to Congress about the general prospect of normalization with China. Brzezinski disagreed, and Carter, as was becoming increasingly routine, sided with his national security advisor.[32]

Carter's surprise announcement touched off a furor, though some of the criticism was misdirected. Instead of focusing on the anti-Soviet context of the normalization deal, critics complained about the administration's supposed negotiating failures concerning Taiwan. Most of them did not realize the legacy of secret diplomacy that Carter had inherited from Nixon, Ford and Kissinger, who had previously agreed to normalization on essentially the same terms Carter had arranged.

Some congressmen argued that Carter should have obtained a promise from China of a peaceful settlement of Taiwan's future. Yet Nixon and Kissinger had also attempted to obtain those assurances and, after failing, settled for the same solution of a unilateral American declaration that Carter also got. Senator Jesse Helms charged that Carter was proposing to "sell Taiwan down the river." The problem was that it had already been sold well before Carter had arrived in the White House.

These congressional critics of normalization can be excused for not knowing the secret negotiating record that had been carefully kept from them. They can hardly be faulted for refusing to embrace an outcome they did not realize had been in the offing for years.

In a few cases, however, the political attacks on Carter's handling of the Taiwan issue reflected little more than opportunism. Among the leading critics was George Bush, one of the few Republican leaders who had had some familiarity with Kissinger's diplomacy. Bush, who by December 1978 was already competing with Taiwan's staunchest ally, Ronald Reagan, for the 1980 Republican presidential nomination, wrote a misleading article for the *Washington Post* suggesting that Chinese leaders would have been willing to put off normalization for a long time. During top-level meetings while he was in Beijing, Bush asserted,

> [Taiwan] was always a distinctly secondary issue. "You have time, there is no hurry," they said over and over again. . . . The terms that the Carter Administration has accepted, and even trumpeted, are the same terms that have been available for the past seven years. But they were always refused before because we knew . . . that in the absence of sufficient guarantees, they were but a figleaf for an abject American retreat.[33]

Bush did not mention that, only three years earlier, while he himself was serving as head of the U.S. liaison office in Beijing, Deng and other Chinese leaders had reacted furiously to Ford's inability to follow through on promises to normalize relations. The Chinese had been mollified only when Ford promised to do so after the 1976 elections. Nixon and Ford had refused to complete normalization not because of a dispute with Beijing over the terms, but because of an unwillingness to incur the high political costs in the United States. Carter was now paying those costs, obtaining the terms on Taiwan that the Republicans had earlier indicated to Chinese leaders they would accept.

By this time, Bush had already secretly courted Chinese leaders' support for his presidential campaign. The article attacking Carter underscored his continuing eagerness to court the Republican right. The words he wrote in 1978 would come back to haunt him. "China needs us more than we need them," Bush declared in his written attack on Carter's normalization. Virtually the same words would be used by critics of Bush's conciliatory policies toward China when, more than a decade later, he succeeded in winning election to the presidency.

TAIWAN WAS hopelessly unprepared for the news that its closest ally and patron was about to break off relations. In Taipei, U.S. Ambassador Leonard Unger woke up President Chiang Ching-kuo (the son of Chiang Kai-shek) at 2:30 a.m. to give him a few hours' notice of Carter's announcement. Chiang told Unger the United States was making a big mistake. "He said his government represented the real China, and that it would in due course take its place on the mainland," Unger recalled.[34]

Taiwan's ambassador to the United States, James Shen, was doing local television interviews in Phoenix when he received an urgent call from Taipei instructing him to return to Washington immediately. Over the following two weeks, the Republic of China embassy shipped some files back to Taipei and destroyed others. It transferred bank accounts to individuals, so that the Beijing government couldn't lay claim to them. It transferred Twin Oaks, the ambassador's spacious Washington residence, and the chancellery to a private corporation, so that Chinese officials couldn't take them over, either.[35]

Carter sought to assuage Taiwan's anger by dispatching Christopher, his deputy secretary of state, to Taipei. It was to be the final visit to Taiwan by any senior American official in the White House, State Department or Defense Department.

Christopher landed in Taipei on December 27. At the airport, Vice Foreign Minister Frederick Chien greeted him with an anti-American speech in which he spoke of the "disastrous damage wrought by this mistake." When Christopher and Unger got in the ambassador's car to drive to a downtown hotel, they were soon surrounded by thousands of people.

"It wasn't just a demonstration, it was an attack on the car, first with tomatoes, then with rocks," Christopher recalled many years later. "Then, when they broke the windows, they began to put in long bamboo poles. . . . I sensed we didn't have an experienced driver. An experienced driver would have sped through all this. It was a long time, a mile or two, in which we went through this very intense crowd. Frankly, it was not a pleasant experience." [36]

Christopher suffered some cuts, and Unger's glasses were broken. They decided to spend the night at a hillside retreat for fear of further demonstrations in downtown Taipei. Carter called them there and offered to withdraw Christopher, but he decided to proceed. The next day, still shaken, he met with President Chiang to lodge a protest and to ask "if we could expect to be treated in a civilized and diplomatic way," Christopher recalled. "He did give assurances, in a rather grudging way." [37]

Thus did the Democrats became the targets of Taiwan's fury—a rage that Nixon, Ford and Kissinger had provoked through their secret negotiations, but had been unwilling to see directed at their own administrations. Many years later, a senior Taiwan official would admit that police had looked the other way and thus, in effect, permitted the demonstrations against Christopher. [38]

In the early months of 1979, Congress gave considerably more concrete, legislative support to Taiwan than Carter had expected. The administration had prepared a bill aimed at paving the way for America's continuing, nongovernment ties with Taiwan. Congress took the State Department's legislation and bolstered it by adding elements the administration neither expected nor wanted. It put into the law a guarantee of future arms sales to Taiwan, saying the United States would supply "such defense articles and defense services in such quantity as may be necessary to enable Taiwan to maintain a sufficient self-defense capability." The law also included a vaguely worded statement of American support for Taiwan's defense, saying the United States would consider any military action, boycott or embargo against Taiwan to be "a threat to the peace of the Western Pacific area and of grave concern to the United States."

Chinese leaders were enraged. Nevertheless, the Taiwan Relations Act passed both houses of Congress by overwhelming, veto-proof margins, and Carter reluctantly signed it, giving Taiwan a degree of American protection it would not have otherwise obtained.

CHAPTER FIVE

Carter's Cold War

THE TWO YEARS FOLLOWING Carter's recognition of the People's Republic of China were in many ways the most significant and least understood period in the modern-day history of the two countries. After America and China had finally recognized one another, they could begin to define the nature of their relationship. How would the two countries deal with one another? What would be the priorities?

Carter's conception, as it turned out, was linked intrinsically to America's immediate needs in the Cold War. Above all, China was viewed in Carter's White House as a partner whose size, population, strategic location and army could help America in its struggle against the Soviet Union. Following the revolution in Iran, and with inflation at home reaching 20 percent, the Carter administration had too many short-term problems to think about the long run, in China or elsewhere.

During 1979–80, America's relations with China turned increasingly to military cooperation. The administration gave America's ties to China such a pronounced anti-Soviet, Cold War cast that this became the dominant element in the relationship. Other concerns, like human rights, were often swept aside on grounds that China was too strategically important for such side issues.

These American military links with China proved not to be the basis for an enduring relationship. Little more than a decade later, after the Berlin Wall was torn down and the Soviet Union collapsed, America's ties to China deteriorated rapidly, because they had been based too heavily on the exigencies of the Cold War. Moreover, in the 1990s as the United States began to complain about human rights violations, Chinese leaders were plausibly able to counter with accusations of inconsistency:

During the Cold War, American officials hadn't seemed to care much about Chinese repression.

Of course, the Cold War also colored America's relations with China under other presidents, too, from Richard Nixon through George Bush. But the special Washington view of China—that it was not so much a country as a military strategy—reached its apogee under Carter and Brzezinski. After diplomatic recognition was accomplished, America and China could have taken any of a number of different paths. They chose the military road.

FROM JANUARY 28 to February 5, 1979, Deng Xiaoping made a celebratory tour through the United States, starting in Washington and stopping in Atlanta, Houston and Seattle. Deng's trip is now remembered in America for some of the pictures and feature stories it produced: the diminutive Deng waving a 10-gallon hat at a Texas rodeo, staring up at the Harlem Globetrotters at the Kennedy Center in Washington, driving through a Ford plant in Atlanta, taking the controls of a space-shuttle simulator at the Johnson Space Center in Houston.

"The Texans just fell in love with him," recalls James Schlesinger, who as Carter's energy secretary escorted Deng to Houston. "Here we were, down in Texas, bitterly anti-Communist Texas, seeing oil and other business executives who regularly proclaimed their belief in free-market principles. And they fell in love with a Marxist dictator." [1]

However, in addition to the photo opportunities, Deng and the Carter administration also had important, though secret, items on their respective agendas. For the United States, one of the top priorities was in the field of intelligence collection. As a result of the Islamic revolution that had overthrown the shah, Muhammad Reza Pahlevi, the United States had just lost its two vital intelligence collection stations at Tacksman in northern Iran, from which the CIA had obtained information about Soviet missile tests. The administration wanted especially to be able to monitor Soviet testing of anti-ballistic missiles from the Soviet testing range in Sary-Shagan, Kazakhstan. Without this intelligence, it feared it might not win approval for a new SALT treaty, because critics could argue that the United States was unable to monitor Soviet compliance.

American and Chinese officials had talked about joint intelligence collection during Brzezinski's visit to Beijing the previous year. The publication *Electronic Warfare/Defense Electronics* reported after that trip that Brzezinski had offered China "eyes and ears of the West." Shortly before Deng arrived in the United States, he stopped in Japan and hinted he was ready for an intelligence deal, making a few vague statements about the importance of strategic cooperation between China and the West.

In Washington, during discussions with Deng led by Brzezinski, the United States and China reached an agreement in principle to set up new signals-intelligence stations in western China to replace the ones the United States had lost in Iran. The details were ironed out over the following months. These stations were to be installed, equipped, staffed and serviced by the CIA with help from the National Security Agency; Chinese personnel would also help run them, and China would share the intelligence gathered at them.[2]

With this agreement, the United States and China formalized their intelligence cooperation. It extended far beyond an occasional briefing on Soviet deployments by some American official visiting Beijing. Under the Carter administration, the intelligence agencies and bureaucracies of the two countries began working side by side.

For American intelligence agencies, the monitoring stations in China were a treasured asset. Ironically, they also became, over the long run, something of a liability for American policy toward China. Whenever there was tension between Washington and Beijing, whether over Taiwan or the Tiananmen Square crackdown, Chinese officials would hint that China might close down the monitoring stations.[3] American officials had to remind themselves that China needed the intelligence about the Soviets more than they did.

DENG'S OWN top priority for the Washington talks was winning American support for China against Vietnam.

During the last months of 1978, China had prepared for the possibility of war. At the end of the year, Vietnamese troops had invaded Cambodia, overthrowing Pol Pot and his Khmer Rouge regime, which China had supported. By the time of Deng's trip to the United States, the Chinese leaders had already made the decision for military action: China would attack Vietnam and then withdraw its forces within a few weeks. It was to be a demonstration of China's military power, similar to a brief Chinese war against India in 1962. However, China needed to be careful to guard against Soviet intervention in the conflict: Hanoi had become a treaty partner of the Soviet Union. The phrase Chinese leaders used was that they intended to "teach Vietnam a lesson." They did not want the Soviets to interfere with their pedagogy.

On the first night of Deng's trip, during a dinner at Brzezinski's home in McLean, Virginia, the Chinese leader told the national security advisor that he wanted to have a private talk with Carter about Vietnam. The following afternoon, after a round of White House talks involving a large contingent of American and Chinese officials, Deng said he had something confidential he wanted to discuss with a smaller group. All the

Americans left except for Carter, Vice President Mondale, Brzezinski and Vance. To them, sitting in the Oval Office late in the afternoon, a few hours before a state dinner and Kennedy Center gala in Deng's honor, the Chinese leader outlined his plans for a punitive strike from Chinese territory across the border into Vietnam. He also pointedly discussed what the various Soviet responses might be. What China was looking for was simply America's moral support, Deng explained.

In his memoirs, Carter insisted that he tried to discourage Deng. He told the Chinese leader the invasion might prove to be counterproductive, because it could arouse world sympathy for Vietnam. However, the president also did not condemn or directly oppose China's plans. Brzezinski was pleased by Carter's seeming tolerance of the use of force; he later wrote:

> I was worried that the President might be persuaded by Vance to put maximum pressure on the Chinese not to use force, since this would simply convince the Chinese that the United States was a "paper tiger."

The following morning, in a session with only Deng and an interpreter present, Carter handed Deng a note that simply urged restraint in what even Brzezinski acknowledged would be overt military aggression.[4]

Carter's reaction amounted to a green light for the Chinese invasion. The best summation of how Carter handled the news that China would attack Vietnam is in the memoir of former CIA Director Robert F. Gates, who served in the Carter White House and is largely sympathetic to the former president. Carter's decision merely to urge restraint, wrote Gates,

> had to have been the best signal Deng could have hoped for. No mention of disruption of normalization. No mention of a change in the direction of economic and military cooperation. No principled objection to the invasion of another state. Just the mildly— albeit firmly—expressed worry that it might create problems. Further, no indication that the secret just shared would be violated to warn the intended victim or complicate Chinese plans.[5]

Deng's eagerness for military action aroused nothing but admiration in Brzezinski, who wrote, "I secretly wished that Deng's appreciation of the uses of power would also rub off on some of the key U.S. decision makers."[6]

China launched its invasion on February 17, less than two weeks after

Deng's return home from the United States. The People's Liberation Army launched rocket attacks and fired long-range guns into Vietnam, then stormed across the border. Over the following two weeks, more than a quarter-million Chinese troops entered into battle, often against Vietnam's second-line forces, since the country's best units had been dispatched to Cambodia. The results were so unimpressive that Deng and Chinese military leaders spent a decade trying to learn their own lessons from the invasion. Chinese casualties (killed, wounded and missing) numbered about 20,000, and the forces found themselves hampered by outmoded equipment and poor logistics. On March 5, after 17 days, China announced that its troops had achieved their objectives, and it immediately began to withdraw.[7]

What remained secret was the extent of America's day-to-day involvement in the Chinese invasion. At the White House, Brzezinski met with Chinese Ambassador Chai Zemin virtually every night throughout the military conflict to turn over American intelligence on Soviet deployments. This was vital information, the product of American satellite reconnaissance, which gathered far beyond anything Chinese intelligence could have collected.[8]

The U.S. support for China's invasion was also a remarkable demonstration of just how much America's role in Asia had changed. A decade earlier, the United States had gone to war in Vietnam largely because (so the American people were told) Chinese expansion in Asia had to be stopped. Over the following years, America had learned that Vietnam was anything but a proxy for China; the two countries were, in fact, adversaries. Now, in early 1979, came the crowning irony: The United States was clandestinely helping China as it moved across the border into Vietnam.

THE DEFENSE of human rights was one of the signature elements in the Carter administration's foreign policy elsewhere in the world, but not when it came to China. Indeed, Carter and his aides gave China virtually a blanket exemption from the human rights policies they so readily applied elsewhere.

The Carter administration's overall human rights policy grew out of the confluence of two developments. One was the Helsinki accords of 1975, which required governments, including those of the Soviet Union and Eastern Europe, to respect human rights. The other factor was congressional pressure: Increasingly, during the mid-1970s, members of Congress complained that the United States was giving military and economic aid to repressive regimes, such as those of Philippine President Ferdinand Marcos or South Korean President Park Chung Hee. Under the leadership of Representative Don Fraser, Congress enacted legislation requiring the State Department to file annual reports on the human rights practices of countries receiving American aid.

When it came to Soviet dissidents, Carter was outspoken and sympathetic. In the first month of his administration, he wrote a letter of encouragement to the Soviet physicist Andrei Sakharov, incurring the wrath of Leonid Brezhnev and the Politburo in the process; news photographs transmitted throughout the world showed Sakharov holding up the letter with Carter's signature. Carter also met at the White House with another dissident, Vladimir Bukovsky. Later on, his administration carried out hard and tough negotiations to persuade the Soviet Union to release an imprisoned dissident, Anatoly Shcharansky.

The president and his aides had no such interest in similarly championing human rights in China. At the outset of the administration, this might have been excused as understandable. China was less repressive than it had been during the early days of the Cultural Revolution. (The Cultural Revolution was, however, a particularly low standard by which to judge China; after all, no one attempted to explain away the Soviet Union's policies of the 1970s by saying that they were better than during the worst days under Stalin's terror.) Moreover, China's political climate seemed, for a time, to be moving toward liberalization.

Chinese leader Deng Xiaoping had seemed to hint at support for the causes of democracy and the right to dissent when in late 1978 he was consolidating his control over the Chinese Communist Party. That December, the Democracy Wall movement burst forth in Beijing and spread to other Chinese cities, including Shanghai, Tianjin, Nanjing, Wuhan, Chongqing and Guangzhou. Ordinary Chinese gave speeches and put up wall posters criticizing their political system, calling for freedom and democracy. Others gathered around the wall posters, with one Shanghai rally attracting about 10,000 people.[9]

On December 7, 1978, Carter gave a speech on the general importance of human rights in American diplomacy. What he said did not go unnoticed in China. The following day, a wall poster went up in Beijing that was an open letter to the American president. It said:

> The demand for basic human rights is common to all. Your concern for Sakharov, Shcharansky and Ginsburg was very moving, but . . . you should not only protest against unsuccessful oppression, because successful oppression is even more fearful. . . . We would like to ask you to pay attention to the state of human rights in China. The Chinese people do not want to repeat the tragic life of the Soviet people in the Gulag Archipelago.[10]

Still, Carter—who was, at the time, in the last stages of completing the agreement on normalization with Beijing—said nothing in support of the Democracy Wall movement.

What followed made a mockery of Carter's human rights policy, showing just how selectively it was applied. In early 1979, two months after Deng's visit to the United States, the Chinese leader reversed course and began suppressing the outpouring of dissent. On March 29, Wei Jingsheng, the young author of the famous wall poster called "The Fifth Modernization—Democracy," was arrested. Official Chinese newspapers launched attacks on the democracy movement. Over the next six weeks, about 30 activists were arrested in Beijing alone. One Chinese province after another issued new regulations restricting wall posters. Young activists who had come to Beijing from around China to take part in the Democracy Wall movement were sent home. By the end of the year, the Democracy Wall in Beijing was closed, although not before one last poem was put up that began: "The people have no rights." [11] Eventually, under Deng's leadership, Chinese authorities amended the Constitution to abolish earlier guarantees of the right to speak out freely, hold debates and put up wall posters.

Wei Jingsheng was put on trial on October 17, 1979, in a courtroom open only to the official Chinese press and government workers. After a six-hour proceeding, a judge found him guilty of counterrevolutionary offenses and sentenced him to 15 years in prison. That action prompted the Carter administration to issue its first and only negative statement about the ongoing Chinese repression. A State Department spokesman said merely that the United States was "surprised and disappointed at the severity of the sentence," leaving the impression that it might otherwise have had no quarrel with Wei's trial and conviction. [12]

In short, during these crucial months in which Deng was, in effect, setting the rules for Chinese political life in the post-Mao era, the Carter administration said and did as little as possible. It kept its distance from Chinese dissidents and avoided condemning Chinese repression, in a way that contrasted markedly with its behavior toward the Soviet Union.

Carter's hands-off attitude toward the Democracy Wall movement was merely one part of a larger pattern of behavior by his administration in dealing with China. At the beginning of 1980, the administration was obliged for the first time to include China in its annual report to Congress about the human rights situation around the world.

The question of what to say about China led to open warfare within the Washington bureaucracy. The State Department's human rights officials wanted the report to be as critical of China as it had been of many other countries; the Bureau of East Asia and Pacific Affairs, led by

Richard Holbrooke, wanted the language about China to be positive and encouraging. "Richard Holbrooke and [Assistant Secretary of State for Human Rights] Pat Derian had a brawl over the human rights report for China," says Stephen B. Cohen, a Georgetown University law professor who worked as an aide to Derian. "He [Holbrooke] tried to understate human rights issues, because we had a new relationship with China, and he didn't want to offend China."

Although Holbrooke and his staff watered down the text, they were forced to include some critical material when the U.S. embassy in Beijing submitted a detailed report candidly describing some of China's repressive policies. When Derian testified before Congress in 1980 about China's arrests and prosecutions of dissidents, Holbrooke sent a deputy to give Congress a different, more upbeat picture. The aide, Deputy Assistant Secretary of State John Negroponte, asserted that "an encouraging trend has begun to emerge in the direction of liberalization." [13]

Overall, the Carter administration established the pattern of inconsistency on human rights that would govern American policy for the following decade. Human rights was considered a suitable subject for high-level American diplomacy with the Soviet Union, but not with China. In 1987, when China was engaging in one of its occasional crackdowns on intellectuals, Deng boasted to other Chinese Communist Party leaders that China had been able to lock up dissidents with impunity. "Look at Wei Jingsheng," he said. "We put him behind bars, and the democracy movement died. We haven't released him, but that did not raise much of an international uproar." [14]

Even after leaving the White House, Carter, so carefully attuned to the rights of Soviet dissidents, seemed blind and deaf to their Chinese counterparts. In 1978, when Shcharansky was convicted in the Soviet Union of charges strikingly similar to those against Wei Jingsheng, Carter, at the White House, eloquently declared: "We are all sobered by this reminder that, so late in the twentieth century, a person can be sent to jail simply for asserting his basic human rights."

By contrast, in 1987, while the former president was visiting Beijing, he was asked at a press conference about Chinese dissidents. He said he didn't know of any specific examples. How about Wei Jingsheng? suggested one reporter. "I'm personally not familiar with the case that you described," said Carter. [15]

THE CARTER administration was willing to venture into new fields with China when these fit into the needs of the Cold War relationship it was forging. Two areas, in particular, would have vast ramifications for the future: the admission of Chinese students to American universities and the extension to China of most-favored-nation (MFN) trade privileges.

Educational exchanges between the United States and China began even before the onset of diplomatic relations. In July 1978, Presidential Science Advisor Frank Press visited Beijing and worked out an agreement under which China would send 500 to 700 students and scholars to the United States in the 1978-79 academic year. In return, Chinese officials agreed to permit about 60 Americans to study in China. Although both countries spoke of this program as a reciprocal arrangement, from the outset the number of Chinese scholars and students coming to the United States dwarfed the number of Americans in China, and the imbalance widened considerably in future years.

The Chinese students were overwhelmingly concentrated in the fields of science and technology. Of the first group of students, about 20 percent were in physics, 12 percent in chemistry or chemical engineering, 10 percent in computer sciences, 8 percent in mathematics, 8 percent in mechanical engineering, 8 percent in biology, 7 percent in medical sciences and most of the remainder spread through other scientific disciplines. In contrast, the American students in China tended to study language and culture.[16]

For China, whose education system had been devastated by the Cultural Revolution, the chance to send scholars for advanced training in America was viewed as an important step in the drive toward modernization. Chinese officials wanted to make the country stronger, and the Carter administration was eager to help. "It is in our interest to contribute to China's efforts to strengthen her agricultural and civil industrial capabilities," wrote Press in one letter.[17] In the process, America would help to bring along China as a more powerful partner against the Soviet Union.

For the United States, the main benefit of these exchanges was more indirect. Carter administration officials believed that by educating students and scholars from China, they were cultivating a future generation of Chinese leaders who would, a few decades hence, steer Beijing toward policies sympathetic to America. "The Chinese studying here will go back to their country and become influential, and it is helpful to have them familiar with our society," explained Press.[18]

However, the new educational programs evolved in ways that neither American nor Chinese officials had anticipated. Both sides seemed convinced at the outset that the Chinese students would come to America, complete programs of limited duration (such as, for example, four years of doctoral training) and then go home. These expectations were best expressed by one diplomat in Beijing, who told a reporter in the fall of

1978 that he expected students who reach the United States "to study hard and quietly and then return to China, perhaps with heightened expectations of what life there should be like." [19] Perhaps a few Chinese students might stay on in the United States, but not many, American and Chinese officials believed. "We'll lose a few, but so what?" Deng Xiaoping told one group of visitors in mid-1978.

These expectations misjudged the realities, both in China and in America. The chance to study abroad quickly became the single most coveted privilege among young urban Chinese; American consulates in China and universities in the United States were swamped with letters and applications. Once in the United States, Chinese scholars, like other graduate students, often lingered in doctoral programs for six or seven years. Meanwhile, the students landed so many jobs as laboratory and research assistants that they constituted a significant portion of the campuses' high-tech labor pool, one that American universities developed a stake in preserving. Those students who returned to China often found that they were offered meaningless or menial jobs in institutions where they were sometimes viewed as a threat to the established order.

The result was that Chinese students came to the United States in far greater numbers than had been originally expected and stayed in America for much longer periods of time. Over the decade beginning in 1979, about 80,000 students and scholars came to America. In 1989, about 43,000 were still in academic programs in the United States, and an additional 11,000 had become permanent residents. Most of the rest had visited the United States for only a few months. [20]

Some senior Chinese officials became queasy about the way the educational exchanges worked. In 1985, Li Peng, who was then the Chinese vice premier in charge of education, complained bitterly to Vice President George Bush that Chinese students were staying in the United States for too long. He and other Chinese officials suggested that the U.S. government tell American universities to force the students to return home, perhaps by denying them permission to extend their studies. Chinese newspapers launched a brief propaganda campaign in the mid-1980s that depicted the lives of Chinese students in the United States as bleak, full of drudgery and poverty. [21]

These efforts failed to stem the tide. American universities were unwilling to clamp down on the Chinese students, and Washington lacked the power or interest to require them to do so. In China, the regime's efforts to stop the outflow were never more than brief and half-hearted. Although Li Peng complained, other senior Chinese officials were willing to let the students stay in America for protracted periods.

Many of China's most powerful leaders, of course, including Deng and his successor, Jiang Zemin, had sent their own sons and daughters to American universities.

CARTER'S EXTENSION to China of most-favored-nation trade privileges was an even more momentous step, and one linked more closely to America's prosecution of the Cold War.

U.S. officials had been talking about expanding trade with China since the time of the Nixon opening. Throughout the 1970s, however, the American plan had been to develop commerce with the Soviet Union and China on an equal footing. The notes Nixon prepared for his meetings with Chou Enlai in Beijing show that, at 6 a.m. on February 23, 1972, under the heading "Trade and Technical Assistance," he had scrawled:

> You want to be self-reliant. It is in our interest to see China prosper & be strong. Russ want it [trade]—We want you to have same.[22]

Without most-favored-nation trade benefits, countries like China and the Soviet Union were forced to export their goods to the United States under the extraordinarily high duties of the Smoot-Hawley Tariff. That made it all but impossible for them to sell the sort of low-technology industrial goods that Japan, South Korea and Taiwan exported to America.

As early as November 1973, during talks in Beijing with Chou Enlai, Kissinger talked about what would be required for China to win MFN benefits. At the time, as part of its policy of detente, the Nixon administration considered granting MFN status to the Soviet Union, and Nixon and Kissinger wanted to bring China along, too.

Ironically, in light of how important MFN would later become, China at first wasn't particularly interested. Even two years later, on October 22, 1975, Deng Xiaoping told Kissinger, "China doesn't need MFN, as long as the Soviets don't get it."[23] It was a modern-day version, with a reverse twist, on the Chinese emperor's lofty 1793 rebuff to the emissary of King George III: "We have never valued ingenious articles, nor do we have the slightest need of your country's manufactures."

During the first two years of the Carter administration, even after Brzezinski's trip and the establishment of diplomatic relations with Beijing, Carter wanted to grant MFN to both the Soviet Union and China at the same time. Carter noted in his diary on December 31, 1978:

As we moved toward a most-favored-nation relationship with the PRC, we must face the need to do the same thing with the Soviet Union.

In his memoirs, Carter recalled being afraid that if China got MFN and the Soviet Union didn't, that would result in "an imbalance in our relationship with the two major communist countries."[24]

Nevertheless, others in the administration, notably Brzezinski, wanted precisely the imbalance between Moscow and Beijing that Carter feared. Although Vance argued determinedly that the United States should be "evenhanded" in its policies toward the Soviet Union and China, Brzezinski had espoused an open, avowed American tilt toward China. In 1979, Carter switched ground and adopted Brzezinski's viewpoint. MFN became the key issue in this larger symbolic struggle over America's relations with Moscow and Beijing.

The administration's first step was to deal with one impediment blocking China's MFN privileges: the Jackson-Vanik Amendment. This law, passed in 1974, required that MFN benefits be withheld from any country that fails to permit freedom of emigration; enacted over Kissinger's vehement objections, it was an effort to pressure the Soviet Union to permit Soviet Jews to leave the country. In theory, the emigration provision applied to China, too, which didn't allow its citizens to travel at will.

At a White House meeting on January 30, 1979, Deng Xiaoping brushed away this problem with a memorable one-liner. When the president raised the subject of the Jackson-Vanik Amendment, Deng quipped, "If you want me to release 10 million Chinese to come to the United States, I'd be glad to do so." Carter and his aides laughed. It was a deft way of deflecting attention away from the question of whether China allowed its people to leave the country without restriction, and toward the obvious point that the rest of the world wasn't exactly clamoring for Chinese emigration. (American leaders sometimes drew this distinction between the Soviet Union and China more pithily. During the Bush administration, some White House officials wondered aloud why the Jackson-Vanik requirement of free emigration had never applied to China. Bush looked at his national security advisor, Brent Scowcroft, and murmured knowingly, "No Jews in China.")[25]

By the time of Deng's 1979 visit, China's policy had changed. Chinese officials now eagerly wanted MFN, and Deng eagerly pressed for the trade benefits during his meetings in Washington. If China got MFN status, he forecast, its trade with the United States would be ten times larger than American trade with Taiwan; that turned out to be an extravagantly optimistic prediction. Moreover, the Chinese leader said, once trade was established, America would be able to sell its technology to China. As usual, Deng was not modest in his requests. He said to Carter's Cabinet, "We want your most up-to-date technology, not even that of the early 1970s, do you understand?"[26]

Deng's proselytizing worked. Over the next few months, American officials carefully laid the groundwork to give China MFN status. In the midst of China's invasion of Vietnam, Secretary of the Treasury Michael Blumenthal was sent to Beijing to negotiate a formal trade agreement opening the way for MFN. Vance and other State Department officials proposed canceling Blumenthal's trip as an expression of America's unhappiness with China's military venture; they pointed out that under similar circumstances, the United States had canceled Cabinet-level trips to Moscow. Brzezinski, backed by Carter, decided Blumenthal should go. Soon after his arrival in China, the secretary voiced some condemnations of the Chinese invasion, but Brzezinski hurriedly cabled Blumenthal to shut up and stick to trade issues.[27]

State Department officials argued that Carter should hold off a little longer on awarding MFN to China, until he was ready to extend the benefits to the Soviet Union, too. By this time, it was too late. In the summer of 1979, on the eve of a visit to China by Vice President Mondale, Carter ended his two-and-a-half-year policy of treating China and the Soviet Union on an equal footing. He decided to recommend MFN benefits for China without waiting for the Soviet Union. Then, taking the logic of this decision a step further, Carter decided to extend to China a series of other American economic benefits that had long been denied to both Communist superpowers, including Export-Import Bank financing and an easing of export controls.

When the Carter administration formally asked Congress to grant MFN benefits for China for the first time, there was a brief foretaste on Capitol Hill of the controversy over MFN that would burst forth many years later. When one business executive predicted (inaccurately, as it turned out) that extending the trade benefits to China would help reduce America's overall trade deficit, Representative Richard Schulze, a Republican from Pennsylvania, retorted:

> We are talking about human rights. The way I read your state-
> ment—you correct me if I'm wrong—the hell with human rights,
> we are worried about making a buck.[28]

Such outbursts were rare, however. Congress authorized the first MFN benefits for China without much debate, not seeming to realize how important they would become for the economic relations between the two countries.

After it was approved, MFN then disappeared as a political issue in Sino-American relations for a decade. In asking Congress to approve MFN for China, Warren Christopher, Carter's deputy secretary of state, had asserted: "It is in our interest for China's next generation of leaders to look back in 1990 upon the relationship we are now building with a sense of satisfaction and to view the United States as a reliable partner in development."

Neither Christopher nor anyone else could have predicted at the time how America and China would view the MFN issue in 1990.

ONCE IT was official American policy to tilt toward Beijing, the Carter administration moved to take the final and most important step: forging a military relationship with China.

Since the early 1970s, when Michael Pillsbury made his first tentative contacts with the People's Liberation Army, the idea of military ties had been explored, both in private and in public. It had gained increasing support in the Pentagon. At the same time, a remarkably diverse amalgamation of forces was opposed to the idea.

Some of America's leading China specialists—those who had fought for decades for recognition of China, who sympathized with the Chinese leadership and favored virtually all other kinds of advances in American links with Beijing—were opposed to military ties. These ties "would not necessarily result in stronger United States–China relationships over the long run," A. Doak Barnett, the veteran China specialist, told Congress, in words that would sound prophetic two decades later.[29]

Many Soviet specialists, too, were opposed to American military ties with China on grounds that they would needlessly anger Moscow and convince Soviet leaders that there was no point in trying to please the United States. This was, essentially, the position of the State Department. Vance argued that developing security ties with Beijing "is less likely to produce moderation in Soviet behavior than strategic claustrophobia and irrationality."[30]

Other critics warned of the long-term consequences if the United States helped strengthen China. "Is it our true purpose to promote the rise of the People's Republic to superpower status?" asked military strategist Edward Luttwak in *Commentary* magazine. "Should we become the artificers of a great power which our grandchildren may have to contend with?"[31] Former American Ambassador to Moscow Malcolm Toon went still further, telling members of Congress:

It does seem to me that far down the road, a China armed to the teeth, as she intends to be, with a fairly strong economy, probably is not going to be very benign in her attitude toward the United States, because they are against the sort of things we stand for.[32]

All these concerns were brushed aside in the Carter administration's determined drive to solidify China as a partner in an anti-Soviet entente. By late 1979, only Vance was opposed to an American military relationship with Beijing; Carter, Mondale and Defense Secretary Harold Brown all sided with Brzezinski.

Throughout the previous decade of rapprochement, there had still been no top-level contact between the defense establishments of America and China. At Brzezinski's suggestion, however, Mondale secretly broached in Beijing a suggestion that it was time for America's secretary of defense to visit the People's Republic. Not surprisingly, Chinese leaders embraced the idea. In public, meanwhile, Mondale insisted nothing was changing. "We do not have and do not contemplate a military relationship with the People's Republic of China," he said at a Hong Kong press conference.[33]

Brown's trip was scheduled for January 1980. A few weeks before, Carter set careful limits on what Brown could offer China: no arms sales, no formal military relations. On December 29, 1979, however, the Soviet Union sent its troops into Afghanistan on behalf of a coup d'état engineered by the KGB. Shortly afterward, Brezhnev told Dobrynin, the Soviet ambassador to Washington, "It'll be over in three to four weeks." Soviet leaders didn't believe the invasion would affect relations with Washington. Their miscalculations were of epic proportions. As Dobrynin later explained, "It was the hinge that turned a decade of detente under Nixon and Ford to the years of confrontation under Reagan."[34]

The Carter administration reacted quickly. Carter postponed Senate ratification of the new SALT treaty, blocked grain sales to the Soviet Union, fostered an American boycott of the 1980 Olympics in Moscow and adopted a new security policy in which the Persian Gulf was defined as a vital American interest. In addition to these steps, Brzezinski seized the opportunity to push China policy in the direction he had wanted. He argued

that we use the Soviet invasion of a country in a region of strategic sensitivity to Asia as a justification for opening the doors to a U.S.-China defense relationship.[35]

He asked Carter to lift some of the restrictions he had earlier imposed on Brown's visit to Beijing. The president agreed. Hours before Brown's departure, Carter authorized the sale of what was called "non-lethal" military equipment to China. The Chinese would for the first time be permitted to obtain an array of American hardware that would improve their military capabilities, including air defense radar, electronic countermeasure devices, radio and communications equipment and transport helicopters. As Brown prepared to board his plane, embarrassed administration staff members found themselves hurriedly calling members of Congress to say, "We [Brown's delegation] may do more [in Beijing] than we told you." [36]

As a concrete symbol of America's new willingness to help China, Brown told Deng the United States would be willing to sell a ground receiving station for the Landsat photo reconnaissance system. Officially, this technology was to be used for civilian purposes like oil exploration and agricultural production. But it also amounted to a breakthrough for China's satellite reconnaissance program, giving Chinese military and intelligence officials the means to improve greatly the resolution capabilities of their satellites. [37]

The die was now cast. America was selling China what it had long sought: hardware and advanced Western technology with military applications. The United States had for many years refused to sell such equipment and know-how to the Soviet Union, and it continued to do so. The equal treatment of China and the Soviet Union had ended. At the time, this was seen as a major achievement.

THE ADMINISTRATION'S leading authority on military technology was a former mathematics professor named William Perry who happily identified himself as a technocrat. Many years later, he would become the secretary of defense. Under Carter, he served in the more obscure post of undersecretary of defense for research and engineering.

In September 1980, Perry led to China an American delegation that included three-star generals and civilian experts on defense technology and manufacturing. Their mission was to look at China's defense industries from the bottom up and to see how America might help. [38]

It was an unprecedented and extraordinary trip, the first step toward concrete American support for strengthening the People's Liberation Army. For nearly two weeks, Perry and his delegation toured China's defense plants. They were taken to the missile-test range on the edge of the Gobi Desert and to the tank factory near the Mongolian border. They visited China's most modern computer and laser plants and the factory where China manufactured its Badger bombers.

The Americans were fascinated. Perry, who had chosen the sites, recalled in an interview that he had observed the plants "by other means [that is, through intelligence collection] for a good many years." Some members of the delegation even took tape recorders with them to dictate notes of what they saw.

What they found surprised them. In 1980, China was using obsolete technology obtained from the Soviet Union in the 1950s. American experts had for many years watched and studied China's nuclear and missile programs, which seemed competent. Now, Perry and his delegation realized that China had been steering the overwhelming share of its resources and its best personnel to those two programs. The talent so devoted, Perry concluded, "was not reflected in the design of airplanes and tanks, and in computers and lasers."

China wanted massive amounts of new American military technology. Perry says he concluded during the trip that this was a bad idea. The main reason was what he called "the incongruity between the two systems." China was too far behind the United States to try to assimilate American defense technology. Perry told Chinese officials they ought to concentrate on developing their infrastructure and civilian technology.

Perry also had qualms during this trip about where China was headed in the future. He said he could see that if China succeeded in modernizing its armed forces,

> in time they would become a formidable military power, and [with] no particular reason to be friendly with us. And therefore, I thought that the advantages of offsetting the Soviet threat, the temporary advantage of that, might be more than offset by the long-term disadvantage of seeing a military threat eventually develop from the Chinese.[39]

After returning to Washington, Perry filed a classified report about his trip. Perry later said he had advised against supplying American military know-how to the PLA. "Not selling weapons systems, not transferring military technology, that was my recommendation," he recalled.[40]

That is not what other American officials remember. Some in the 1980 delegation say Perry's trip was an important step toward a new arms and technology relationship between Washington and Beijing. "We started talking about various kinds of possible cooperation in the military area, what kinds of weapons we might be prepared to sell them," recalled Roger Sullivan, the National Security Council aide who accompanied Perry. "The Chinese were trying to show us we didn't have anything to fear. It was a nice touch. The message was, 'Look how crummy our stuff is. You don't have to worry about these things threatening Taiwan.' "[41] Sullivan remembers China specifically asking the Pentagon officials to help improve the PLA's jet fighters and the guidance systems for its tanks.

The written record supports Sullivan's memory over Perry's. A copy of Perry's 1980 report does not include warnings against providing arms or technology to China. On the contrary, the 24-page report is devoted almost entirely to the subject of how the United States could help modernize the PLA. Perry wrote:

> We need to expedite action on pending dual use and military technology cases, and developing further guidelines on the level of technology which can be considered for transfer to the PRC.[42]

The report does note the wide disparity between the levels of technology in the United States and China. Perry wrote at one point of trying to persuade Chinese officials to accept "more limited objectives" in their desire for a defense relationship. But his report looked ahead to the day when the United States might lift its restrictions on selling military equipment to the PLA; it specifically explored the possibility of helping China obtain anti-tank missiles, surface-to-air missiles, and better jet fighters.[43]

By the time Perry's report was filed, Carter had been defeated in the November elections. As a result, for a time nothing happened. Gradually, though, the United States moved toward strengthening China's armed forces.

THE CIA was equally interested in jumping onto the China bandwagon. For years, the agency had participated on the margins of the American rapprochement with China, offering Kissinger and other high-level policymakers some intelligence to share with the Chinese about Soviet troop deployments. With Deng's 1979 visit to Washington, the CIA had obtained the use of western China as a prime location for collecting signals intelligence about the Soviet Union.

By 1980, the CIA was ready and eager to establish its own liaison relationship with China, one in which senior intelligence officials of the two countries would meet on a routine basis to share secret information. To formalize this new relationship, the CIA agreed to send its director on the obligatory visit to Beijing.

The director, however, did not travel to China in the same open fashion as other top American officials. At China's insistence, the meetings were handled like covert operations. At the end of December 1980, CIA Director Stansfield Turner made the first in a decade-long series of clandestine visits to China by directors of the agency. Turner was kept out of the public eye; he stayed away from the American embassy and otherwise avoided places where he might be recognized. He even grew a mustache for the trip. The effort almost failed. Turner and an aide, future CIA Director Robert M. Gates, were taken on a tour of the Forbidden City at the same time as a Senate delegation. They scurried down an alley to avoid being noticed.[44]

Over the following decade, CIA Directors William Casey, Gates and William Webster all visited China. None of the trips was made public; the directors flew into and out of a special military airfield outside Beijing. In each instance, Chinese officials turned the visits into clandestine operations, although the American officials sometimes chafed at the restrictions.

"The Chinese suggested I wear a disguise," recalled Webster. He rejected the idea and refused to grow a mustache. Webster, like Turner, was taken to the Forbidden City, and he too ran into Americans he knew: A voice shouted out, "Hey, Bill Webster, it's Emmitt from St. Louis!" An aide, Bill Baker, was dispatched to warn Emmitt he should never say he had seen the CIA director in China.[45]

In order to disguise Casey, Chinese officials gave him a large hat with earflaps that covered his face. They also ordered that he not go into public places where he could be seen by other Americans. Casey grew so restless under the Chinese controls that at one point, in Shanghai, he demanded to eat with ordinary Chinese. "I don't want to be followed around and eat in empty rooms," he said to his Chinese hosts. "I'm going home if I don't get a good Chinese meal in a real restaurant with real people!" Chinese officials cleared out a restaurant and filled it with intelligence and military people in civilian clothes. When Casey was brought in, he said, "Yeah, this is what I want." Apparently not looking too closely at the other diners, he sat down and ate contentedly.[46]

The agendas for these directors' visits were highly orchestrated. During Gates's trip, he tried at one point to raise a subject that hadn't been planned. Let's talk about North Korea, Gates said: It looks like the Soviets are putting reconnaissance aircraft there and that China is losing all its influence.

Gates's host was the director of Chinese military intelligence, a notoriously hard-boiled operator named Xu Xin. He never even bothered to answer. "It's time for dinner," Xu said. He got up from the table and walked out of the room.[47]

China set the rules, and Americans were supposed to follow them.

CHAPTER SIX

Ronald Reagan and Taiwan

U NLIKE RICHARD NIXON, Ronald Reagan did not enjoy overseas travel. He rarely left the United States. In April 1978, however, the former governor of California flew off on a trip aimed at bolstering his credentials as a presidential candidate. One of the principal destinations was Taiwan.

Reagan traveled with his wife, Nancy; with Richard Allen, his principal adviser on foreign policy; and with Peter Hannaford, who had been one of Reagan's aides in Sacramento and whose small California lobbying firm received a $30,000-a-year retainer from the government of Taiwan. Reagan and his entourage saw several of Taiwan's leaders, including President Chiang Ching-kuo.

Reagan, who by then had been the leader of the conservative wing of the Republican Party for more than a decade, gave a luncheon speech in Taipei. "It is hard for me to believe that any sensible American who believes in individual liberty and self-determination would stand by and let his government abandon an ally whose only 'sins' are that it is small and loves freedom," he declared.[1]

Allen had hoped the Taiwan stop would pave the way for Reagan to visit China, too. Reagan was considerably less ambitious. "He had no taste for it," recalls Allen. "He actually didn't want to go to Moscow, either." Instead, after Japan and Taiwan, the delegation stopped in Hong Kong and then flew to Iran, carrying the Iranian Ambassador to Washington Ardeshir Zahedi with them, because Nancy Reagan wanted to meet the shah.[2]

.   .   .

THE ASCENDANCE of Ronald Reagan in 1980 suddenly reopened the contentious issue of Taiwan, which American and Chinese officials thought they had settled.

Over the previous decade, Reagan had ranked, along with Barry Goldwater, as one of the two most fervent supporters of Taiwan in American politics. He had opposed normalization of relations with China during his unsuccessful 1976 campaign against Ford for the Republican nomination. In the early months of the 1980 campaign, Reagan's standard speech ended with an emotional declaration: "There's one message I want to deliver more than anything in the world as president—no more Taiwans, no more Vietnams, no more betrayal of friends and allies by the U.S. government." He had also suggested on several occasions that if elected president, he would support the reestablishment of "official relations" with Taiwan.[3]

By the summer of 1980, as Reagan wrapped up the Republican nomination and prepared to run against Carter, Reagan's advisers grew nervous that his support for Taiwan was becoming a liability. The Democrats warned that Reagan would cause a rupture in the new American relationship with Beijing. Chinese leaders had made plain that they would never accept an American consulate or governmental presence on Taiwan; yet this was exactly what Reagan seemed to advocate.

Allen was eager to defuse the issue before the fall campaign got under way. Shortly after the Republican convention, at a strategy session in California, he came up with an idea: George Bush, Reagan's vice presidential nominee, should visit Beijing, tell Chinese leaders what Reagan would do as president and work out some accommodation with them. The aim was to make use of Bush's experience as former head of the U.S. liaison office in Beijing to smooth over ties between China and the Reagan campaign.

"I went to Reagan and said, 'I'd like you to let Bush and me go to China,' " recalled Allen. " 'They will listen to him, and we will offset the terrible damage being done to us. Because we're going to have this [questions about Taiwan] at every campaign stop. . . . This is going to be a millstone hanging around your neck, unless you do something dramatic.' "[4] Bush was happy to take on the assignment, and Reagan, though skeptical, gave his approval.

Bush flew to Beijing, accompanied by Allen and by James Lilley, who had served as the CIA station chief under Bush in Beijing and had also worked with Bush at the CIA in Washington. Allen, who had never traveled to China before, didn't trust Bush; he feared the vice presidential candidate might stray from Reagan's positions on Taiwan.

In China, Allen stuck close by Bush at all times, even making sure to ride in the same limousine with him. He discovered Bush was so loyal that he had nothing to worry about. "George was perfect. He did exactly what was expected," Allen concluded.

Speaking to Chinese Foreign Minister Huang Hua, Bush explained that Reagan did not want to reestablish diplomatic relations with Taiwan or to recognize two separate Chinese governments. Don't be deceived by the rhetoric, and read Reagan's language very carefully, Bush urged: We are not calling for any change in policy. But Huang demanded to know what Reagan had meant in calling for "official" relations with Taiwan.

The next day, August 22, 1980, Bush and his delegation had a meeting with Deng Xiaoping. In the midst of the session, an aide handed Deng a slip of paper with news from the United States. Reagan had just made another vague campaign statement, suggesting once again that he favored some sort of "official" relationship with Taiwan.

Deng was irate. If you do what Reagan is suggesting, you will set the clock back, he told Bush. The Chinese leader pointed out, correctly, that the Republicans had been planning to normalize relations with China during the Ford administration on essentially the same terms that Carter later worked out. I have my own country to run, and I don't plan to take out American citizenship, Deng fumed. He singled out for attack one of Reagan's advisers, Ray Cline, a former CIA station chief in Taiwan who had long been one of the Nationalist government's closest allies in Washington. "What's he doing in your campaign entourage?" Deng asked the delegation.[5] It was a stunningly tense, frosty session. After it ended, and the Americans headed home, the official Chinese press branded Bush's mission a failure.

The most important confrontation was still to come: that between the advisers and Reagan himself. On the way back across the Pacific, Allen and Lilley drafted a careful statement for the Republican candidate, trying to gloss over the Taiwan issue so that it wouldn't dominate the fall presidential campaign. The statement formally acknowledged that Reagan wouldn't try to undo or renegotiate the terms of America's formal recognition of China.

When Allen and Lilley arrived in Los Angeles, they showed the Republican presidential nominee what they had written. "Oh, no, I'm not giving that statement," Reagan replied. "This really isn't what I want to say."

Bush talked privately to Reagan. Allen, separately, also saw the Republican nominee, warning him once again that they had to make the Taiwan controversy disappear at the start of the fall campaign. At one point, Reagan sat down and began to draft his own statement on a yellow pad; Lilley thought that if those words had ever been uttered, the United States and China might have come close to war. The issue was left unresolved overnight, while those who had just returned from China got some sleep. Reagan had already scheduled a press conference for the following day.

The next morning, Reagan's high command gathered once again. This time Ed Meese, another Reagan adviser whose conservative credentials were impeccable, urged the candidate to deliver his advisers' statement. It was the pragmatic thing to do, he argued. "This is something that has been drafted, it has George Bush's support, and Dick Allen's behind it," Meese told Reagan. "I think this is something you can go along with."

In the middle of the tense meeting, Reagan began to tell stories. One anecdote followed another: He spun out jokes, yarns, tales. Those who hadn't seen Reagan in action had no idea how entertaining he could be. On the other hand, there was an important decision to make, and Reagan didn't seem to be focusing on it. The clock was going round. It was about five minutes before the press conference was supposed to start.

Finally, Reagan asked, "You still think I ought to make this statement?" Everyone in the room nodded. A few minutes later, he walked out and read to the press what had been written for him about Taiwan, acting as though the words represented his deep and long-settled convictions.

"I would not pretend, as Carter does, that the relationship we now have with Taiwan, enacted by Congress, is unofficial," Reagan insisted. However, this was a semantic subterfuge: Reagan agreed to accept and leave undisturbed the terms of the Carter administration's recognition of China.[6]

From a political standpoint, it worked. Taiwan subsided as an issue in the fall campaign. The controversy would return in a new form, however, after Reagan won the election.

WHEN REAGAN took office, China became one of the principal battlegrounds for bloodletting within the new administration. Throughout 1981 and the first half of 1982, American policy toward China and Taiwan was the subject of infighting between the moderate and conservative wings of the Republican Party; between the White House and the State Department; and ultimately, between President Reagan and his secretary of state, Alexander Haig.

Reagan arrived in the White House as an outsider, eager to bring about change, but also to win acceptance from the Republican establishment. At the 1980 convention, he had even flirted briefly with a deal that would have brought back Ford as vice president with special authority over foreign policy and would have returned Kissinger to secretary of state. Reagan ultimately rejected this arrangement, concluding he would have to yield too much of his power. Yet the episode revealed both his insecurity toward foreign affairs during the 1980 campaign and his uncertainty about the strength of his conservative base.

Reagan had proceeded to name Haig (who had been Kissinger's deputy, Nixon's White House chief of staff and the commander of NATO) to be his first secretary of state. That choice had once again seemed to suggest continuity with past Republican administrations. Such impressions, however, were misleading. Reagan, who often appeared passive and detached, did in fact want to control policy and, eventually, to change it. As time went on, the new president became ever less willing to defer either to tradition or to people like Haig.

When it came to China policy, Haig was a far cry from his mentors Nixon and Kissinger. He had all of their paranoia and none of their subtlety or syntax. For Nixon and Kissinger, forging a strong relationship with China had been a response to specific circumstances around the world; they viewed China as a means to the ends of a peace settlement in Vietnam and detente with the Soviet Union. Haig, by contrast, saw close relations with the Chinese regime as an end in itself; he portrayed himself as the keeper of the faith he had learned during his years in the Nixon administration. He would later assert in his memoirs,

> In terms of the strategic interests of the United States and the West in the last quarter of the twentieth century, China may well be the most important country in the world. . . . The Chinese do not believe that the United States and its allies can bring about the neutralization of Soviet adventurism without the participation of China, or that China can do so without the participation of the United States and the West.[7]

Haig did not seem to understand at first that Reagan and others in the new administration might not share these views, or that by maximizing China's importance to the United States, he might also be minimizing America's leverage. He would probably not have survived in the Reagan administration in any case, because of his continuing bureaucratic struggles with the White House over his authority as secretary of state; but China was undoubtedly one of the contributing factors in his downfall. In their memoirs, both Haig and Reagan listed China as one of the principal issues on which they had disagreed.[8]

The main problem confronting the Reagan administration was what to do about American arms sales to Taiwan. This was the question that had been left unanswered by Carter and Deng Xiaoping when they had hurriedly concluded the deal for normalization of relations at the end of 1978. China had refused to give its assent for a continuing American flow of weaponry to Taiwan, and the United States had refused to give up the arms sales.

By the time Reagan took office, Taiwan was seeking new weapons systems from the United States. The Nationalist regime was particularly eager to obtain a new American fighter plane called the FX for Taiwan's air force. One of America's leading defense firms, Northrop, had developed the FX with the aim of selling it to Third World countries, at a time when the Carter administration would not allow the export of America's more sophisticated jet fighter, the F-16. Soon after taking office, however, Reagan reversed this Carter policy and allowed F-16s to be sold overseas, suddenly leaving Northrop with virtually no demand for an expensive plane it had paid to develop. Taiwan was one of the few prospective buyers for the FX, because the United States was not prepared to offend China by letting Taiwan purchase a plane so advanced as the F-16.[9]

Several members of the Reagan administration's new foreign policy team were considerably more sympathetic to Taiwan than was Haig. They included Allen, who had become national security advisor; Secretary of Defense Caspar Weinberger; and Lilley, whom Allen had installed as the National Security Council specialist for China. Before long, the question of arms sales to Taiwan became the main battleground in the war within the administration over Reagan's China policy.

At the State Department, Haig came up with an approach that seemed to be aimed at purchasing China's tolerance for weapons sales to Taiwan. His first initiatives attempted to open the way for American arms to China itself; Haig's hope was that once the Chinese regime was receiving its own weaponry from the United States, Beijing might complain less about continuing U.S. sales to Taiwan.

In June 1981, Haig made his first and, as it turned out, only foray to China as secretary of state. Before leaving Washington, he had won approval from the administration to bring to Beijing several gifts. First, Haig told Chinese leaders that the United States was ready to treat China as a "friendly, non-aligned country," eligible to receive much greater amounts of American technology than the Soviet Union.

Haig then offered Chinese leaders an even more significant change: The Reagan administration, he said, was prepared to suspend the American prohibition on arms sales to China. The Carter administration had taken the first step by clearing the way for "nonlethal" military equipment, such as trucks; now, Haig told Chinese leaders the United States would be ready, on a case-by-case basis, to consider selling lethal weapons systems to China, too. He invited a top official of China's People's Liberation Army, Vice Chief of Staff Liu Huaqing, to Washington to explore further exactly what weapons China might buy.[10] As a test of how far the Reagan administration might be willing to go, Chinese officials quickly said they would be interested in purchasing several American weapons systems, including Hawk missiles, Mark 48 anti-submarine torpedoes and armored personnel carriers.[11]

Haig was supposed to dangle the prospect of American arms sales before Chinese leaders in secret meetings but say nothing about the subject in public. He had pressed the State Department to develop the idea, hurriedly, in the final weeks before his trip. The concept of making China eligible to buy arms had been cleared with the White House, but without the usual, exhaustive reviews within the Washington bureaucracy. The formal National Security Decision Directive (NSDD) worked out within the administration before Haig's trip said the new policy of American arms sales to China was not to be revealed for several months, until after a follow-on trip by a Chinese defense official to Washington.[12]

Instead of keeping the idea quiet, however, Haig revealed this far-reaching change in American arms policy at a press conference in Beijing, proudly proclaiming that his trip marked a new step forward toward security cooperation between the United States and China. Even Haig's aides at the State Department were stunned by the disclosure; the idea of selling arms to China had not yet been discussed at all with America's allies in Asia. Haig's performance particularly unsettled two members of the American party: Lilley and Richard Armitage, the Pentagon specialist on East Asia. Both men had been relegated to the margins of Haig's delegation; they had been required to ride in the back of Haig's plane and to share a hotel room together in China, while State Department officials of equal rank were given single rooms.

These two outsiders realized that they couldn't send messages back to Washington through regular State Department channels, because Haig would see them. Instead, Lilley—who, as a former CIA station chief, was thoroughly familiar with the various secure communications systems at the American embassy in Beijing—secretly informed Allen in Washington that Haig had gone much further with the Chinese than the administration had expected. Armitage sent a similar message back to Weinberger. In Washington, Allen took the news of Haig's improvised, unapproved disclosure directly to the president, and Weinberger may have done so, too.[13]

A few hours before Haig was to depart from China, Reagan appeared at a news conference in Washington. "I have not changed my feelings about Taiwan," he declared. "We have an act, a law called the Taiwan Relations Act, that provides for defense equipment being sold to Taiwan. I intend to live up to the Taiwan Relations Act." [14] Chinese officials were taken by surprise; Reagan's tone seemed strikingly different from Haig's. The administration seemed to be trying to pressure Beijing to accept its agenda on Taiwan.

Haig expected to be seen off at the Beijing airport by the foreign minister, the usual custom. Instead, only a deputy appeared. He pulled Haig aside to complain about Reagan's remarks. "Who makes American foreign policy?" the official asked.

Haig was furious that the White House had undercut him. He even tried briefly to bar Lilley and Armitage from returning home on his Air Force plane. The episode illustrated the extraordinary divisions over China policy within the new administration. [15]

Back in Washington, Haig continued to argue that by selling arms to China, America might be able to end Beijing's objections to the sale of the FX fighter plane to Taiwan. When John Holdridge, the assistant secretary of state for East Asia, said he was having trouble winning approval from the Pentagon to sell China the missiles and armored personnel carriers it wanted, Haig blew up. "Get it through your thick head," he ordered. "We're going to sell arms to China in September, so we can sell arms to Taiwan in January!" [16]

The Chinese, however, were no happier with Haig's idea than was the White House. Haig seemed to be suggesting that China didn't care about the continuing American military support for Taiwan, so long as it got its share. In Beijing, Foreign Minister Huang Hua had warned Haig that China would not accept American weapons as a bribe. One Chinese press commentary warned that any policy seeking a trade-off between American arms for China and American arms for Taiwan was "doomed to failure." [17]

China gradually increased the pressure on the new administration, creating a sense of crisis over Taiwan. Early in 1981, China had formally downgraded its diplomatic relations with the Netherlands by permanently withdrawing its ambassador there in retaliation for the Dutch sale of a submarine to Taiwan. Within months, Chinese officials began threatening to do the same to Washington if the Reagan administration persisted in plans for arms sales to Taiwan. Throughout the summer, China repeatedly postponed the visit by Liu Huaqing.

Once again, as it had in 1977, the Chinese leadership registered its displeasure with a new administration by rolling out the red carpet for those American politicians who had just left office. During the summer of 1981, no fewer than eight alumni of the Carter administration were welcomed to China.

Carter himself was among them; Deng Xiaoping told the former president that "we Chinese will never forget" his role in breaking off American relations with Taiwan. Chinese television broadcast an unusual prime-time interview with Carter, in which he pointedly said Taiwan was "a very difficult and sensitive issue" that should be resolved by the Chinese people "without interference from my country."

Carter's former assistant secretary of state, Richard Holbrooke, had a ready explanation for the sudden rush of out-of-office Democrats to Beijing. "With U.S.-China relations still a slight question mark, there is the sense that the Carter people represent continuity," he said. But there was another aspect to this phenomenon; former American officials were increasingly making commercial use of the contacts with Chinese officials they had made while in government.

By the time of Holbrooke's mid-1981 visit to Beijing, he had become a consultant for Lehman Brothers, the investment banking firm, and an adviser to Nike and Seagram. Carter's energy secretary, James Schlesinger, also visited China for Lehman Brothers. Carter's treasury secretary, Michael Blumenthal, came as chairman of Burroughs Corp., and Carter's agriculture secretary, Bob Bergland, visited for Farmland-Eaton World Trade.[18]

Chinese officials were discovering that American politicians, after they left office, often sought to make money from their China connections. And the leaders quickly learned to treat the out-of-office politicians well, realizing that many of them still had influence back home and might be back in office someday.

IN THE early fall of 1981, the Reagan administration was still weighing the possibility of selling American fighter planes to Taiwan. China decided to prevent this from happening by making a series of demands that went well beyond anything it had previously sought from Carter or Reagan.

At a meeting in Cancun, Mexico, Foreign Minister Huang Hua told Haig the United States would have to set a date by which all American arms sales to Taiwan would end. Moreover, Huang said, China expected the United States to limit both the quantity and quality of its arms to Taiwan to the levels of the Carter administration, and then to reduce these weapons sales year by year.[19]

Until then, Reagan administration officials believed their troubles with China were merely over the sale of the FX fighter to Taiwan.

Huang's message amounted to a breathtaking ultimatum. Beijing was, indirectly, asking the Reagan administration to abandon Taiwan, leaving it without the military supplies on which the regime depended for its security in the absence of a defense treaty with the United States. Had Washington gone along with China's request, its action would have forced Taiwan not merely to negotiate its future with China, but to do so from a position of increasing military weakness.

A few days later, on a visit to Washington, the Chinese foreign minister repeated his demands and added a new one. In a meeting with Reagan, Huang said that the United States should also immediately stop all arms supplies, even minor ones, to Taiwan until after it negotiated with Beijing a long-term arrangement to end the arms shipments; if not, China would downgrade its relations with the United States. By this time, even Haig was irritated with China's lengthening list of demands. He warned Huang Hua that he was putting at risk everything that had been built up between China and the United States over the previous decade.[20]

Almost immediately, however, Haig sought to ease the tension by making plain he was willing to accept one of China's requests. While insisting the United States could not set a date to end arms sales to Taiwan, he suggested the United States would be willing to limit these sales to a level no greater than that of the Carter administration. It was a significant concession, one that would circumscribe American policy in the years to come.

In a memorandum to Reagan on November 26, 1981, Haig justified this new limit by arguing that America's relations with China were at a "critical juncture," and that it was important to avoid "a setback which could gravely damage our global strategic posture." Moreover, Haig argued, American arms sales to Taiwan in Carter's last years had been substantial (slightly more than $500 million a year). "We must recognize that mainland capabilities and intentions do not require a level of U.S. arms sales [to Taiwan] above the final year of the Carter Administration, which provided an unusually high ceiling," Haig wrote.[21]

At the beginning of 1982, the Reagan administration offered China another major concession. In January, Holdridge was dispatched to Beijing to inform Chinese officials that the administration would not sell Taiwan the FX fighter or any other advanced fighter plane. Instead, the United States would merely allow Taiwan to obtain or produce the same, older-model fighter planes, called F-5Es, that its air force already possessed. Reagan approved the decision after American defense and intelligence officials completed a study showing that Taiwan didn't need the FX; it could easily defend itself against China's relatively weak air force with its existing planes. Reagan finally gave up on the FX sale after a weekend meeting with advisers at Camp David.[22]

This decision on the FX might well have ended the entire affair, if it had been offered the previous summer. By early 1982, however, China wanted to test how much more the United States would give. Haig was willing to go to great lengths to preserve what he considered America's strategic relationship with China. Furthermore, Richard Allen had just resigned from the NSC in a scandal over his acceptance of Japanese gifts, temporarily strengthening Haig's hand.

Administration officials thought China would be pleased that America would not sell Taiwan the FX. Instead, the Chinese pocketed this new concession and came back for more. They complained about a decision by the Reagan administration to sell some spare parts to Taiwan. They also expressed dissatisfaction that Taiwan might obtain more of the old F-5E fighters. Above all, Chinese officials kept pressing for the United States to set a date to cut off all arms sales to Taiwan.[23]

Over the following six months, they brought all of their negotiating skills to bear in an effort to wring this last concession from the Reagan administration. They were very nearly successful.

The tenth anniversary of the Shanghai Communique was approaching. State Department officials suggested the idea of honoring the occasion with a new communique, one that would limit arms sales to Taiwan and would also proclaim America's and China's cooperation around the world. Chinese officials seemed interested, but then submitted language that would have forced the United States to phase out American weapons supplies to Taiwan. The Reagan administration balked, and the tenth anniversary of the Nixon trip passed with little celebration.

In May, Bush visited Beijing, urging Chinese officials to recognize that the United States could not possibly set a date to stop supplying Taiwan. The vice president tried to persuade Deng of the Reagan administration's good intentions. Like other American officials, he was also treated to a diatribe from Huang Hua. "He just battered Bush, saying this is a two-China policy," recalls Don Gregg, who accompanied Bush on the trip. "Bush kept saying, 'No, it's loyalty to our friends.' " Huang told the American delegation nothing had been accomplished since his trip to Washington the previous autumn. The State Department officials were stunned; they had already made several significant concessions, yet Huang was claiming there had been no progress.[24]

The arms dispute was still unsettled when, on June 25, 1982, Haig suddenly resigned, after the last in his unending series of battles with the White House over his authority as secretary of state. "The only disagreement was over whether I made policy or the Secretary of State did," Reagan noted in his diary.[25]

Haig was not quite finished with his work, however. Following the announcement of his resignation, he summoned subordinates at the State Department for a final talk about China policy. Within days, he wrote Reagan a memo summarizing where things stood in the negotiations over Taiwan arms sales. Haig recommended giving way to China on the final concession it had sought: a promise to end American arms sales to Taiwan.

According to William Rope, the head of the State Department's China desk who drafted the memo and agreed with its contents, Haig said he thought Reagan should accept language that spoke of "a day when arms sales [to Taiwan] will end." That was the promise China had long sought, its ultimate negotiating goal. Haig predicted gloomily that without such a concession from the Reagan administration, China was going to downgrade its relations with the United States.[26]

Haig's resignation deprived Beijing of its strongest supporter in the top ranks of the administration. At the same time, his recommendation brought the prolonged Taiwan arms controversy to a point where it was ready for a resolution: The administration had to decide how far it would go to accommodate China.

What Haig had written reflected the beliefs of many of the China experts at the State Department. Indeed, the administration was, by this time, considering seriously the idea of ending arms sales to Taiwan. Lilley, who at the beginning of 1982 had been sent to Taiwan as head of America's unofficial office there, was recalled to Washington and instructed to see if Taiwan might go along with the idea.

"They wanted me to go back and convince Taiwan that there should be a terminal date for arms sales," Lilley said. Instead, after returning to Taiwan, he cabled back that the idea wasn't going to work. His message annoyed Bush, who had been Lilley's patron and former boss. "It was the first time he [Bush] was ever upset at me," recalled Lilley. "He said, 'You've got to realize where the big relationship is.'" Taiwan, Bush was saying, didn't count nearly as much as China.[27]

In the end, the issue was settled by Reagan himself. In July, aides brought the president the Haig memo arguing that the United States should agree to end arms sales to Taiwan. Reagan refused to sign it. He was willing to agree to limits on the sales and to other concessions, but not to a cut-off. Instead, he approved what was termed a "final offer" to Deng Xiaoping: a written agreement that spoke vaguely of America's hopes for a "final resolution" of the dispute over arms sales but set no date for the sales to end.[28]

After another month of testing to see if the administration might retreat a bit more, China finally agreed to the deal, which was enshrined in a communique on August 17, 1982. Haig had been wrong: Despite the refusal to set a date for the termination of arms sales to Taiwan, China did not downgrade its relations with the United States.

THE 1982 communique was the most controversial agreement ever reached between the United States and the People's Republic of China. Although the Reagan administration did not promise to end all arms sales to Taiwan, it did agree to set strict limits on these sales, where none existed before.

In the days after the agreement was announced, the administration made public a series of assurances it had given to Taiwan's government in an effort to make the deal more tolerable. The administration promised that the United States would not consult with China about the kinds of arms to be sold to Taiwan; that America would never try to mediate between China and Taiwan; and that America would not pressure Taiwan to negotiate with China. Acting on Washington's instructions, Lilley had carefully negotiated the wording of these assurances with Chiang Ching-kuo.[29]

Still, these palliatives could not overcome the agreement itself. Over a period of ten months in 1981–82, the administration had repeatedly yielded ground in the talks with China, only to have Beijing ask for more. American objectives, such as obtaining a concrete pledge from China not to use force against Taiwan, were progressively weakened. The concessions Haig made in the early months of the talks might well have been part of a final package. In the years to follow, even those American officials who were the most sympathetic to China would describe the Taiwan arms negotiations as a classic illustration of how not to negotiate with Beijing.

The aftermath of this affair has never been made public. Shortly after the arms communique with China was issued, Reagan moved, secretly and unilaterally, to eviscerate what he had just signed. He dictated a terse, one-page memorandum that explained his own interpretation and understanding of what he had done. The United States would restrict arms sales to Taiwan *so long as the balance of military power between China and Taiwan was preserved* [author's emphasis], Reagan wrote. If China upgraded its military capabilities, the United States would help Taiwan to match those improvements. These were important qualifiers, not to be found in the language of the agreement itself.

Reagan's memo was placed in a safe at the National Security Council. Over the years, whenever any question arose about arms sales to Taiwan, the presidential memo would be pulled out of the safe. Here is how Reagan believed his deal with China should be interpreted, American officials told one another.

As a result, Taiwan obtained most of what it needed, and the dispute between America and China over arms sales subsided for another decade. Taiwan survived, and China, having tested America's resolve, turned its attention elsewhere.[30]

AMONG THOSE in the Reagan administration especially irked by the way the Taiwan arms issue had been handled was a young State Department official named Paul Wolfowitz. In the first years of the new Reagan administration, he was the department's director of policy planning, charged with developing long-term strategies for American foreign policy.

Wolfowitz represented a new breed in American thinking about China. When it came to the Soviet Union, he was a hawk; in the 1970s, on issues like detente and the Soviet military buildup, he had been a certifiable hard-liner. In the policy debates of the Carter administration, he would clearly have sympathized with Brzezinski over Vance.

Yet unlike Brzezinski and many of these hawks of the 1970s, Wolfowitz didn't think China was of much help to America in dealing with the Soviet Union. He believed that American foreign policy in general, and Haig in particular, vastly overestimated China's strategic importance to the United States. China was important within East Asia, in places like Korea and Indochina, Wolfowitz argued. But the idea that it was the key to changing the worldwide behavior of the Soviet Union struck Wolfowitz as wrong. Indeed, he felt that the notion of China's global strategic importance had been largely manufactured by Kissinger to make himself look smart and to help justify the opening to China.[31]

The bottom line, Wolfowitz argued, was that China needed the United States far more than the United States needed China. It was China, not the United States, that was being threatened by a Soviet invasion. Washington had considerable leverage in negotiations with Beijing but wasn't making use of it. The Carter administration should never have agreed in 1978 to a moratorium on arms sales to Taiwan, Wolfowitz thought: At the time of those negotiations, China was preparing to invade Vietnam and wanted desperately to solidify its ties with the United States. By overestimating China's importance, America was making concessions it didn't have to make.

For the Reagan administration, Wolfowitz's line of thinking offered a way to bridge the 1970s disagreements over China between the anti-Soviet right wing and the pro-Taiwan right. Wolfowitz was arguing that if you kept China's importance in perspective, you could be a staunch Cold Warrior without abandoning Taiwan. His view was also in line with some of the changing military realities of the Cold War. The People's Liberation Army had been unimpressive in its invasion of Vietnam. The administration, meanwhile, had launched a massive American military buildup to confront the Soviet Union. By the early 1980s, Washington did not think China would be nearly so crucial in the event of a U.S.-Soviet conflict as it had thought a decade earlier.

During the negotiations over Taiwan arms sales, Wolfowitz had twice criticized in writing Haig's reverence for China. In mid-1981, he sent along a broadly worded memo, drafted by an assistant, Sean Randolph, which argued that the United States was inflating China's strategic significance. In the spring of 1982, Wolfowitz wrote a paper attacking the State Department for making too many concessions to China in the Taiwan arms negotiations.

Haig was infuriated. He ordered that his director of policy planning be cut out of all further information about the talks between Washington and Beijing, and Wolfowitz never heard anything more about the communique until after it was signed.[32]

Nevertheless, Wolfowitz's thinking about China attracted the attention of others within the Reagan administration, among them Haig's successor, George Shultz. The new secretary appointed Wolfowitz to be his assistant secretary of state for East Asia, replacing John Holdridge, who had served with Haig on Kissinger's National Security Council staff. It was a classic illustration of a personnel shift that represented a dramatic change in policy.

Shultz embraced many of Wolfowitz's ideas. In Shultz's memoirs, written a decade later, he said he had sought to "alter the thinking" underlying American policy toward China:

When the geostrategic importance of China became the conceptual prism through which Sino-American relations were viewed, it was almost inevitable that American policymakers became overly solicitous of Chinese interests, concerns and sensitivities. Indeed, while President Nixon's historic opening to China in 1972 gave both countries some leverage with the Soviets, it is also true that the opening gave the Chinese leverage over us. As a result, much of the history of Sino-American relations since the normalization of relations in 1978 could be described as a series of Chinese defined "obstacles"—such as Taiwan, technology transfers, and trade—that the United States had been tasked to overcome in order to preserve the overall relationship.[33]

Along with these ideas that had been earlier espoused by Wolfowitz, Shultz brought his own insights. As a former businessman and secretary of the treasury, he was impressed more by economic and industrial strength than by military power; in this respect, he was the opposite of Haig. Moreover, as a former labor negotiator, Shultz understood the bargaining process. "I am convinced that in international relations, as in labor relations, the road to a bad relationship is to place too much emphasis on the relationship for its own sake," he wrote, speaking of America's approach to China.[34]

In early 1983, Shultz and Wolfowitz added the last, crucial element in their new Asia policy: the notion that Japan, not China, should be the primary focus of American attention.

During a speech in San Francisco outlining his ideas, the secretary praised lavishly Japan's growing economic power. He also spoke of the importance of democracy. "We believe that democratic nations are more likely to follow the just and sensible policies that will best serve the future of the region and the globe," Shultz declared. Frictions between the United States and China were inevitable, he argued, not just because of Taiwan, but because of "differences between our social systems."

Shultz's speech represented a subtle but remarkable change in the assumptions that had guided American policy toward Asia. For the first time, America was redirecting its foreign policy to take account of Asia's growing prosperity. The non-Communist governments of Asia—not only Japan, but South Korea and the nations of Southeast Asia—had been treated as sideshows in the Cold War for decades; Washington depicted them mostly as wards to be protected from Communism. Now, they were portrayed as important for their own sake, as future powers to be courted.

Even more strikingly, in the San Francisco speech Shultz discussed China without ever once using the favorite Kissingerian adjective "strategic." Instead, he talked of China's "regional role," suggesting that China's importance to American foreign policy lay mostly within Asia itself, rather than against the Soviet Union. This was, of course, also a considerable change for American policy: Kissinger, Brzezinski and Haig had all contended that China's support was essential for America in the Cold War.

Shultz's reorientation of American policy also reflected changes in China's own view of the world. In the 1970s, China had often been the cheerleader, indeed provocateur, seeking confrontation with the Soviet Union, at a time when the United States was pursuing detente. That phase ended after the invasion of Afghanistan, when China began to worry that it might be caught up in a dangerous conflict between Washington and Moscow. As Reagan increasingly challenged the Soviet Union around the world, China began to distance itself from the United States. In the fall of 1982, Communist Party General Secretary Hu Yaobang told a Party Congress that China would carry out an independent foreign policy, separate from that of either the Soviets or the Americans. The anti-Soviet partnership of Kissinger and Chou, or of Brzezinski and Deng, was not entirely eliminated, but it was being scaled back.

Soon after Shultz's speech, the *Far Eastern Economic Review* published a cover story called "Leaning Toward Japan," showing America's secretary of state at a street corner, following a sign marked "Ginza" and heading away from another one marked "Tiananmen." Shultz "does not view the Pacific through the dreary and emotional prism of Washington's Asian wars," the story said.[35]

AFTER HIS first two years in office, Ronald Reagan had, however haphazardly or inadvertently, come up with the personnel and the approach to China that suited him. The ideas propounded by Shultz and Wolfowitz were to guide American policy toward China for the remaining five years of the Reagan administration.

Shultz lost little time in putting these ideas into practice. Before his first trip to China in February 1983, State Department officials let it be known that the secretary was not carrying any surprise gifts or policy changes to Beijing, as other American visitors like Brzezinski and Haig had done in the past.[36]

In Beijing, Shultz had a testy confrontation with a group of American executives eager to do more business with China. During a lunch at Beijing's new Jianguo Hotel, the Americans repeatedly asked the secretary why Washington wasn't doing more to help them win business contracts. One of them observed that Japan and West Germany issued export licenses for China much more quickly than did the Reagan administration.

"Why don't you move to Japan or Western Europe?" Shultz asked. When another representative asked him why the administration had refused to grant Westinghouse the right to sell nuclear power plants in China, the secretary retorted, "The problem of proliferation is a distinct problem, and I think the question suggests in a rather cavalier fashion that [we] brush it off. I don't brush it off."

Shultz told the business leaders many of their questions implied that "there is something wrong with the United States." Some, he went on, "sign deals even though they know the technology cannot be exported, and then say to the U.S. government, 'We made this financial commitment: now you've got to approve it.' Buddy, that's your problem when you do that. Don't complain to the government."

In his memoirs, Shultz complained that the American business leaders had espoused "the standard Chinese line." His confrontation at the hotel had left him "with a sour taste," Shultz said. The contretemps illustrated how little influence the business community had over American policy toward China in the early 1980s. Eleven years later, during the Clinton administration, when Secretary of State Warren Christopher had a similar meeting in Beijing with American executives, the dynamics between business and government were strikingly different.[37]

THE DISPUTE over arms sales to Taiwan left a legacy of acrimony and factionalism that endured a decade or more.

In the years after Nixon's rapprochement, many other battles had been fought within the U.S. government over China. Most of these, however, were conflicts between the executive branch and Congress, or among Cabinet-level officials: between Kissinger and Rogers, for example, or between Brzezinski and Vance.

The Reagan administration's internal divisions over arms sales to Taiwan filtered down through the bureaucracies to a far greater extent than these other disagreements. Competing networks emerged within the government: one network of officials whose highest priority was close ties with China, and another of those who placed greater emphasis on relations with Taiwan, Japan and the rest of East Asia. The pro-China faction included men like John Holdridge and William Rope; its intellectual leader was Charles W. Freeman Jr., the deputy chief of mission at the American embassy in Beijing. The pan-Asia faction included Reagan's aides William Clark and Gaston Sigur at the National Security Council as well as Wolfowitz, Armitage and Lilley.

Each network was intensely suspicious of the other. The pro-China faction was accused by its opponents of wanting to abandon Taiwan, or at least wishing it would disappear. (On that last point, at least, the critics were often right. One U.S. official was amazed to hear Holdridge joke, in his State Department office, that it would be nice if a tidal wave hit Taiwan.)[38] The other, pan-Asia faction was portrayed by its adversaries as a bunch of interlopers who couldn't understand Chinese culture and didn't respect or honor the foreign policy legacy of Nixon and Kissinger.

In the aftermath of the 1982 communique, the pan-Asia faction triumphed within the Reagan administration. Wolfowitz became assistant secretary of state, and Reagan appointed Sigur to succeed him three years later. Armitage, their close ally, was in charge of Asia policy at the Pentagon. Once a week, these men gathered together to work out the administration's Asia policies; it was something between a regular meeting and a cabal. One of its purposes was to make sure the administration continued to approve arms sales to Taiwan.[39]

By contrast, those State Department China hands who had worked most closely on the Taiwan arms agreement gradually found themselves further and further removed from American policy toward China. It wasn't exactly a full-scale purge, but it wasn't random, either. Holdridge was sent off to be ambassador to Indonesia. Freeman stayed at the American embassy in Beijing through 1984, but then was given assignments elsewhere; he wasn't involved in China policy for nearly a decade.

Rope, the youngest and lowest-ranking member of the pro-China faction during the Taiwan arms negotiations, was unable to obtain any State Department job for any country in East Asia after his time ran out as head of the China desk in 1983. Finally, he gave up and became a specialist on Turkey.

ALEXANDER HAIG'S fortunes were unaffected, however. Following his resignation, Haig worked as a consultant for United Technologies, where he quickly adopted the formula he had so unsuccessfully put forward for the U.S. government as secretary of state: He tried to sell arms both to China and to Taiwan.

In the months after the 1982 communique was worked out, the Reagan administration went about the task of deciding exactly what sorts of arms and other equipment Taiwan should be allowed to buy under the new agreement. To their astonishment, State Department officials soon found themselves receiving phone calls from Haig.

Their former boss urged them to approve the sale by United Technologies of advanced Sikorsky helicopters to Taiwan. His lobbying effort was unsuccessful; the State Department did not let Taiwan buy these aircraft, but it approved the sale of less-advanced helicopters also made by Sikorsky.[40]

This did not mean, however, that Haig had somehow become partial to Taiwan. He soon appeared in Beijing, too, eager to sell weapons systems to China. In November 1984, Assistant Secretary of Defense Lawrence Korb visited China on a Pentagon delegation aimed at helping the Chinese army improve its logistics. While there, he ran into Haig. On a walk in the garden of China's state guest house at Diaoyutai, the former secretary of state told him the Reagan administration ought to open the way for the sale of more military hardware and technology to China.

"We ought to give them [China] whatever they want," Haig told Korb. "They're not going to use it against us."[41]

CHAPTER SEVEN

Reagan and the Golden Years

WITH HAIG'S DEPARTURE and the end of the acrimony over arms sales to Taiwan, the United States and China entered their golden years. Surprisingly, between 1983 and 1988, the Reagan administration forged a closer, more extensive working relationship with China's Communist regime than the two governments had before or have had since.

American and Chinese military commanders who fought against one another during the Korean War crisscrossed the Pacific, offering warm toasts to the friendship between the People's Liberation Army and the American armed forces. Intelligence agencies worked together to fight large-scale covert wars in Afghanistan and Cambodia. American defense contractors supplied weapons systems to China, and U.S. warships for the first time visited ports on the Chinese coast. Chinese leaders sent thousands of the country's best and brightest students to American universities. U.S. Cabinet secretaries offered Chinese government ministers the best in American training and technology in fields ranging from agriculture to securities law.

In the days of Kissinger and Brzezinski, the collaboration between America and China had often been close, but not deep: It had been confined to the highest levels of government. Throughout the 1970s, the two countries had been somewhat constrained by the lack of diplomatic relations. By the early 1980s, America and China were ready to do serious business with one another. Though neither country realized it at the time, this decade would come to be viewed as the apogee in relations between the two countries.

What brought about this halcyon era? At least on the surface, it ran contrary to expectations. The first two years under Reagan had been rancorous. Moreover, many of China's strongest allies within the U.S. gov-

ernment—those who, like Haig, believed most strongly in the importance of a strategic relationship between America and China—had by
1983 either lost their jobs or declined in influence.

Several factors were behind this era of good feeling. One was simply
that America and China had tested one another to the point of exhaus-
tion. Each side had probed the other's limits. China had discovered how
much the United States would give concerning Taiwan, and what it
wouldn't. Both countries recognized that despite their differences over
Taiwan, they still had a great deal to offer one another. Both remained
wary of the Soviet Union's military power and Soviet intentions in
Asia. China wanted American technology, and America was becoming
ever more interested in pursuing its old dream of selling to the China
market.

Another dynamic at work during this period might be called the
phenomenon of reverse expectations. In its relations with America, Chinese officials have often been considerably more demanding of those
Americans considered China's "friends," such as Kissinger, Bush and
Haig, than of other U.S. officials. Those Americans whom China calls *lao
pengyou,* old friends, can be repeatedly asked to deliver favors, where others are treated more pragmatically. China's dealings with Reagan, Shultz
and Wolfowitz—none of them considered friends—were less turbulent
and more businesslike.[1]

The final and most important factor propelling the two countries
toward one another was China's domestic politics. The 1980s were the
peak period for the Westernization of Chinese society and culture. The
country was emerging from the straitjacket of Maoism. Deng Xiaoping
emphasized the importance of education, technology and expertise that
China could best obtain from America and its Western allies.

Communist Party Secretary Hu Yaobang and Premier Zhao Ziyang,
the two leaders whom Deng said he was grooming to succeed him in
running the country, sometimes seemed considerably more eager to support the values of the West than Deng was. Zhao appeared in public in
Western suits. Hu sometimes went further than Zhao: In the mid-1980s,
he touched off a furor by suggesting that the Chinese people should eat
with silverware instead of chopsticks. "We should prepare more knives
and forks, buy more plates and sit around the table to eat Chinese food in
the Western style, that is, each from his own plate," he said. "That way, we
can avoid contagious diseases."[2]

Hu's and Zhao's embrace of Western culture was reflected throughout Chinese society in the 1980s: China experimented with Western
music, art, law, journalism, political science, business and finance in ways
that had not been permitted a decade earlier, and without so many of the

political conflicts that would arise in the 1990s. The Communist Party did not yet view American influences and ideals as a threat to its rule over China, in the way that it did after 1989.

Thus, ironically, under Ronald Reagan and George Shultz, both considerably less enamored of China than their predecessors, America and China for a few years forged the sort of close working partnership of which Richard Nixon and Henry Kissinger had once dreamed.

NOTHING COULD better symbolize the depth of the intelligence cooperation between America and China in the 1980s than the Afghan mules.

After the invasion of Afghanistan in 1979, the United States launched its biggest covert intelligence operation since World War II, aimed at supporting the *moujeheddin* rebels in their guerrilla war against Soviet forces. The CIA, working closely with Pakistan's intelligence service, rushed to arm, train and support the Afghan resistance.

China was a partner in these clandestine operations. Starting with CIA Director Stansfield Turner's visit to Beijing in late 1980, American and Chinese intelligence agencies had established a formal working relationship. China, like the United States, was happy to see the Soviet Union bogged down in a protracted war, one that might teach Moscow the dangers of trying to expand its power in Asia.

One of the main logistical problems for the *moujeheddin* was finding ways to distribute arms and ammunition to its fighting units. Soviet forces controlled the roads and the air. For resupply, the Afghan rebels relied on pack animals, moving overland at night. As the fighting in Afghanistan intensified, the *moujeheddin* discovered that there simply weren't enough four-legged animals inside the country to support their operations. The rebels desperately needed mules.

Enter America and China. The CIA studied briefly the possibility of transporting mules from the United States to Afghanistan, but finally decided that the idea wouldn't work; transportation was expensive, and American mules weren't sturdy enough. Instead, the CIA turned to its Chinese partners and agreed to buy thousands of Chinese mules. Chinese intelligence officials arranged to have mules bred inside China and then marched along the Karakoram Highway, the route of the old Silk Road, from Xinjiang Province in far western China into Pakistan. There, the mules were laden with mortars, machine guns, rocket launchers and other guns and ammunition and sent on another journey into Afghanistan.[3]

While the mules were the symbol of the Sino-American intelligence cooperation on Afghanistan, arms were the substance of it. Chinese intelligence supplied many of the weapons used by the *moujeheddin,* under a similar arrangement with the CIA: The United States paid the costs, and China supplied the goods.

For American intelligence, buying Chinese weapons served several purposes. China was relatively close to Pakistan, and the two countries were already allies, so it made sense to set up a flow of weapons from China to Pakistan to the Afghan guerrillas.

Furthermore, the Chinese arms enabled the CIA to maintain the fiction that the United States was not supplying the Afghan resistance. Through the first half of the 1980s, it was official American policy to make sure that the weapons used by the *moujeheddin* came from Communist countries, so that the Soviet Union could not accuse the United States of direct involvement in the war.

The CIA obtained some of the arms it needed for Afghanistan from Egypt, which had stocks of Soviet-built weaponry. In addition, the agency found that Israel was happy to sell some of the Soviet-made weapons it had captured during the war in Lebanon; the Afghan *moujeheddin* didn't realize that their *jihad* against Soviet forces was being fought with the indirect help of the Israelis.[4]

Despite these other sources of supply, however, the overwhelming share of the CIA's arms purchases for Afghanistan, particularly during the early stages of the war, came from China. At the Pakistan port of Karachi, Chinese ships unloaded cargoes of small arms, assault rifles, mines, anti-tank and anti-aircraft guns, rocket launchers and 107 mm rockets. Mohammed Yousaf, the general who headed Pakistan's Inter-Services Intelligence (ISI) Directorate operations to supply the *moujeheddin,* estimated that the Afghan resistance received 10,000 tons of weapons in 1983. The arms supplies increased year by year to a level of 65,000 tons in 1987, with most of the shipments coming from China, Yousaf later wrote. By some estimates, China made $100 million a year through its weapons sales to the CIA.[5]

Years later, the CIA's massive payments for Chinese arms would seem ironic. By the late 1980s, the United States was complaining about China's proclivity for selling arms, missiles and other weapons overseas, particularly in the Middle East. American officials sometimes accused the Beijing government, Chinese arms industries and the People's Liberation Army of crass commercialism. Never was it noted that one of China's earliest, biggest and most profitable customers for arms exports was the CIA.

FOR MICHAEL PILLSBURY, the covert operations in Afghanistan represented the fulfillment of the decade-old dream of American military cooperation with China.

By the beginning of the 1980s, Pillsbury had become part of a network of right-wing activists in Washington, a loose alliance of congressional staff aides and other conservatives whose main interest was in weakening and challenging the Soviet Union.[6] On Capitol Hill, Pillsbury's hawkish views attracted the support of several important Republican legislators, including Senators Orrin Hatch and Gordon Humphrey. After Reagan took office, he landed a job in the Pentagon as an assistant to Fred Ikle, the undersecretary of defense for policy.

Pillsbury was by nature both intelligent and conspiratorial. Secretary of Defense Caspar Weinberger later complained that Pillsbury had been "a loose cannon who was really in the department on sufferance because of his political friends."[7] Such remarks reflected a common view of Pillsbury among top-level officials, not only at the Pentagon but at the State Department and CIA. Pillsbury was skilled at building up pressure on high-level officials to do things they hadn't wanted. He was, in many ways, a provocateur, whose talent lay in knowing how to work the executive branch and Capitol Hill on behalf of the causes that interested him.

During the 1980s, his cause was defeating the Soviets in Afghanistan, and the means he seized upon was the Stinger missile. As Ikle's coordinator for Afghan affairs, Pillsbury spearheaded a campaign to give these missiles to the *moujeheddin*.

In 1985, as the Soviet Union stepped up its efforts for a military victory in Afghanistan, Washington was divided over what to do. Some of the more hawkish officials in the Pentagon and CIA, together with their allies on Capitol Hill, urged the administration to intensify its efforts against the Soviet forces. Increasingly, they focused on the Stinger missile as a new weapon that could change the course of the war. The Stingers were portable and highly accurate weapons that might enable the Afghan rebels to shoot down Soviet aircraft.

More cautious officials, including Weinberger, worried that if the *moujeheddin* were given the Stingers, some of these missiles might be lost and fall into the hands of potential adversaries. Moreover, some officials feared that introducing the Stingers might prompt the Soviet Union to retaliate against Pakistan. In support of these arguments, opponents of giving Stingers to the rebels pointed out that the Pakistani government itself was cool to the proposal.

To help win the argument, Pillsbury made use of his China connections. In Washington, he enlisted the backing of Morton Abramowitz, the head of the State Department's intelligence service. Abramowitz had been one of Pillsbury's earliest patrons; in the 1970s, he had played a key role in winning acceptance in the Pentagon for Pillsbury's idea of an American military relationship with China. He was decidedly not part of the right-wing political coalition that made up the core of Pillsbury's support; yet Abramowitz feared that without the Stingers the Afghan rebels would lose the war.

On a trip to Beijing in early 1986, Hatch, Ikle, Pillsbury and Abramowitz persuaded Chinese intelligence officials not only to support the idea of giving the American-made Stingers to the Afghan resistance but also, more significantly, to lobby Pakistani President Zia ul-Haq to endorse the idea. That was an important change, undercutting the argument in Washington that Pakistan didn't want the *moujeheddin* to obtain these new weapons.[8]

After China persuaded Pakistan to request the Stingers for the Afghan guerrillas, the opposition to the idea in the administration evaporated, and the way was cleared for the Stingers. During the last half of the 1980s, the United States sent roughly 1,000 of the missiles to the *moujeheddin,* at a cost of at least $30 million.

As the proponents had argued, the missiles proved to be effective, particularly against helicopters, although disagreement persists over how much of a factor they were in producing the Soviet withdrawal. As the opponents feared, hundreds of the Stingers sent to Afghanistan were lost or diverted; some were obtained by Iran. In the years after the war, the CIA launched what was called Operation MIAS (Missing-In-Action Stingers), spending tens of million dollars in an effort to buy back the Stingers that had been lost.[9]

To the annoyance of the Reagan administration, Pillsbury became involved in the minute details of the Afghan war. One former CIA official recalls Senator Humphrey and Pillsbury, in a Capitol Hill hideaway office, telling American intelligence officials exactly which buildings and other targets they should try to hit in Kabul.[10]

Pillsbury was not to be deterred. The covert Afghan war enabled him finally to put into practice the idea that America and China should team up to fight the military power of the Soviet Union.

BEGINNING IN 1983, the Reagan administration progressively opened the way for China to obtain American arms and technology. It was the final step in the process that had begun under Carter and had continued when Haig sought to win Chinese assent for arms sales to Taiwan.

In May 1983, Commerce Secretary Malcolm Baldrige was dispatched to Beijing with the news that the Reagan administration would loosen its controls on high-technology exports to China. The administration decided to treat China like other countries in Europe, Asia and Africa that were considered friendly but were not allies. After Baldrige's trip the administration approved the export of several specific items of "dual-use" technology (goods with both military and commercial applications) that could not have been sold to the Soviet Union or its allies in Eastern Europe.

With these liberalized export controls, American defense and high-technology industries rushed to sell hardware to China. In 1982, U.S. firms obtained licenses for about $500 million in exports to the People's Republic; by 1985, the dollar value of these sales had jumped to $5 billion.[11]

Later in 1983, Weinberger traveled to China to revive the formal Sino-American military relationship that had started during the last year of the Carter administration. To demonstrate China's importance to the Pentagon, Weinberger carried a huge delegation of American officials with him, including Armitage, Wolfowitz, Ikle and General Colin Powell, who was then Weinberger's military assistant.

The Reagan administration had by this time concluded China was not so strategically important as American officials had believed during the 1970s. Nevertheless, Weinberger's Pentagon delegation tended to view China primarily through the prism of the Cold War. Weinberger said he hoped his trip would demonstrate to Chinese leaders "that they did not need to resume or strengthen their military ties to the Soviet Union."

He delivered warnings in China about Soviet naval and air power in the Pacific. In one toast, he likened the People's Liberation Army to a modern-day Great Wall blocking the "threat from the north," an unmistakable reference to the Soviets. It was reminiscent of the visit to China a half-decade earlier when Brzezinski had inveighed against the Soviet "polar bear."[12]

Weinberger found, however, that the Chinese were more interested in obtaining American technology than in talk of an anti-Soviet alliance. They pressured the Americans to approve the export of entire categories of new defense technology, so that Beijing did not have to ask for each item, one by one. Weinberger was unwilling to go so far. He did, however, announce that the administration had decided to approve export licenses for 32 specific items of military and dual-use technology that the Chinese had been trying to buy since 1981.[13]

Weinberger's visit opened the way for much closer defense ties between America and China. The Pentagon and the People's Liberation Army launched their most extensive series of exchanges ever. Over the following six years, American generals, admirals and service secretaries traveled to China, often offering American know-how or some new technology along with their toasts. In January 1985, General John W. Vessey Jr., chairman of the Joint Chiefs of Staff, became the highest-ranking American military official to visit China since 1949; he exchanged toasts of Chinese mao-tai and Missouri corn whiskey with Yang Dezhi, the PLA's chief of staff, who had once commanded troops in their "human wave" attacks against American forces in Korea.[14]

One of the administration defense officials who took part in these exchanges with China was Lawrence Korb, the Pentagon's assistant secretary of state for logistics. To Korb, a civilian, the U.S. military acted as though it was rekindling its old love affair with China—one that dated back to the days in World War II when American and Chinese soldiers had joined together against Japan. American military officers made sentimental returns to Chongqing, the locus of Chiang Kai-shek's wartime government, or to other cities in China where they had served.

In their more private moments, Korb observed, American and Chinese military officers swapped stories about their shared dislike for the Russians and the Japanese. "The whole thing was so Cold War–oriented," Korb said of the Pentagon's military exchanges with China. "It was, 'How do we keep the Soviets in a box and keep [Soviet military] pressure away from Europe?' No one looked beyond the end of the Soviet empire. It was a classic case of the old adage, 'The enemy of my enemy is my friend.'"[15]

As the American and Chinese armed forces began to do business with one another, arms sales became the medium of exchange. They were what China most wanted from the United States. "It turned into an arms sales relationship," one senior Pentagon official acknowledged in a subsequent interview. "Our judgment is that pre-Tiananmen [before 1989], 60 to 70 percent of the military relationship was arms sales."[16]

By early 1984, leaders of the People's Liberation Army and of China's defense industries were being brought to the United States for shopping tours of American companies and military installations. Among the visitors were He Ping, Deng Xiaoping's son-in-law, and He Pengfei, the son of the famed PLA Marshal He Long. A decade later, during the 1990s, these two men would be depicted in Washington as arms dealers eager to sell Chinese weapons, missiles and technology to the Middle East and other dangerous parts of the world. Few Americans realized that both men, and other Chinese arms dealers like them, had during the 1980s received a warm welcome at the Pentagon.[17]

In June 1984, Reagan made China eligible for America's Foreign Military Sales program, enabling Beijing both to buy weapons directly from the U.S. government and to obtain American government financing for these purchases. Over the next half-decade, China acquired a series of American weapons systems. It paid $22 million for American help in modernizing its factories to produce artillery ammunition and projectiles. China spent an additional $8 million for American torpedoes,

$62 million for artillery-locating radar and more than $500 million for American help in modernizing its jet fighters.[18]

China also entered into several commercial transactions, in which it bought American hardware directly from U.S. defense firms. The most notable of these was the purchase of 24 Sikorsky S-70C helicopters from United Technologies Corp. Alexander Haig had helped make the deal. China thus was able to obtain helicopters similar to those that United Technologies had not long before sold to Taiwan.

By this time, Haig's pervasive role in selling weapons systems overseas had attracted congressional attention. Speaker of the House Jim Wright, whose Fort Worth district included one of United Technologies's main rivals, Bell Helicopter, complained to George Shultz that Haig was exploiting his former position as secretary of state to influence decisions on arms sales.[19]

These American arms sales helped Chinese military officials to modernize some parts of their defense industries. Nevertheless, China never achieved all that it wanted from America during the 1980s. Its ability to buy weapons systems from abroad was limited by the high costs. During this decade, the leadership was tightly controlling its defense spending.[20] Moreover, the Pentagon remained cautious about what it would permit China to purchase, worrying about the impact on Taiwan, Japan and other neighbors.

According to Armitage, who was in charge of Asia policy at the Pentagon, the general concept was to let China buy only military hardware "that the Soviets [already] had, that would serve them against the Soviets, and wouldn't be used in a way that would be a particular threat to others."[21] In practice, officials found that it was not so easy to say which weapons systems might threaten China's neighbors. Taiwan did, in fact, lobby against American arms sales to the Chinese navy and air force, even though administration officials insisted these sales would not undermine the island's security.[22]

These arms deals were in many ways a symbol of the entire relationship between the United States and China in the 1980s. In military matters, as in virtually all other aspects of life, China looked with extravagant expectations toward the West and particularly toward the United States. China had been forced during the 1950s to depend on Soviet military technology in a partnership that had ended badly. Since that time, Chinese military officials had relied on their own resources, trying where possible to devise improvements for Soviet factories and technology.

In the 1980s, as Deng Xiaoping opened China to the outside world, the Chinese often tried to buy the best, most advanced Western goods they could find. Military officers were no different from anyone else. The problem was that the highest level of technology wasn't always the one that was suitable for China. There were many instances where China didn't have the infrastructure or the skills necessary to absorb the most advanced levels of technology. Sometimes, the best of the West was a misfit for China.

All of these problems came together in the largest single American arms sale, a deal in which China paid for American help to upgrade its F-8 jet fighters. This Chinese plane had been modeled on the Soviet Mig-21 and therefore, by the mid-1980s, was based on technology that was a quarter-century old. The administration agreed to sell China about $550 million in avionics kits (radar and navigational equipment) to improve the performance of 55 of these jets. The project, which Pentagon officials code-named Peace Pearl, was to be carried out largely by the Grumman Corp. in Bethpage, Long Island.

Years later, Pentagon officials would admit that Peace Pearl had been a mistake. The avionics kits proved to be difficult and expensive to install in the older Chinese planes. There were cost overruns, which in turn led to money disputes between America and China. Moreover, the kits weren't enough to turn the F-8 into a high-performance plane. For that, China needed a new jet engine, and the United States was unwilling to sell China these engines.

The project was, in short, a piecemeal approach that didn't solve the larger problem: China needed a completely new plane. "To take a dog aircraft and try to make it better, that was mistake one," explained Carl Ford, who served as the deputy assistant secretary of defense for East Asia during the Bush administration. "Mistake two was that at such a primitive level of aircraft production, you can't mass-produce avionics systems and weapons to put in it. And third, they had no agreement from anybody to get a jet engine." [23]

Nevertheless, Peace Pearl went forward, with costs and frictions between America and China mounting, until 1989, when the project became the subject of another, still more contentious dispute between the two countries.

I T WAS inevitable that Ronald Reagan himself would visit Beijing, along with virtually all other senior officials of his administration. Reagan and his advisers began discussing a visit to China in early 1983. Such a trip, they thought, would not only dramatize the growing cooperation between the United States and China; it would also, not incidentally, provide colorful film footage that could be used to bolster Reagan's foreign policy credentials in his 1984 campaign for reelection.

Reagan's staff at first wanted him to go to Beijing in November 1983, while he was visiting Japan and South Korea. By going so early, they felt, he could avoid charges that the trip was part of the 1984 campaign. At the State Department, Wolfowitz balked. Several American Cabinet members were visiting China in 1983, but no senior Chinese leader had agreed to come to the United States. American officials had suggested that Premier Zhao Ziyang visit Washington, but China had not agreed. Wolfowitz argued that if Reagan flew to Beijing to court its leaders so quickly after American Cabinet members did, his trip would undercut the sense of reciprocity between America and China; it might also reinforce the old notion that foreign leaders go to China to pay tribute.

Finally, the decision went up to Reagan, who backed Wolfowitz and the foreign policy team over Michael Deaver and the political advisers. I will go to China, but not until Zhao Ziyang comes here first, the president wrote. China soon announced that Zhao would visit Washington in January 1984, opening the way for Reagan to go to China in April.[24]

The struggle over Reagan's itinerary underscored how America's perceptions of how to deal with China were changing. The heady days of Kissinger's secret diplomacy were by now more than a decade old. No longer was America willing to dispense with the niceties of protocol in order to transact business almost exclusively on China's home turf. In an ideal world, such details might not matter. Yet China certainly cared about the setting and symbolism for doing business with the United States; American leaders had decided that they too should care about such details.

For the Chinese leadership, the mere fact of Reagan's visit was vastly more important than any business conducted while he was there.

Reagan was the world's best-known anti-Communist. In 1979, at the time Carter had established diplomatic relations with Beijing, Reagan had branded the People's Republic "a statist monopoly founded on violence and propaganda, and destructive of the humane tradition of the Chinese people themselves." By traveling to Beijing and treating Chinese leaders with respect, he seemed to be conveying an acceptance of their legitimacy.

So, too, in visiting China, the president was demonstrating the limits of U.S. backing for Taiwan. Reagan was America's most conservative president in two generations and over the previous decade had been one of the staunchest American supporters of Taiwan. Yet he, like his three predecessors in the White House, intended to do business with Beijing. America would make sure Taiwan had the weaponry it needed to defend the island, but Reagan's trip to Beijing eliminated any lingering doubts among Taiwan's leaders about the finality of America's recognition of the Beijing government.

Stopping in Honolulu on his way to China, Reagan met Senator Barry Goldwater, for years a fellow supporter of Taiwan. Goldwater was just returning from Taipei. "Barry was upset about my visiting China and made little attempt to hide it," Reagan recalled in his memoirs. "He suspected I was getting ready to give up on Taiwan, and I don't think I convinced him otherwise." Associates of Goldwater say he told Reagan, "You sold out Taiwan!" [25]

In fact, Taiwan survived Reagan's trip and, after finally recognizing the limits of American support, made the changes it needed to adapt to the new environment. During the last half of the 1980s, the government gradually discarded its old and spurious claims to govern the entire Chinese mainland. The Nationalist leadership also phased out its authoritarian controls over Taiwan, opening the way for a more democratic government, one that could attract greater support in America. Reagan's trip to China may actually have helped Taiwan by teaching its government not to cling to the past.

IN BEIJING, Reagan received what was, in retrospect, a lesson on the vagaries of China's domestic politics. In addition to meeting with Deng and Premier Zhao Ziyang, he met with Hu Yaobang, who was Deng's top aide and the titular leader of the Chinese Communist Party. Hu informed the American president that Chinese politics was stable and orderly. There was, he said, no serious opposition to the party leadership's reform program. America need not fear chaos after Deng's departure, Hu told Reagan, because a younger generation of leaders was being groomed to take over.

In fact, the opposition within China to the reforms was considerably greater than Hu realized, and so was the power of party elders. As it turned out, the younger generation of Chinese leaders taking power after Deng Xiaoping would not include Hu Yaobang. [26]

Reagan and his aides had one revealing contretemps with the Chinese leadership. White House officials had been told that China would broadcast on television, live and unexpurgated, a speech he gave to a select audience at the Great Hall of the People. In fact, however, the speech was videotaped and censored; Chinese authorities deleted the portions of the speech that inveighed against the Soviet Union and those that preached the values of democracy and free enterprise.

In one of the deleted passages, Reagan declared that "American troops are not massed on China's borders," an unmistakable reference to the Soviet Union. Foreign Ministry spokesman Qi Huaiyuan explained that "it is inappropriate for the Chinese media to publicize the comments by President Reagan on a third country." China was just beginning to mend fences with the Soviet Union; from its point of view, the days when Americans and Chinese joined together to denounce the Soviet Union had passed.

China also censored Reagan's declaration that Americans "have always drawn tremendous power from two great forces—faith and freedom." In still another deleted passage, perhaps the most sensitive of all, Reagan asserted, "Abraham Lincoln defined the heart of democracy when he said, 'No man is good enough to govern another man without the other's consent.' "[27]

Reagan's speech engendered some friction within the administration, particularly between Wolfowitz and Charles Freeman, deputy chief of mission at the embassy in Beijing. The two men were powerful intellectual forces, each representing a different point of view: Freeman was the strongest proponent within the U.S. government for a close relationship between America and China, while Wolfowitz was the leading skeptic about the value and wisdom of such ties.

According to Wolfowitz, Freeman was extremely upset that Reagan's speech had included words so provocative they had to be censored. "I remember Chas Freeman running up to me with his hair on fire, saying, 'We told you guys not to do that. See what happens?' And I said, it just means we said something they don't like. It probably means that three million senior cadres are going to ask to see the speech." Freeman, in an interview, said he did not recall the incident.[28]

Reagan tried a second time to have some of these ideas broadcast to a Chinese audience. Appearing on Chinese Central Television, he told an interviewer that America had "no troops massed at your borders," again alluding to the Soviet Union. He also asserted that "economic growth and human progress make their greatest strides when people are secure and free to think, speak, worship, choose their own way and reach for the stars." Once again, these passages were deleted from the interview before it was published.

Finally, in Shanghai on the final stop in his trip, Reagan tried a third time. He appeared before a group of students and faculty at Fudan University, one of China's most prestigious educational institutions. This time, he denounced the Soviet Union as an "expansionist power" that had engaged in "an evil and unlawful invasion of Afghanistan." He also praised what he called "my own values" of faith in God and free markets. This time, the speech was carried live on Shanghai television, but without any translation into Chinese. Reagan had managed to get his points across in a fashion, but only to English-speaking residents of Shanghai.[29]

Reagan's worst moment came on the way out of China. Flying back to Alaska aboard Air Force One, he gave a rare interview, his first in a year and a half, to the pool of reporters assigned to cover him. Tired and no doubt happy to have finished a successful trip, he referred to China as a "so-called Communist country."

Reagan recalled in the interview how he had visited a joint venture in Shanghai where an American firm, the Foxboro Company, was manufacturing industrial-control equipment with a Chinese state enterprise. "American concerns can create branches of their own in China, in this so-called Communist China," the president told reporters on his plane.[30]

He was deluding the American public, if not himself. On the very day he left Beijing, Tiananmen Square had been decorated with huge portraits of Marx, Engels, Lenin and Stalin, the pantheon of Communist heroes, for the traditional May Day celebrations. Though Reagan was alluding to the economic reforms that for the first time permitted foreign investment in China, his words suggested that China's political system had fundamentally changed.

The offhand remark underlined an important change in America's approach to China. Richard Nixon had never tried to deny that he was doing business with a Communist government. Indeed, the thrust of Nixon's underlying political message throughout his career had been that he, Richard Nixon, was the American leader tough enough and clever enough to sit down with (or stand up to) Communists.

Reagan, who during the 1970s had often attacked Kissinger's obsession with realpolitik, seemed to believe he needed a moral justification for dealing with the Chinese leadership, in a way that Nixon did not. His solution was to suggest that its rulers were not really Communists.

Reagan's remark about "so-called Communists" epitomized the delusions and the China euphoria that swept America during the 1980s. The effect was damaging. America believed China was changing its political system more than it in fact was. The disillusionment would come in 1989.

CURIOUSLY ENOUGH, America's romantic view of China in the 1980s was sometimes belied by the realities that Reagan and other officials confronted during their visits to Beijing. A tension always existed between American officials' public portrayals of a steadily reforming, opening country and their private experiences of a Chinese system that never changed as much as the Americans thought. Indeed, the level of private mistrust between American and Chinese officials remained high, even during the 1980s era of good feeling between the two countries.

Years later, in his memoirs, Reagan acknowledged that during his 1984 visit to Beijing, American security officials had found five listening devices hidden in the rooms where the president and his close advisers were lodged at China's state guest house. He did not say anything in public about them.[31]

Shultz and Weinberger had similar experiences during their 1983 trips. Neither described them at the time, since they would have undercut the American image of China as a friendly country; yet both men were impressed enough to record what happened in their memoirs. "I constantly reminded myself to turn my sensitive papers face down because of possible cameras in the ceiling," wrote Shultz. "I was told that even the garden was wired and therefore provided no refuge."[32]

The only truly secure location for American officials to talk with one another in Beijing was "the tank," the specially designed room inside the American embassy. On high-level visits like those of the secretaries of state and defense, however, logistical obstacles made it hard to use the tank regularly. The American embassy is located east of Tiananmen Square, miles away from the state guest house west of the square where important American visitors stay. It would have been impossible for delegations to visit the embassy every time they wanted to talk privately about their plans and negotiating strategies.

And so the CIA provided Shultz and Weinberger with special devices, called hush-a-phones or voice protectors, that were supposed to enable them to talk with their aides on trips to Beijing without being overheard by Chinese security. Each person put a mask over his face, and then talked through a long tube to another person, similarly masked. The devices came with a noise machine, also supplied by the CIA, which produced a cacophony of meaningless sound meant to drown out the secrets being transmitted back and forth inside the tubes.

The devices didn't work particularly well. It proved impossible to have a meeting in which several people could talk at once. The CIA's phones did, however, succeed in making the American officials look and feel silly. Weinberger compared the devices to the ether masks used in hospitals many years ago. Shultz thought he and an aide looked like Siamese-twin elephants joined at the trunk. Other colleagues thought the hush-a-phones made the American secretaries look and sound like Donald Duck. American officials decided not to try to use the phones on Reagan's presidential visit in 1984.[33]

Working-level Americans were monitored at least as intensively as Cabinet-level visitors. One senior U.S. intelligence official who traveled to China during the 1980s found that he was the subject of more snooping in China than he had been in supposedly more hostile countries. "I've been to Russia, I've been to Syria, I've been to a lot of different places. But China's the only place where there actually was evidence to suggest that my bags were gone through," he said. "I was in a guest house, and I fixed my bags so that I could know if somebody got into them. I never was expecting to find this, but I came back and found that they had been opened." Nothing of importance was inside, the intelligence official said.[34]

The Americans were not above some ploys of their own. One of the many Pentagon delegations to China included a young Marine who had never been in China before but who, unbeknownst to the Chinese, spoke fluent Mandarin. His job was to be silent, observe and listen to what Chinese military officials were saying to one another. The Marine discovered a bit of the enduring reality of China: The officers in China's field armies were much more worried about the central army leadership in Beijing than they were about the Soviet Union, the United States or any other country.[35]

In short, American defense and intelligence officials often treated China during the 1980s as a past adversary that might become a present one in the future. They prudently gathered information and tried to guard themselves against Chinese intelligence.

The view of China inside the U.S. government during the 1980s was often different from the one presented to the American people. The Cold War was not yet over, and China remained a potential partner against the Soviet Union. The positive images of a friendly, changing China were for public consumption. The darker images, the reminders of a more adversarial relationship, were exchanged privately in Washington or saved for the memoirs.

EVEN THOUGH by the 1980s the CIA and its Chinese counterparts had a formal liaison relationship with one another, each intelligence service continued to spy upon the other. Some of the skirmishing was inconsequential, but at times it was considerably more serious.

In late 1985, American intelligence agents in China assisted a young, well-placed official for China's Ministry of State Security, its foreign intelligence service, to flee the country. The Chinese official, Yu Zhensan, was the son of Yu Qiwei, one of the leaders of the Chinese revolution; he was also reportedly a protégé or adoptive son of Kang Sheng, who had been Mao Tsetung's intelligence chief. In a hurried, tense intelligence operation, Yu was provided with a false identity and spirited out of China.[36]

When he was debriefed, Yu offered American intelligence a startling revelation: The CIA had been penetrated for many years by an agent for the Chinese intelligence service. The Chinese mole was Larry Wu-Tai Chin, who had been spying for Beijing at least since the time of the

Korean War while working as a CIA translator and analyst. Chin had held a security clearance since 1970; he had been stealing and photographing classified documents and then passing them along to a Chinese contact named Lee during occasional visits to Toronto. For his services, he had received about $10,000 a year in a Hong Kong bank account, much of which he had lost during gambling trips to Las Vegas casinos.[37]

Chin was arrested on November 22, 1985. As was customary in such cases, the State Department decided to lodge an official protest with the Chinese government for its spying activities. The usual protocol would have called for the deputy assistant secretary of state dealing with China to call in Chinese Ambassador Han Xu and lodge the American complaint. At the time, the deputy assistant secretary happened to be James Lilley, the CIA's former station chief in Beijing, who had spent a good part of his career spying on China. While willing to deliver the protest, Lilley thought it would have prompted a lot of snickering from both American and Chinese officials. Finally, another State Department official was assigned the task.[38]

Chin was convicted of espionage at a federal court in Alexandria, Virginia. On February 21, 1986, while he was in jail awaiting sentencing, he committed suicide by asphyxiating himself with a brown plastic trash bag, thus limiting the CIA's efforts to learn more about his Chinese contacts and what information he had compromised.

Later that year, Chinese officials politely asked Lilley for help in contacting Yu Zhensan. They said they wanted simply to learn more about Yu's activities. The Chinese must believe we're gullible, Lilley thought: Their interest in a face-to-face meeting with Yu Zhensan could hardly be so benign. Only a year earlier, the Reagan administration had been embarrassed when a Soviet defector, Vitaly Yurchenko, suddenly decided to return to Moscow after a few months in Washington. Despite the supposed friendship between America and China, the administration turned down the request.[39]

AMONG THE many other visitors to the Diaoyutai state guest house during the early 1980s were Margaret Thatcher, the first British prime minister ever to visit China, and her foreign secretary, Geoffrey Howe. They were attempting to negotiate with Chinese officials the future of Hong Kong, a subject of considerable interest to the United States as well.

Under the three treaties Britain had imposed upon the weak Qing Dynasty in the nineteenth century, it held permanent title to about 8 percent of the land in Hong Kong, including the heart of its business and retail districts, Hong Kong Island and Kowloon. But Britain held the remaining land under a 99-year lease that was to expire in the year 1997. The British could have attempted to keep the vital downtown districts while returning the remainder to China. However, they realized that Hong Kong depended upon China for its water, vegetables and other services, and that Hong Kong, which had been seized by Japan during World War II, was, in military terms, virtually indefensible.[40]

It was a situation ripe for negotiation. Unfortunately, Thatcher and her top aides approached the Chinese government in the style once exemplified by a British phrase book intended for English-speaking travelers to Asia: "What is your bottom price? I don't like bargaining." In talks that began in 1982 and ended with the signing of a final agreement in 1984, Thatcher and her aides made concession after concession.

Britain's position at the outset was that it might possibly be willing to think about returning to China the 8 percent of Hong Kong over which it held permanent sovereignty if China would agree first to let Britain keep running all of Hong Kong. China would thus have titular sovereignty to Hong Kong, while Britain would continue to govern. In September 1982, Thatcher, fresh from her military triumph in the Falklands, tried to persuade Deng to accept this idea. She failed; Deng was understandably insulted by the suggestion that Hong Kong could be run only by Britain.

British officials then bargained their way backward in piecemeal fashion. First, they said they would definitely be willing to return Britain's 8 percent to Chinese sovereignty, in exchange for a promise of British administration of Hong Kong. China refused this offer, too. In early 1984, Howe, with Thatcher's assent, made the key concession by dropping the request for British administration. After abandoning their original negotiating objectives, they then went to work on a deal for Hong Kong's autonomy under Chinese sovereignty—an agreement both looser and weaker than it might have been because Britain had conceded points that would have given it more leverage.

Britain's Hong Kong negotiations served as another textbook example of how not to do business with China. Virtually all of the important discussions took place on Chinese soil. At one typical session, Howe and his aides found themselves struggling to work out their strategy amid Chinese eavesdropping:

> We held our group meeting to consider this offer away from the microphones of the Diaoyutai, pacing up and down in the shade of a flowering thorn tree in the garden. (Who knows if we were "secure" even there?)[41]

So, too, British officials let China employ a common negotiating ploy by setting an artificial deadline. A study of Chinese negotiating behavior, prepared for the CIA, found that China often tries to "control the pace . . . so that the counterpart government must make its final decisions under the pace of a time deadline." In the case of Hong Kong, China announced that there would have to be a negotiated deal by September 1984. In setting that date, China managed "to establish a time deadline where none really existed," the study for the CIA concluded.[42]

Most important of all, Britain took upon itself, rather than sharing with China, the burden of preserving Hong Kong's economic prosperity. Whenever the talks seemed to flag, and fears arose in Hong Kong of capital flight and a flood of refugees, it was Britain that made concessions to put the negotiations back on track. The British never seemed to recognize that China's stake in Hong Kong's future prosperity was even larger than Britain's own.

Indeed, Britain's series of negotiating retreats was foreordained because of its unwillingness to look seriously at other options for Hong Kong's future. Thatcher flirted with the idea of trying to create an independent entity out of Hong Kong Island and Kowloon. There was talk, too, of developing democratic government and letting Hong Kong Chinese run the colony. Yet none of her advisers was interested in these ideas.[43]

Above all, London's position in negotiating with China over Hong Kong was undercut by Britain's restrictive immigration policies: Thatcher and her aides were never willing to say (or threaten) that they would accept into Britain anybody who wanted to leave Hong Kong. A more liberal British immigration policy would have given China a stronger incentive to guarantee Hong Kong's citizens genuine political autonomy after Britain's departure; China didn't want to take over a city devoid of people. As it was, most of the residents of Hong Kong had no choice: They knew they could not leave, and would have to accept whatever deal Britain and China worked out.

On September 26, 1984, the two governments reached a final agreement under which Britain agreed to return all of Hong Kong to Chinese sovereignty in 1997, in exchange for loose Chinese assurances that it would preserve Hong Kong's economic system and its "way of life" for 50 years after the handover.

The Reagan administration's position during these Sino-British negotiations was one of neutrality. Declassified documents make clear that the administration did not want to be perceived as having supported Britain (or the people of Hong Kong) against China.

During Shultz's first trip to Asia as secretary of state in early 1983, he stopped in Hong Kong after visiting Beijing. The purpose of the visit was for the secretary to attend the annual meeting of all American ambassadors and chiefs of mission in Asia. While there, however, Shultz had lunch with Hong Kong Governor Edward Youde.

The briefing materials prepared for Shultz by the State Department warned that "there may be efforts by the press to cast your visit as a show of U.S. support for the continuation of Hong Kong's current status." The State Department paper cautioned the secretary that the principal American objective was "to avoid giving the impression that the U.S. is taking sides on the issue of Hong Kong's future."[44]

American officials kept careful watch over the talks between Britain and China. The job was carried out largely by Charles Freeman, the embassy's deputy chief of mission. When the talks started in the summer of 1982, Freeman felt that the United States couldn't play much of a role in them; at the time, the administration was in the midst of its own highly contentious skirmish with Beijing over American arms sales to Taiwan. A year later, as America's relations with China improved, Freeman became more active, operating as what he called a friend of the two parties. He kept in close touch with Zhou Nan, the steely Chinese negotiator for the Hong Kong talks, and also with Ambassador Percy Craddock and Tony Galsworthy at the British embassy, as the deal was being made. One correspondent for a British newspaper found that in the last days of the Hong Kong negotiations, Freeman was so well-informed that he knew the Chinese position before the British government did.[45]

In Washington, the story of the Hong Kong negotiations had an extraordinarily important aftermath. Soon after the deal was concluded, Deng Xiaoping launched an intensive effort, largely secret, to settle with the Reagan administration on the fate of Taiwan.

Thatcher signed the Hong Kong agreement in December 1984, during a brief trip to Beijing. While she was there, Deng gave her a message to deliver to Reagan. Now that Hong Kong's future is settled, the Chinese leader asked, why don't we apply the same formula of "one country, two systems" to Taiwan?[46]

Deng apparently expected that his message would be taken seriously, hoping that Thatcher would use her considerable influence with Reagan to get him to think again about Taiwan. Perhaps Deng also felt that the British prime minister might be eager to defuse criticism of the Hong Kong deal by persuading the Americans to accept a similar arrangement for Taiwan.

In any case, Deng misjudged. Thatcher came to Washington shortly afterward for talks with the American president but never delivered Deng's message; she either forgot about it or deliberately decided not to bother. Soon after Thatcher departed, Chinese officials in Washington began quietly asking their American counterparts what they thought of Deng's proposal. Reagan administration officials were mystified by these questions until they finally discovered, with the help of the British, what had happened.[47]

At this juncture, American friends of China began weighing in with the administration, urging that Deng's "one country, two systems" offer for Taiwan was important and worth considering. At the State Department, Wolfowitz found that there was a lot of quiet lobbying at high levels to persuade Shultz to consider Deng's idea. Among those weighing in on China's behalf was Henry Kissinger, Wolfowitz discovered. The idea of a "one country, two systems" settlement for Taiwan began quietly gathering momentum in Washington.[48]

The Americans lobbying on behalf of Deng's offer argued that it represented an historic opportunity. No Chinese leader in the future would be as strong as Deng or as able to make a deal for Taiwan's future like the one he was offering, proponents contended. Wolfowitz—who was opposed to any bargaining with China over Taiwan—countered that if this argument was correct, then future Chinese leaders would also be less willing than Deng to carry out such an agreement. Moreover, Wolfowitz noted, if the United States embraced the idea of "one country, two systems" for Taiwan, it would be violating promises it made when it agreed to limit arms sales to Taiwan in 1982. At that time, the administration agreed it would not pressure Taiwan's government to negotiate with China or to serve as an intermediary between the two governments.

In the end, Deng's initiative on Taiwan failed. Shultz supported Wolfowitz, and the administration sent a message to China that it would not take up the offer for talks on Taiwan's future. Reagan himself would have rejected the idea, even if the State Department had supported it; his brief visit to China had not prompted him to abandon utterly his support for Taiwan. Having refused two years earlier to end American arms sales to Taiwan, Reagan would not likely have taken the larger step of negotiating a Hong Kong–type deal for Taiwan.[49]

Taiwan was different from Hong Kong. It had its own government and its own army. There was no 99-year lease about to expire for Taiwan. The Reagan administration, despite its improving relations with Beijing, had no interest in letting Taiwan's future be determined by the example of the way Britain had treated Hong Kong.

CHAPTER EIGHT

Trouble in Paradise

O N A COLD, grimy evening in December 1984, a thousand students at Beijing University, China's best-known and most prestigious institution of higher learning, lit firecrackers, burned makeshift torches, put up wall posters and marched to the university administration building. They were protesting a new policy of cutting off electricity to student dormitories at 11 o'clock each night. At the time, a relatively young Chinese technocrat newly promoted to the top leadership ranks, Vice Premier Li Peng, defended the blackout, citing "an acute shortage of power supply" in China.

One month later, at a nearby campus, Beijing Normal University, another demonstration occurred, this time one with political overtones. In their wall posters, the students at this school complained about rising prices.[1]

The students' grievances were seemingly mundane. The demonstrations were, however, the first sign of dissent or unrest in Beijing since the repression of the Democracy Wall movement five years earlier. They were also the beginning of a chain of events that would expose the contradictions inherent in America's Cold War partnership with the Chinese Communist Party.

Over the next five years, the Reagan and Bush administrations consistently underestimated the tensions and cleavages that were emerging in China, both among ordinary people and in the leadership. American officials failed to recognize how intense was the appeal of Western-style political values in these early days when China was opening itself up. Still more problematically, the U.S. government also didn't appreciate the depth of the opposition to change, particularly among the elderly leaders of the Communist Party, and the broader discontent the economic reforms were producing in Chinese society.

Deng Xiaoping's first reforms, at the end of the 1970s and the beginning of the 1980s, had been launched in the countryside. The communes established by Mao Tsetung had been disbanded, and peasants had been allowed to grow their own plots. The impact was remarkable. Agricultural output increased year by year to the point where, in 1984, China had the largest single grain harvest in its history—no small achievement for a country with a history of famines and starvation.

That year, the leadership turned its attention to urban China. This second phase of Deng's reforms was not so simple, either economically or politically. Prices of food and other consumer goods, which had been fixed at artificially low prices for decades, were allowed for the first time to float in response to market forces. Many ordinary Chinese were confronting for the first time such elementary economic principles as the law of supply and demand.

The result was a period of uncertainty and upheaval. Elderly Chinese, who remembered well the hyperinflation of the last days of China's civil war, began stockpiling goods. When some residents of Beijing started buying eggs in amounts of 10 pounds or more, an official newspaper published assurances that the price of eggs would not go up. Elsewhere, Chinese hoarded sugar and soap. Others took their small savings and bought durable goods, such as refrigerators and television sets.[2] Such prudence was well-founded: For the first time under Communist rule, inflation crept upward in Chinese cities.

It was a volatile mix: Young Chinese were flirting with Western political values, while their elders, including some within the Communist Party leadership, were growing unhappy with the impact of the new economic reforms. Before long, the effect could be seen in protest demonstrations on the streets of Chinese cities.

POLITICAL PROTEST in the People's Republic of China has some peculiar traditions. In a nation where the Communist Party has a monopoly on power, those Chinese who want to register dissent have often found some safe political cover for their protests—that is, to demonstrate in the name of some cause so unassailable that authorities find it awkward to interfere. One such cause is the death of a revered Chinese leader, such as Chou Enlai. The other all-purpose vehicle for protest is anti-Japanese sentiment; no Chinese leader is eager to stop a demonstration that is supposedly aimed at expressing nationalist sentiments against Japan.

In the fall of 1985, China was suddenly struck by a series of anti-Japanese demonstrations. Unlike the smaller protests of the previous winter, these were not confined to campuses. As many as a thousand students marched from Beijing University to Tiananmen Square, which had seen no demonstrations for nearly a decade; the students protested Japanese "militarism" on the 50th anniversary of the Japanese invasion of Manchuria. Other demonstrations followed throughout China. When Vice President George Bush visited the city of Chengdu in October 1985, an outburst of anti-Japanese protests there prompted American officials to hurriedly switch his motorcade from Toyotas to Chinese-made vehicles.

At the outset, this student unrest appeared to have some high-level support among conservatives within the Chinese leadership. The protests may have been designed to embarrass reform-minded leaders, particularly Party General Secretary Hu Yaobang, the Chinese leader closest to and most admiring of Japan.

As the demonstrations spread, however, they took on a life of their own. Chinese students complained about price increases, corruption and special privileges for the families of high-ranking officials. Later, some students raised broader questions: They spoke of freedom and democracy. The Chinese leadership countered with warnings that democracy could lead to the sort of anarchy the country had experienced during the Cultural Revolution. In December 1985, the regime ordered an end to the demonstrations, and they quickly ceased. In public, the leading role once again was played by the orthodox Vice Premier Li Peng; he warned students that the regime intended to keep out of the country "the capitalist concept of value and decadent way of life, because they conflict with our socialist system."[3]

One year later, in late 1986, Chinese students took to the streets once again in considerably larger numbers. This time the demonstrations openly embraced Western political ideals. In the remote town of Hefei in rural Anhui Province, a middle-age astrophysicist named Fang Lizhi, then the vice president of the Chinese University of Science and Technology, encouraged students to protest the lack of any choice among candidates in elections for the local legislature. "Rights are in the hands of every citizen. They are not given by top leaders of the nation," Fang told students in one of a series of provocative speeches.[4] The demonstrations in Hefei grew from 1,000 students to 3,000 and spread to other cities.

By late December, the protest movement had reached Shanghai, where as many as 30,000 young Chinese mobbed the streets in the largest demonstration anywhere in China since the end of the Cultural Revolution. In People's Square in Shanghai, students carried huge placards saying, "Long Live Freedom" and "Give Us Democracy." Other students met with the city's new mayor, a party technocrat named Jiang Zemin, urging that the Chinese press be allowed to report on the demonstrations. When Jiang appeared at Shanghai's Jiaotong University, some of the students heckled the mayor and asked who had elected him.[5]

This round of demonstrations produced an upheaval in the top ranks of the Communist Party. As the student movement began to spread from Shanghai to Beijing, the leadership ordered an intense nationwide campaign against "total Westernization" and "bourgeois liberalization." Fang Lizhi and two other leading intellectuals accused of embracing these trends were expelled from the Communist Party.

The most astonishing of the political changes was announced less than a month after the Shanghai demonstrations: The leadership forced the resignation of Hu Yaobang, the ranking official of the Communist Party and Deng's second-in-command. Zhao Ziyang, the premier, replaced Hu as party secretary.

Hu Yaobang had been at odds with elders within the Communist Party for other reasons, such as his efforts to install younger leaders and his attacks on privileges and nepotism. Nevertheless, the issue that provoked Hu's ouster was his willingness to support political liberalization and greater intellectual freedom in China. The political changes reflected the fissures that were emerging in China, both at the grassroots and in the top levels of the Chinese leadership.

IN WASHINGTON, these unfolding political events in China attracted scant attention. Those who noticed them at all tended to minimize their importance. A senior State Department official told reporters that Hu Yaobang's downfall and the accompanying political changes in China were "a little bump on the road, but perhaps no more than that."[6] Some in Washington suggested that Hu had been dismissed primarily because of his mercurial personality, rather than because of a larger debate about the extent of economic and political change in China.

The main reason for the inability to grasp these emerging tensions was that doing so might have unsettled what were then entrenched American convictions about China. The American viewpoint of China throughout the 1980s rested upon two firmly held assumptions: first, that China was reforming smoothly and steadily; second, that Deng Xiaoping was in complete command of the country.

Winston Lord, who had come to Beijing as the U.S. ambassador in 1985, gave voice to these prevailing American beliefs when he told one interviewer: "There have been extraordinary changes [in China]—both the kind you can see and other, less tangible but equally important changes in mood. Almost all of these changes seem to be going in a generally positive direction."[7]

This optimism was shared by Reagan administration officials in Washington, and was furthered by American news magazines and television features. In 1985, the first year Deng Xiaoping's reforms ran into serious difficulty in China, he was named *Time* magazine's Man of the Year. The rising popular discontent over inflation and the divisions within the leadership over political liberalization were dismissed as minor and temporary difficulties.

Virtually all of the American analyses judged China almost exclusively against the standard of the Cultural Revolution. By these standards, to be sure, China looked good. However, as the 1980s wore on, ordinary Chinese judged the situation in China not just against that benchmark, but against their own lives as they had been two or four years earlier, and the lives of others in China in the 1980s. By these standards, increasing numbers of ordinary Chinese grew unhappy with the progress of the reforms.

From the distant perspective of Washington, the American preoccupation with Deng Xiaoping seemed logical. American officials had found during the late 1970s and early 1980s that Deng was the virtually unchallenged authority on relations between America and China. It was he who had made the deal for establishing diplomatic relations with the Carter administration in 1978, and he who had settled the dispute with the Reagan administration over arms sales to Taiwan.

The problem with this reasoning was that Deng's authority over China's domestic economy and politics was not nearly so absolute. Others within the Chinese leadership were willing to let Deng handle relations with the United States, but wanted to have their own say on what happened inside China. In one noteworthy illustration of the divisions within the leadership, Chen Yun, China's senior economic planner and a leader nearly equal to Deng in seniority, warned party leaders against an over-reliance on market forces; he openly scored party officials who he said have "forsaken the socialist and communist ideal." [8]

Every few months, Deng would shift the direction of his policies in an effort to accommodate the views of Chen and other conservatives. From the distance of Washington, American officials, reinforcing their own beliefs in Deng's omnipotence, would portray him as a sailor in command of his ship, tacking with the gentle breezes. In China, however, the winds felt stronger, and it was sometimes harder to determine whether Deng was the sailor or the weathervane.

During the late 1980s, Washington received occasional warnings about the problems China was encountering. At the American embassy in Beijing, for example, one experienced intelligence analyst, Lee Sands, who was responsible for studying the Chinese economy, wrote extensively about the rising unhappiness with and opposition to the reforms. His reports had little impact. After Sands returned to Washington, he was relegated to an obscure job in the Foreign Broadcast Information Service, where, disillusioned, he left intelligence work. In the 1990s, he became America's leading trade negotiator with China.[9]

Some of the developments in China gave the more optimistic American views some plausibility. In the year after Hu Yaobang's resignation, the economic reforms went forward. With Zhao as Communist Party secretary, the leadership, after an interval of a few months, once again tolerated a modicum of intellectual ferment. At Chinese universities, faculty and students held workshops at which they freely discussed the possibility of political liberalization.

On the surface, nothing seemed to have really changed. But in fact China's problems were mounting, and America would soon be swept up in them.

OF ALL the American officials who have dealt with China in the modern era, Winston Lord was probably the least likely to emerge as an agent for change. He had, by the late 1980s, already been involved in American policymaking toward China for nearly two decades. He was, indeed, the embodiment of the old relationship Richard Nixon and Henry Kissinger had formed: Lord was the functionary who sat by Kissinger's side in the 1971 meeting with Chou Enlai and was the young staffer who accompanied Nixon and Kissinger to their first meeting with Mao Tsetung.

Lord was not a daring individual; he rarely challenged authority or conventional wisdom. When Nixon invaded Cambodia in 1970, Lord and a fellow staff member at the National Security Council, Anthony Lake, strongly disagreed with the widening of the Vietnam War. Lake resigned, but Lord did not. Instead, he stayed on as Kissinger's loyal aide for six more years. When the Republicans left office, he became the president of the Council on Foreign Relations, an organization designed to perpetuate the traditions of American internationalism.

He had never held any job that did not involve foreign policy. Other American officials found themselves obliged to work for private companies, or to teach at universities, after the presidents for whom they worked left office. Lord didn't need to do so: He was a wealthy man, the heir to the Pillsbury baking fortune. His wealth made him incorruptible, in the sense that he didn't have to worry about his future job prospects. Yet it also left him narrow in his range of experience.

In private or in comfortable surroundings, Lord could be witty and self-deprecating. He realized how others perceived him. Asked once why Jesse Helms, the zealous conservative on the Senate Foreign Relations

Committee, had opposed his nomination as ambassador to China, Lord rattled off a list of his liabilities: "Rich kid from New York, Yale, Skull and Bones, more importantly I was president of the Council on Foreign Relations." [10] In public, though, Lord spoke in dull policy formulations, the dry idiom of the think tanks. He was a borrower and a polisher of ideas, not someone given to creative insights of his own.

One aspect of Winston Lord's life distinguished him from other mandarins of American foreign policy: his marriage to Chinese-American Bette Bao. Born in Shanghai, she had been brought out of the country as a little girl amid the upheavals of the Chinese civil war; her family had close ties to Chiang Kai-shek's Nationalist government. (After meeting at the Fletcher School of Diplomacy, the couple had married at Twin Oaks, the sumptuous Victorian-style residence of Taiwan's ambassador to Washington. That fact was rarely mentioned during the era of the Nixon opening to China—although Kissinger, while charmed and impressed by Bette Bao, was also careful enough to make sure that Lord kept the preparations for his 1971 trip to Beijing secret from his Taiwan-connected wife.) [11]

Bette Bao was at least as ambitious as her husband, and considerably earthier and more vivacious. In 1978, she returned to China for the first time, seeing relatives and gathering information. The result was a novel, *Spring Moon,* that became a best-seller and launched her on a career as a popular author.

Since the days of the Nixon rapprochement, Bette Bao Lord had served as, in effect, the tutor for America's highest-ranking leaders in the ways of Chinese culture and thinking. It was Bette Bao, not the CIA, who offered Kissinger the interpretations he came to accept about some of Mao Tsetung's delphic utterances. [12] In 1984, when Ronald and Nancy Reagan were preparing for their trip to Beijing, Bette Bao Lord once again emerged as the principal White House adviser on matters Chinese. Secretary of State George Shultz recalled in his memoirs:

> Winston Lord and his wife, Betty [*sic*] Bao Lord, and four China scholars were present. After the scholars had said their piece, we turned to Betty for some personal observations about the Chinese people. . . . [She] vividly described how the Chinese deal with others, and how she thought it best to respond. Putting herself in the shoes of the first lady and then the president, she role-played how conversations might proceed. [13]

After his nomination was held up by Senator Helms for months, Lord finally arrived in China in late 1985. In his work as ambassador, he proved to be attuned, far more than his predecessors, to the world of the American power elite. While in Beijing, he seemed more comfortable dealing with famous visitors from Washington or New York than with a lowly municipal official from Guangzhou or a diplomat from Bangladesh; he appeared, for a long time, more familiar with the details of the Kissinger diplomacy than the streets of Beijing. Lord was not a trained China scholar ("A China expert is an oxymoron" was a regular line in his repertoire), nor did he speak Chinese.

His wife, however, did. Arriving in China with plans to write another book, Bette Lord soon became immersed in the world of Chinese culture, social life and literary politics. She cultivated friendships with leading Chinese writers, actors and critics, such as the author Wang Meng and the actor Ying Ruocheng, at a time when they and other artists were beginning to test the limits of artistic freedom in China.

The younger and more daring members of Beijing's cultural and literary elite began appearing at nighttime parties at the U.S. embassy, where Bette Bao Lord would ceaselessly make the rounds, encouraging them to dance to American music. She enjoyed poking fun at the humdrum routines of ordinary embassy life—and even, once a while, at her husband. "The Wasp's away, let's play," she joked at the beginning of one party while the American ambassador was out of town. When Congressman Stephen Solarz asked during a trip to Beijing if he could talk with any dissident who had served time in a Chinese prison, it was Bette Lord who made the arrangements for a furtive nighttime interview.[14]

The Lords were not popular within their own embassy. To those working underneath him, Winston Lord seemed to care far too much about what the press might write or what Washington officials and congressmen might think, and to care far too little about the concerns and day-to-day life of an ordinary American diplomat. To embassy personnel, Bette Bao Lord seemed a bit imperious and also too remote in a different way: She thought more about Chinese literary lions than the lives of other residents of Beijing, the ordinary Chinese or working Americans who held nine-to-five jobs. Her predecessor, Betty Lou Hummel, the wife of Ambassador Arthur Hummel, was no less bright but considerably less ambitious; she had served a motherly role by regularly baking cookies for the American community in Beijing. (Years later, back in Washington, the American officials and business personnel who had lived in Beijing held occasional reunions at which they could swap old memories and exchange phone numbers. While Lord's predecessors and successors as ambassador all regularly attended these get-togethers, the Lords never came. They had never been part of the crowd.)

During the first years in Beijing after his 1985 arrival, Winston Lord showed few signs of being changed by his surroundings. He continued to talk and think in the idiom of geopolitics he had learned under Kissinger. Like George Bush in Beijing a decade earlier, Lord was careful to preserve, from the distance of China, his position within the Washington establishment; in early 1988, when *New York Times* columnist William Safire did a column about the up-and-coming figures who might run foreign policy in a Bush administration, he mentioned Lord as a leading candidate for national security advisor.[15]

Whenever he was questioned about China by American visitors or resident correspondents, Lord responded with the conventional American viewpoint: China is progressing, and the reforms are on track. Signs of a darker, more repressive and more troubled China were dismissed with the usual formulations: two steps forward, one step back.

Nevertheless, merely by living in Beijing for an extended period of time, Lord was gradually exposed to a China different from the one he had seen on the Kissinger trips. And by virtue of his wife's contacts with intellectuals, he was also obtaining a perspective on Chinese life that was not ordinarily available to American diplomats.

ON JUNE 1, 1988, the official car for the U.S. embassy in Beijing, a black Cadillac with a small American flag on the front, rolled through the gates of Beijing University. Out stepped Winston and Bette Lord. The couple wandered over to an outdoor gathering of students. Though the event was seemingly ordinary, it had far-reaching consequences for America's relations with China's Communist Party leadership.

The American ambassador had been invited to talk to the Beijing University students. He was an instinctively cautious speaker, who punctuated virtually every statement with a series of qualifications. What Winston Lord had to say was not particularly stirring or even encouraging to the students. With his wife translating, he talked about the importance of Sino-American relations, the cause with which he had been involved since Kissinger's mission of 1971. It was a casual give-and-take; some of the questions posed to Lord were personal rather than political. The ambassador was asked, for example, what it was like to have an interracial marriage.

When one Beijing University student questioned how the United States could maintain strong ties with a China regime that was still fundamentally committed to Communism, Lord responded that ideology was not so important. "It's true we have values in our society, and we are concerned about human rights. But we respect other countries, and do not try to impose our values," he explained. "We look at how a country performs on the world stage, rather than at its ideology." [16] It was the sort of answer Lord's mentor Henry Kissinger would have given.

So unexceptional were Lord's remarks to the Chinese students that the following day, a Hong Kong newspaper carried a short article about the speech with a caption saying that the American ambassador had praised Deng Xiaoping. From the standpoint of China's senior leadership, however, Lord's measured words mattered far less than his presence on the Beijing University campus and the audience to which he was speaking. That spring, a group of students—among them Wang Dan, later one of the leaders of the Tiananmen Square movement—had organized a series of informal open-air meetings to explore various political issues, including democratic reforms. These sessions came to be nicknamed the "Grass Salon." The first speaker in the series had been Fang Lizhi, the astrophysicist who had encouraged the student demonstrations in late 1986. Lord had addressed the fifth and final spring meeting of this salon. [17]

What followed Lord's seemingly uneventful talk was never made public and was unprecedented in the nearly two decades of American rapprochement with China. A few days later, Deng Xiaoping himself sent word to Lord, through an intermediary, that he should not have appeared on the Beijing University campus. The message was phrased as a "cautionary" warning by Deng to the American ambassador; he appealed to Lord as an "old friend" of China. [18]

The message angered Lord, and he said so. He told the intermediary that the United States would never tell a Chinese ambassador to Washington that he could not speak to young Americans, or that he could not appear at a university in the United States. Lord noted that he hadn't even said anything to the Beijing University students with which Deng could disagree. "Please tell the chairman [Deng], with all due respect, that this is unacceptable," Lord retorted. "I am not going to be restricted in my access. I spend most of my time with [Chinese] officials, but I have an obligation to get out and meet all people, including young people." [19]

Not long afterward, the Lords visited Shanghai, where the ambassador had been scheduled to appear before a policy institute and Bette Lord had been invited to speak at Fudan University, another of China's elite schools. At the last minute, the appearances were canceled. Fudan University officials told the Lords that the timing was not right because students were taking exams.

Lord reported these events to the Reagan administration in a restricted cable. Separately, American intelligence also reported that Deng Xiaoping was angrily complaining about Lord's willingness to meet with the Beijing University students. [20] Back in Washington, among

China specialists within the U.S. government, there were some raised eyebrows and pointed questions. Why was Lord causing trouble for American policy toward China?

All of this was kept secret, known only to a select few American and Chinese officials. It was, however, an epochal event in defining the relationship between the United States and China. At issue was this question: How should one define the China with which the United States was dealing? Was Washington supposed to do business with China exclusively through the Communist Party leadership, or through the Chinese people and society as a whole?

From Lord's point of view, the visit to the university campus was hardly unreasonable. In the turbulent political climate that prevailed in Beijing and Shanghai at the time, Chinese intellectuals were thinking and talking about new political ideas; in doing so, they appeared to have some encouragement from the political leadership. Lord had come to Beijing believing that one of his tasks as ambassador was to develop ties with a broader segment of Chinese society, particularly young people.[21] If America were to base its relationship too narrowly on the top levels of the Communist Party, those ties might not last; the United States might find itself clinging to an eroding leadership, as it had with the shah of Iran.

Elsewhere in Asia, the Reagan administration had already taken much bolder steps in support of democratic reforms: Over the previous two years, in 1986–87, American officials had pressured two authoritarian rulers, Philippine President Ferdinand Marcos and South Korean President Chun Doo Hwan, to yield power and give way to democratic elections. In this instance, Lord was not preaching democracy at all, but merely meeting with a group of students.

Of course, there was a difference: This was China, a Communist regime, not South Korea, an American ally. Yet in other Communist countries, too, the United States had also taken steps toward contact with the society at large and toward recognition of the right of dissent that went quite a bit further than the ambassador's casual talk to the Chinese students. Indeed, on May 30, 1988, the very week that Lord visited Beijing University, Ronald Reagan met with 96 Soviet dissidents at the American ambassador's residence in Moscow. Ignoring complaints by Soviet President Mikhail S. Gorbachev that the meeting amounted to an interference in his country's internal affairs, Reagan had told the dissidents that the United States would remain "unshakable" in its commitment to human rights.[22]

Judged in the context of American policy toward other nations, then, Lord's meeting was hardly unusual. By the standards of American policy toward China, however, it was indeed an earthshaking departure from the past. The relationship America had built up with China since the time of the Nixon administration had been almost solely with the Communist Party leadership and not with broader segments of Chinese society. This had been part of the implicit Cold War bargain Washington had struck with Beijing since the days of Nixon and Kissinger.

Ever since 1971, China's Communist Party leadership had been given virtually an exclusive franchise on dealings with the United States. All contacts, at least those of any significance, went through the party leadership and were cleared by it. In the 1970s, several organizations were set up in China and the United States to enable the Chinese government to monitor and control the scholarly, cultural and economic exchanges between the two countries. Washington had handed the Chinese regime effective control over American programs in which other governments had no say: In selecting Fulbright scholars to study in America, for example, the United States regularly accepted the students recommended by the Chinese government, where elsewhere in the world American officials made their own independent selections.[23]

It was this system, this longstanding American willingness to deal with China only through its party leadership, that Lord's talk at Beijing University threatened to undermine. Moreover, his appearance took place at a time when the Chinese were becoming especially jittery, both because of tensions within the leadership and because of rising unrest throughout urban China.

At a Communist Party Congress the previous fall, Zhao had won renewed support for economic reforms. At the same time, however, the party gathering opened the way for Li Peng, the traditionalist most popular with party conservatives, to become the premier. By the summer of 1988, the economic reforms were in greater trouble than ever before. As the government talked of phasing out subsidies and letting the prices for more consumer goods be set by the market, panic buying once again swept Chinese cities. Official estimates put inflation at 19 percent for the year 1988, and the actual rate was probably 25 percent or more. In the factories, workers feared that the reforms could mean not only higher prices but layoffs. In the face of these problems, Zhao and his reformist allies lost some support within the top leadership, and Li Peng and the conservative forces gained in strength.[24]

Lord's visit to Beijing University had little impact. The students he addressed didn't revolt. His talk was indeed the sort of routine session American ambassadors around the world might have had with students. In the context of China's political situation in the spring and summer of 1988, however, it took remarkably little to make Deng Xiaoping and other Chinese leaders extremely nervous. Their hold over Chinese society was considerably more tenuous than Americans realized.

THE GROWING unrest in China was not the only dark cloud gathering over America's seemingly tranquil, trouble-free romance with the Chinese leadership in the last half of the 1980s. There was, in addition, the new problem of China's missile exports.

America's Cold War relationship with China had been built not merely with the assumption that the two countries shared the goals of combating the Soviet Union and bringing about stability in East Asia, but also upon the notion that Washington and Beijing had no serious conflicts of interest elsewhere in the world. This idea had seemed plausible enough in the 1970s. American officials occasionally objected when China supported the Palestinians and other liberation movements at the United Nations. On the whole, however, American officials could take comfort in the belief that this was merely the usual Third World rhetoric, and that what China said didn't matter much.

Under Mao Tsetung, China had supplied arms for free, primarily to its Asian neighbors: North Vietnam, North Korea and Pakistan. At the beginning of the 1980s, however, China began selling arms overseas for profit. It quickly emerged as a leading supplier of low-cost weaponry around the world, particularly in the Middle East. From 1980 to 1987, China sold $8.7 billion worth of arms in the Third World. The overwhelming share of these sales were to Iran and Iraq; China supplied each side in the Iran-Iraq War with billions of dollars in weaponry. Many of the rocket launchers, artillery shells, jet fighters and missiles flying across the Persian Gulf had been made in China.[25]

By 1987, these supplies became an increasingly troublesome problem for American foreign policy. U.S. intelligence discovered that Iran was constructing missile launch sites near the Strait of Hormuz, the narrow waterway through which oil tankers must pass to and from the Persian Gulf. Iran, it turned out, had purchased new Chinese Silkworm land-to-ship missiles, able to carry 1,100 pounds of explosives—five times as large as the payload for the missiles Iran had previously used to attack ships in the Gulf.

American officials became particularly worried about the Chinese arms exports after May 1987, when the Reagan administration agreed to reflag Kuwaiti oil tankers so that they became, effectively, American ships entitled to the protection of the U.S. Navy. The Chinese Silkworms "represent for the first time a realistic Iranian capability to sink large oil tankers," explained Assistant Secretary of State Richard W. Murphy.[26]

The administration discovered, however, that when confronted by complaints, China responded with denial. To the Americans' astonishment, Chinese officials refused to acknowledge selling any arms at all to either side in the Iran-Iraq War. "Those reports are sheer fabrication," Li Jinhua, a spokeswoman for the Chinese Foreign Ministry, told reporters. At one point, Undersecretary of State Michael H. Armacost showed Chinese officials pictures of the missiles leaving China and then arriving, on the same ship, at the Iranian port of Bandar Abbas. Even then, the denials continued.[27]

For the Pentagon, the dispute over the missiles served as a warning that China was more than simply a potential partner in the Cold War. "The frustration level at the Pentagon in the latter half of 1987 rose steadily as the Chinese continued to avoid the Silkworm issue," wrote Eden Y. Woon, an air force officer working on the Pentagon's relations with China. "This lack of candor . . . eroded the earlier goodwill toward China felt by many in the U.S. defense establishment. Some even questioned the basic worth of a military relationship with China."[28]

The result, finally, was the first series of economic sanctions America imposed upon China since the establishment of relations. On October 23, 1987, the Reagan administration announced that it would restrict the export of high-technology products to China as a protest against the missile sales. In practical terms, the action was a mild one: The United States merely froze the ongoing process in which it had been gradually liberalizing the controls on high-technology exports to China. Yet this represented a considerable change in America's approach to China, and it was a harbinger of what was to come.

Although the trade restrictions were strongly opposed by the American business community, they appeared to be effective. Within a few months, China promised to cut off the flow of Silkworms to Iran, without ever quite acknowledging that it had been selling the missiles. "China has adopted strict measures to prevent what you call the Silkworm missiles from flowing into Iran through the international arms market," Chinese Foreign Minister Wu Xueqian told the National Press Club during a visit to Washington in March 1988. The Reagan administration responded by lifting the restrictions it had imposed six months earlier.[29]

The settlement of the Silkworm controversy, however, was soon overshadowed by the revelation of another Chinese missile transfer, one that was considerably more serious. American intelligence belatedly discovered that China had secretly sold 36 of its intermediate-range CSS-2 missiles to Saudi Arabia. These missiles, first deployed in China in 1971, have a range of up to 1,700 miles and had been developed in China with the aim of carrying nuclear weapons.[30]

The sale of the CSS-2 missiles was the result of more than two years of clandestine negotiations between Saudi Arabia and China. Prince Khaled bin Sultan, later to serve as the Saudi military commander during the Gulf War, claimed that the idea for the purchase had come directly from King Fahd, who thought that "we needed a weapon powerful enough to deter any potential enemy from attacking us." From the Saudi perspective, the potential enemies were either Israel, its longtime adversary, or Iran, which at the time was firing missiles across the Persian Gulf at Iraq. Saudi officials explained that they decided to buy the Chinese missiles after the Reagan administration turned down their requests to purchase F-15 combat planes.

Both Saudi and Chinese officials had gone to extraordinary lengths to conceal their actions from the United States. Their success in doing so was particularly awkward for American intelligence officials. The United States considered both China and Saudi Arabia friendly countries; both had ongoing intelligence ties with the United States; and the CIA was supposed to keep a close eye on military developments in both countries. Compounding the agency's embarrassment, it turned out that the initial overtures for the deal had been made in Beijing by Prince Bandar, the Saudi ambassador to Washington, who was a friend of CIA Director William Casey. The later negotiations were conducted by Prince Khaled and Yang Shangkun, vice chairman of China's Central Military Commission and Deng's closest political ally.[31]

In order to evade the detection of American or Israeli intelligence, Khaled and other Saudi officials met their Chinese counterparts in Hong Kong hotel rooms, where they read documents under umbrellas opened indoors to protect against the possibility of hidden cameras. The Saudis were a boon for the Hong Kong hotel industry: Each time Khaled needed to call home to Saudi Arabia, he rented another room in a different hotel, strictly for a single phone call.

In the Arabian desert, meanwhile, a secret training base was set up at which Chinese technicians could teach Saudis about the missiles; once brought to the desert base, Saudi trainees were not allowed to leave, and even their phone calls home were monitored to make sure they did not disclose to their families where they were.

The result was that Saudi Arabia possessed, for the first time, missiles that enabled it to hit Tehran, Tel Aviv or any other area of Iran or Israel. The Reagan administration was furious, first of all at the Saudis. At the Pentagon, Assistant Secretary of State Richard Armitage called in Bandar and gave vent to the American frustration. "I want to congratulate you," Armitage told Bandar bitterly. "This is the law of unintended consequences. You have put Saudi Arabia squarely in the targeting package of the Israelis. You are now number one on the Israeli hit parade. If the balloon goes up [war breaks out] anywhere in the Middle East, you're going to get hit first." [32]

The administration was also angry at China. When Foreign Minister Wu Xueqian arrived in Washington for the March 1988 visit designed to smooth over the earlier dispute over Silkworm missiles, he was greeted on the night of his arrival by Shultz and General Colin Powell, then Reagan's national security advisor. The two senior officials told Wu the United States had learned of the sale of the CSS-2s to Saudi Arabia; they sought details of the transaction and an explanation. In a private letter to the foreign minister a few weeks later, Shultz wrote, "The introduction of Chinese intermediate range ballistic missiles into the Middle East has the potential to create serious doubts in the U.S. and elsewhere over China's policies and intentions." [33]

Chinese and Saudi Arabian officials informed the Reagan administration that the missiles had been modified in such a way that they could not carry nuclear warheads. These assurances, however, did not alleviate the American sense of unease over the sale. U.S. officials became increasingly aware that Chinese arms exports could alter the military balance in the Middle East.

The discovery of China's sale to the Saudis prompted fears in Washington that still worse surprises might be coming. China appeared to be preparing to sell newer, more advanced missiles to other Middle Eastern countries that were considerably less friendly to the United States than was Saudi Arabia.

The CSS-2 missiles were based on 1960s-era technology. They used liquid fuel, which is difficult, dangerous and time-consuming to transport; nearly two hours of preparation are required to launch the missiles. But by the late 1980s, China had developed more modern missiles, known as the M-9 and the M-11, which operate on solid fuel, so that they are more mobile and require as little as a half-hour to launch. These new missiles also have better guidance systems, making them more accurate than earlier Chinese missiles. The M-9 missile had a range of 375 miles, while the M-11s could travel about 180 miles.

These Chinese missiles had been developed for export as well as for the use of the People's Liberation Army. Nothing was secret about their existence. Indeed, in 1986, well before the missiles had been flight-tested, they had been put on public display at an Asian Defense Technology Exposition in Beijing and had been described in the *Beijing Review,* China's principal magazine for overseas readers. [34]

In the late spring of 1988, American intelligence found that China had concluded a tentative deal to sell its new M-9 missiles to Syria, and that officials were also trying to make additional sales to Iran, Pakistan and Libya.[35] With this discovery, the subject of China's arms exports jumped to the top of the agenda between the United States and China.

When George Shultz traveled to Beijing in July 1988, he warned Chinese officials about the "particularly destabilizing potential" of missile sales in the Middle East. The secretary said afterward he had been promised that China had not yet made any final sale, beyond the one to Saudi Arabia.[36] Yet China's assurances were vague and less than conclusive.

Shultz's effort was only the beginning of a decade-long process of missile diplomacy. In the coming years, the subject of whether and to what countries China might sell these new M-9 and M-11 missiles was to preoccupy the Bush and Clinton administrations as well. China's missiles were to become the subject of secret talks, public maneuvering and outright haggling. China proved adept at parceling out concessions, making a series of promises, each slightly less vague than the last, often seeking something in exchange from the United States.

Shultz had been told only that China had not *yet* made any final sale of missiles except to the Saudis. In September 1988, Defense Secretary Frank Carlucci visited Beijing, looking for promises China would not export the M-9 missiles. Carlucci emerged with a dubious bargain, in which the United States traded a far-reaching new economic benefit to China for an assurance about missile sales that was less than conclusive.

After a meeting with Deng, Carlucci proudly told a press conference that China had agreed to conduct itself with restraint in selling missiles. "The Chinese have said that their future sales [of missiles] . . . will be very prudent and very serious," Carlucci declared. In fact, American officials say Deng privately promised that China would not sell intermediate-range missiles—an assurance that left hanging the crucial question of how the phrase "intermediate-range" was to be defined. No one knew whether Deng's promise applied to the new solid-fuel missiles China had been trying to sell in the Middle East.[37]

In exchange, Carlucci offered China a lucrative reward. He announced that the administration would clear the way for export licenses that would permit American-made commercial satellites to be launched in China on the Chinese Long March rockets. China was proposing to launch satellites at fees of $15 million to $30 million, well below the rates charged by companies bidding in the West. The United States had never before approved the launch of an American-made satellite by anyone other than one of its Western allies.[38]

Reagan administration officials may well have wanted to approve the export of the satellites for commercial reasons that had nothing to do with the missile diplomacy. The administration was being lobbied by Hughes Aircraft, the manufacturer of the satellites that Asian and Australian firms were hoping to launch in China. (On the other hand, other American companies that produced rockets, such as General Dynamics and Martin Marietta, lobbied against these export licenses, which would help China to undercut American prices for satellite launches.)[39]

The central fact was that for approving the export of the satellites, the Reagan administration got remarkably little in return with respect to the M-9 missiles. In public, China had gone merely from saying it had not yet approved missile sales to declaring that it would be prudent in doing so. In private, China had promised not to sell intermediate-range missiles, without saying whether this statement applied to the M-9s.

No one in Washington knew for sure what China's unclear promises meant in practice. Within only a few months, CIA Director William Webster was asked by Pentagon and State Department officials to try to nail down from Chinese military intelligence chief Xu Xin something more specific about missile sales than Carlucci had obtained. Webster tried, but failed. Xu merely repeated the bland words Deng Xiaoping had given Carlucci.[40]

"I hope that we can now put this issue behind us," Carlucci had said of the Chinese missile sales at his press conference in Beijing. That was a false hope; he had conceded much and obtained little. It would be left to successors to attempt to obtain specific promises that China would not sell its new missiles to Syria or other countries in the Middle East. Within weeks after taking office, the Bush administration was trying to pin down what Carlucci hadn't.

THE RISING social discontent in China and the Chinese missile sales were both major new developments, signs of important changes in the relationship between the United States and China. Each one was, in its own way, an indication that the old Nixon-Kissinger ties with China were eroding.

The budding Chinese democracy movement raised important questions about the scope and the durability of those old ties. Nixon and Kissinger had dealt with Mao Tsetung and Chou Enlai at a time when China was rigidly controlled. By the late 1980s, however, Chinese society was opening up. Would it be sufficient for America to deal with China only through its top leaders, or would that prove too fragile a basis for an enduring relationship? Should America seek to establish links with other elements in Chinese society?

So, too, China's arms exports presented the United States with difficulties it had not confronted in the 1970s: Chinese foreign policy was potentially in conflict with that of the United States in the Middle East, one of the most vital regions of the world for American foreign policy. A decade earlier, U.S. officials had thought of China almost exclusively for what it could do for American interests in Asia and with the Soviet Union; Chinese policies toward the rest of the world had seemed to be of little consequence.

The Reagan administration didn't recognize the seriousness of these new developments. Instead, in its last years, it sought mostly to perpetuate the era of good feeling with China. The political and military leaders of America and China continued to court one another as though nothing was changing. Neither American nor Chinese leaders had any inkling that the Cold War relationship built up over the previous two decades was coming to an end.

ON MAY 16, 1987, Karl Jackson flew to Honolulu for a special mission. The Pentagon had made him responsible for the care and feeding of Yang Shangkun, vice chairman of China's Central Military Commission. Yang was not only Deng's oldest and most trusted associate within the Chinese leadership but also, next to Deng, China's most senior military leader. He had been invited to visit America for two weeks as head of a large Chinese military delegation, and the Reagan administration had decided to give these Chinese officials the royal treatment.

In Honolulu, Yang was taken on a tour of Pearl Harbor. In Washington, Vice President Bush treated him to a nighttime cruise on the Potomac River aboard the presidential yacht *Sequoia;* while Bush listened raptly, Yang told old stories about how he had swept floors during the Cultural Revolution. In New York City, the Chinese leader saw Wall Street and visited Mayor Ed Koch, who asked undiplomatically, "Are you going to invade Vietnam again?" In St. Louis, Yang ate a bag and a half of popcorn on a boat ride down the Mississippi River. In Omaha, he and his delegation saw a Strategic Air Command installation; in San Diego, they toured an American aircraft carrier. In Los Angeles, they made the ritual visit to Disneyland, where Yang Shangkun had his picture taken together with Jackson and with Goofy.[41]

Jackson, a former Berkeley professor, was the deputy assistant secretary of defense in charge of dealing with Asia. He spent most of his time in Washington attending meetings and writing policy papers. He had dreaded the prospect of spending day after day with Yang, an octogenarian who spoke little English and had traveled little outside of China. Before the trip, Jackson expected nothing but boredom and stilted conversation.

In fact, Jackson was charmed and delighted. Yang proved to be energetic and intellectually curious. He inquired about housing prices and about American patterns of divorce. He reminisced about the war against Japan. He talked about his own brother, who had been in Chiang Kai-shek's Nationalist Party and had died during China's civil war.

Rarely did any of the problems America was soon to confront with China come up during Yang's visit. At the time of the visit, Yang had already taken the forward role for the Chinese leadership in secretly negotiating the sale of the intermediate-range missiles to Saudi Arabia; however, American intelligence had not yet detected the transaction. Yang would also become, two years later, one of the two key figures (along with Deng) in China's decision to have the People's Liberation Army launch its bloody assault on the Tiananmen Square demonstrations in Beijing. At the time of Yang's 1987 visit to America, however, the prevailing view in Washington was that China was in the midst of a long, steady reform process, in which there might be only a few bumps along the way, nothing more.

For one brief moment, late in the trip, Karl Jackson felt he was seeing Yang's other, darker side. At a banquet for the Chinese community in Los Angeles, someone asked Yang about the aftermath of Hu Yaobang's resignation as Communist Party secretary. The questioner wanted to know whether China's reforms would continue and whether the leadership would continue to let Chinese students come to America.

Yang dispensed with his prepared text and delivered a steely response. Yes, the reforms would continue, and the students could still study in the United States, he answered. However, he went on, some things in China would never change. China would remain a Communist country, and it would continue to be ruled by the Communist Party.

Yang was saying no more than was official doctrine in China. He was repeating what is enshrined in China's Constitution, which says that China will continue to be governed by the "people's democratic dictatorship" under the leadership of the Communist Party. In the United States, however, these unpleasant realities had often been downplayed because they got in the way of winning public support for America's Cold War partnership with China. It was much easier for American leaders to speak of the China that was changing than of the China that wasn't.

Yang's flash of toughness made a strong impression on Jackson. Much later, in the spring of 1989, when American leaders were wondering what the Chinese Communist Party leadership might do about the throngs of people gathering in the streets of its cities, Jackson remembered the Los Angeles dinner. These Communist Party leaders are not going to give up their monopoly on power, he thought. They won't roll over or be steamrolled. Yang Shangkun was not like Ferdinand Marcos.[42]

CHAPTER NINE

A New President Confronts
Upheaval in China

GEORGE BUSH WAS, IN many ways, the antithesis of other American presidents of the modern era in dealing with China. After the Nixon administration, everyone else elected to the White House has taken office with the intent of altering the style or the substance of American policy toward China. In the end, these other presidents have tended to preserve far more than they changed. Bush, by contrast, came to the White House committed to continuing the existing U.S. relationship with China. Ironically, he was fated to preside over the greatest series of changes between America and China in the modern era. Indeed, the more Bush tried to perpetuate the past, the more he unintentionally ushered in the new.

Bush was perceived, throughout his four years in office, as an inveterate China lover, someone who had consistently favored close ties with the leadership in Beijing. It was an understandable impression, but a superficial one, belied by Bush's own record. On China issues, in fact, Bush had been all over the lot. During Nixon's and Henry Kissinger's opening to Beijing, it was Bush, as U.N. ambassador, who fought hard to prevent the loss of Taiwan's seat in the United Nations; in doing so, he had clashed with Kissinger. In 1978, when Jimmy Carter established diplomatic relations with Beijing, Bush became one of the leading Republican critics of the deal, arguing that normalization should have been delayed and that the Democrats had given away too much. In the 1980 election, however, when Ronald Reagan and his supporters suggested they might backtrack on the terms the Carter administration had worked out for recognizing China, Bush opposed any retrogression. Once diplomatic ties had been established, he emerged as a strong proponent of close ties with China's Communist Party leadership.

The common thread in all these seemingly disparate positions was that, above all, Bush approved of established authority and the existing order, whatever these might be at a particular time. There was rarely a status quo Bush didn't cherish, whether in China or elsewhere. As president, he favored Soviet President Mikhail Gorbachev when he was challenged by Boris Yeltsin; he resisted the independence of the Ukraine; he was willing to go to war to restore the boundaries of Kuwait—though after doing so, he decided to leave Saddam Hussein in power. In this sense, Bush's approach to China was not unique; it reflected his general outlook toward the world.

Valuing personal relationships, Bush felt close to others in positions of power, those with whom he had done business regularly. China's leaders were among them. Deng Xiaoping had even endorsed Bush's campaign for the White House. During Defense Secretary Frank Carlucci's visit to China in September 1988, Deng had recalled for reporters how Bush had headed the U.S. liaison office in Beijing during the 1970s. "We had a lot of contact with him then. I hope he'll win the election," announced Deng, whose government sometimes complained about American interference in China's internal affairs. (Carlucci later quipped, "I gave him [Deng] about a billion absentee ballots.")[1]

As Bush began to put together his new administration, Winston Lord let it be known he was ready to leave China after three years as ambassador there, and that he would be interested in a top-level job in Washington. None was forthcoming; there were others with whom Bush felt more comfortable. He selected James A. Baker III, his oldest and most trusted political ally, to be secretary of state. Brent Scowcroft (like Lord, a former member of Kissinger's White House staff) was named the national security advisor, a job he had held while Bush was CIA director in the Ford administration.

During the Christmas season before Bush moved into the White House, the president-elect visited the Washington residence of Chinese Ambassador Han Xu, one of China's oldest America hands, who had been dealing with Bush since the 1970s. It was a gesture reflecting Bush's desire for a close working relationship with China during his tenure in the White House.[2]

BUSH'S INITIAL test on China policy came within weeks after taking office. It was a harbinger of what was to come. The new president was confronted by evidence of China's domestic tensions, and he responded by seeking to placate the Chinese leadership.

On January 6, 1989, two weeks before Inauguration Day, Emperor Hirohito died in Japan. Bush decided to attend the February funeral, along with many other heads of state. He and his new foreign policy team then concluded that while the new president was in northeast Asia, he should also stop in South Korea and China.

They viewed the trip as an opportunity to display Bush's expertise in foreign policy, including his special interest in Asia and close associations with Asian leaders. Bush's aides told the press that the stopover in Beijing, in particular, would be a "sentimental journey" back to the place he had once lived and worked. The Bushes planned to visit the Chongwenmen Protestant Church where their daughter Doro had been baptized as a teenager in 1974. White House spokesman Marlin Fitzwater told reporters that Bush would be visiting "his old friend," Deng Xiaoping.[3]

The White House decided that Bush should host a large banquet on his second night in China. The American embassy in Beijing was asked to draw up a list of guests, covering a broad cross section of Chinese society. Lord told the various sections of his embassy to recommend illustrious Chinese who should be invited. Both the embassy's science and technology section and the political section put onto their list of recommendations the name of the astrophysicist Fang Lizhi.

By this time, Fang was no longer an obscure researcher from a remote province. He was China's principal proponent of democratic reforms, the most outspoken critic of the Chinese Communist Party. He was regularly compared to Andrei Sakharov, the Soviet dissident who was also a physicist. Fang had attracted notice not just in China but also in the United States. Indeed, in its issue of February 2, 1989, which came out just as the new Bush administration was planning its trip to Beijing, the *New York Review of Books* published an article by Fang that amounted to a scathing critique of the Chinese leadership. "Forty years of socialism have left people [in China] despondent," Fang wrote. "There is no rational basis for a belief that this kind of dictatorship can overcome the corruption that it has itself bred."[4]

Embassy officials believed that China's top leaders were willing and able to tolerate such rhetoric. The Chinese regime had at one point stopped Fang from traveling to an international conference, but it otherwise had done little to stand in his way. Fang continued to work in Beijing, attended meetings and talked regularly with reporters—all activities the authorities could have stopped. U.S. diplomats foresaw little problem in inviting him to a dinner with Bush.[5] Fang was merely the most prominent of several proponents of political liberalization in China who were put on the guest list; others included political scientist Yan Jiaqi and Marxist theoretician Su Shaozhi.

Lord himself was happy to put Fang and these other critics on the guest list, which also included diplomats and business people. After all, he reasoned, Fang Lizhi wasn't a bomb thrower, merely an academic critic, a recognized scientist working for a government research institute. The ambassador also believed that while advancing America's other interests in China, the president should demonstrate some concern for human rights.[6] Putting Fang on the guest list represented, in a sense, an extension of the approach to dealing with China that Lord had first displayed in his visit to Beijing University the previous year.

The embassy in Beijing cabled the guest list to the White House. Ever careful, Lord added a warning next to a few of the names, pointing out that they were critics of the Communist Party leadership; in one paragraph, the cable focused upon Fang as the best-known of these critics. A few days later, the embassy submitted a revised guest list, with a few Chinese names added; once again, the cable included a cautionary note about Fang.[7]

Bush and his top advisers may not have read these cables. In any case, they paid little attention to the warnings. On the weekend before departing for Asia, Bush, Scowcroft and Baker met at Camp David with a group of academic and government specialists on China, Japan and Korea. The plans for the dinner were mentioned briefly during this planning session, and some of the scholars debated the merits of having the United States identify itself with any particular proponent of human rights and democracy in China. Two days after this Camp David session, the American invitation to Fang was reported in the *Los Angeles Times*.[8] Even then, the public disclosure seems to have attracted considerably more attention among Chinese leaders in Beijing than among Bush and his top aides in Washington.

China's expressions of outrage began at a relatively low level. A Chinese protocol official approached Lord's deputy chief of mission and suggested that bringing Fang to a dinner with Chinese leaders might not be a good idea. Embassy officials assumed this was the sort of low-level complaint they could ignore. However, after Bush flew to Tokyo, Chinese Vice Foreign Minister Zhu Qizhen called in Lord to deliver a tough ultimatum. If Fang Lizhi attended Bush's banquet, Zhu said, then the delegation of Chinese leaders invited to the dinner (headed by Yang Shangkun, by this time the president of China, and including also Premier Li Peng) would not come.[9]

The threat of a high-level boycott caught the attention of the president and other top administration officials. "Who IS Fang Lizhi?" Bush is said to have roared to his advisers as he learned aboard Air Force One that he faced the prospect in China of an empty head table at his own banquet.[10]

Several rounds of intensive, secret negotiations followed. Lord's deputy chief of mission took part in some of the talks; after Bush arrived in China, Scowcroft and Deputy Assistant Secretary of State J. Stapleton Roy took charge. Chinese officials nervously asked whether Fang would be at Bush's head table or whether there would be any toasts to him. Of course not, the Americans responded.

These clandestine talks ended with what the Americans believed was a compromise. Fang would be allowed to attend the American president's dinner, but would be seated in a distant location out of sight of Yang and other Chinese leaders. Bush and others at the head table would not make the rounds of the tables, mixing with dinner guests. In that way, there was no chance that the president of the United States would come face-to-face with China's leading proponent of democracy.[11]

Meanwhile, Bush went about his business in Beijing, both serious and ceremonial. He gave Premier Li Peng a pair of black leather cowboy boots, one with an American flag, the other with a Chinese flag, accepting in return a pair of Chinese Flying Pigeon bicycles for himself and his wife, Barbara. The president also tried without much luck to get from the premier a more tightly worded promise not to export China's new missiles to the Middle East than Carlucci and Webster had been able to obtain. Li's responses were sufficiently imprecise that American officials spent the rest of the year trying to find out whether or where China would export its M-9 missiles.

On Sunday night, February 26, American and Chinese leaders attended Bush's banquet at the Great Wall Sheraton Hotel, a sleek silver high-rise structure towering over northeastern Beijing. Throughout the dinner, those few Americans who knew about the previous days' negotiations concerning Fang assumed that he was at the dinner, sitting at one of the back tables of the banquet hall as they had arranged.[12]

They were wrong. Chinese security officials had physically blocked Fang from reaching the hotel. Fang and his wife, Li Shuxian, set out for the dinner from their Beijing apartment with Perry Link, an American professor living temporarily in Beijing. Two blocks from the hotel, the Links' driver was stopped for a supposed traffic violation, and the car was surrounded by uniformed, armed Chinese policemen. Fang tried to walk to the hotel, but was repulsed; he showed the police his invitation to the dinner, to no avail. The group attempted to take a taxi to the American embassy, but the taxi, too, was stopped. When Fang tried to ride a public bus, Chinese security officials instructed the driver not to pick him up. Finally, tailed by Chinese plainclothes officers, the group walked to a distant apartment, where they contacted American embassy officials only to discover that Bush's banquet was already ending.[13]

In nearly two decades of top-level meetings between the United

States and China since the Nixon opening, there had never been such an ugly moment. The Chinese regime had used the muscle power of its security apparatus to prevent an invited Chinese guest from attending a dinner of the American president. Chinese officials had, moreover, disregarded a negotiated compromise in such a way that American officials were lulled into believing that Fang would be at the dinner.

The episode demonstrated, once again, how extraordinarily nervous the Chinese regime had become. The American perception of a strong, stable Chinese leadership, steadily reforming the country with strong domestic support, seemed increasingly to be at odds with the day-to-day realities inside China. After Bush returned home, the perplexed American embassy cabled to Washington a new analysis of China's internal situation. Something is rotten here, the cable argued: The Chinese leadership should not be so threatened by a mild-mannered professor.[14]

IN WASHINGTON, the fallout from the Fang Lizhi affair proved to be even more significant than the event itself.

China's heavy-handed treatment of Fang received extensive news coverage in the United States. The contretemps became the most well-remembered aspect of Bush's two-day stay in Beijing. A trip aimed at displaying the new president's experience and foreign policy skills had, instead, illustrated new discord between the United States and China. Bush and his top advisers were furious.[15] Departing from China the following morning, the president expressed "regret" over China's handling of Fang. However, the brunt of the recriminations was soon to fall elsewhere.

Three days later, reporters for a few of America's leading newspapers were summoned to the White House for a "background" briefing, given by a senior administration official who was not to be named in their stories. His message was that Lord and the American embassy in Beijing should bear the blame for the Fang Lizhi episode.

" 'Blunder' at Beijing Dinner: U.S. Chides Embassy," declared the headline in the following day's *New York Times*. Washington bureau chief R. W. Apple Jr. wrote:

> A senior White House official said today that inviting a prominent dissident to a dinner in Beijing last week honoring the country's leaders had not been President Bush's idea, and he suggested that the resulting contretemps was the fault of the American Embassy there. . . .
>
> The official, who accompanied Mr. Bush on his five-day Asia swing, said the embassy, which is headed by Winston Lord, had sent

a proposed guest list to Washington some time ago. He said neither the embassy nor the State Department had "flagged" Mr. Fang's name to suggest that a dinner invitation might stir a controversy.[16]

Similar stories appeared in the *Los Angeles Times* and the *Washington Post* the same day.

This account by the Bush White House was simply untrue. Declassified cables, obtained for this book under the Freedom of Information Act, show clearly that Lord and his embassy in Beijing had, in fact, "flagged" Fang's name on two separate occasions.

The very first cable about the guest list for Bush's dinner had informed Washington:

> The list includes at least three prominent dissidents [The cable described Fang Lizhi, his wife, and Su Shaozhi.]. . . . These dissidents, though they retain their official status, are vocal representatives of the group of young, well-educated Chinese officials and intellectuals who strongly advocate greater, more comprehensive and quicker political reform, freedom of expression, and democratization throughout Chinese society . . .
>
> . . . If these dissidents attend, there will be press attention. The dissidents, especially Fang, could very well speak to the media at the banquet and cause some annoyance on the part of the Chinese authorities. We nevertheless recommend that the three be invited.

A subsequent embassy cable gave even greater prominence to Fang. It said near the top of the message:

> We are still planning to invite noted dissidents Fang Lizhi and his wife. Following are the changes we have made to the list . . .[17]

The unnamed White House backgrounder was National Security Advisor Brent Scowcroft, a fact that Lord was able to discover with little difficulty. It seems unlikely that Scowcroft would have given the briefing on his own, without the knowledge of the president. Blaming Lord represented Bush's and Scowcroft's way of smoothing over relations with the Chinese leadership by distancing themselves from the decision to invite Fang to dinner. The background briefing was not a full apology to China, but it certainly came close.

In Beijing, Lord was stunned. He called together his embassy aides, told them they had all done a good job on the president's trip, and ordered them not to contradict the White House in talking to the press.

Then, infuriated, the ambassador sat down and wrote a private, personal message to Scowcroft, complaining bitterly about the news stories.

This is the wrong way to deal with China, Lord argued in his memo: It was the Chinese who had misbehaved and whose actions required an explanation, not the Bush administration. By disavowing the invitation to Fang, the administration was conveying an impression of weakness on human rights issues. Lord argued that the administration should have been more firm, that it was wrong to start off a new administration by making it appear to the Chinese that the United States felt defensive about an invitation that was legitimate. Lord also noted that the news stories had destroyed his own credibility as ambassador to China, making it appear that he was a freelancer operating independently of the White House.[18]

The acrimony between the ambassador and the White House reflected a blend of personal antagonisms, conflicting ambitions and a substantive disagreement over how to deal with China. Bush and Scowcroft had just taken office and were not nearly so confident in their foreign policy judgments as they would later become. Scowcroft no doubt believed, correctly, that Lord would have liked to have his position as national security advisor. Years earlier, Lord had served as Kissinger's top henchman, the deliverer of the boss's bad news and recriminations—and Bush and Scowcroft had been among those on the receiving end.

For his part, Lord was not accustomed to public criticism, and particularly not from another member of the foreign policy establishment. It was one thing for Lord to be attacked by a right-wing ideologue like Jesse Helms; it was another to be singled out for blame by the White House.

Nevertheless, to dismiss this dispute as stemming from merely a clash of ambitions would be inaccurate. Bush and Scowcroft reflected a view of China very different from Lord's.

Lord and the American embassy in Beijing saw Fang and the handful of other dissidents and intellectuals they invited to the dinner as part of a new element in Chinese society. Those calling for political reform seemed to be an established part of life in Chinese cities in the 1980s, and embassy officials thought American policy should give recognition to this new reality. As it turned out, the embassy overestimated the extent to which China's top leadership would tolerate these signs of an emerging civil society.

Bush and Scowcroft, by contrast, based their views of China largely on their experiences and the images of the controlled society of the 1970s. They didn't see the changes taking place in Chinese cities and (if they thought about the subject at all) didn't place much importance on talk about political reform in Beijing. Therefore, they felt no particular need for any change in American policy, which had been, since the Nixon era, focused on China's top leadership. While the embassy overestimated the regime's willingness to accommodate the political opening of the late 1980s, Bush and Scowcroft underestimated the strength of the broader forces for change building up within Chinese society.

Amid these disagreements, there was one fallacious assumption that the American officials—Bush, Scowcroft and Lord—all shared. None of them had expected, in advance, that the Chinese regime would react with such fury and crudeness to the invitation to Fang. Their reasoning may have been different: In the Bush-Scowcroft 1970s view of China, political reformers like Fang were so insignificant that they could not possibly be a threat to the regime; in Lord's 1980s view, the reformers were so well-established that they seemed to have a degree of support and tolerance from the top leadership. Still, all the American officials believed, wrongly, that China's top leaders could tolerate a simple dinner invitation to a critic of the regime. The American invitation to Fang "shouldn't have been offensive in principle," observed one chagrined senior State Department official. "Was it an affront? Only if the Chinese chose to make it one." [19]

After writing his angry protest note to the White House, Lord hung onto it in Beijing for two days, reading it over and over to make sure that it was not an overly hasty or intemperate response. Then he sent it off as a back-channel message, using restricted CIA communications rather than the open cable traffic of the State Department. Lord's memo was addressed to Scowcroft; he sent a copy to James Baker.

Lord later checked to see that his message had been delivered. Familiar with the ways of the Washington bureaucracy, he even obtained the date and the exact time it was handed by the CIA to Scowcroft. He thought perhaps he might get a response saying that "we respectfully disagree," or that "we're sorry you have to take the fall for this one," or asking him to stop by for a talk the next time he was in Washington. Instead, Lord never received a reply. [20]

It was a bitter end to Winston Lord's career as a rising star and office seeker for Republican administrations.

AFTER BUSH returned home, the American embassy in China quickly turned its focus to the trip to Beijing that Soviet leader Mikhail Gorbachev was planning to make in May 1989.

Officially and in public, the United States took the position that there was no reason to be worried about Gorbachev's visit. Relations between China and the Soviet Union had been gradually improving since the early 1980s, and this summit-level meeting was simply one more step. Professing a lack of concern, Defense Secretary Frank Carlucci had told reporters the previous fall: "We think the relaxation of tensions between the Soviet Union and China would be healthy for world peace and stability." [21]

Privately, American officials were more nervous than they let on. Since the Nixon administration, the greatest fear in Washington had been that China and the Soviet Union would overcome their differences and enter into some partnership with one another. By 1989, these American anxieties had eased somewhat, because Nixon's strategic opening to China had by then endured for nearly two decades. Still, Gorbachev seemed to be a dynamic figure, and his bold initiatives were unsettling. Soviet troops were withdrawing from Afghanistan, and Gorbachev had also pledged to remove most of the Soviet troops from their positions in Mongolia near the Chinese border—thus easing two of the longstanding disputes between Beijing and Moscow. What might he do in Beijing?

Peter Tomsen, the embassy's deputy chief of mission, knew that Gorbachev's visit was of extraordinary importance. He summoned Mark Mohr, a member of the political section, and told him he should take the lead role in reporting on the Soviet leader's trip; all others in the embassy should coordinate their work through him. [22]

A few weeks after Mohr began, however, the embassy was sidetracked by what seemed, at first, to be a brief distraction. On Saturday, April 15, Hu Yaobang, the former Communist Party secretary who had been ousted from his job two years earlier, died of a heart attack in Beijing. Within hours, wall posters went up at Beijing University. "A great man has died, but false men still live," said one of them. Over the next two days, a few hundred Beijing students marched from various universities to Tiananmen Square to lay wreaths in Hu's honor at the base of the Monument to the People's Heroes.

By early the following week, there were several thousand people in the square. The Tiananmen demonstrations grew larger, spread to other cities and refused to subside.

AT THE White House, Bush moved quickly to replace Lord after the dispute over Fang Lizhi. On March 15, he nominated James R. Lilley as the next U.S. ambassador to China.

It was a logical choice. Lilley was close to the president. He had been CIA station chief in Beijing while Bush headed the U.S. liaison office, and they had remained associated ever since. Lilley had worked on China for a quarter-century, serving at the CIA, State Department and

National Security Council. China announced that it welcomed the appointment.[23]

In Beijing, the Lords packed their bags and said their farewells. The demonstrations over Hu Yaobang's death were just beginning to gather strength as the Lords made their last rounds. On April 19, the ambassador went in for a formal good-bye session with Premier Li Peng.

There was one awkward moment, a fleeting reminder of Lord's inability to speak Chinese. He said he wanted to voice special thanks to everyone who had helped over the previous four years, and especially to Liu Huaqiu, the vice foreign minister in charge of China's relations with the United States. However, Lord mispronounced Liu's name Hao-chi [How-chir], which means "loves to eat" in Chinese.

"Loves-to-eat? Who's that?" a startled Li Peng whispered to Liu. "It's me. I'll tell you later," Liu murmured to the premier.[24]

The incoming and outgoing American ambassadors to China had dinner together in Washington at the end of April, a few days before Lilley departed for Beijing. In style, background and viewpoint, Lilley could not have been more different from Lord. The two men illustrated the contrasting personalities of a policymaker and an intelligence operative. Lilley, the CIA veteran, was genial where Lord was remote. Lilley loved to talk to business executives, Asian reporters and American scholars. Doing so was part of his background: In the world of intelligence, you never knew where you were going to learn something. In Lord's experience, what counted above all were foreign policy elites: Nixon and Kissinger, Mao Tsetung and Chou Enlai. Lilley paid more attention to what was happening within armies and intelligence services and in the streets.

Whenever Lord talked about America and China, he always spoke in the idiom of diplomacy. He qualified his statements, smoothing over differences, minimizing controversy, so as to give others in Congress or the press as little as possible to criticize. Lilley, on the other hand, always chose tough language, emphasizing the conflicts, the power plays, the hustles, what was going on beneath the veneer.

As the two men dined at the Metropolitan Club that night, a television showed news coverage of the growing Tiananmen Square demonstrations. Lilley was intensely interested. "Is this thing for real?" Lilley asked Lord. "This isn't the China I know from the 1970s." Yes, replied Lord, what was happening was really important.

But Lord was as eager to talk about Washington as about Beijing. He poured out his anger at how Scowcroft had treated him after the presidential visit. "I did the right thing. I cleared it [the Fang invitation]," Lord said. "They didn't do their homework, and then they stuck it to me."[25]

Lilley was taken aback by Lord's outburst. He quietly sent word back to Scowcroft and others in the White House. Watch your step with Lord, cautioned Lilley. This guy is very well plugged in. He's got ties to the Council on Foreign Relations, the *Washington Post,* the *New York Times.* He's going to screw you unless you talk to him. It was a prescient warning, which the White House did not heed.

IN CHINA, the demonstrations grew in size throughout late April and early May. Young Chinese took to the street in 80 cities across China, ranging from the biggest metropolitan areas like Shanghai, Guangzhou and Tianjin to smaller provincial capitals. When Chinese leaders gathered on April 22 in the Great Hall of the People for a memorial service for Hu Yaobang, the crowd outside in Tiananmen Square reached 30,000. A few days later, after an editorial in the *People's Daily,* the official Communist Party newspaper, condemned the demonstrations, the crowds for the first time swelled to more than 100,000.

As Lilley prepared to leave Washington for Beijing, Bush asked his new ambassador essentially the same question Lilley had earlier posed to Lord. "Is this a genuine movement?" the president asked. "What do you think?" He was perplexed. This did not seem like the Chinese society he thought he had come to know from the embassy in Beijing 14 years earlier.

Lilley said he thought so. The movement did seem to be genuine. It wasn't clear how the Chinese leadership was going to handle the demonstrations, Lilley told the president. However, he went on, this was a potentially explosive situation in China; the demonstrations could be a serious threat to the regime.[26]

THE HISTORICAL record is often humbling to the work of governments, in America as elsewhere. As crises mount, as events move slowly toward their climax, the record often demonstrates that officials and bureaucracies go about their daily business, busying themselves with the mundane, failing to grasp the importance of what is about to occur.

And so it was in Washington in the spring of 1989. Documents show that in the fateful months leading up to China's Tiananmen Square massacre, officials at the White House, State Department and Pentagon were swept up by two items of business between the United States and China. Both of them were treated as matters of utmost importance at the time. Both turned out to be, in the end, of little consequence.

One of these preoccupations was a visit to Washington by Wan Li, one of Deng Xiaoping's closest associates. Wan was a senior Chinese official, a member of the Politburo and the chairman of the National

People's Congress, China's legislature. He was also a leading reformer. Wan was not, however, as the coming weeks would show, a man who by himself had the ability to influence the course of events in China.

Nevertheless, the awesome power of Washington's bureaucracy was set to work churning out plans, memos, talking points and arrangements on behalf of the Wan Li trip. "Memorandum for Brent Scowcroft. Subject: Request for Presidential Meeting and Tennis Game," wrote the State Department in one document. "Request for Presidential Aircraft," said another. State Department officials planned Wan Li's dinners and drafted talking points for President Bush and Vice President Quayle to use in meetings with him.[27]

One reason for this special attention was that Wan Li's visit was viewed by some American officials as a way of counteracting the impact of Gorbachev's trip to Beijing. "Believe it would be useful for media purposes to work in a dimension portraying Wan Li visit in context of Sino-Soviet summit," Peter Tomsen of the American embassy argued in one cable. Wan Li's trip, he said, could be used to demonstrate that America and China were still working together, despite Gorbachev's summit meeting in Beijing.[28]

Washington's other consuming interest was a plan for U.S. Navy ships to make a port call in China. American warships had made one previous such visit in 1986, but that had been to the relatively remote, quiet city of Qingdao. This time, Pentagon officials made plans for the American ships to sail up the Huangpu River into Shanghai in what they felt would be a demonstration of the continuing military cooperation between the two countries.

This event, too, was viewed in Washington as a way to upstage the Gorbachev visit to China, about which American officials professed publicly not to care. Indeed, the port call was intentionally scheduled to take place the very day after a Gorbachev stopover in Shanghai. "That [timing] wasn't coincidental," a State Department official boasted to the *New York Times.* "Nothing could send a more graphic signal to the West than this ship visit," a Western diplomat told the *Washington Post.*[29]

BOTH OF these events, Wan Li's visit and the navy port call, had been rendered all but meaningless by the time they took place. They lost their significance amid the drama of the continuing Chinese demonstrations.

By the time Gorbachev arrived in China on May 15, approximately half a million people filled Tiananmen Square. Chinese officials were forced to move the welcoming ceremonies for the Soviet leader from Tiananmen Square to the Beijing airport. Within two days, the crowd grew to a million. Gorbachev went about his meetings with Deng

Xiaoping, Chinese Party Secretary Zhao Ziyang and Premier Li Peng, but he was obliged to cancel many other activities in Beijing.

In Shanghai on May 18, Gorbachev found similar crowds. China's largest cities were increasingly in turmoil. That night, astonished Chinese witnessed on television a confrontation between their proper, orthodox Premier Li Peng and Wu'er Kaixi, a 21-year-old student engaged in a hunger strike. While the cameras rolled, Wu'er Kaixi, clad in pajamas, upbraided the premier for being late for their meeting.

Lilley had arrived in China at the beginning of May, a new ambassador with no time to ease quietly into his job. His schedule called for him to take up his post in Beijing for two weeks; to visit Shanghai for the U.S. Navy's port call; and then to return from there to the United States to participate in Wan Li's meetings in Washington.

On May 19, the U.S. Navy command ship USS *Blue Ridge* sailed up the Huangpu River into Shanghai, flying the American and Chinese flags, flanked by the cruiser *Sterett* and the guided missile frigate *Rodney M. Davis*. As the ships moored a few hundred yards from the Soviet consulate, the 1,600 Americans aboard lined the decks to look out at the city.

What they saw was not what the Pentagon had originally expected. On the streets of Shanghai near the waterfront were more than 200,000 demonstrators shouting slogans for political reform and attacking the Chinese leadership.[30] Lilley and other American officials arriving by air from Beijing had trouble reaching the ships for the welcoming ceremonies. They had to weave through and around demonstrations.

By this time, the idea of using the navy's port call to embarrass Gorbachev or to make a point about Sino-American relations seemed farcical. The event was barely attracting any attention at all, either in China or in the United States. The original plan had been for Vice Admiral Henry Mauz, the commander of the American Seventh Fleet, to travel from Shanghai to Beijing for further ceremonies. Chinese officials politely suggested to Lilley that the time might not be opportune. The ambassador hurriedly agreed. The American ships departed from Shanghai quickly and without fanfare.

At that point, Lilley made a snap decision.[31] He was supposed to board a plane and fly to Washington for the Bush administration's talks with Wan Li. But China seemed to be coming unstuck. With the benefit of satellite reconnaissance, American military and intelligence personnel reported that Chinese armies were moving toward Beijing from other points around the country: from Shijiazhuang to the south and from Shenyang in the northeast.

The ambassador decided to stay in China. When he informed officials in Washington, some of them were unhappy. You should be here for the meeting between Wan Li and the president, Lilley was told. It's a good way to start your job in China on the right foot. I'm not coming, Lilley replied. The situation in China is too ugly for me to leave now. The ambassador won the argument.

He was eager to return to Beijing but had no plane ticket, only a reservation to Washington. Instead, Lilley took the return ticket to Beijing held by his wife, Sally, leaving her to search in Shanghai for another ticket or a hotel room. By the time Lilley arrived in Beijing late that Friday night, Premier Li Peng was on television announcing that martial law had been declared in the city.

After Li's proclamation, Chinese television, which had been temporarily freed from the usual controls, sarcastically played the movie *Paper Moon,* suggesting that the regime's assertion of power should not be taken seriously. But the time for subtlety or satire in China was running short.

THAT WEEKEND, Wan Li stopped in Toronto on his way to Washington. There, the aging reformer offered words of sympathy for the student demonstrators. "We will firmly protect the patriotic enthusiasm of the young people in China," the Chinese official said, according to the temporarily uncontrolled New China News Service. "All these problems should be settled through democracy and [the] legal system."[32]

In Beijing, Chinese troops called in to enforce the martial law edict had been blocked by crowds from entering the center of the city. Meanwhile, reformers who supported the demonstrations had begun to challenge the legality of Li Peng's declaration of martial law, on grounds that only the National People's Congress could impose such an order. These reformers began circulating petitions calling for a special session of the Standing Committee of the National People's Congress, which Wan Li headed.[33] Suddenly, Wan Li took on a central role in the political crisis.

After Wan Li arrived in Washington, the Chinese embassy there began to receive a series of conflicting messages for him, reflecting the intense divisions and turmoil within the leadership. One message instructed Wan to return to China immediately, while another told him to stay in the United States.[34] Wan agonized about what he should do, before finally deciding to return home. Keeping up appearances, the Chinese official hurried through a day and a half of meetings; he talked with Baker, Quayle and, finally, President Bush, although the White House announced that the Bush-Wan tennis game had been canceled because it would be "inappropriate" in the midst of China's political crisis.

Wan Li flew back across the Pacific. When he landed in Shanghai he was led off and kept in seclusion by a group of officials, among them

Shanghai's Communist Party Secretary Jiang Zemin. By some accounts, Wan may have been kept against his will in a mild form of house arrest.[35]

Whatever the circumstances, Wan came to realize that China had not reached the stage where the legal system could be used to restrain brute force. After a couple of days, he succumbed and publicly declared that he would support martial law. Gone was his talk of the previous week about the importance of democracy and the patriotism of the students. In the end, Wan Li had not mattered, and neither had his trip to the United States.

ON THE Monday after martial law was declared, a Chinese Foreign Ministry official called Mark Mohr, the American embassy official who had been told to report on Gorbachev's trip to China. Acting as though it were an ordinary, routine day, while People's Liberation Army troops ringed the city and demonstrators chanted in the streets, the Chinese official told Mohr that the formal briefing he had long before requested on the Sino-Soviet summit meeting would be held within an hour.

Mohr, dressed in jeans, wasn't ready for the briefing. He had almost forgotten about the request. He called the State Department to tell Washington about the unexpected offer. "Okay," shrugged Jeffrey Bader, the deputy chief of the China desk. "But Mark, I hope this doesn't hurt your ego too much, nobody's going to read your cable."[36]

By this time, few in Washington cared about Gorbachev's visit. The attention of the government was riveted to China's political crisis. In Beijing, embassy officials discovered to their surprise that Lilley was doing his own reporting rather than relying on his subordinates. It was an unusual role for an ambassador, particularly a newly arrived one, but Lilley was harking back to his experience as CIA station chief.

During the week after martial law was declared, Lilley believed Washington was under the delusion that the crisis might still have some peaceful outcome. The president, he thought, was being given the false impression that violence might be avoided because Deng was in charge and always knew how to make things come out well. The ambassador thought differently: Deng was an Old Testament character; the Chinese leadership was being humiliated by the demonstrators, and revenge was in Deng's blood.[37] Lilley put his thoughts into a cable that argued that the Tiananmen Square showdown would have no happy ending. There was going to be bloodshed.[38]

Some State Department and White House specialists on China later insisted that, despite Lilley's claims, they had been under no illusions. They had been watching, day by day, the reports of how much military force was gathering outside the city of Beijing. For a time, Washington had hope that the regime would not use force, these officials acknowledged. However, they said, as core military units began moving toward China's capital, Washington, too, realized what was about to happen.[39]

Nevertheless, some evidence shows that during the two-week period between China's declaration of martial law and the June 3 Tiananmen crackdown, Washington became lulled into thinking the regime might not resort to violence. A confidential summary of events that is prepared each morning by U.S. intelligence officials for the secretary of state reported on June 2, 1989, that the "stalemate continues" in Beijing. "Hard-liners remain unable to resolve the leadership crisis or to remove students from Tiananmen Square," the report says.[40]

Bush himself, in his first press conference after the crackdown, suggested he believed the army assault was the result of a last-minute decision, one that had taken him by surprise. "They [Chinese officials] showed restraint for a long time," Bush said. "And I don't, I can't begin to fathom for you exactly what led to the order to use force because, even as recently as a couple of days ago, there was evidence that the military were under orders not to use force."[41]

The American embassy in Beijing believed the military assault upon the city would come over the Memorial Day weekend. Instead, the standoff endured for another week. Deng Xiaoping was apparently using the extra time to overcome the objections of some military and civilian leaders who did not want to use force; he was also making sure that virtually every unit of the People's Liberation Army, every branch and service, had a role in the operation, so that none could say afterward that it had not been involved.

In those last days, Bush attempted to send private messages to the Chinese leadership. He urged Deng and his colleagues to act with restraint, because doing so would be important for relations with the United States. Lilley found, however, that he had to deliver even presidential communications from Washington through the regular, lower-level Chinese Foreign Ministry channels. No matter how persistently the American ambassador asked, he could not get access of any kind to China's senior leaders.[42]

It was a telling comment on just how limited were the ties between American and Chinese leaders. At a time when it mattered, Bush's friendship with Deng Xiaoping didn't count for much. The president couldn't pick up the phone, couldn't send a letter or even a message through his ambassador.

On the night of June 3, 1989, China's six weeks of demonstrations for political change came to an end. The regime launched its military assault upon the city of Beijing. Units of the People's Liberation Army moved into the city toward Tiananmen Square from all directions, shooting unarmed civilians on their route. The number of dead has been variously estimated as between 700 and 2,700.[43]

American television broadcast images of the crackdown to a huge, horrified audience in the United States. In a single night, the Chinese leadership altered irrevocably the American perceptions of a steadily reforming China and the friendly relationship that had been so carefully nurtured since the days of Richard Nixon.

THOSE IN America who sought to minimize the fallout from the Tiananmen crackdown would later advance a number of arguments aimed at justifying what the Chinese leadership had done.

Some contended that the regime was simply inexperienced at crowd control. This view was first advanced by Premier Li Peng a month after the massacre. Li claimed that Chinese troops had to fire on demonstrators because they did not have enough tear gas, rubber bullets or water cannon.[44] Yet the regime's use of deadly force had also served an important purpose, one that tear gas and rubber bullets could not have accomplished: It terrorized the Chinese population into submission. This result, so helpful to the regime's survival, most likely was intentional rather than accidental.

Others have maintained that America's public reaction to the events in Beijing resulted from the fact that the crackdown was seen on television. Because of the impact of instantaneous news coverage, this argument goes, the American public saw an exaggerated or distorted view of the crackdown. This claim, too, seems too simplistic to withstand scrutiny. Indeed, the American television public never saw the full fury of the crackdown. By happenstance, almost no television cameras were along the street leading west from Tiananmen Square where most of the killings took place. Had those deaths been televised, the American outrage over the massacre might well have been even greater.

Finally, some Americans, led by former Secretary of State Kissinger, contended that the Chinese leadership simply had to do something about the Tiananmen Square demonstrations. "No government in the world would have tolerated having the main square of its capital occupied for eight weeks by tens of thousands of demonstrators who blocked the area in front of the main government building," Kissinger wrote a few weeks after the crackdown. That argument deftly shifted attention away from the means China chose; Kissinger ignored the question of whether other governments would have called in troops to fire on protesters.[45]

What might the Bush administration have done differently in the months leading up to the Tiananmen crackdown? Perhaps the American warnings against the use of violence might have been made more noisily. Perhaps U.S. officials might have given the Chinese leadership a clearer picture of how seriously China's relations with the West, and particularly with the United States, would be damaged by the use of force against the demonstrators.

Yet it is not likely that any of these actions would ultimately have produced a different outcome. What the United States said and did in the spring of 1989 could have had little impact, one way or another, on the leadership's decisions. The events inside China had a life and logic of their own.

The problem was not in the actions or inactions of the Bush administration in the spring of 1989, but rather upon the larger relationship between the United States and China that had been gradually developed over the previous two decades. The friendly partnership between Washington and Beijing rested not merely upon a shared opposition to the Soviet Union, but also upon the assumption that China would not do what it did on June 3–4, 1989. During the 1980s, Americans had been told that China was changing, and that it was different from other Communist regimes; China was thought to be, in Ronald Reagan's words, only a "so-called Communist" country. In the Tiananmen Square crackdown, China had shown itself to be as Leninist as any other Communist state, and certainly no less brutal.

For the two decades before 1989, American policy toward China had been made almost exclusively in the executive branch of government. To be sure, American presidents and their underlings at the White House, Pentagon and State Department had kept a watchful eye on Congress and American public opinion. Yet these had not, until 1989, been the driving forces underlying American policy toward China. Indeed, Congress had given the executive branch of government relatively wide latitude in dealing with China.

After the Tiananmen Square crackdown, the dynamics changed. Congress and American public opinion would no longer permit as amicable a relationship with China as the executive branch often sought to pursue. Although President Bush and his aides did not realize this at the time, there could be no return to the partnership between America and China that had existed before June 3, 1989. The relationship forged in the era of Richard Nixon and Henry Kissinger was forever altered.

CHAPTER TEN

The Immediate Aftermath of Tiananmen

Bob Kimmitt already had plans in Washington for Sunday, June 4, 1989, that were of considerable sentimental importance. Kimmitt was an alumnus of the U.S. Military Academy, and June 4 happened to be the 20th anniversary of his graduation. He and his West Point classmates had decided to observe their reunion in a somber fashion. They agreed to convene not at a restaurant or hotel, but at the Vietnam Memorial, in order to honor the 17 members of their class who had been killed during the Vietnam War.

At the time, Kimmitt was also serving as the undersecretary of state for political affairs, one of the inner circle of aides running American foreign policy under Secretary of State James A. Baker III. The State Department's operations center, the communications hub through which information flows in to the department from around the world, had notified Kimmitt of the People's Liberation Army assault in Beijing and of the high death toll. Kimmitt, acting on Baker's behalf, was responsible for organizing the Bush administration's first responses to the massacre.

And so on a sunny, glorious Sunday in Washington, Kimmitt found himself rushing back and forth between his spacious seventh-floor office at the State Department and the Vietnam Memorial on the mall, where more than a hundred of his West Point classmates and their wives were gathered. He couldn't help but think of the irony. As a paratrooper, Kimmitt had himself been wounded in Vietnam by a mortar shell that had been fired by the Viet Cong but had been made in China. During that war, America had viewed China as an adversary. In the intervening years, Kimmitt had trained as a lawyer and worked at the National Security Council, where China had reemerged as a friendly partner for American foreign policy in its efforts to combat the Soviet Union.

As Kimmitt walked back from the Vietnam Memorial to the State Department, he thought to himself that in the two decades since his West Point graduation, events had come full circle. Here America was, trying to figure out what to do about China again.[1]

THAT DAY, Kimmitt chaired a meeting of officials from throughout the U.S. government. There were experts on China, on human rights, on international law and on international finance.

In Kennebunkport, Maine, President George Bush issued a formal statement deploring the use of force by the Chinese regime. Beyond that, Bush said as little as possible. Relaxing at his vacation home after a visit to Europe, Bush went outside for an early-morning jog. When reporters asked him about the reports that hundreds of Chinese had been killed, he dismissed them abruptly. "Not while I'm running," he said.[2]

However, in the Washington meeting led by Kimmitt, American officials were not so dismissive. In fact, they began looking at a range of actions the Bush administration might take against China. The contrast between the president's casual response in Kennebunkport and the tougher, policy-oriented approach of the government was to set a pattern that continued through the Bush administration. Bush himself consistently failed to give voice to the public outrage Americans felt over the deadly crackdown on the Tiananmen Square demonstrations. However, often acting under congressional pressure, his administration adopted policy measures that sometimes had a considerable impact on China. Because Bush's rhetoric never matched the actions, and because the administration took steps to undercut the impact of some of its own policy measures, Congress and the American public sometimes assumed inaccurately that the Bush administration had done nothing at all.

The officials gathered at the State Department that Sunday decided that the administration's first response should be to halt the military relationship between the United States and China. This freeze applied both to American sales of military equipment to China and also to contacts between the American military and the People's Liberation Army.

Pentagon officials did not oppose this action. They felt that it was the very least the administration could and should do in response to the Chinese crackdown. Moreover, they believed that the suspension of the military ties could be viewed as a sacrifice—a way of preserving America's larger political and strategic relationship with China, which the Pentagon valued. After all, Pentagon officials reasoned, if the administration did not take some action, Congress would have pressured it to go much further.[3]

While the cutoff in military associations was thus adopted with little debate, its consequences were far-reaching. In a matter of days, the

United States uprooted the network of military connections with China that had been nurtured for more than 15 years during the Ford, Carter and Reagan administrations—thus raising questions about the wisdom of placing such a heavy emphasis upon them in the first place.

It would be nearly a half decade before American army officers would be permitted to meet or talk business with their friends and contacts in the People's Liberation Army. The freeze on military sales was of even more lasting effect. At the time, in June 1989, the halt was viewed by some Pentagon officials as temporary; in fact, the decision reached that Sunday would mark the end of the many years of efforts by the United States to sell military equipment to China.

Over the previous decade, the United States had entered into deals worth hundreds of millions of dollars to sell ammunition factories, torpedoes, radar and avionics equipment to the PLA. China had been hoping and lobbying for more and better weapons systems. Instead, in the years after 1989, the Pentagon found itself struggling merely to settle accounts on these earlier sales. Over the following decade, China's military leaders would turn to other countries, especially Russia, to obtain the arms they had once sought to buy from America.

Bush announced the freeze on the military relationship with China at a White House press conference the following day. It was the only policy change he made public at the time. However, the officials at Kimmitt's meeting had also tentatively decided upon another action, one that would hurt China in the pocketbook. They agreed to invoke an American law that could cut off China's ability to borrow money abroad.

One of the officials at that Sunday gathering was Richard Schifter, the assistant secretary of state for human rights. Schifter was one of the moderate-to-conservative Democrats, originally allied with Hubert Humphrey, who had joined the Reagan administration in part because of concern that the Democratic Party had become too conciliatory toward the Soviet Union. As the State Department's leading human rights official through the last half of the 1980s, Schifter had devoted most of his energy to combating human rights abuses in the Soviet Union and Eastern Europe.

Until the Tiananmen Square demonstrations, Schifter had paid little attention to China. He and his staff were required to file an annual human rights report about the situation in China, as they did for more than 100 other countries. But aside from these annual reports, Schifter hadn't seen the need to do anything about China. Despite the intermittent stories of continuing repression, despite the regime's detention of Democracy Wall dissidents such as Wei Jingsheng for long periods of time, Schifter had accepted at face value the assumptions about China that were commonplace in America during the 1980s: that the country was gradually opening up, politically as well as economically, and that the government was moving in the right direction.[4]

Now, in Kimmitt's meeting, Schifter listed a number of provisions of U.S. law that either required or authorized the president to take action against countries that commit gross violations of human rights. There was little question that China's use of the army to shoot unarmed civilians protesters qualified as a "gross violation."

The most important of the laws cited by Schifter called upon the United States to oppose lending by international financial institutions to a country engaging in gross violations of human rights. That provision was of extraordinary importance, because it covered the World Bank loans that were important for China's economy.

China had become a special favorite of the World Bank, indeed the bank's largest single borrower. Beijing appeared to use the money it borrowed more efficiently than other borrowers in Asia and Africa, and the reform-minded officials in China led by Communist Party Secretary Zhao Ziyang had relied heavily on the World Bank's advice. In the year before the Tiananmen crackdown, the bank had lent $1.3 billion to China, and for the year afterward, 1989–90, the bank had been scheduled to lend $2.3 billion.[5] China regularly obtained hundreds of millions of dollars more through loans from the smaller Asian Development Bank. All of this lending could be blocked by the opposition of the United States.

The Bush administration did not make public any change in policy on international lending to China for another two weeks. The delay was necessary in order to coordinate America's policy with the policies of Western European governments and Japan. Nevertheless, several of the participants in Kimmitt's meeting recalled that the decision to clamp down on international lending to China was made then, on the first day after the massacre.

The State Department sent out cables informing America's closest allies that the United States intended to try to cut off international loans to China, and saying it hoped other countries would do likewise.[6] This diplomatic effort took some time but was largely successful. Six weeks later, at the time of the annual economic summit of the world's seven leading industrialized powers in Paris, the United States and its allies formally announced that all World Bank loans to China were being postponed. Japanese Prime Minister Sosuke Uno quickly followed suit by announcing that Japan would suspend a multi-year package of $5.6 billion in loans to China. Taken together, the freeze on World

Bank and Japanese loans was a tremendous blow to China's development plans.[7]

The Bush administration moved against China almost apologetically, always aware that if it didn't act, Congress and the American public would demand that it go still further. Nevertheless, within a day after the June 4 crackdown, the administration was heading toward the imposition of a series of sanctions against a Chinese regime that America had, until only a few days earlier, treated as a friend and strategic partner.

ON THAT same Sunday morning of June 4, Ed King's phone rang at his home in Bethesda, Maryland. "This is the senator," said the voice on the line. It was King's boss, Senator George Mitchell of Maine, the Democratic majority leader of the U.S. Senate.[8]

King was Mitchell's legislative assistant for foreign policy. His boss had taken over as majority leader at the beginning of 1989. In his new post, Mitchell's only serious endeavor in foreign policy had been one in which he had worked with, not against, the Bush administration. Secretary of State James Baker had been eager for a deal that would put an end to the years of friction between the Reagan administration and Congress over Nicaragua. Seeking to lay to rest the ugly history of the Iran-Contra scandal, Baker had negotiated, one-on-one with Mitchell, a bipartisan agreement on Central America. The deal, signed in April, had been a huge success.

On that Sunday morning in June, King found that on China, Mitchell had a different, more combative role in mind. He wanted to challenge George Bush's China policy. "I want to make a speech tomorrow on China," he told his assistant. "I want a tough speech. I think this [the Tiananmen Square crackdown] is outrageous. It's murder."

Mitchell upbraided the administration the next day from Capitol Hill. "We ought to make it very clear that the United States government stands with and in support of those who seek freedom and democracy in China and throughout the world," declared the Senate majority leader.[9] Later that week, he urged Bush to take steps against China beyond the initial military sanctions.

Mitchell quickly emerged as the most powerful critic of the administration's policies toward Beijing. Over the next few years, he provided support and leadership for others in Congress who sought, through hearings or legislation, to prevent the administration from steering relations with China back onto the course they had been following before the Tiananmen massacre.

In doing so, Mitchell, in his low-key manner, resisted intense pressures to support the administration. During the following months, the

White House appealed to senior Democratic figures to try to talk with Mitchell and turn him around on China. Veterans from the Carter administration, such as Zbigniew Brzezinski, urged Mitchell to stop challenging Bush.

Business leaders visited Mitchell, too, pleading that his legislative efforts were going to harm their business in China. At one point, Paul Fireman, the chief executive of Reebok, complained to Mitchell that a piece of legislation was going to damage his company's business making shoes in China. Mitchell admired his visitor's hand-sewn leather shoes and asked where they were made. "Austria," replied Fireman. Mitchell was wearing black rubber-soled shoes made at the last shoe factory in his home state that hadn't closed down. "If you need a place to make shoes, I've got about 20,000 unemployed shoe workers in Maine who could use the jobs," he told the Reebok executive.[10]

To his detractors in the Bush administration, Mitchell was prompted by sheer partisanship. This was, certainly, one part of his motivation. During his four years in the White House, George Bush won the Gulf War and presided over the fall of the Berlin Wall, the collapse of the Soviet Union and the reunification of Germany. There was not much grist for Democratic opposition there. China was an issue where the Democrats in Congress could oppose the Republican administration and know, with certainty, that they had public opinion on their side. It was the one foreign policy issue where Bush was clearly out of touch with the views of ordinary Americans. If George Bush wasn't going to convey the country's outrage over Chinese repression, then the Democrats in Congress would happily volunteer.

Nevertheless, to write off Mitchell's motivation as merely partisan would be inaccurate. In private conversations, Bush sometimes acknowledged that Mitchell's behavior could not be explained by partisanship alone. "I just can't understand Mitchell," he told Ambassador James Lilley at one point. "What's he got in his craw on this one?"[11] Indeed, when it came to China, Mitchell would later become nearly as much of a problem for a Democratic president, Bill Clinton, as he had been for the Republicans. He was genuinely outraged by Chinese repression; he believed in what he was doing.

Before coming to the Senate, Mitchell had served as a U.S. attorney and federal judge. His experience and outlook were based upon law and legal process. He represented a consistent school of thought in America about China: that when it came to American policy, China should be treated like any other country. The American China experts who tried to talk to Mitchell usually made precisely the wrong arguments: They contended that China had to be treated with special care, because it is a huge and powerful nation with its own unique history, traditions and culture. But to Mitchell, the heart of the matter was that even powerful countries should be held to the same standards as everyone else.

Over the two decades before 1989, American policy toward China had been largely bipartisan. There had been a few momentary exceptions—as when Republicans like Bush attacked President Carter after he established diplomatic relations with Beijing. On the whole, however, neither political party had mounted a sustained challenge to the China policy of the other party.

With Mitchell taking the lead for the Democrats, and with Bush both unable and unwilling to give voice to the views of ordinary Americans about Chinese repression, that tradition of bipartisanship ended with the Tiananmen Square crackdown.

ON THAT Sunday morning of June 4, 1989, Zhao Haiqing was working in a chemistry laboratory at Harvard, doing research on the molecular structure of proteins. By the end of the day, Zhao was on the road to Washington, along with many other Chinese students.

Zhao, a post-doctoral student in biochemistry at Harvard, knew almost nothing about American politics. The previous month, however, as the Tiananmen Square demonstrations swelled ever larger in Beijing, about 200 Chinese students at Harvard began organizing political activities in support of the movement. Zhao was appointed to a seven-member committee in charge of the Chinese students in Boston. Working with other Chinese students at the Massachusetts Institute of Technology, Boston University and other Boston campuses, the new student organization staffed phone lines and began sending faxes to universities in China.

A rally of Chinese students had already been planned for Monday, June 5, in Washington, to support the Tiananmen Square demonstrations. Suddenly, after the massacre, this rally took on profoundly greater importance. Attendance, originally expected to be about 2,000 students, was 5,000 to 10,000.

Zhao drove through the night from Boston to Washington, picking up one Chinese friend in New York City and another in Princeton. Some of the students had decided that instead of merely demonstrating, they should also try to meet with members of Congress. Most of the students were dressed in their customary attire of T-shirts and jeans, but a few of them, including Zhao, had decided to wear sports jackets and ties. Those who had dressed up became the designated Washington lobbyists for the Chinese students.

Years later, Zhao remembered how perfectly everything had worked out on that Monday. The rally was held at the Capitol. At least 12 members of Congress showed up to show their support, ranging from liberal Democrats like Senator Alan Cranston to conservative Republicans like Senator Jesse Helms. Later, when the students marched past the White House, Jesse Jackson joined them.

The Chinese students became America's poster children. They were the vehicle through which a new generation of Americans paid tribute to the humble, enduring virtues of the Chinese people: The students were an educated, English-speaking version of Pearl Buck's romanticized heroes of the 1930s. By this time 43,000 Chinese students were in America, spread out among colleges and universities across the United States; there was virtually no member of Congress who didn't have at least a few students at some school within his or her district. The students were bright, sincere, idealistic and diligent.

They also became amazingly well-organized. Virtually all of them were graduate students, most of them in the sciences. The Chinese students were the low-cost, well-educated labor pool that kept America's university and research laboratories running. Virtually all of them had access to computers at their universities; even in the 1980s, at a time when most of America had not yet discovered the Internet, the Chinese students had become familiar with it in the course of their research work. Beginning in 1986, when a group at Texas A&M University created a computerized forum called CHINANET, Chinese students throughout the United States had been swapping news and information, gossiping and debating with one another through on-line networks like the China News Digest and VISANET.[12]

Two days after the rally, the student leaders sat down to work out their agenda and priorities. Some argued that the students should press efforts to have the United States and other countries put economic pressure on China. Some favored a boycott of the Asian Games, which were to be held in Beijing in 1990. Some proposed that the students should seek legal changes that would protect them from being required to return home and would instead enable them to remain in the United States.

At the meeting, the student leaders decided to pursue all three objectives. But over the coming months, it was the Chinese students' effort to stay in the United States that gradually captured America's attention.

EARLY ON the morning of Monday, June 5, shortly before 7 o'clock, Jeff Bader, the deputy director of the State Department's China desk, stopped at the operations center on the way in to his office. Anything happen in Beijing overnight? Bader asked.[13]

Well, yes, Bader was told. The duty officers said that at about noon that day in Beijing, Fang Lizhi, China's leading proponent of democratic reforms, had come to the American embassy, accompanied by his wife, Li Shuxian, and their son. They said they were afraid for their safety and sought refuge inside the embassy compound. Nevertheless, two American officials, Raymond Burghardt and McKinney Russell, had persuaded them to leave the embassy and go back out onto the streets.

Fang had told the American officials he was on top of a list of people whom the regime intended to arrest and blame for the Tiananmen Square protests. Fang's wife was considerably more distraught than he was. The talks had gone on for several hours, over a lunch of peanut butter and crackers, while gunfire occasionally erupted on the streets outside. The American officials told Fang that no Chinese had ever been granted protection inside the Beijing embassy; that it was unclear how long Fang might have to stay inside; and that if he took refuge at the compound, the Chinese regime might use that fact as a way of blaming the democracy movement on foreign powers. Maybe we can get you a visa to try to leave China for the United States, the American officials told Fang, but we don't want to take you into the embassy.

Fang didn't think a visa would be of much help. He was rightly skeptical that Chinese officials would allow him to pass through the airport and leave the country without stopping him. Nevertheless, he left his passport in the hands of the American diplomats and agreed to come back for a visa the next day.[14]

In discouraging Fang, these embassy officials believed they were merely following instructions from Washington. Over the previous weeks, the State Department in Washington had held secret discussions with the American embassy in Beijing about what should be done if there were a crackdown and, as a result, large numbers of Chinese sought refuge in the embassy. Ambassador James Lilley had feared the embassy might be faced with the task of dealing with thousands of Chinese. The State Department had agreed that it wanted to avoid such a situation; long and troublesome stalemates had occurred inside embassies elsewhere in the world, such as when seven Russian Pentecostalists took refuge in the Moscow embassy and stayed in its basement for five years.

Nevertheless, when Bader heard on Monday morning that American officials had urged Fang to leave, he was furious. Those earlier instructions had been intended for a situation in which throngs of ordinary, nameless Chinese came to the embassy. They had not been meant for China's leading dissident. People's Liberation Army units were roaming the streets of Beijing. China's security apparatus was just beginning to search for and arrest those who could be held responsible for the Tiananmen Square demonstrations. What if Fang were picked up and harmed, or even executed, after U.S. officials had politely declined to grant him refuge inside the American embassy? What would the American people think of their government then?

Bader felt he had little time. He made a couple of quick calls—one to Kimmitt and one to a staff member at the National Security Council—to get approval for what he was about to do. Then he telephoned the American embassy in Beijing. There was no secure line available, but Bader was in a hurry and didn't care. He talked over an open phone line to Mark Mohr, from the embassy's political section.

"What the fuck are you doing?" he shouted into the phone. Have someone get out there, Bader went on, and tell Fang that he's welcome to stay inside the American embassy if he's afraid for his safety outside.

Turning Fang away had not been Mohr's decision in the first place. He reminded Bader that guns were still firing on the streets of Beijing. I'm not telling you to endanger your own life to deliver this message to Fang, Bader replied. But as soon as it's possible, do it.

In Beijing, American diplomats tracked down Fang and his family in a room at the Jianguo Hotel near the embassy. Perry Link had persuaded an old friend, *Washington Post* correspondent Jay Mathews, to let Fang stay in his hotel room temporarily while Mathews went off on assignment to Shanghai.

It was nearly midnight in Beijing when Burghardt called Fang at the hotel. "This is the friend you talked with this afternoon," he said carefully and anonymously. He and Russell said they were coming to Fang's room. There, contradicting the message they had given Fang earlier that day, the two diplomats made clear that he and his family could come to the embassy. They told Fang he would be a "guest of George Bush." [15]

What followed had all the trappings of a covert intelligence operation. The diplomats hurriedly escorted Fang, his wife and their son out the back door of the Jianguo Hotel into a waiting minivan, where they were driven to the embassy residence of Ambassador Lilley and installed in the front guest bedroom. Lilley and his family, who had arrived in China only a month earlier, were still living in a hotel, waiting for their possessions to arrive and for their embassy residence to be renovated.

As a result, Fang and his family found themselves alone in an empty building in darkness, ordered by the Americans not to turn on any lights or do anything else that would attract the attention of Chinese officials. Fang would later recall these first nights, creeping around vacant rooms, unsure whether Chinese security officials would rush in to seize him, as especially terrifying.

Chinese authorities found out about Fang quickly. In Washington, the White House confirmed that Fang had taken refuge in the embassy. The Chinese regime reacted rapidly and angrily. Two days later, Lilley was summoned to the Chinese Foreign Ministry. He was told that Fang had helped instigate the Tiananmen demonstrations and was, therefore, a criminal counterrevolutionary. By lodging him in the American embassy, the United States was interfering in China's internal affairs. Lilley felt it was an especially unpleasant conversation. The Chinese seemed to suggest that Fang was a creature of the United States and that America had been behind the Tiananmen Square demonstrations.[16]

In Washington, Bush defended the American decision to take in Fang. "It is awful hard for the United States, when a man presents himself, a person who is a dissident and says that his life is threatened, to turn him back," the president told a news conference. "That isn't one of the premises upon which the United States was founded. So we have a difference with them [Chinese leaders] on that. But I hope it can be resolved."[17]

In fact, the standoff would not be settled for a year. Fang's presence inside the American embassy in Beijing became both the heart and the symbol of the new political differences between the two countries. Four days after Fang entered the embassy, Secretary of State Baker began meeting with Chinese Ambassador Han Xu in Washington to try to resolve Fang's fate, but without success.

Over the following year, the Bush administration became increasingly swept up in the problem of how to win China's permission to let Fang leave the country. The Chinese regime, meanwhile, came to see Fang as a valuable hostage, who could be kept inside the embassy until the United States offered other policy concessions in exchange for his freedom.

In short, within only days after the Tiananmen Square crackdown, America and China were set on a new course, one without precedent in the previous two decades. The Bush administration said it wanted to preserve America's existing relationship with China. Yet the U.S. government was also imposing sanctions on the Chinese regime and giving refuge to China's leading dissident. Chinese students had launched what would become an extraordinarily successful nationwide campaign for American support, and Democratic leaders in Congress were attacking the administration for failing to take stronger action.

THROUGHOUT THE following weeks of June 1989, Beijing launched a nationwide campaign of repression to enforce its authority over an unruly nation. Thousands of dissidents were arrested, and some were quickly put on trial. Chinese television showed almost daily pictures of proceedings in which defendants with shaved heads, weary voices and bruised bodies were marched before judges who sentenced them to long prison terms or, in several cases, executions.

The Chinese footage was rebroadcast in America, destroying whatever slim hopes the Bush administration had that the passions inspired by the massacre would subside. In Congress, complaints mounted that the mere suspension of military contacts was too mild a response to the Chinese crackdown. "As the executions began, we decided to take more stringent actions," Baker wrote in his memoirs.[18]

On June 20, Baker was scheduled to testify before the Senate Foreign Relations Committee. Realizing that he would be interrogated about the administration's China policy, the politically attuned secretary of state decided to seize the initiative by unveiling a new set of sanctions against China.

Baker told the senators the United States would seek to freeze lending to China by the World Bank and other international financial institutions. This was the action that the administration had privately decided to pursue on the first day after the June 4 crackdown. Then the secretary added another new action: He said he had recommended to the president that the United States suspend high-level contacts between Americans and Chinese.

The White House was caught off guard. Earlier that day, White House spokesman Marlin Fitzwater had suggested to reporters that new sanctions against China would be counterproductive. Nevertheless, by that evening, the White House had embraced Baker's recommendation as official U.S. policy. Fitzwater formally announced the freeze on international lending and high-level contacts, saying the United States was responding "to the wave of violence and reprisals by the Chinese authorities against those who have called for democracy."[19]

Underlying this White House announcement were elements of intrigue, hypocrisy and drama that would be recognized only many months later. Bush was, at that very moment, arranging a secret trip to Beijing by National Security Advisor Brent Scowcroft. Scowcroft's visit would turn the new prohibition on contacts into a meaningless exercise, at least for its impact on the Chinese leadership. However, Bush and Scowcroft believed that no one would find out about Scowcroft's trip.

According to Douglas Paal, who was serving at the White House as the China specialist on Bush's National Security Council, Baker had not told the president what he planned to announce until minutes before testifying in Congress. Paal then delivered the news about the ban on high-level exchanges to Scowcroft, his boss. "What I did not know at the time was that Scowcroft was planning to go [to Beijing] in July," Paal explained in an interview. "And so when I went to Brent and told him [about the prohibition on contacts], he was surprised."[20]

The official White House announcement said that the United States was suspending all "high-level exchanges of government officials with the People's Republic of China." A half-year later, after Scowcroft's July trip had been made public, Bush administration officials would explain that the word *exchanges* had been a term of art, applying not to all high-level meetings between American and Chinese officials, but only to a handful of formal, structured joint commissions in which American Cabinet members had been meeting with their Chinese counterparts to discuss matters like trade and investment.

But at the time of the announcement on June 20, Bush administration officials did not offer such a limited interpretation of their action and, to the contrary, encouraged the broader interpretation that was widely given to their action. "A senior administration official said Bush's order . . . would bar visits from Washington-based officials to Beijing or official trips by Chinese officials to this country," reported one White House correspondent.[21]

The initiative for the Scowcroft trip had come from Bush, who had sent a letter directly to Deng Xiaoping suggesting the mission. At the outset, the only two other American officials who knew about the proposal were Scowcroft and Baker. The secretary of state had been intimately involved in the planning. Not wanting to cede turf to Scowcroft's NSC, he had insisted that Scowcroft take a senior State Department official with him, and Deputy Secretary of State Lawrence Eagleburger was assigned to go along. On June 25, Bush received a reply that Deng would agree to see the two administration representatives.[22]

The administration went to great lengths to conceal its clandestine diplomacy. Lilley was suddenly recalled to Washington and told of the mission only after he arrived there; Bush, Scowcroft and Baker feared that any cable sent to Lilley in Beijing might leak. Baker didn't tell even his closest advisers, including Kimmitt, who was in charge of China policy for the secretary of state. Kimmitt would later remember just how closely held Scowcroft's mission had been: It was the only piece of information Baker had kept secret from Kimmitt, except for the starting times for the Panama invasion and the Gulf War.

State Department officials realized, however, that something was going on. During the early weeks of June, officials from the department's East Asia bureau sat in on several talks between Baker and Chinese Ambassador Han Xu. Suddenly, in late June, they were told that lower-level officials would not be allowed to attend the meetings.[23]

Scowcroft and Eagleburger left Washington before dawn on June 30 in an air force plane. It was refueled in the air so that it would not have to stop over at Guam or any other Pacific island where they might be observed. They were in China only for a day, seeing Deng Xiaoping, before they returned home. The administration said nothing about the mission in public, either at the time or for nearly a half-year afterward.

The obvious question is, What was the aim of this trip? What message did Bush want to convey to China? What, exactly, was worthy of such remarkable secrecy?

By all accounts, one purpose was to appeal to Deng to limit the repression in China and let him know of the impact the show trials and mass arrests were having in the United States. A list of themes drawn up for the Scowcroft-Eagleburger mission—dated June 29, 1989, the day before the two men left for China—shows that Bush wanted to ask Deng to ease the crackdown. "Further arrests and executions will inevitably lead to greater demands in the U.S. to respond," says the memo, which was obtained under the Freedom of Information Act. "Efforts at national reconciliation, on the other hand, will find a cooperative U.S. response." How China dealt with its citizens was "of course an internal affair," the memo conceded, but how the U.S. government and the American people viewed China's actions was its own internal affair, too, and Americans had been "shocked and repelled" by the Tiananmen crackdown.[24]

"They [Bush, Scowcroft and Baker] thought they could curb this Chinese tendency to take vengeance," explained Lilley in an interview. "And they asked me, 'Do you think this would be able to stop it?' And I said to them, 'You can only get it stopped in public. If that happens, at least you won't have these lugubrious films on TV. But they [the Chinese leadership] aren't going to stop punishing. They're going to get these guys, one way or another.' "[25] Baker, in his memoirs, offered a similar account, saying the president wanted to appeal to Deng to end the repression.

A second purpose was to reopen a direct channel from the White House to Deng Xiaoping. During the Tiananmen crisis, Bush had found, to his dismay, that he was unable to send messages to Deng. He had attempted to do so both through Lilley and, at one point, by trying to telephone directly, but Deng and other Chinese leaders refused to take the call. The Scowcroft mission was designed "to keep channels open," explained Paal. "If you don't talk to Deng, and he's running the country, you're not talking to anyone that matters."[26]

Still, these purposes by themselves seem inadequate to explain the mission. Another message, one the Bush administration officials were considerably less eager to advertise, was that the sanctions the United States was imposing on China would not be so serious or long-lasting as the American people were being led to believe. The very presence of Scowcroft and Eagleburger in Beijing, less than two weeks after the administration announced its ban on high-level contacts, conveyed this message. According to Lilley, one part of the mission was to tell the Chinese regime that "Bush wanted to preserve the relationship, and we had to sanction them because of the public pressure in the United States." [27]

The memo of talking points prepared for the secret mission shows that Scowcroft and Eagleburger were to assure Chinese leaders that "the President intends to do all he can to maintain a steady course" and that he considered "the long-term relationship" between the United States and China to be of great importance. "He wants to manage short-term events in a way that will best assure a healthy relationship over time," the memo says. "But he is not the only factor in the American democratic system. The Congress is a co-equal branch of government." [28] It was, in a way, telling that Chinese leaders needed to be reminded of this fact a full decade after diplomatic relations were established.

Finally, the Scowcroft mission may well have been aimed at telling Deng that despite the differences over the Tiananmen crackdown and the American sanctions, the United States wanted to continue its security cooperation with China against the Soviet Union—and particularly to keep in operations the clandestine intelligence facilities in China that monitored Soviet missile and nuclear tests. The memo prepared for the secret mission talks extensively about the benefits both China and the United States had derived from their security ties over the previous decade or more; the memo contained one passage that was deleted before its release, and which may well concern intelligence cooperation between the two countries. In interviews for this book, Bush administration officials declined to discuss this subject. Lilley acknowledged, however, that some lower-level Chinese officials had suggested or threatened the possibility of closing down these intelligence monitoring stations in the tense period after the Tiananmen Square crackdown. [29]

When Scowcroft and Eagleburger returned to Washington, they reported privately that Deng and other Chinese leaders had been "as inscrutable as ever," according to Baker. At the time, their efforts to keep the trip secret were largely, though not completely, successful.

There was one mishap. Chinese officials, always meticulous on questions of money, wrote up a bill to charge the United States for the costs of refueling the U.S. Air Force plane while Scowcroft and Eagleburger were in Beijing. The bill, written in Chinese, was forwarded to the Pentagon, which had to call in its China specialists to explain what it said.

Gradually, within the Pentagon, word leaked out about the secret trip. Congress and the American public, however, remained in the dark.[30]

This mission had a number of significant consequences. To the Chinese leadership, it conveyed the message that the Bush administration still wanted and needed to preserve as much as possible of the relationship with Beijing that had existed before 1989; in simplest terms, the trip told Deng and other leaders not to take so seriously what the administration said and did in public in response to the Tiananmen Square crackdown. Scowcroft was cast into the role of the visiting emissary from abroad, showing respect and paying tribute to the Chinese leadership less than a month after it had used force against its people.

The trip had consequences in Washington, too. Power over China policy shifted increasingly from the State Department to the White House. State Department officials saw that Bush and Scowcroft had been unhappy with Baker's hasty announcement of a ban on high-level contacts with Beijing.[31] Baker, meanwhile, seemed to grasp that China was a foreign policy problem on which little was to be gained in domestic political terms and was in any case a problem that Bush and Scowcroft intended to handle in their own way. He began to devote himself increasingly to the Soviet Union and the Middle East, leaving the White House to take the initiative on China.

So, too, the Scowcroft mission created an unmistakable divide, a degree of alienation—not only between the Bush administration and the American public, but even between the top officials of the administration (that is, Bush, Scowcroft and Baker) and the working-level bureaucracy. Those Americans who worked regularly on China policy came to realize that they were often being kept in the dark. It became a standing joke that the U.S. government's desk officer for China, the person handling all the daily details of relations between Washington and Beijing, was George Bush.

CHAPTER ELEVEN

George Bush Misjudges

Z HAO HAIQING TURNED OUT to be the perfect Washington lobbyist for the Chinese students. He dressed well but not flashily, spoke humbly but in impeccable English, and was firm but not confrontational with those who questioned him. With his Harvard training and doctorate in biochemistry, he set at ease powerful figures, such as members of Congress.

Zhao was willing, where more flamboyant and renowned Chinese student leaders were not, to delve into the minute details that are important to the passage of legislation. His businesslike manner and nondescript appearance belied the reality of a life that was anything but normal: For five years after the Tiananmen Square crackdown, he never called or wrote his parents in China, fearing that contact with him of any kind could put them in jeopardy, until finally his parents could win permission to follow Zhao and his sister to America.[1]

By July 1989, the Chinese student movement was beginning to shift its focus from China to America, from Tiananmen Square to Capitol Hill. Some of the leaders of the Beijing demonstrations, such as Wang Dan, had been arrested inside China. Others had fled to Hong Kong and from there to France or the United States.

In America, these student leaders were being treated as celebrities. On the ABC television program *Nightline,* Wu'er Kaixi cockily reminisced with host Ted Koppel about his televised confrontation with Premier Li Peng two months earlier. From a television studio in Chicago, he declared to Koppel, "We have this aim: to overthrow the government headed by Li Peng."[2]

Yet power was slowly shifting from these newly arrived exiles to the Chinese students who had been studying in the United States for some time—that is, to those students who spoke English and understood the ways and customs of America. During the five years after the Tiananmen Square crackdown, Zhao Haiqing would come to exert a vastly greater influence over American policy toward China than did Wu'er Kaixi.

Most of the 43,000 Chinese students in America had come with the sponsorship of the Chinese government. Their visas required them to return home for a period of at least two years as soon as they completed their studies.

As part of his first response to the Tiananmen Square crackdown, President Bush had announced that he would permit Chinese students at American universities to remain in the United States for at least another year. Upon learning the details of Bush's action, however, many students were dismayed. Anyone who accepted the administration's offer, without exception, would have been required to return to China after one more year; such students would have had no ability to extend their visas in America for other reasons.

Since well before the Tiananmen massacre, many of these students had been prolonging their stays in the United States. The reasons had little to do with politics. If the students returned to China, they faced low-paying, unchallenging jobs; the work units to which they were assigned back home were usually headed by older, less educated cadres who resented anyone coming back from overseas. And so, the students had resorted to a variety of ploys—switching majors, transferring to other universities or extending their graduate work—to avoid being classified as having completed their studies.

After the Tiananmen crackdown, these students faced not only these longstanding problems, but also some important new political reasons to avoid returning home. Yet the administration's initial offer seemed to offer less protection than they had enjoyed in the past.

Quickly, the students turned to Capitol Hill for legislation that would grant them new legal guarantees against being required to return home. Zhao Haiqing became the leader and spokesman for this cause.

Members of Congress introduced several different bills on behalf of the students. One of them, proposed by Republican Senator Slade Gorton, even suggested giving the students permanent resident status in America. Zhao shrewdly decided Gorton's legislation was so far-reaching that it could never be enacted. Instead, he decided to support another, more moderate bill, one that would temporarily suspend the requirement that Chinese students return home. This bill was sponsored by a relative newcomer to the House of Representatives, a Democrat named Nancy Pelosi.

Pelosi's congressional district in downtown San Francisco was one of the most progressive in the nation; it also contained one of the highest concentrations of Asian-Americans. The district had been held for many years by Phil Burton, one of Congress's most masterful legislators, and later by Burton's wife, Sala. Pelosi, a protégé of Phil Burton, won the seat in 1987 after Mrs. Burton's death.

Pelosi was easy to underestimate. She had a perpetually wide-eyed look, and she talked in a halting fashion, often mulling over her thoughts and shifting direction in midsentence. But Pelosi had the experience to blend together the modern, television-driven politics of California and the older, more traditional backroom politics of America's cities. She knew how to create sound bites and how to count votes.

She had been introduced to politics virtually at birth. Her father, Thomas (Tommy) D'Alesandro Jr., had been a New Deal congressman and, from 1947 to 1959, the mayor of Baltimore; at age 6, she had been photographed swearing in her father as mayor. She had moved to California to marry Paul Pelosi, a businessman whose brother was a San Francisco supervisor. By the time she came to Capitol Hill, Nancy Pelosi possessed millions of dollars in real estate and bond holdings and appeared regularly among the top 20 in listings of the wealthiest members of Congress.[3]

During the late 1970s and early 1980s, Pelosi had become a Democratic Party activist and insider in California, rising to serve as state party chair. She was also one of the California party's best fund-raisers—so good, in fact, that in 1986, she was appointed by George Mitchell to serve as finance chairman for the Democratic Senatorial Campaign Committee. It was a winning combination. The Democrats regained control of the Senate that year, and after Pelosi came to Washington, her successful partnership with Mitchell proved to be of extraordinary significance for American policy toward China.

Pelosi at first seemed to view her proposed student legislation as a low-key effort on behalf of a constituency important to her San Francisco district. Nevertheless, her bill soon took on a significance she had never intended.

On July 20, at a hearing before the House Judiciary Subcommittee on Immigration, Zhao Haiqing and his organization, the Federation of Chinese Students, gave a ringing endorsement to the Pelosi bill, arguing that many of the students who had supported the Tiananmen demonstrations would be in political jeopardy if they returned to China. "We do not seek to remain as guests in your country merely because we faced repression when we left," Zhao told the committee. "Rather, it is in large part because we have been guests in your country that we face repression when we return."

Richard Williams, the head of the State Department's China desk, did not oppose Zhao or the Pelosi bill. He stated that the continuing, nation-wide crackdown in China since June 4 provided "ample reason for the fears and anxieties of Chinese students." As a result, the legislation to sup-port the students won quick approval from the subcommittee.[4] By the fall, the bill was moving through the full committee and headed for the floor of the House of Representatives.

By this time, the students were fully mobilized. They had won the help and support of some young congressional staff members; in the office of House Majority Leader Richard Gephardt, for example, an ambitious young staff aide named George Stephanopoulos became one of the students' closest allies on Capitol Hill.

The students also attracted experienced Washington lawyers to their cause. A Chinese intern at the firm of Arent Fox Kintner Plotkin & Kahn persuaded his superiors to represent the students on a pro bono basis. When in Washington, Zhao Haiqing made phone calls and granted interviews while working out of Arent Fox's plush offices on Connecti-cut Avenue.

More importantly, the students were also making political use of their computerized network to an extent that was, at that time, unprece-dented. Students in Boston or Los Angeles, or for that matter rural Maine or Montana, were able to keep track of the progress of the Pelosi legisla-tion, learning the details of every small step in Washington within hours after the events. At one point, Zhao discovered that he had a problem with Lamar Smith, the head of a House subcommittee on immigration. He sent out an appeal over the computer network to Chinese students, and within a day, Smith's congressional office was besieged with several hundred phone calls, many of them from within his district, urging him to change his mind.[5]

The Bush administration had little idea of what was happening with the Pelosi bill. During this period, Bush and his senior advisers—always more attuned to the elite world of foreign affairs than to the progress of domestic legislation—were devoting their attention to the strategic aspects of American policy toward China, such as the trips to Beijing planned for the fall of 1989 by Richard Nixon and Henry Kissinger. Administration officials were still operating on an assumption about China policy that had proved valid at the time of the Nixon opening and its aftermath: If the White House took the lead, Congress would eventu-ally go along.

One night Jeffrey Bader, the deputy director of the China desk, wrote a rare "overnight memo" to the White House—a brief internal message about something so important that it should be called to the president's attention immediately. Bader warned that Pelosi's student legislation was sailing through Congress and might soon be approved. At that point, Bader discovered that Bush, Scowcroft and White House Chief of Staff John Sununu didn't know what the Pelosi bill was.[6]

Formally, the administration had taken the position during the summer hearings and the early autumn that it was not opposed to the Pelosi bill. At the time, it hadn't taken the measure seriously. But when administration officials looked more carefully at the legislation in the late autumn, they were strongly against it for several reasons.

The measure was certain to antagonize the Chinese leadership, which had originally permitted the students to come to America with the understanding that they would return home to work in China. From the standpoint of Beijing, the requirement that the students return home also served to inhibit their political activities while in America—since they would know they could be punished after returning to China if they were too outspoken overseas. Second, administration officials feared that the legislation, if enacted, might jeopardize future educational exchanges between China and the United States.

Finally, although administration officials never made this argument in public, they felt it was in America's strategic interest to have the students return home. The underlying rationale for bringing the students to America in the first place had been to help educate a core of future leaders in Beijing, who would be familiar with and therefore perhaps sympathetic to the United States. Just as Chinese Premier Li Peng's beliefs in central planning reflected to some extent his training in the Soviet Union, American officials had hoped that a future generation of American-educated leaders would take back to China the values and beliefs they had learned in the United States.[7]

Suddenly, in mid-November 1989, as the Pelosi bill was about to come up on the floor of the House of Representatives, the administration tried to kill it. Abandoning their earlier position, White House and State Department officials argued that its passage could bring an end to future education exchanges between the United States and China.

For the first time, the administration was forced to confront how little public and congressional support existed for its China policy. University presidents and other American education officials rushed to support the cause of the Chinese students, who constituted a sizable, if not irreplaceable, segment of their graduate programs and laboratories. With their computer network, the students were able to attract grassroots support. "I represent Texas A&M, which has over 300 Chinese students,"

President Richard Nixon stops in Hawaii while en route to China in February 1972. Behind him stands his wife, Pat, and Secretary of State William Rogers. In Hawaii, Nixon wrote down his thoughts and plans for the secret diplomacy to be conducted in China. *AP/Wide World Photos*

National Security Advisor Henry Kissinger toasts Premier Chou Enlai during the state dinner on Nixon's 1972 trip. *AP/Wide World Photos*

President Richard Nixon talks to Chairman Mao Tsetung at their first and only meeting in February 1972, as Premier Chou Enlai looks on. To Henry Kissinger's left sits his aide Winston Lord, whom Kissinger brought along to occupy the chair that Secretary of State William Rogers would have wanted. *Courtesy of Winston Lord*

Vice-Premier Deng Xiaoping tries out the controls of a space shuttle simulator at the Johnson Space Center in Houston, Texas, during his visit to the United States in early 1979. *AP/Wide World Photos*

President Ronald Reagan and Secretary of State George Shultz toast Chinese Premier Zhao Ziyang *(far right)* in 1984. Behind the president stand the intellectual leaders of two opposing factions on China policy during the Reagan administration: Assistant Secretary of State Paul Wolfowitz *(left)* and Charles W. Freeman Jr., deputy chief of mission at the U.S. embassy in Beijing. *Courtesy of Paul Wolfowitz*

As ambassador to China, Winston Lord *(with interpreter Jim Brown)* addresses an outdoor gathering at Beijing University in June 1988. Shortly after this event China's leader, Deng Xiaoping, sent a warning to Lord that he shouldn't have spoken to the Chinese students. *AP/Wide World Photos*

Barbara Bush and Betty Bao Lord tour the rock garden at the Forbidden City during President George Bush's February 1989 visit to Beijing. Although the two women were smiling, their husbands were at odds over how America should deal with China. *AP/Wide World Photos*

Chinese soldiers with automatic rifles parade in front of the American embassy in Beijing following the Tiananmen massacre in June 1989. At that time, China's leading dissident, Fang Lizhi, was living in another embassy building. The armed guards were removed after Richard Nixon visited Beijing and told Chinese officials, "I find this repugnant." *AP/Wide World Photos*

Brent Scowcroft, President Bush's national security advisor, toasts Chinese Foreign Minister Qian Qichen in December 1989. The pictures of this toast brought forth an upsurge in public and congressional criticism of the Bush administration's policy of reconciliation with China. *AP/Wide World Photos*

Nancy Pelosi, the congresswoman from San Francisco, appears at a press conference in January 1990 with Zhao Haizing, the leading congressional lobbyist and spokesman for Chinese students. After sponsoring legislation to let Chinese students stay in the United States, Pelosi emerged as the Democratic Party's leading critic of the Bush administration's China policy. *Congressional office of Nancy Pelosi*

U.S. ambassador to China James R. Lilley is greeted by Chinese Communist Party leader Jiang Zemin. *Courtesy of James R. Lilley*

Fang Lizhi, China's leading proponent of democracy, took refuge inside the American embassy in Beijing for more than a year after the Tiananmen massacre. Here, Fang, dressed in an American embassy T-shirt, poses with Ambassador James R. Lilley and their wives, Sally Lilley and Li Shuxian. *Courtesy of James R. Lilley*

In the midst of the 1992 presidential campaign, President Bush visits a General Dynamics factory in Fort Worth, Texas, and announces that he will open the way for Taiwan to buy American-made F-16 warplanes. Workers at the plant had been complaining that the restrictions on arms sales to Taiwan were costing jobs in Texas. *Rodger Mallison / Forth Worth Star-Telegram*

President Bill Clinton signs his 1993 executive order linking trade and human rights in the presence of Senate Majority Leader George Mitchell and Representative Nancy Pelosi. The order required China to make a series of changes if it wanted to renew its most-favored-nation trade benefits the following year. When China didn't meet the conditions, Clinton abandoned the order. *White House photograph*

Taiwan President Lee Teng-hui receives an award as a distinguished alumnus of Cornell University. Lee's 1995 visit to the United States was the first one ever made by any president of Taiwan; China reacted with outrage. *AP/Wide World Photos*

Republican Representative Joe Barton said in one speech on the House floor. "We must do all we can to protect the Chinese students."[8]

Despite the administration's opposition, the House of Representatives voted 403 to 0 to approve Pelosi's bill, and the Senate passed the measure by a voice vote a day later. Bush then vetoed the bill. To prevent Congress from overriding his veto, however, the president also announced that, through his own executive order, he would grant the students the same legal protection that they would have received from Pelosi's legislation—a waiver of the requirement that they must return to China after finishing their studies in the United States.

Thus, in his handling of the student bill, the president managed to jeopardize congressional backing for his larger China policy and to give Democrats an issue to use against him, without gaining anything tangible in return. He had demonstrated to Beijing that it could count on his support against Congress, but that in practical terms, this support might not count for much. After Bush announced that he would, on his own, give new legal protection to Chinese students, the regime lodged a bitter protest—contending, plausibly, that Bush's executive order seemed to bring about the same result that Pelosi's bill, if enacted, would have. The Chinese government and people cannot "swallow this bitter pill," declared Vice Foreign Minister Liu Huaqiu.[9]

The skirmishing over the student legislation was a milestone, the first manifestation of the new dynamics that would affect American policy toward China throughout the coming years. The legislative battle lines were being drawn. On one side were the administration and the Chinese government, in an uncomfortable partnership aimed at avoiding changes in the relationship that had been built up before 1989. On the other side were members of Congress, led by (but not confined to) the opposition Democrats.

Pelosi was only a second-term member, and her bill had not been designed, at the outset, as a broad-based challenge to Bush's China policy. But the administration had elevated the importance of her bill, increased Pelosi's own interest in China, and, in the process, won considerable publicity for the congresswoman, who soon began to think about other ways in which she could raise China as an issue in Congress.

So, too, the contretemps over the Pelosi bill underlined for the Democratic leadership for the first time the possibilities of invoking China as a political issue against Bush. Republican members of Congress were agonizing at being asked to cast votes for the China policy of their own president.

George Mitchell immediately proclaimed Bush's veto of the China legislation to be "a grave mistake." The president, Mitchell said, "has made it easier for the Chinese government to succeed in its campaign of intimidation to silence the students' cry for democracy in China." [10] Such criticism was merely a harbinger of what was to come.

UNDERLYING THESE political conflicts lay some fundamental, though rarely articulated, disagreements about what America should do about China in the aftermath of the Tiananmen crackdown.

Bush, Scowcroft and others in the administration continued to operate on the assumption that American policy should and would return to the essential outlines of what it had been in the many years between the Nixon opening and 1989. That policy was guided by the strategic concerns of the Cold War, and these had not changed: China remained a large, powerful country and a crucial partner in American efforts to restrain the Soviet Union.

To Bush, the Tiananmen crackdown was only a bump in the road in China's overall progress. He made this plain in his formal message vetoing the Pelosi bill. "I believe that China, as its leaders state, will return to the policy of reform pursued before June 3," the president wrote. "I further believe that the Chinese visitors [to America] would wish to return to China in those circumstances." [11]

By contrast, to critics of Bush's policy and to large segments of the public as well, the Tiananmen upheavals showed that America's partnership with the Chinese regime before 1989 had been far too friendly and uncritical. In this view, there could be and should be no return to the close relationship between America and China that had existed before the Tiananmen crackdown; the earlier strategic partnership between Washington and Beijing had been based upon false assumptions that China was gradually opening up its political as well as its economic system.

What Bush failed to recognize was that the earlier China policies had always rested implicitly on public support. However much noise the Washington friends of Taiwan might make from time to time, the American public had been willing to normalize relations with the People's Republic of China. Nixon had skillfully nursed along that support, defusing the right wing in the process; all of his successors, too, had gone to great lengths to maintain a domestic base in America for their policies toward China.

Without this bedrock of public backing, America's cozy, secretive, elite-based partnership with China could not have been established in the first place. Now, after the Tiananmen crackdown, Bush was seeking to reestablish the old relationship with China at a time when he had little or no approval from the country to do so.

The rules for dealing with China were changing. Not only the Bush administration, but congressional leaders, too, discovered in the aftermath of the Tiananmen massacre that the old ways of operating got them into serious political trouble.

In the summer of 1989, a senior member of the House Foreign Affairs Committee, Republican Representative Robert J. Lagomarsino of California, quietly lobbied the State Department to grant a small company in his district an exemption from the administration's post-Tiananmen ban on the sale of military equipment to China. The company, Quintron Systems, had signed a $2 million contract to sell advanced television surveillance systems to the trading arm of the Chinese military. At the time of Lagomarsino's request, Chinese television was still broadcasting film of the Tiananmen protesters that had been taken by more primitive surveillance systems.

Lagomarsino was persistent. He even telephoned Deputy Secretary of State Lawrence Eagleburger to see if there might be a way around the sanctions. He was turned down, and word of his lobbying effort leaked to the press. "I can't imagine anything more offensive to a large number of Americans," explained one State Department official.

It was, for Lagomarsino, a costly mistake. Three years later, he lost his congressional seat when a wealthy challenger named Michael Huffington defeated him in a Republican primary; Huffington's principal campaign issue, the subject of numerous television and newspaper advertisements, was Lagomarsino's attempt to help sell surveillance systems to China.[12]

IN EARLY December 1989, Bush made his second political mistake on China policy, one that proved to be more costly and enduring than his belated attempt to kill the Chinese student bill. He decided to send Scowcroft and Eagleburger to China for the second time.

This second Scowcroft trip had been planned for weeks. It represented to some extent the work of Richard Nixon and Henry Kissinger, the two founding fathers of the modern-day American relationship with China. By some accounts, Nixon and Kissinger had also worked behind the scenes in advising Bush on the first Scowcroft mission the previous July.[13]

During the fall of 1989, Nixon and Kissinger had made separate trips to Beijing. Neither was formally representing the administration, but both were talking to and working closely with the White House, particularly Scowcroft. Both were testing the waters to see if they could restore some version of the strategic relationship they had forged nearly two decades earlier. Both sought to tell Chinese leaders how the Tiananmen crackdown was undercutting China's support in the United States.

The Nixon trip was the more important of the two. The former president met for an hour and a half with Deng Xiaoping, and saw the rest of China's leaders as well. Saying he was speaking more in sorrow than in anger, Nixon, the American most respected in Beijing, reminded the Chinese he was a politician, and then bluntly told them how strong the feelings about the Tiananmen Square crackdown were in America.

In one of the Beijing sessions, Nixon told the Chinese he had just been at the American embassy and had seen a phalanx of security men ringing the compound outside, carrying guns. This menacing detail had been stationed there after Fang Lizhi had taken refuge inside the embassy. "I find this repugnant," Nixon told the Chinese. Not long after Nixon left, the security detail disappeared from the embassy's perimeter.[14]

Nixon brought back to the Bush White House a message from the Chinese leadership. The Chinese held out the prospect that they were ready to be accommodating on some of the outstanding issues dividing Washington and Beijing; at the same time, they made clear that they also had some things they wanted from the United States. This Nixon initiative gave Bush the idea to send Scowcroft and Eagleburger to China once again.[15]

WHAT DID the administration want from this second Scowcroft mission? By this time, in the last months of 1989, Bush was looking for a broad accommodation with China, one that would both resolve a series of practical problems and restore an amicable working relationship between the two governments. In the half-year since the Tiananmen crackdown and the imposition of sanctions, leaders in both Washington and Beijing had attempted to resume doing quiet business with one another but had run up against a series of obstacles.

The administration was struggling with the consequences of its own sanctions. In July, the president had to approve a special waiver of his ban on sales of military equipment in order to permit Boeing to sell four commercial jets to China; the navigation systems for these jets had possible military uses and were, therefore, covered by the new sanctions.

In October, the administration quietly eased the impact of its military sanctions by quietly allowing Chinese officials to go back to work at the Grumman plant on Long Island and at Wright-Patterson Air Force Base near Dayton on the $550 million Peace Pearl project to upgrade Chinese fighter planes. The administration got around the June sanctions by decreeing that the ban on providing military equipment or technology to China applied only to the final transfer of the hardware and not to the development work beforehand.[16]

By December, the White House was facing a more serious problem. The sanctions imposed after the crackdown stood in the way of a large and groundbreaking business deal: the proposed export of two satellites from Hughes Aircraft to China, which had been approved in the last months of the Reagan administration. The Chinese government had agreed to launch these satellites for Australian and Hong Kong companies, the first time any Communist regime had entered the commercial satellite business. However, because the satellites had potential military uses, their export was blocked by the American sanctions. Both Hughes and the Australian government had been lobbying the Bush administration to ease the sanctions enough to allow the deal to go forward. They were pushing for a decision before the end of the year.[17]

These problems with the sanctions were only the beginning of a long list of items the administration wanted to discuss with China. Politically, it wanted to persuade the Chinese regime to lift martial law, an action that would enable Bush to demonstrate to Congress that the repression inside China was easing. American officials also wanted China to stop jamming the Voice of America; in May, after the imposition of martial law, Chinese officials had begun blocking transmissions for the first time since the establishment of diplomatic relations in 1979.[18]

In addition, the administration was desperate to find some way of getting Fang Lizhi out of China. Fang had been transferred from inside Lilley's home to what had been a small nursing station on the grounds outside, but he remained confined inside the embassy compound, as he had been for the previous six months.

Fang's presence in the compound had become by far the greatest single source of tension between the two governments. The dispute was, at times, almost comic. In October 1989, Chinese Vice Foreign Minister Liu Huaqiu summoned Lilley to demand that the embassy cancel its Halloween costume party because some Americans had been joking about wearing Fang Lizhi masks. China was afraid the Americans might use the cover of the costumes to try to sneak Fang out of the embassy.

Lilley, dressed in jeans on a Saturday morning, told Liu that Washington would be "rolling in the aisles" to hear of China's latest protest and the Halloween party went ahead as scheduled. However, China's fears about an American attempt to spirit Fang out of the country were not entirely groundless: Baker acknowledged in his memoirs that Lilley had on at least one occasion suggested this possibility.[19]

There are some indications that obtaining Fang's release was one of the main objectives for the second Scowcroft trip. Inside the embassy compound, while Scowcroft was in China, a U.S. official instructed Fang and his wife to pack their bags and be prepared to leave the country on short notice. After Scowcroft departed, the disappointed official told Fang his situation had not been resolved.[20]

For its part, China, too, sought several objectives from Scowcroft's December mission. The leadership was deeply in need of recognition and respect. In the months since the June crackdown, presidents and prime ministers throughout the developed world had canceled their trips to China. On October 1, at the celebrations for the 40th anniversary of Mao Tsetung's founding of the People's Republic of China, the only American willing to stand on the podium with Chinese leaders was Alexander Haig, the former secretary of state, a man who had never seemed bothered by the massacre and who, more than any other American official of the modern era, viewed a close relationship with China's Communist regime as an end in itself.

China also wanted approval for the export of the Hughes satellites and an easing of the American sanctions. It hoped for assurances that Bush would work to make sure that his veto of the Pelosi student legislation was not overridden in Congress. Most importantly, China wanted the administration to lift the freeze on World Bank loans; the inability to borrow new money from overseas had, in the months after the June crackdown, contributed to a dramatic slowing of the economy.

While each government had its specific goals, ultimately both of them seemed to be seeking something broader—that is, a return to the relationship that had existed between the two countries before the assault upon the demonstrators.

This second Scowcroft trip would later be called "secret" by its critics in America, but this characterization was not entirely accurate. Unlike the first, truly clandestine Scowcroft trip the previous July, the December mission was meant to be kept secret only in its beginning stages, before Scowcroft and his delegation landed in China. From that point onward, the trip was clearly intended for public consumption: It was designed to change public opinion, to galvanize the American people into realizing that the United States needed to keep on doing business with China— much as the Kissinger and Nixon trips in 1971–72 had been intended to spur Americans into recognizing the necessity of acknowledging China's existence.

"It [the Scowcroft trip] sends a political signal that we are now ready to resume relations on a more normal basis," one official told the *New York Times* the day after the mission was announced. "We hope that we have reached the point where time heals all wounds, and that once the public gets used to more normalized contacts, it won't be focused on the past." [21]

In other words, Bush sent Scowcroft to China the second time in part because he thought the American public was ready, six months after the June crackdown, to let bygones be bygones. In this respect, he badly misjudged the mood of the country.

Scowcroft and Eagleburger landed in China on December 11. Their delegation also included Lilley, the American ambassador; Douglas Paal, Scowcroft's China expert; and Chase Untermeyer, the White House personnel director. The inclusion of Untermeyer demonstrated how much the president wanted to show Chinese leaders that the purpose of the mission extended beyond routine business. Untermeyer was one of the president's oldest and most loyal aides: He had begun to work for Bush during his 1966 congressional campaign in Texas. One of his tasks was to contact an old friend, Yang Jiechi of the Chinese Foreign Ministry (who had gotten to know Bush and Untermeyer during their 1977 tour of China), and deliver a personal message from Bush. The assignment underscored Bush's belief in the power of personal relationships to overcome policy differences.[22]

During their two days in Beijing, the members of the Scowcroft delegation saw all of China's highest-ranking officials, including Deng. They also had time for a banquet with Chinese leaders, which produced the enduring image of the trip. Photographs transmitted to America showed Scowcroft clinking glasses with a smiling, satisfied Foreign Minister Qian Qichen and other Chinese officials.

In a toast delivered at the same banquet, Scowcroft seemed to suggest the United States was ready to let pass the events of Tiananmen Square. "We believe it is important that we not exhaust ourselves in placing blame for problems that exist," he declared. He also appeared to be proposing a partnership between the Bush administration and Chinese leaders against their domestic critics—thus seeming to equate hard-line forces in China with the administration's critics at home. "In both our societies, there are voices of those who seek to redirect or frustrate our cooperation," Scowcroft said. "We must both take bold measures to redirect these negative forces."[23]

Many of the ideas incorporated in this banquet toast had come from Lilley and others at the American embassy. Lilley thought he was following some advice offered many years earlier by America's most renowned China scholar, John K. Fairbank. When you're dealing with China, Fairbank had said, you shouldn't be put in the position of becoming either an enemy or a best friend; instead, you should always reject the two extremes and take the middle road.

Several years later, Lilley admitted that at the time of the Scowcroft mission, he had no idea of the degree of public outrage in America about the Tiananmen massacre. He had supported Scowcroft's trip, though he felt his advice wouldn't have mattered; Bush and Scowcroft were going to go ahead with the mission, no matter what he said. Still, from the distance of Beijing, Lilley had no concept of the domestic politics involved.

The White House was supposed to know the pulse of the country, to know what American people would and wouldn't support. With years of hindsight, Lilley reflected that the Bush administration had mishandled the Scowcroft trip. Senior officials within the administration really hadn't talked enough beforehand about the wisdom and ramifications of the mission.[24]

Just before Scowcroft left for Beijing, Lilley had talked privately in Washington with Paul Wolfowitz, who was then serving in the administration as undersecretary of defense. Wolfowitz didn't know about the mission until Lilley informed him. "Do you think it's a good idea?" Wolfowitz asked the ambassador. "I don't."

Wolfowitz was not alone in his unease. One of the officials asked to work on the secret preparations for the second mission remembers being surprised at what the administration was about to do. The trip seemed to run directly contrary to the ban on high-level contacts with China. We'd better get something good in return, the official remembers thinking to himself; the only thing that could possible make this worthwhile is if Fang Lizhi comes out of China on the plane with Scowcroft.[25]

Even before Scowcroft and his aides returned home from Beijing, the mission was greeted with criticism in America. Over the following days, Bush defended the trip by pointing to some of the tangible results that had been obtained. The president said that Scowcroft had obtained assurances that China would not sell its new M-9 missiles in the Middle East. That explanation was roundly denounced: Even the most dispassionate China scholars pointed out that this was merely a new version of the assurances China had given over the previous 18 months. "How many times do we get that concession?" asked Harry Harding of the Brookings Institution.[26]

In fact, it quickly became clear that Bush and his foreign policy team had made a political miscalculation. The Scowcroft trip solidified the opposition to Bush's China policy. Americans did not want to return to a normal relationship with China; or at least they were not ready to do so six months after they had seen tanks on the streets of Beijing.

Bush had not consulted Congress before sending Scowcroft and Eagleburger. He had not prepared the press or the public for the announcement of the mission. He had hoped to follow the model of Kissinger's trip to Beijing for Nixon in 1971—but the reaction was far different this time, primarily because Congress, the press and the American public were not ready to support what the president wanted to do.

The contrast to Nixon's political handling of the opening to China is striking. Nixon had quietly prepared the way with Congress for nearly two years before the Kissinger trip of 1971. The public had been treated to a series of lesser steps, such as "ping-pong" diplomacy. Kissinger's trip had merely confirmed that American policy toward China was, in fact, going in the direction that previous public signs indicated it was heading. Scowcroft's second trip was made with far less political preparation, and it showed that American policy was heading in the opposite direction from that which the sanctions and other public pronouncements had indicated. Kissinger had traveled to a country with which Americans were fascinated; Scowcroft was doing business with a regime whose conduct only six months earlier had shocked and infuriated the American people.

In Congress, George Mitchell denounced the mission as "an embarrassing kowtowing to a repressive Communist government." Republican leaders, by contrast, were at best lukewarm in their support; Senate Minority Leader Bob Dole backed Bush, but others, including House Republican Whip Newt Gingrich, spoke out against the China policy.

The press coverage was scathing. "The President should not be making placatory concessions to a repressive and bloodstained Chinese government," declared the *Washington Post*. "Mr. Bush failed to grasp the most hard-headed point of all: Beijing's present rulers need his approval far more than he needs their strategic help," said the *New York Times*.[27]

Most of the critical editorials and commentary made the point that the administration did not need to send high-level officials to Beijing; the government could have transacted whatever business needed to be done on a lower level. The critics invariably observed that the Scowcroft mission ran counter to Bush's apparent ban on high-level visits announced the previous June.

At first, the critics reacted only to the December mission. Less than a week after Scowcroft's return, however, CNN broke the news that Scowcroft and Eagleburger had made a trip in July, less than two weeks after the sanctions were imposed.

That disclosure intensified the furor. Democratic leaders by now clearly realized the depth of popular unhappiness with Bush's policy, and moved to capitalize on it. "President Bush has demonstrated yet again that he doesn't see the connection between human lives, human rights and an effective foreign policy," said Democratic National Committee Chairman Ron Brown—who later, as President Clinton's secretary of commerce, would reverse course and favor close American ties with Beijing.

AMID THE outcry over Bush's China policy came unprecedented criticism from a new and unusual source: the recently retired American ambassador to Beijing. On December 19, the *Washington Post* carried an article by Winston Lord on its op-ed page entitled "Misguided Mission." It was a frontal attack on the Scowcroft mission and the logic behind it.

"Let us conduct necessary business with the Beijing authorities in workmanlike fashion, not with fawning emissaries," Lord wrote. He argued that the trip would hearten only hard-line leaders in Beijing. "They take satisfaction that once again, the foreigner pays tribute," he said. He also challenged the need for Scowcroft's mission from the perspective of Kissinger-style realpolitik; "the geopolitical dimension" of the ties between China and the United States, Lord argued, had changed with the advent of Soviet leader Mikhail Gorbachev. "Beijing needs to worry more about fast-moving U.S.-Soviet relations than Washington does about Sino-Soviet relations," Lord asserted.[28]

Lord's article was, in its own way, a watershed. It demonstrated that not only had the bipartisan consensus in Congress over China policy shattered, but that there were intense disagreements within the foreign policy elite, too. Lord had not only been America's top representative in Beijing for most of the previous four years, he had also been Henry Kissinger's right-hand man. He had participated in the history of the American opening to China to an even greater extent than Bush or Scowcroft.

Despite the contretemps with the White House over the Fang Lizhi dinner invitation in early 1989, Lord had not, until that article, publicly opposed the administration's policy toward China. His willingness to speak out bolstered the credibility of the critics. With Lord on their side, they could not be accused of a lack of sophistication about foreign policy or an ignorance of the history of Sino-American relations.

The following month, when the Senate Judiciary Committee held hearings on the possibility of overriding Bush's veto of the Pelosi legislation, the star witness was Winston Lord. Lord declared: "The veto, if sustained, would reinforce the mind-set and the mandate of those who have proceeded from massacre to repression; those who predict America will be lulled by cosmetic gestures and return to business-as-usual; those who dismiss the Chinese as a people apart from the global winds of change."[29]

It was the beginning of Lord's three years as a foreign policy mandarin in exile. He became perhaps the most improbable dissident in America—an innately respectful and circumspect individual whose entire career had been spent in the federal government and the Council on Foreign Relations. In public speeches and on television, Lord talked in the idiom of foreign policy and strategy. He hedged virtually every statement with qualifiers ("this is not to say . . . " "to be sure"), as if he were guarding against attackers from all directions. Once, speaking to a forum on China at Johns Hopkins University, he confessed self-mockingly, "I don't speak with passion, my wife does."

In some instances, Winston Lord, the reincarnated champion of human rights in China, staked out positions directly contrary to the ones he had espoused in earlier years. As ambassador in the 1980s, he had regularly insisted that there was no "double standard" in America's different treatment of human rights issues in China and the Soviet Union, its seeming eagerness to attack Soviet repression and to ignore similar conduct by the Chinese regime. The situation inside China appeared to be better than that across the border in the Soviet Union, Lord had sometimes argued while he was ambassador. He had also contended that human rights problems in China should be handled through quiet diplomacy rather than in public. "Human rights cannot dominate our relations with any country," he told one reporter as he was ending his tour as ambassador in Beijing. "Remember, the Chinese human rights situation is infinitely better now than it was 15 years ago."[30]

Now, beginning in December 1989, Lord confessed that he had for years given the wrong answer on the question of a double standard. Yes, a double standard *had* long existed in America's disparate policies toward Moscow and Beijing, he now admitted, but for good reason: China had not been a threat to the United States in the way that the Soviet Union was.[31]

To Lord, this was merely a conceptual reformulation—a new logic that would still have led (before 1989) to the same result: American policies that favored China over the Soviet Union. Left unsaid was the fact that by acknowledging the existence of a "double standard," Lord was also changing his interpretation of what the political situation had been in China and the Soviet Union, the world's two main Communist powers.

For years, the American people had been told by the country's top officials, including Lord, that the Soviet regime was far more repressive than was China. Now, Lord was recanting. He was admitting, in effect, that in the interests of what he called geopolitics, America's leaders had given the public a distorted picture of political reality in the world's biggest nation, the Soviet Union, and in the world's most populous nation, China.

CHAPTER TWELVE

Stirrings of a New Decade

A T THE BEGINNING OF 1990, American policy toward China appeared to be running on inertia. The Bush administration was seeking to restore a close working relationship with the Chinese leadership primarily because of the momentum that had been generated during the previous two decades. Just as a quarter-century earlier America had failed to adjust its foreign policy to take account of the Sino-Soviet split, so now the United States clung to a China policy forged during the latter stages of the Cold War, despite changes in both Moscow and Beijing.

The situation called for a reexamination of the fundamental assumptions underlying America's China policy—the same sort of reexamination that Richard Nixon and Henry Kissinger conducted during Nixon's first administration. Yet there was no sign of any such questioning. Indeed, Nixon and Kissinger themselves—both influential at high levels of the Bush administration—had by 1990 become powerful conservative forces, proponents of preserving the old special relationship with China. Both were eager to ensure that their greatest foreign policy triumph should be preserved.

In the months following the Tiananmen Square crackdown, those who sought to justify a reestablishment of ties with Beijing once again revived the arguments of the Cold War, warning that China might still prove to be an invaluable partner for America in dealing with the Soviet Union. "The United States needs China as a possible counterweight to Soviet aspirations in Asia," Kissinger warned in July 1989.[1] Such arguments seemed increasingly out of place at a time when Mikhail Gorbachev was trying ever harder to work out a new accommodation with the United States.

At the end of 1989, the Cold War rationale for restoring the old China relationship collapsed with the fall of the Berlin Wall and the downfall of the Communist regimes in Eastern Europe. These events had a profound impact in both Washington and Beijing. For China's leaders, the revolutions in Eastern Europe exacerbated the sense of unease and paranoia that had existed since the time of the Tiananmen demonstrations. They showed that Communist leaders could be overthrown, either by popular uprisings or, worse, as in Romania, by their own security forces.

In America, the events of late 1989 virtually eliminated the fear of Soviet domination of Western Europe, demonstrating conclusively that Gorbachev represented a dramatic change from his predecessors. For American policy toward China, the consequences were profound: The United States did not need China to counterbalance a Soviet threat. Moreover, the proof in Eastern Europe that Communist governments might be toppled from power heartened those Americans who did not want to do business with the Chinese leadership.

At the beginning of 1990, the Bush administration was struggling to come up with new, non–Cold War justifications for preserving strong ties with the Chinese government. Yet these efforts only raised more problems. During one press conference, the president seemed to suggest that the United States needed China as a counterweight not to the Soviet Union but to the growing power of Japan—a theme that had been raised a few months earlier by Kissinger. Japan, however, was a nonnuclear democracy and America's closest ally in Asia. The notion that the United States had to prop up China, a nuclear-armed Communist regime, against a country with which it had a military alliance was subsequently disavowed by administration officials.[2]

On February 7, Lawrence Eagleburger was dispatched to testify before the Senate Foreign Relations Committee on the administration's policy toward China. It was the first time any official had appeared before Congress to answer questions about China policy in a half year, and also the first testimony about Bush's decision to send the two Scowcroft missions to Beijing.

Eagleburger's testimony was a landmark. The administration now conceded that the anti-Soviet rationale that had driven American policy toward China for the previous two decades had all but disappeared. "We all recognize that the dramatic reforms occurring in Eastern Europe and the Soviet Union have altered the strategic scene," Eagleburger told the committee. The Cold War basis for a strong U.S. relationship with China, Eagleburger said, was still "marginally important, but the changes in the Soviet Union and Eastern Europe are so fundamental . . . it is not by any means a dominant or controlling factor as it would have been a decade ago."[3]

Instead, the administration, through Eagleburger, advanced new justifications for preserving close American ties with Beijing. "While United States–Soviet tensions may be declining, the strategic value of our relationship with China is not," Eagleburger asserted. He cited, in particular, China's importance in coping with international problems such as "the proliferation of missiles and nuclear weapons, chemical weapons proliferation and environmental pollution."[4]

This strategic formulation was to set the tone for the new American foreign policy toward China in the 1990s. The emphasis was on the weapons of mass destruction—the missiles, nuclear technology and chemical weapons ingredients—that China could sell to other countries, if it chose to do so. The rationale was implicitly negative in its outlook: China was now important to the United States not because of the help it could provide (against the Soviet Union), but because of the potential harm it might do (by exporting missiles and nuclear technology).

The new formulation also established a paradox: China could succeed in demonstrating its strategic importance to the United States by threatening to sell dangerous weapons overseas. If, on the other hand, China *stopped* exporting missiles and other deadly weaponry, it would have less strategic importance to Washington. In other words, the administration's new rationale for its China policy gave Beijing an incentive if not to act in menacing ways, at least always to appear to be on the verge of doing so.

The administration's policy was guided by other considerations as well, though they were not articulated in public. At this time, Bush and his top aides were preoccupied by the upheavals in Europe; they had little time, energy, attention or resources to devote to China. "The whole rest of the world was flying down, straining every resource we had," explained Douglas Paal, the NSC China specialist. "We were not interested in adding China to the list of basket cases. We had no interest in pushing them [China] over the edge."[5]

There was, in fact, a commonplace belief in Washington that the repressive Chinese leadership would not last long. Under this thinking, Premier Li Peng, the devout traditionalist who had summoned the People's Liberation Army into Beijing, and Communist Party General Secretary Jiang Zemin, who had been installed to replace Zhao Ziyang after the Tiananmen crackdown, would probably fall from power within a couple of years.

This notion that China's post-Tiananmen leadership was only temporary was put forward by both defenders and opponents of the administration. Some administration officials contended that it made no sense to try to confront or seek changes from the Chinese leadership, because the regime was not going to survive. According to this argument, it didn't matter whether the Scowcroft mission helped reinforce or perpetuate China's hard-line regime, because it was doomed anyway.

In 1990–91, senior U.S. intelligence officials, too, were willing to suggest the possibility that China's Communist regime might not endure. During his confirmation hearings to become CIA director, Robert Gates testified that the demise of Communist regimes in Eastern Europe and Moscow had taught the American intelligence community to "think the unthinkable. . . . Clearly we need to be thinking about alternative futures for China as well." [6]

At the same time, critics of Bush's policies contended that it was not worthwhile for the administration to conduct serious business with China's leaders, because they would fall from power before too long. "The current discredited regime is clearly a transitional one," wrote Winston Lord in *Foreign Affairs.* Testifying in Congress at the beginning of 1990, Lord predicted that within three years, "there will be a more moderate, humane government in Beijing." [7] That assumption was wrong, but at the time, it was prevalent on both sides of the debate over American policy toward China.

OVER THE weekend of January 6–7, 1990, the leaders of the Chinese student movement and their political allies in Washington came together for a conference at Harvard University's Fairbank Center to talk about their goals and tactics. It was, as it turned out, a fateful meeting.

Zhao Haiqing and approximately 35 other student representatives took part, along with their unpaid American political adviser John Sasso, who had been the manager of Michael Dukakis's unsuccessful presidential campaign in 1988. Joining them were about ten congressional staff members, including George Stephanopoulos, the young aide to Senate Majority Leader Richard Gephardt. The sole member of Congress present was Nancy Pelosi, the sponsor of the legislation guaranteeing Chinese students the right to remain in the United States. [8]

The meeting had been called to talk about Pelosi's student bill. Although Bush had vetoed the bill, a congressional vote was scheduled for later in the month on whether to override the veto. Yet the participants realized that the fight over the student bill would end, in one fashion or another, within a few weeks.

Thus, during the meetings at Harvard and the social gatherings at the nearby Charles Hotel, the talk turned to what should happen next. Was there some other vehicle through which to keep Congress's attention focused upon China? Was there some other tool that could be used to further the causes of human rights and political change?

Gradually, the answer emerged: The next target should be China's most-favored-nation (MFN) trade status. Some of the students had been pressing since the June crackdown for the use of economic sanctions as leverage against China. Moreover, when he was lobbying for the student legislation during the fall of 1989, Zhao Haiqing had found that sympathetic congressional staff members had also suggested casually the idea of economic sanctions against Beijing. At the Harvard meetings, the participants for the first time zeroed in on MFN benefits as the most far-reaching of all the possible economic sanctions that could be imposed against China.

China's MFN benefits were the very core of the economic relationship between the two countries. With MFN status, China could trade with the United States on the same basis as virtually every other nation in the world; without MFN benefits, Chinese products would be subject to duties so prohibitively high that it would be difficult, if not impossible, to sell them in the United States.

In the decade since Congress had first approved Jimmy Carter's extension of MFN status to China in 1980, those trade benefits had been renewed over and over again without debate, to the point where they were taken for granted. Nevertheless, China, as a Communist country, was still subject to the provisions of the Jackson-Vanik Amendment, the law requiring that the president formally renew the benefits each year; Congress could reject this presidential decision, if it chose to do so.

The deadline for presidential action was in June each year. In the immediate aftermath of the Tiananmen massacre, China's MFN benefits had been quietly renewed for another year, largely because no one had thought to mount a challenge. Zhao later said that until the end of 1989 he hadn't even known what the letters MFN stood for.[9]

By this time, few in Washington could even remember the controversies of the 1970s, in which the United States, after years of debate, had finally decided to extend MFN status to China while denying it to the Soviet Union. Fewer could have explained why Washington maintained this favoritism for Beijing over Moscow after Gorbachev's reforms and the Tiananmen crackdown.

Indeed, during one visit to Washington, Gorbachev accused the United States of sheer hypocrisy in its MFN policies. When Senate Minority Leader Bob Dole warned that the United States might not grant MFN benefits to the Soviet Union unless Moscow eased its menacing policies in the Baltics, the Soviet president erupted in fury.

"You have given MFN to China after Tiananmen," Gorbachev told

Dole. "What are we supposed to do, declare presidential rule [that is, declare martial law] in Lithuania?"[10]

None of those at the Harvard conference could have recognized the long-term consequences of their decision to target China's MFN benefits. None was aware that they were starting a series of annual legislative battles that would continue through most of the decade and would prove far more enduring that the Chinese student movement itself.

In Washington two weeks later, Congress took up the issue on whether to override Bush's veto of Pelosi's student bill. It was a largely symbolic vote; the president had already granted the Chinese students the same legal protection that was offered in the legislation. Nevertheless, the bill gave members of Congress their first chance to take a public stand on Bush's China policy since the Scowcroft trip. The House voted 390 to 25 to override Bush, with even House Republican Whip Newt Gingrich deserting the Republican president. The Senate voted 62 to 37 in favor of the override, four votes short of the two-thirds margin necessary for passage of Pelosi's legislation.[11]

Officially, Bush had won the battle. However, these overwhelming congressional votes showed how little support there was in Congress for the way he was dealing with Beijing. Bush's opponents, encouraged, quickly shifted their attention to China's MFN benefits.

In March, Pelosi circulated a letter inviting colleagues to join a new congressional working group on China aimed at opposing Bush's policies. From the outset, this group attracted a bipartisan coalition. Some 30 Democrats and 11 Republicans responded; at their first meeting, the top item on the agenda was what to do about MFN.[12]

Meanwhile, Zhao Haiqing found himself being courted by Democratic senators eager to take on MFN as an issue. In March, Nancy Soderberg, then the foreign policy specialist for Edward M. Kennedy's staff aide, informed Zhao over lunch that Kennedy would be happy to take the lead in sponsoring legislation restricting China's MFN benefits. Soon afterward, Ed King, the staff aide to George Mitchell, told Zhao that *his* boss wanted to take the initiative. Zhao had become skillful enough as a lobbyist to recognize the importance of the Senate majority leader. He held Kennedy at arm's length and began working with Mitchell.[13]

In this earliest skirmish in Congress over China's MFN benefits, the Chinese students—who in later years would vanish as a factor in the annual debates—were a strong influence in Congress. By contrast, the American business community, which would later become the dominant constituency in the MFN argument, was relatively weak. During the first congressional hearings on curbing China's MFN benefits, on May 16, 1990, relatively few American business groups showed up to testify.

To be sure, the Toy Manufacturers of America told Congress that if toymakers had to stop buying from China, "Christmas 1990 would definitely be lost; Christmas 1991 quite possibly would be lost as well." The National Association of Wheat Growers wrote that a revocation of MFN would be "simply too high for U.S. wheat producers to bear." (These efforts by the wheat growers seemed to be well-rewarded. On May 22, the Agriculture Department announced that China had purchased 400,000 metric tons—one of many occasions over the years in which China seemed to time its wheat purchases to coincide with the MFN debate in Washington.) [14]

On the whole, however, the Fortune 500 companies were noticeable by their absence from this first round of the debate. The business community was no doubt caught off guard by the suddenness with which the challenge to MFN status had arisen. Moreover, at the time, the corporate interest in selling to China was far less than it would later become: In the immediate aftermath of the Tiananmen Square upheavals, China carried out an austerity campaign so drastic that industrial growth, in the first quarter of 1990, was zero. The U.S.-China Business Council, the umbrella group for American firms doing business in China, was losing members rapidly and cutting its budget and staff. Many corporate executives, too, were reluctant to lobby for China's MFN benefits, either because they found the Tiananmen Square crackdown to be morally repugnant or because they felt it would be bad public relations to be lobbying for China's trade benefits so soon after the massacre.

Initially, the Chinese students, backed by Mitchell and Pelosi, pressed for outright revocation of China's MFN status. However, a compromise soon emerged, in the form of what was called conditional legislation: Congress would renew China's MFN benefits for a year, but impose a series of human rights conditions that China would have to meet for further renewals. This compromise was pushed forward by Representative Stephen J. Solarz (D-N.Y.), the head of the House Foreign Affairs Subcommittee on Asia, and won the endorsement of Winston Lord. When the Democratic Congress held its first hearing on the possibility of imposing conditions on China's MFN benefits, Lord was the first witness called to testify on behalf of the idea.

This switch to legislation imposing conditions on China's MFN benefits instead of cutting them off entirely was originally tactical in nature. It was aimed at winning support from those in Congress who might be afraid of the consequences of outright revocation, but who wanted to do something about the repression in China. Nevertheless, though the idea represented a short-term compromise, the conditional approach took on a life of its own, with subtle but far-reaching political consequences that would affect China policy over the next few years. The compromise created a political dynamic in which a series of sometimes overt, sometimes subterranean battles would be fought over what the specific legislative conditions should be.

In the next two years, for example, Tibetan organizations put intense pressure on Pelosi to add to her legislation a provision saying that China would have to make improvements in Tibet in order to win renewal of its MFN benefits. Pelosi turned down the request the first year, arguing that the MFN bill should not address special issues like Tibet. But with the support of Senator Daniel Patrick Moynihan, the Tibetan groups were successful a year later in getting a Tibet provision added to the MFN legislation.

Eventually, almost every group and organization with an interest in China policy wanted to be part of the action in drafting the specific MFN conditions. For example, the Bush administration favored having no conditions at all; but if Congress was going to insist upon stipulations, then one part of the government, the United States Information Agency, wanted a provision that would require China to stop jamming the Voice of America.

So, too, Pelosi and the Chinese student leaders had hoped that MFN conditions would focus, specifically and narrowly, on human rights. But in 1991, Senator Joe Biden (D-Del.) insisted that the MFN legislation include some language requiring China to curb its arms proliferation. Pelosi gave in to Biden, explaining to the students that in the Senate, unlike the House, the opposition of a single member could prevent the passage of a bill.[15]

In 1990, the legislation imposing conditions on future renewals attracted widespread support. The House voted 384 to 30 in favor of a bill that would have required the president to certify that China had made progress on human rights before extending MFN benefits for another year. In October, in the final hours of an outgoing Congress, the legislation died when Mitchell declined to call it to the Senate floor. He was, at the time, preoccupied with budget negotiations, but he may also have been accommodating senators who did not relish the prospect of having to cast a vote on MFN status for China.

The dynamics of a new decade were now being established. The MFN issue was becoming the focal point of the efforts by Congress to influence American policy toward China.

AFTER SCOWCROFT'S second visit to China, the Bush administration tried to reach a working accommodation with the leadership in Beijing. At the turn of the new year, the administration took a series of steps aimed at mollifying the Chinese leadership and at showing American goodwill. In exchange, Beijing made a policy concession that the administration had been seeking.

Like Congress, the administration was establishing what was to become a new pattern in dealing with China. The steps that followed the Scowcroft trip were the first in a series of concerted attempts at reconciliation between Washington and Beijing. Several others were to follow, both under Bush and later under Bill Clinton.

These efforts usually ended in disappointment on both sides. Once or twice a year, the United States and China engaged in intense negotiations aimed at ending the friction between them and restoring a working relationship. After each attempt at reconciliation, the climate would sour within months. Officials on both sides discovered that the larger changes they had hoped would follow were not forthcoming, and that the political differences between the two countries pulled them apart once again. It was impossible to return to anything like the relationship that existed before 1989—yet for years, American officials proved unable to recognize this fact.

Scowcroft's early-December trip to Beijing was, of course, itself a substantial White House concession toward the Chinese. On December 19, President Bush took two more steps: He opened the way for the U.S. Export-Import Bank to resume loans to American companies doing business in China, and he approved the export of Hughes Aircraft satellites that were to be launched in China.

These actions were of considerable financial benefit both to China and to companies doing business there. Within weeks, the Export-Import Bank loaned the China National Offshore Oil Corporation $9.75 million to buy engineering services from a New Orleans company, the first such loan since the Tiananmen crackdown.

In the case of the satellites, Bush's action also aided the government of Australia, which was to own the Hughes satellites. The president's action drew strong criticism from Congress, including the future vice president of United States. "This is a fresh insult to the memory of those who died for democracy in Tiananmen Square," said Senator Al Gore.[16]

In addition, the following month, the president eased the freeze on World Bank and other international loans to China—the sanction that had had the most serious impact upon the Beijing leadership. The White House announced that it would open the way, on a case-by-case basis, for World Bank loans to China if these loans were aimed at earthquake relief or other "basic human needs." For the time being, the administration continued to oppose a full-scale resumption of World Bank and other loans to China, but the door had been opened a crack.

In response to these American actions, China took one important step of its own. On January 11, 1990, the regime lifted the martial law that had been imposed upon the city of Beijing the previous May. Premier Li Peng made the announcement, declaring that China had achieved a "great victory" over a "counterrevolutionary rebellion." At the same time, in order to be sure no one got the impression that the regime was easing up, authorities deployed large numbers of police and paramilitary units in Beijing, particularly near Tiananmen Square. One elderly man took the occasion to run up to two police officers at the Monument to the People's Heroes in the center of Tiananmen Square and shout, "The dead cannot be brought back to life, and the living should not die." He was quickly taken away.[17]

By late January 1990, therefore, the Bush administration had sent its national security advisor on a public mission to Beijing, removed two important economic restrictions on American business in China and eased its opposition to World Bank lending there. For its part, China had lifted martial law.[18] The two countries appeared, on the surface, to have entered a period of rapprochement.

Yet this first try at reconciliation proved short-lived. China's official press kept up its anti-American rhetoric, denouncing America as a "hegemonist" power. The jamming of the Voice of America continued. No noticeable change occurred in the political climate inside China.

When Chinese Ambassador Zhu Qizhen, during a private dinner at Nixon's home in New Jersey, urged a wider and speedier resumption of World Bank loans to China, one guest, former Democratic Party Chairman Robert Strauss, rebuffed the envoy. Bush had already gone as far as he could without major changes in Beijing, Strauss said. Nixon told the ambassador he agreed.[19]

Bush himself said in a television interview in March 1990 that despite his efforts, "there hasn't been much give" from the Chinese leadership. Vice President Dan Quayle went further, admitting in public that the results of the Scowcroft mission had been "a disappointment. . . . China refuses to recognize reality, and that's freedom and democracy eventually."[20]

Quayle's words underscored the reason why such efforts at reconciliation foundered. Detailed programmatic concessions—high-level visits or economic concessions on the part of the United States, or limited actions such as prisoner releases on the part of the Chinese—could go only so far. They did not alter the changed political and ideological realities dividing the two countries.

At the time of the opening to China, Nixon and Kissinger had told Chinese leaders that America cared only about China's behavior abroad, not about its policies at home. During Kissinger's secret trip of 1971, when Chou Enlai had sought to talk with him about the Cultural Revolution, Kissinger "demurred that this was China's internal affair," he later wrote. The following year, when Nixon first met Mao Tsetung, he told the Chinese leader: "What brings us together is a recognition of a new situation in the world and a recognition on our part that *what is important is not a nation's internal philosophy*. What is important is its policy toward the rest of the world and toward us" [emphasis added].[21]

After the Tiananmen crackdown, no American president or secretary of state could possibly claim such a disinterested approach to China's domestic policies. Such a position was no longer politically acceptable. As a result, a curious new dynamic took hold. In order to justify conciliatory policies toward China, American leaders frequently attempted to argue that these U.S. efforts would, over the long run, lead to freedom and democracy—or, alternatively, that China's Communist system was doomed to failure. Over the following years, countless other political leaders in the United States voiced sentiments similar to Quayle's. In 1997, President Clinton told a press conference that liberty was bound to come to China, "just as eventually the Berlin Wall fell. . . . I just think it's inevitable."[22]

However, whenever American leaders made such remarks, they merely reinforced suspicions in Beijing that the United States was trying to undermine or overthrow China's Communist system. Indeed, in the aftermath of the Tiananmen Square crackdown, hard-line elements in Beijing argued that America was carrying out a strategy called "peaceful evolution." According to this theory (which the Chinese traced back to John Foster Dulles, Eisenhower's secretary of state), the United States was trying to overthrow Communism not by military means but through softer methods, such as economic, educational and cultural interchanges.

Paradoxically, then, the Chinese sometimes seemed less threatened by their toughest critics in the United States than by their supposed American friends—who were preaching conciliation but also proclaiming that their policies were a more sophisticated way of bringing about the eventual downfall of Chinese Communism.

After each attempted reconciliation, the Chinese watched to see whether the United States was now prepared to accept their Communist system without trying to change it. They were regularly disappointed. American leaders wondered whether their attempts at reconciliation were opening the way for some broader, more fundamental change in China's system—an easing of repression, an end to anti-American rhetoric, a tolerance of dissent. They, too, were more often than not disappointed.

·   ·   ·

THE SCOWCROFT trip had failed to resolve the dispute over the presence of China's leading proponent of democracy, Fang Lizhi, in the American embassy. In June 1990, after a new round of intensive negotiations, the administration finally worked out a deal to permit Fang's departure from China. This arrangement represented the second attempted reconciliation with China by the administration. However, like the Scowcroft trip and its aftermath, the impact proved to be transitory.

The negotiations over Fang's release had centered on three issues.[23] One was China's desire for Fang to sign some form of written confession to wrongdoing. The second was where the dissident would go and what kinds of restrictions would be imposed upon his political activities after leaving China. The third was whether Fang's grown son, Fang Zhe—who was living in Beijing but not inside the American embassy—would leave China with his parents. This last issue was not merely personal, but had political significance; Chinese authorities realized that if Fang Zhe, who was in his 20s, remained behind, Fang Lizhi would likely be more restrained in criticizing the regime from abroad.

The larger question was what China would get in return. The Chinese repeatedly asked the administration to lift all of the sanctions that had been imposed upon China after the Tiananmen massacre, but they were refused.[24]

In the early months of 1990, the Bush administration turned to private channels to try to win Fang's release. Several overseas Chinese volunteered to serve as go-betweens. The administration also secretly sought to work on Fang's release through Trammell Crow, a Dallas real estate developer who was building a large trade center in Shanghai. Crow, who had contributed at least $100,000 to Bush's presidential campaign, had come to know Party Secretary Jiang Zemin when Jiang had been a government minister and mayor of Shanghai. In the aftermath of the Tiananmen crackdown, when Jiang was brought to Beijing as general secretary of the party, Crow had been the first major American businessman to meet with him.[25]

Ultimately, these private efforts foundered, and the Bush administration worked out Fang's release through official government channels. James Lilley conducted a three-sided negotiation. He met daily with China's Deputy Foreign Minister Liu Huaqiu. He talked with Washington over a secure phone line, sometimes to the State Department but also, in the last days, directly to Brent Scowcroft. And he spoke regularly with Fang Lizhi and his wife, who were still living in the nursing clinic.

At one point, Lilley told Liu, "I'm only the mailman for Fang

Lizhi."[26] What he meant was that the U.S. government was merely an intermediary in the talks. That was not entirely true, however. The administration didn't want to pressure Fang to accept a deal he didn't like, but it also had a strong interest in getting him out of the embassy. When Lilley tried to persuade China to release Fang on humanitarian grounds, because of a mild heart murmur, Fang at first balked at the idea. "I don't have a heart problem," he told the ambassador. "No, no," Lilley shot back. "You have a heart problem."

Liu insisted that Fang should not be allowed to become the focus of political opposition to the regime after he left the country. Lilley felt China's underlying fear was that Fang would become a modern-day version of Sun Yat-sen, who at the turn of the century had used his time as an exile in the United States to organize revolutionay activities against the Qing Dynasty.

We don't want you Americans setting up an operation against China behind Fang, Liu told Lilley. We're not going to do that, the ambassador replied, but we can't muzzle him, either. Like everyone else in America, Lilley went on, Fang would be entitled to First Amendment guarantees of free speech.

The most bizarre aspect of the negotiations involved Fang's son. At first, Lilley worked out a tentative deal for the release of Fang and his wife. But in Washington, administration officials insisted that the deal should include Fang Zhe, too—worrying that otherwise, Chinese authorities would use the son as what amounted to a hostage. Lilley dutifully went back and renegotiated for Fang Zhe's departure. Chinese officials complained, but eventually relented and said Fang's son could leave the country. Fang Zhe was put in a safe house run by Chinese security officials to await his departure.

Then a new obstacle emerged: Fang Zhe announced he was in love and wouldn't leave the country until he was married. Moreover, he wanted to bring his new bride out of China with him. That last request was too much for the Chinese. Finally, an arrangement was worked out in which Fang Zhe would be permitted to get married and to leave the country shortly after his parents, while his wife stayed behind.[27]

On June 25 the deal was consummated. Fang Lizhi and his wife, Li Shuxian, were escorted by American officials to the Beijing airport. It was their first time outside the embassy in more than a year. They were put aboard a U.S. Air Force plane specially sent from Japan, and flown to Great Britain, where American officials said Fang would continue his work in astrophysics. China announced that it had allowed Fang to leave the country for medical reasons.[28]

The Bush administration's deal was favorable to Fang. The statement he agreed to sign fell far short of the confession China had been seeking. Fang formally acknowledged that he was opposed to the "four cardinal principles" in the Chinese Constitution—the critical language requiring allegiance to Marxism, socialism, the people's democratic dictatorship and the leadership of the Communist Party. His "admission" thus represented a violation of the Constitution, but it was also one in which he could take pride. Fang also agreed not to take part in activities "whose motive lies in opposing China." That wording was sufficiently vague, because it said nothing about the Chinese government or leadership; Fang could claim that he was trying to help China by combating the Chinese Communist Party.

Moreover, there were no restrictions on Fang's political activities in exile. After a half-year in Britain, Fang moved to the United States, where he worked briefly at Princeton before settling at the University of Arizona in Tucson. He occasionally gave speeches and wrote articles on behalf of the cause of democracy in China. None of them was as threatening to the Chinese regime as his work inside the country during the three years before the Tiananmen Square demonstrations.

While the Bush administration did well for Fang Lizhi, China was also richly rewarded for letting him go. With Fang's release, and with American acquiescence, China got its international loans back. The deal was thus worth billions of dollars to China. At a time when the Chinese economy was in a post-Tiananmen slowdown, and when the leadership was sorely in need of funds from abroad, these loans proved of considerable importance in stimulating a new era of rapid growth.

China's main sources of loans from abroad were Japan and the World Bank. Before the Tiananmen massacre, the Japanese government had agreed to a five-year, $5.6 billion package of subsidized loans to China, with much of the money designed for railroads, harbors, power stations and other projects; Japanese companies were supposed to get approximately half of the contracts for these projects. All of these loans had been held up by the sanctions imposed in the summer of 1989.

The World Bank had loaned China more than $10 billion in the decade before the 1989 upheavals, and had expected to lend another $2.3 billion in the 1989–90 fiscal year. Roughly half of this credit was in the form of interest-free loans that did not have to be repaid for at least 35 years. These favorable loans were designed for the world's poorest countries; China qualified because of its low per-capita income. But the World Bank loans, too, remained largely frozen by the post-Tiananmen sanctions. Only a few projects for "basic human needs" were being approved.

The suspension of lending to China had irritated the international business community. Without loans, China couldn't buy goods or pay for services from overseas; it couldn't go forward with the contracts it had signed before June 1989. Japanese companies were pressuring their government to open the way for the blocked yen-loans to China. Similarly, European companies were also urging their governments to support a resumption in World Bank loans, so that China could use the funds to buy dams, helicopters and power plants.

On July 10, two weeks after Fang's release, America and its allies cleared the way for a resumption of World Bank loans to China. In Houston, attending their annual economic summit meeting, the world's seven leading industrialized nations announced that they were willing to go along with World Bank loans not just for "basic human needs" in China, but also loans that would contribute to "reform of the Chinese economy"—a far broader category that covered a wide variety of projects.[29] In explaining the allies' policy reversal, former World Bank President Barber Conable Jr. later observed, "Procurement won out over idealism."[30]

In 1990–91, during the year after this Houston summit, China obtained $1.6 billion in World Bank loans, nearly as much as it had expected before the Tiananmen massacre. The following year, the loans amounted to $2.5 billion, more than to any other nation. China, in other words, regained within less than three years the credit it had lost after the Tiananmen massacre.

Whenever the World Bank voted on these loans, the United States abstained. Yet this was largely a charade. During 1989–90, the Bush administration had actively encouraged its allies in Europe and Japan to stop or delay World Bank loans to China. After Fang's release and the Houston summit, the administration relented. It let the World Bank open the flow of money to China again.

Even more importantly, the Houston summit gave Japan the political cover it had been seeking to resume doing business in China. The Japanese government headed by Prime Minister Toshiki Kaifu had not wanted to stand alone in lending money to the Chinese regime. As soon as the summit leaders in Houston altered their policy on World Bank loans, Kaifu, who had been actively supporting such a change, immediately announced that Tokyo would move forward with its $5.6 billion package for China. Bush once again was accommodating, telling reporters that Japan "is a sovereign nation that can make up its own mind on a lot of questions."[31]

Thus, Fang was effectively ransomed in exchange for a resumption in international loans to China. The main beneficiaries were the Chinese economy, which obtained an injection of several billion dollars, and the countries and private companies doing business in China.

Overseas, the biggest winner was Japan. In 1991, following the deal for Fang's release, Japan's exports to China grew by 40 percent as its suppliers often increased their share in the Chinese market at the expense of American and European competitors. The CIA later concluded that the rising Japanese sales to China "probably reflect a political decision on Beijing's part to reward Tokyo for the important role it played in supporting an early return to normal economic relations with China following the Tiananmen crackdown." [32]

White House spokesman Marlin Fitzwater called China's release of Fang "a far-sighted, significant step that will improve the atmosphere for progress in our bilateral relations." [33] In fact, the atmosphere did not change much, if at all. Fang's confinement inside the American embassy had been a byproduct, not a cause, of the differences between the United States and China.

THE MOST visible critics of the Bush administration's China policy were Democrats like Mitchell and Pelosi. But behind the scenes, the administration confronted some particularly energetic, though less well recognized, opponents from within the Republican Party, such as William C. Triplett II.

Triplett, the minority chief counsel to the Senate Foreign Relations Committee and a staff aide for Senator Jesse Helms, was Washington's most tenacious campaigner against the Chinese government. He was also one of the best illustrations of how American foreign policy can be made or undone in ways that are not covered in civics texts.

As the administration sought to restore American relations with China, Triplett labored frenetically in the opposite direction. China's behavior gave him no small amount of material with which to work. During the late 1980s and early 1990s, Chinese arms dealers, sometimes working for or allied with the People's Liberation Army, offered missiles and other technology for sale throughout the Middle East.

Triplett became Capitol Hill's principal drafter of legislative sanctions, particularly those aimed at China. He knew how to slip a provision onto the huge authorization bills for the State or Defense Departments that would require penalties against China for exporting dangerous weapons.

His own interest in China dated back to the 1960s, when he had served in the Vietnam War and as a low-level American intelligence operative in East Asia. One of his unpleasant assignments had been to examine the corpses of drowned Chinese refugees that washed up from the waters near Hong Kong to see if they were carrying any letters or other revealing information. He also had taken part in American intelligence operations against the Chinese military occupation of Tibet. In the early 1970s, he landed briefly at Robert R. Mullen and Company, a public relations firm that served as a cover for CIA operations. There he worked out of the office that had been occupied, only a short time before, by Watergate burglar E. Howard Hunt.[34]

After wandering through other jobs in and out of government, Triplett went to work on Capitol Hill in the mid-1980s as a congressional staff member, emerging as Helms's point man on China. Following a staff shake-up in the 1990s, he stayed on as an aide to other Republican senators, including Larry Pressler of South Dakota and Robert Bennett of Utah.

On Capitol Hill, Triplett purveyed a steady stream of facts, rumors, threats and legislative maneuvers, all of them designed to expose wrongdoing by China and to frustrate and embarrass those who were trying to improve America's ties with Beijing. His principal weapon was the telephone, where he talked endlessly and conspiratorially in colorful, street-savvy language.

"These are *baaaad* people, doing *baaaad* things!!" Triplett would say of the Chinese regime. He sometimes referred to Helms, his powerful boss, as "the 900-pound gorilla." His friends and sources within the Pentagon, the intelligence community and State Department became, in Triplett's entertaining terminology, "the mice" or "the midnight patriots." Once, when he was spinning out a convoluted theory of the internal workings of the Bush administration, he began referring to a "Mr. Flower." A perplexed reporter asked who that was. Triplett paused, as if stunned by such ignorance. "Lily!" he exclaimed, referring to Ambassador James Lilley.[35]

Beneath this bluster lay a considerable cunning. In the terminology of Capitol Hill, Triplett was adept at working "across the aisle," cultivating liberal Democrats as assiduously as he did conservative Republicans. He was as responsible as anyone for the unlikely bipartisan coalition that emerged in the 1990s on behalf of tougher policies toward China.

On human rights issues, Triplett swapped information regularly with the staffs of Mitchell and Pelosi. When he came across new information about Chinese arms sales, he would call up the offices of Democrats interested in arms proliferation, like Gore, John Glenn or Joseph Biden. His Democratic collaborators never advertised that they were working hand-in-hand with the staff of Jesse Helms. Triplett kept in close touch with union officials, too, recognizing that an issue like China's use of prison labor could bring together the AFL-CIO and protectionist textile manufacturers. He became the principal congressional supporter of Harry Wu, the Chinese-American who had served time in a Chinese labor camp and had documented China's exports of goods made in its prisons.

Triplett was a master of the well-timed leak, the delayed nomination hearing, the planted question at the noontime White House briefing. He would call up State Department officials and urge them to do something because the press was hot on the trail of a story; then he would phone reporters to tell them the State Department was about to change its policy. Other, less creative congressional aides would talk only to the *New York Times* and the *Washington Post,* the sunrise and sunset of their limited horizons. Triplett spoke regularly to elite newspapers, but also knew how to work with the *Washington Times,* the wire services, or even magazines from Japan, Germany or Hong Kong in order to get attention and good display for a story that could later be picked up elsewhere. In this fashion, he could slowly heat up a controversy until it reached full boil.

To be sure, he was, like Helms, an ardent anti-Communist. He worked regularly with human-rights groups and Tibetan organizations. But Triplett's principal interests were the People's Liberation Army and China's proliferation of dangerous weapons (missiles, nuclear technology and the ingredients for chemical weapons) to countries in the Middle East. In this respect, his agenda on China issues closely paralleled those of the governments of Taiwan and of Israel (whom Triplett sometimes jokingly referred to as "my clients").

Taiwan's future depended on making sure the PLA did not grow so much more powerful than Taiwan's own armed forces that it would be forced to negotiate with China from a position of weakness. Israel, although it was highly active in selling its military technology to China, was also intensely eager to stop China from selling missiles and other weapons or technology to its neighbors in the Middle East, such as Iran, Iraq, Syria and Saudi Arabia.

Triplett's legislative efforts were aimed primarily at stopping Chinese exports of military technology. In late 1990, near midnight on the last day of a congressional session, a Triplett-drafted amendment required the imposition of sanctions on any company or country that helped supply missile technology to Iraq. The provision was put into the overall defense bill; in the midst of the Desert Shield operations in the Persian Gulf, Bush needed the bill and couldn't possibly veto it.

The following year, Triplett came up with a new provision that increased the penalties for supplying missile technology to the Middle East. This language—directed specifically at China—was added to an authorization bill in a near-empty Senate chamber, at a time when Triplett and other aides noticed that the State Department official assigned to keep an eye on the legislation had gone to lunch.[36] In 1992, working with other congressional staff members, he helped graft onto the defense bill a provision known as the Gore–McCain Act, which requires sanctions against any country that transfers large amounts of advanced conventional weapons to Iran or Iraq. In all these cases, Triplett's provisions won the backing not only of Helms and other conservative Republicans, but also of Democratic senators worried about weapons proliferation.

After these measures passed, Triplett began publicizing information about Chinese exports that would require the imposition of sanctions. Eventually, the evidence was strong enough that both the Bush and the Clinton administrations were forced to invoke sanctions against China for its exports of missile technology.

Many of the established China scholars loathed Triplett. They complained bitterly that he exaggerated negative information about China. That accusation was sometimes valid; Triplett wasn't interested in context or in nuance. Yet journalists and congressional staff members found that some of his tips checked out. He called attention to the underside of China—the darker aspects of its international behavior, which the White House and State Department would often have preferred to keep hidden from the attention of Congress and the public.

Indeed, in portraying Triplett as the devil incarnate, mainstream sinologists sometimes exaggerated his importance. At times, he was merely a conduit, a one-man medium of exchange. A China watcher in the Pentagon or the CIA might be afraid to call newspapers with new evidence of a Chinese missile sale, for fear of being fired as a leaker. But that same official could legitimately tell Triplett, a congressional staff member, and be confident that the information would make its way into the press. A representative of the United Auto Workers or the International Association of Machinists might not want to appear in public with Jesse Helms, whose record of supporting organized labor was lamentable; but the same union official might work quietly with Triplett in seeking to limit the transfer of American manufacturing technology to China.

There was one China issue in Washington that Triplett avoided. He steered clear of the annual campaigns to revoke or restrict China's most-favored-nation trade benefits. He often argued that for those opposed to the China's Communist regime, MFN was a losing issue, because the power of U.S. corporations would always hold sway in Congress. (It is worth noting that in this respect, too, Triplett's position ran parallel to that of Taiwan. The Taipei government never sought to curb China's MFN benefits, because many Taiwan-based companies were running factories in mainland China, earning handsome profits by exporting their products to the United States.)

In February 1990, when Lawrence Eagleburger appeared before the Senate Foreign Relations Committee to testify on American policy toward China, he was greeted with a barrage of tough, sometimes hostile questions from Helms and several other Republican Senators. How many Chinese are confined in prison and labor camps? the senators asked Eagleburger. Does China have a requirement that the labor camps be profitable, forcing them to make goods for export? What can you tell us about reports of China's nuclear cooperation with Iran? With Pakistan? Is China still trying to sell its new M-9 missiles to Syria? What has the Bush administration done to stop Chinese arms sales to the Middle East?

Eagleburger struggled to answer these questions. He requested permission to discuss China's arms sales behind closed doors, so that classified intelligence would not be disclosed—thus leaving the impression that when it came to arms proliferation, China was doing considerably more than the Bush administration wanted to acknowledge in public.

For Triplett, who had drafted most of these questions, it was merely another day's work.

CHAPTER THIRTEEN

China's Long March Back to Respectability

Slowly, month by month, the Chinese regime worked to bring itself back to respectability, to overcome the stigma of the Tiananmen massacre.

It was a job Beijing carried out with consummate skill. The strategy, in which Foreign Minister Qian Qichen played the leading role, called for a slow, gradual desensitization of outrage. China incessantly pushed each foreign government to ease its sanctions or its shunning of Chinese leaders only a little bit, never too much; then, after each slight change, China began pressing once again until another small change was won. A long journey starts with a single step, says the famous Chinese proverb. In the years after 1989, the world's leading powers all found themselves making long journeys back to China.

For Beijing, the low point came in the last weeks of 1989, when China found itself more isolated in international affairs than at any time since the early days of the Cultural Revolution. The leading industrialized nations—the United States, Western Europe and Japan—were enforcing economic sanctions against China, and their presidents and prime ministers were avoiding meetings with the Chinese. Under President Mikhail Gorbachev, the Soviet Union kept its distance, too; Moscow had clearly opted for political change and a toleration of dissent to a degree unacceptable in Beijing.

When the Chinese staged a lavish celebration in Tiananmen Square for the 40th anniversary of the founding of the People's Republic of China on October 1, 1989, Gorbachev sent only a low-level delegation. China countered by giving top billing to representatives from East Germany and Czechoslovakia, the two Central European governments that were then resisting the changes sweeping the socialist world. East

Germany's Erich Honecker took care to send one of his government's highest-ranking officials to Beijing. The sense of solidarity was short-lived. Over the following two months, both the East German and Czechoslovak Communist Parties fell from power, leaving China out in the cold and even further embarrassed.[1]

China's long comeback started in Asia. Beijing lavished attention on neighbors with whom it had long been at odds. Until the late 1980s, businesses from Taiwan and South Korea had been barred by political restrictions from setting up operations in China. In the wake of the Tiananmen crackdown, as executives from the West and Japan froze and reexamined their investments in China, Taiwanese and South Korean companies began flooding to the mainland, supplying new sources of capital, management and technology. In both Taiwan and South Korea, a "China fever" took hold as legislators and scholars, too, visited the country from which they had long been barred.

In the summer of 1990, China established diplomatic relations with Indonesia and Singapore, two Southeast Asian nations with sizable overseas Chinese business communities, once again clearing the way for new sources of Asian investment. Over a three-year period culminating in 1992, China also moved toward full diplomatic ties with South Korea, a move that stunned and severely undercut China's old ally, North Korean President Kim Il Sung.

China's political and economic courtship of these other Asian countries put intense pressure on Japan. Tokyo was a member of the G-7, a group of the world's seven leading industrialized nations; for a time, it had joined in the international sanctions on China. But Japanese businesses did not want to be left behind as other Asians seized opportunities, and Tokyo was wary of finding itself increasingly isolated within Asia. Eventually, Japan broke ranks with the West. In August 1991, Prime Minister Toshiki Kaifu became the first leader from any of the G-7 powers to visit China since the Tiananmen crackdown.

Britain was the next domino. China's leverage over Prime Minister John Major was its growing power in Hong Kong. Britain had announced plans for a huge infrastructure project in Hong Kong, including a new airport, to be started in the last years before Britain returned sovereignty over its colony to China in 1997. That project was viewed as important for Hong Kong—and also for British companies hoping for design and construction contracts.

In order to get the airport project moving and to secure financing for it, Britain needed China's approval; no one wanted to make commitments while the plans were clouded by uncertainty over what China might do after 1997. China, in turn, made plain that its stamp of approval for the airport project would require a visit to Beijing by Major.

Thus, in September 1991, the prime minister became the first Western European leader to visit China since Tiananmen Square. Major succeeded in obtaining a go-ahead for the airport project. However, his trip also illustrated some of the political dynamics involved in these first visits to Beijing after the Tiananmen crackdown: China had pushed so hard for an early visit by the British prime minister that over the long run, the effort backfired and the Chinese paid a huge price.

Both during and after his trip, the prime minister was excoriated in Parliament and in the press for his seeming deference to the Chinese and his inability to come to grips with the repressive nature of its rule. "Attempts at an impromptu meeting with ordinary people dissolved in chaos when Chinese security police moved in to push back the crowd, pouncing on anyone who offered his hand in greeting to the Prime Minister," reported the London *Independent* in one typical story.[2] In the months after his return to London, Major reacted by taking a much tougher line on China and by changing the personnel responsible for British policy. He decided to replace the governor of Hong Kong, Sir David Wilson, who had followed the traditional British Foreign Office policies of accommodating Beijing, and install his political ally, Chris Patten, as the new governor.

China was furious when, over the following years, Patten pushed vigorously for democratic reforms in Hong Kong. Yet in a sense, Beijing had itself to blame for Patten's appointment and the changes he introduced. They were a consequence of China's post-Tiananmen push for respectability, its insistence on having Major visit Beijing at a time when there was little support back home for his trip.

In dealing with the United States, China's point of leverage was its permanent membership on the United Nations Security Council. China had the ability to veto American initiatives at the United Nations. At a more tranquil moment in history, the threat of a Chinese veto might not have mattered much. In August 1990, however, the Gulf crisis erupted with Iraq's invasion of Kuwait. The Bush administration realized that the support of the U.N. Security Council, including China, would provide the legitimacy it needed for any military action to roll back the Iraqi invasion.

Although Bush had twice sent his national security advisor to China, he had avoided formal, top-level meetings with the Beijing leadership in either China or the United States. A presidential summit was out of the question. Secretary of State Baker refused to travel to Beijing or to meet with Foreign Minister Qian Qichen in Washington. In the 18 months after the Tiananmen massacre, Baker and Qian met several times at international conferences and in out-of-the-way places.

During the months after Saddam Hussein's invasion, the administration asked China to support a U.N. resolution authorizing the use of force against Iraq. Qian Qichen countered by bargaining hard to see what China might get for its vote. The foreign minister suggested a presidential visit to Beijing, or at least one by Baker, and for a lifting of American sanctions. The administration balked at these demands. However, it finally agreed to let Qian visit Washington after the U.N. vote if China went along with the resolution on Iraq. Baker also agreed to send one of his top aides, Undersecretary of State Bob Kimmitt, to Beijing, and to consider making a trip himself the following year.[3]

On November 30, to the Bush administration's annoyance, China abstained from the U.N. resolution on Iraq—not vetoing it, but not supporting it either. The resolution passed, but without the formal endorsement from China that the administration had wanted. A confrontation followed that demonstrated once again the tenacity of China's continuing drive to regain international recognition.

Under the deal that had been worked before the U.N. vote, Qian was scheduled to visit Washington the following day. However, Baker decided that because China had merely abstained on the resolution, the foreign minister didn't deserve a meeting with Bush at the White House.

Overnight, Chinese officials mounted a secret campaign. In the early morning hours, Kimmitt got a phone call at his home in Washington from Chinese Ambassador Zhu Qizhen. Qian would not come to Washington unless he could see the president in the White House, the ambassador said.

Bush administration officials scurried to find out exactly what deal had been reached with the Chinese. It was Baker who had offered Qian the visit to Washington, during a late-night telephone conversation from the secretary's hotel room in Paris. A review of the transcript of that conversation, kept by the State Department's operations center, left unclear whether Baker had said China needed to vote *for* the resolution against Iraq or merely to avoid vetoing it, in order to get a session with the president.

Finally, the administration gave way. Kimmitt reminded Baker that the United States would need China's help on future U.N. votes, too. Qian's planned visit to Washington had already been made public, and Baker felt that if it were canceled at the last minute, American relations with China would become even worse than they already were.

The following day, Qian became the first senior Chinese official to obtain a meeting with the American president since June 1989. At the

White House, with the foreign minister standing alongside him, Bush told reporters, "We have some differences on this whole broad question of human rights, but we have many things in common."[4] Qian's visit was another important step toward breaking down the American resistance: The regime was now being welcomed back to the White House.

A YEAR LATER, Baker relented and decided to visit China himself. The driving force behind the secretary's trip was the ever-increasing American unhappiness with China's continuing sales of missiles and other weaponry throughout the Middle East. Despite the administration's public claims that it had made progress in curbing China's missile sales, officials realized they needed to try again.

By mid-1991, U.S. intelligence agencies had confirmed that China sold missiles or missile technology to Pakistan, Syria and Iran. The agencies also concluded that China had, over time, helped the nuclear programs of Iran and Pakistan, and had sold anti-aircraft weapons to Libya to help protect a secret plant used to produce chemical weapons. In April 1991, the White House imposed a limited new economic sanction, blocking the sales of some American high-speed computers and satellite parts, after it was found that China had sold the launchers for its M-11 missiles to Pakistan.[5]

Deng had vaguely promised the United States in 1988 that China would stop selling intermediate-range missiles. Since that time, however, China had repeatedly avoided being pinned down on what the dividing line was between an intermediate-range missile and a short-range missile. Therefore, it was unclear whether its new M-11 missiles, which had a range of 180 miles, were covered by Deng's old promise. The U.S. government itself was divided over what laws or guidelines should apply to these Chinese missiles.[6]

By late 1991, Baker had won a reputation as a skillful negotiator. He had worked out a series of arms-control and other agreements with the Soviet Union; he had helped pull together the coalition of nations joining with the United States in the Gulf War; and he had played a leading role in bringing about the reunification of Germany.

In dealing with China, however, the secretary had considerably less success. Before agreeing to visit Beijing, he had attempted to obtain promises from Qian that China would make at least some concessions on arms proliferation and human rights during his trip. The foreign minister refused to give any promises in advance, gauging correctly that Baker would come anyway without preconditions.[7] In this way, China could make modest concessions in the last moments of Baker's trip after obtaining something in exchange for them.

The secretary of state—always attuned as much to public relations as to diplomacy—had learned lessons from the furor over Scowcroft's last trip to China. Before he landed, Baker's aides told reporters he would not attend any banquet, but rather would take part only in a private "working dinner." The lack of a banquet meant that there would be no public toasts and no photographs of Baker clinking glasses with Qian Qichen or other Chinese officials.

The distinction between a banquet and a working dinner may not have been quite so great as Baker's aides sought to portray it. Nevertheless, it represented a significant change in the way America dealt with China. The days of warm public toasts to the friendship between China and America, which dated back to Nixon's trip in 1972, were over. Two years later, Baker's successor, Warren Christopher, went a step further by shunning even a private dinner with his Chinese counterparts.[8]

Baker had hoped to meet with Deng Xiaoping. He was carrying a letter from Bush to Deng, and after arriving in Beijing, Baker asked that he be permitted to deliver it in person. Chinese officials turned him down. In the end, the secretary was obliged to read Bush's letter aloud in a room full of lower-level Chinese officials, hoping that at least one of them might pass along the message. Baker's inability to deliver the letter was, once again, a telling sign of the changing relationship between the two countries. No longer could American officials count on Deng's help, as they had for the previous 13 years.[9]

While in Beijing, the secretary attempted to discuss China's up-heavals of 1989 with Premier Li Peng. He later acknowledged that the meeting was so disastrous that he thought fleetingly of walking out of the room. At one point, Baker referred to the Tiananmen crackdown as a "tragedy," a euphemistic terminology that seemed to suggest the events might have been be merely the fault of the gods.

Even this phraseology was too much for Li. He countered, "The actions in Tiananmen Square were a good thing. We do not regard them as a tragedy." Without them, China might have gone the way of Eastern Europe or the Soviet Union, Li said.[10] Since the failed coup in Moscow the previous August and the collapse of the Communist Party in the Soviet Union, Chinese leaders had tirelessly pressed the theme that polit-ical liberalization leads to chaos.

Although Baker didn't realize it at the time, Chinese security officials had resorted to old-fashioned thuggery to make sure the secretary and his aides didn't see or talk with anyone in China who might give them a different point of view. One prominent Chinese dissident, Dai Qing, had agreed to meet during Baker's trip with Assistant Secretary of State Richard Schifter. On the same day Baker met with Li Peng, two plainclothes security officials grabbed Dai Qing and shoved her down a fire escape and into a car. She was first kept in a government "guest house," then was driven out of town, to the seaside resort of Beidaihe. She was kept there until Baker and Schifter left China. Another Chinese dissident, Hou Xiaotian, was similarly detained while Baker was in Beijing.[11]

By the final day of his trip, Baker was still empty-handed. During the last hours, Qian offered only a few minor and well-qualified concessions. He turned down Baker's repeated requests that China grant amnesty to anyone convicted of nonviolent protests during the Tiananmen demonstrations, and also rejected American requests to let the International Red Cross into China's prisons. But Qian agreed to let some dissidents leave China, and he gave American officials a sketchy and incomplete list of what had happened to some of the hundreds of people who had been detained since the Tiananmen crackdown. Baker admitted he was disappointed at China's lack of progress in human rights. Some of his aides suggested turning down Qian's meager offer and simply leaving Beijing.[12]

On arms proliferation, Qian for the first time said China intended to comply with the guidelines of an agreement called the Missile Technology Control Regime (MTCR). Under these guidelines, drawn up by the United States and six of its allies in 1987, countries are not supposed to export any missile system with a range of more than 300 kilometers (about 185 miles) or a payload of more than 500 kilograms (1,100 pounds). Nations are also barred from exporting sensitive technology or equipment that could be used to manufacture these missiles. The MTCR rules clearly covered China's M-9 missiles, and they appeared to cover the shorter-range M-11 missiles as well.[13]

However, Chinese officials sought to weaken this promise by filling it with qualifications. Moreover, Qian said China would abide by its pledge only if the Bush administration would lift its sanctions on the sale of high-speed computers and satellite parts to China. Baker claimed in his memoirs that he decided to reject this last demand. In fact, however, the administration lifted the sanctions three months later, after first making sure that China put in writing what Qian had promised during Baker's trip.[14]

The result was that Baker left Beijing with a still-vague verbal commitment from China to curb its missiles sales. "To us, this means that they [China] will apply the [MTCR guidelines] to any exports of missiles and related technology. We understand that this applies to the M-9 and M-11 missiles," Baker told a news conference—thus leaving unclear whether China had the same interpretation.[15]

On his way home from Beijing, Baker offered his own version of what it had been like to deal with Chinese officials. It was worse than negotiating with Syrian President Hafez el-Assad, he said. "It's like your annual physical," Baker quipped, "the unpleasant part."[16] It was quite a contrast to the era when Henry Kissinger had waxed rhapsodic about the talents and virtues of Chou Enlai.

By the end of 1991, the Chinese regime had nearly regained the international acceptance it had lost two years earlier. European and Japanese prime ministers had made respectful visits to Beijing, as had the American secretary of state. The Chinese foreign minister had been welcomed into the White House.

The next logical step was a meeting between the highest leaders of the American and Chinese governments. Chinese officials turned their attention to this goal. In January 1992, Premier Li Peng made his first trip to Europe since the Tiananmen crackdown. From there, he traveled to New York City for a summit meeting of the 15 members of the United Nations Security Council. Chinese diplomats pressed the White House for a separate meeting between the American president and the Chinese premier.

The administration found it hard to say no. Bush was seeing many of the other world leaders at the U.N. session; and some of them had already agreed to meet with Li Peng. After Baker's visit to Beijing, a session with Li in New York seemed like only one more marginal step further toward recognition of the Chinese regime.

On January 31, 1992, in a small room near the U.N. Security Council, the president of the United States, flanked by his top aides, sat down with the Chinese leader who had played an instrumental role in the massacre in Beijing less than three years earlier. The meeting was on the neutral turf of the United Nations. Bush, sitting between Baker and Scowcroft, kept a solemn expression on his face as photographers took pictures of the gathering.

But Li Peng smiled tightly. He and the Chinese regime had made their way back. They were, once again, respectable in the eyes of the world that had shunned them.

CHAPTER FOURTEEN

A Campaign and an Arms Sale

F OR THREE YEARS AFTER the Tiananmen crackdown, one impor- tant aspect of American policy toward China had remained stable amid the tumult. That was Taiwan. Ever since the Reagan administration had agreed to restrict American arms sales to Taiwan in its 1982 commu- nique with China, Taiwan had been marginalized as an issue between Washington and Beijing. China had grumbled from time to time over America's low-key, continuing support for Taiwan. On the whole, how- ever, the issue remained quiescent, like a dormant volcano.

In 1992, the calm was broken. In the midst of a presidential cam- paign, with his China policy under attack, President Bush reversed ten years of American policy toward Taiwan. That summer, the administra- tion announced that the United States would sell Taiwan F-16 warplanes, the advanced jet fighters that the Nationalist government had been try- ing to obtain for more than a decade. This was more than a routine arms sale; it was a change with profound implications for the armed forces of China, Taiwan and their neighbors in Southeast Asia. The sale also had political and diplomatic consequences, because a modernized air force bolstered Taiwan's position in any future negotiations with China.

Bush's decision was tinged with irony. From the standpoint of the stunned Beijing leadership, the sale of the F-16s was probably the single most infuriating action taken by any American president since the Nixon era; it ended Beijing's delusion that it could regain Taiwan by slowly cut- ting off its access to modern weaponry. Yet the sale was made by Bush, whom the Chinese considered one of their oldest friends in Washington. Over the following years, the F-16 sale did more than anything else to ensure that there would be no restoration of a smooth working relation- ship between America and China of the sort that Bush had sought.

Surprising as Bush's decision was, it had more than two years of antecedents. The People's Liberation Army had found new sources of advanced hardware and technology. Taiwan had been changing, and so had American attitudes toward the island. In the United States, defense contractors were eager for new markets overseas, as the end of the Cold War brought constraints on American defense budgets. Bush's China policy was subjected to ever-increasing political attack during the 1992 campaign. All of these factors combined in prompting the president to break with the past and throw off the earlier American restraints in arming Taiwan.

THE FIRST step in the sequence of events leading to the F-16 sale was the rupture in China's military relationship with the United States.

During the late 1970s and early 1980s, China had looked to the United States to supply some of the advanced equipment and technology necessary to modernize its army, which was still operating with weapons systems it had obtained from the Soviet Union in the 1950s. The Carter administration had started down the path of a U.S. military relationship with Beijing; the Reagan administration had gone several steps further by selling arms and technology to China. Of these American deals, by far the largest and the most significant had been Peace Pearl, the $550 million project to improve China's F-8 jet fighters.[1]

In 1989, when Bush suspended American military ties to China on the day after the Tiananmen massacre, Peace Pearl was put on hold. At the time, however, the Americans and Chinese seemed to believe the furor might blow over. When Pentagon officials visited Beijing in August 1989 for a tense meeting with the Chinese military about the future of Peace Pearl, they decided to keep the project alive. A few weeks later, despite the administration's sanctions, Chinese military officers and engineers were permitted to return to work on Peace Pearl (see chapter 11).

Nevertheless, this effort to resuscitate the arms deal soon foundered. Even before the Tiananmen sanctions were imposed, problems had arisen with the project. Beijing had complained that Peace Pearl was becoming expensive. China, understandably, was not accustomed to the idiosyncrasies of American defense contractors and to the endemic cost overruns to which the Pentagon had become inured.

In early 1990, the Chinese discovered after another review of Peace Pearl that the costs were rising again; American help for the Chinese jets was estimated to run to nearly $800 million, more than $200 million higher than China had expected. Moreover, it was becoming increasingly clear that the American sanctions wouldn't be lifted anytime soon. Thus, even if the work on Peace Pearl were to be finished, China had no guarantee that it would ever receive the equipment being developed in the United States for its air force.

In the spring of 1990, China decided to cut its losses. Beijing told the administration that it was canceling out of Peace Pearl. By this time, China had sunk more than $200 million into the abortive program. China got back nothing in return but a collection of useless prototypes and unfinished equipment, without even the instruction manuals.[2] It was a bitter end to the Sino-American arms-sale relationship forged over the previous decade.

IN BEIJING that spring, Ambassador James Lilley noticed what he first thought was an old Chinese ploy: China was flirting with the Soviet Union. In May 1990, only a few weeks after the cancellation of Peace Pearl, General Liu Huaqing—the vice chairman of China's Central Military Commission and the man in charge of the modernization program for the army—traveled to Moscow to talk about the possibility of buying Soviet warplanes.

Lilley was unconcerned. For years, the Chinese had been staging well-publicized meetings with Soviet officials and suggesting the possibility of a Sino-Soviet rapprochement in order to help them extract the concessions they wanted from the United States. The approach had often worked. Over the years, anti-Soviet hawks in Washington like Senator Henry Jackson had often urged doing whatever was necessary to keep China happy in order to prevent it from gravitating toward Moscow. On this occasion, Liu Huaqing's visit to Moscow seemed to be designed to coax the Bush administration to be more forthcoming with China in negotiations for the release of Fang Lizhi.

This time, Lilley felt, the Chinese maneuver wouldn't go anywhere. In 1990, the United States had a much stronger relationship with Mikhail Gorbachev's Soviet government than China did. Moreover, the Soviet military threat to Europe had virtually disappeared. The world was moving in America's direction. This flirtation with Moscow was the same old stale game China had been playing for years, Lilley believed. Why should the United States worry about it?[3]

However, this time the overture to Moscow was more than a Chinese ploy. Two momentous events of the following year—the Gulf War and the collapse of the Soviet Union—gave Liu Huaqing's visit to Moscow a significance well beyond what Lilley had expected. It was the beginning of a new arms relationship.

The Gulf War demonstrated to China's military leaders the importance of high-technology weaponry, greatly intensifying China's desire to modernize its armed forces. If China wasn't going to obtain advanced military technology from the United States and Western Europe, it would have to get it elsewhere. One source was Israel, which had already been secretly working with China on military projects for more than a decade. After 1989 and the imposition of Western sanctions, Israel emerged as one of the leading suppliers of advanced weapons and technology to China. Still, China continued to look to other countries, notably to Russia.[4]

Politically, the collapse of the Soviet Union was, of course, deeply unsettling to China's Communist Party leaders. They could explain away the toppling of Eastern European Communist regimes in 1989 as merely a series of nationalist revolts against domination by an outside power, the Soviet Union. Such rationalizations did not apply to the downfall of the Communist Party of the Soviet Union. The Chinese made the best of an awkward situation. They pointed to the economic upheavals that followed the collapse of Communism across the border. See what is happening in Russia? We don't want that sort of chaos in our country, the Chinese regime told its people.

In military terms, the Soviet Union's disintegration represented not a threat, but a shopping opportunity for China. Amid the economic upheavals that followed, Russia was eager, indeed desperate, for arms sales. Its defense industries were running out of money; Russian research scientists and engineers were in danger of losing their jobs. For Russia, China was in many ways a very attractive customer. The army was anxious to modernize, and much of China's military equipment—its tanks, artillery, armored personnel carriers, even its AK-47 rifles—had been based on Soviet technology in the first place.

By late 1991, Russian defense industries were offering their products and technology at bargain prices, and the Chinese military flocked to Russia to see what might be worth buying. At first, the sales involved relatively small-scale weapons and technology. In March 1992, however, military leaders of the two countries completed a groundbreaking deal: Russia agreed to sell China 24 of its Sukhoi-27 jet fighters. The Russian Su-27 was an advanced, all-weather plane with a range of more than 2,400 miles.[5]

The number of planes was relatively small, given the size of China's air force. Nevertheless, with the purchase of the Su-27s, China for the first time obtained some of the modern combat aircraft it had long sought—thus beginning to fulfill the needs that had earlier driven China into its Peace Pearl disaster with the United States.

The Su-27 deal attracted considerable notice, especially in Taiwan and also in Washington. Something new was happening. China was starting to increase its ability to project military power outside its borders.

Moreover, the United States had less ability than in the past to control military developments between China and Taiwan. During the 1980s, America had been a leading supplier of military hardware and technology to both China and Taiwan, and thus had been able to limit what each government bought.

Now, China no longer looked to the United States for military technology. It had turned to Russia for help in modernizing its armed forces. Taiwan wanted to improve its military, too, and Taiwan officials were warning that if they couldn't buy advanced equipment from the United States, they, too, would look elsewhere.

IN MAY 1991, Lilley stepped down as American ambassador to China. During his time in Beijing, he had witnessed demonstrations by hundreds of thousands of Chinese, an army assault upon those demonstrations and the wave of political repression that followed. He had run an American embassy surrounded and besieged by Chinese security officials and had served as the host for more than a year for Fang Lizhi. In 1989, before starting as ambassador, Lilley had said he wanted to serve no more than two years. Nothing in China had changed his mind.[6]

At one point, during a 1990 meeting, Chinese Premier Li Peng had told the American ambassador, "You think I'm the hard-liner." (This was Li's way of suggesting that he had been merely the front man, not the architect, of the Chinese leadership's bloody 1989 crackdown.) "No, I'm the hard-liner," the ambassador replied. It was an accurate self-description. Lilley was a man of strong views, far less inclined to explain away the repressive behavior of the Chinese leadership than others in the U.S. government.

As ambassador, Lilley had generally hewed to the Bush administration's line on China, avoiding any public remarks that would diverge from the official U.S. government position. Soon after he returned to the United States as a private citizen, however, the restraints came off. In a series of speeches and articles, Lilley condemned the Chinese regime with which he had done business for the previous two years. The Communist Party leadership was a "decaying dynasty," Lilley said in a speech at Penn State University.[7]

Lilley thus became the second American ambassador to Beijing in a row (following Winston Lord) to become, in retirement, a staunch public critic of the Chinese regime. U.S. ambassadors to Beijing have the opportunity to deal with the Chinese government more regularly and at higher levels than other Americans. The two U.S. ambassadors had both departed with a sense of outrage; the Chinese regime, it seemed, was even less appealing up close than it was from afar.

Lilley went considerably further than had his predecessor. Lord had merely criticized China's repressive human rights policies without challenging the underlying structure of the ties that had been built up under Richard Nixon and Lord's old patron, Henry Kissinger. Lilley, by contrast, questioned the very underpinnings of the Sino-American relationship. From the freedom of retirement, he asserted that China's claims of sovereignty over Taiwan were "anachronistic." American policy toward China has been "locked for too long into the three communiques," Lilley said.[8]

Lilley's attack on the "three communiques," while seemingly obscure, was especially far-reaching. He was challenging America's one-China policy. The United States and China had signed three communiques governing their relations with one another. The first had been the one signed by Nixon in Shanghai during his 1972 trip; in it, the United States agreed not to challenge the idea that Taiwan was part of China. The second was the one signed by Carter, establishing diplomatic relations and acknowledging that Taiwan was part of China. The third was the Reagan administration's 1982 communique limiting American arms sales to Taiwan.

In their dealings with one another, even when they agreed on little else, American and Chinese officials had always paid homage to these three communiques. Now that Lilley was out of office, he was saying publicly what other American officials would say only privately: Perhaps the policies embodied in these communiques ought to be reexamined or updated to take account of the changing realities on Taiwan.

Taiwan was becoming more prosperous and more democratic. Its government was coming to reflect the views of the island's Taiwanese majority, who had been left unmentioned in the words of the Shanghai communique that "all Chinese on either side of the Taiwan Strait" believe that Taiwan is part of China.

In Lilley's view, these changes in Taiwan made the Nixon-era one-China policy hopelessly out of date. "Why not a popular vote in Taiwan and Hong Kong on unification with the PRC?" asked Lilley in one essay published during this period. "This process has been used in highly sensitive areas such as the U.S. in Puerto Rico and Canada in Quebec."[9]

In the months after Lilley left Beijing, he made two trips to Taiwan, seeing old friends and observing the changes on the island. Years earlier, while in the CIA, he had worked with Taiwan's intelligence service. During the Reagan administration, Lilley served for three years as the director of the American Institute in Taiwan, the head of the U.S. government's unofficial presence on the island. He had come to know the Taiwan leadership from top to bottom.

Once, in the early 1980s, Lilley had even toured the island with a rising young politician named Lee Teng-hui, who was being groomed by
President Chiang Ching-kuo as the first ethnic Taiwanese leader to take a
top leadership post in the ruling Nationalist Party. It had been a bonding
experience, meant to teach Lee Teng-hui how the Americans thought.
Lilley was, in effect, Lee's mentor. At the time, the Nationalists were still
dominated by Chinese from the mainland, who had come to Taiwan
with Chiang Kai-shek, the father of Chiang Ching-kuo. By 1991, when
Lilley visited the island, Chiang Ching-kuo had died, and Lee Teng-hui
had become the first native Taiwanese president.

Back in the United States, Lilley became a forceful proponent of
greater American support for Taiwan. Such public advocacy, coming
from a just-retired American ambassador to China, would have been significant enough. As it turned out, however, Lilley would come to wield
even greater influence, because he did not stay retired for long. In
November 1991, Bush appointed him to a top Pentagon job as assistant
secretary of defense for international security affairs. In that position, Lilley was directly responsible for military relations between the United
States and the governments of Asia.

Though Bush did not always agree with Lilley, personal loyalties
counted far more for him than did any potential disagreements over policy. On the wall of Lilley's office hung a picture of the two men at the
White House, taken at the time of Lilley's return from China in 1991.
The president had signed the picture: "Welcome Back—your friend,
and, to a degree, pupil, George Bush"—a subtle reminder that Lilley's
lessons to the president about China did not always take hold. But Lilley
had been Bush's trusted aide for many years, in Beijing, Washington and
at the CIA. Lilley's criticism of the one-China policy did not stand in the
way of the Pentagon job.

Once back inside the Bush administration, Lilley could no longer
speak out in public about his views concerning Taiwan. He could, however, attempt to change American policy.

IN THE autumn of 1991, Zhao Haiqing, the principal Washington lob-
byist for the Chinese students, was teaching a course at Harvard's
Kennedy School of Government. One day, his friend John Sasso told
Zhao that a visitor wanted to meet him. It was one of the candidates
campaigning for the Democratic nomination in 1992: the governor of
Arkansas, Bill Clinton.

Clinton wanted to talk to Zhao about China, Sasso said. The candidate and the Chinese student leader met at Harvard for about 45 minutes.
Zhao gave Clinton his pitch: Clinton should support the imposition of

conditions on any renewals of China's most-favored-nation trading status. He argued that President Bush's China policy would be vulnerable to attack during the 1992 campaign. Zhao came away from the meeting with the impression that Clinton wasn't very knowledgeable about China but wanted to learn and had listened closely.[10]

That night, Clinton was the guest speaker for a small dinner at the Kennedy School. One of those present was Lilley, who was then in his brief interlude between government jobs. The former ambassador urged Clinton to think carefully about what he would say about China in the 1992 campaign. Restricting China's MFN benefits would hurt the wrong people in China, Lilley told the governor; the Democrats should focus on other issues concerning China, such as the need to protect freedom in Hong Kong.

The Democratic candidate wasn't about to take political advice from any Republican, let alone George Bush's ex-ambassador. Clinton pointed out that he had just seen in the newspapers a story about China's proliferation of arms and technology. The United States shouldn't be giving MFN benefits so freely to a country that sold arms to such countries as Iran, Clinton said. Then, eager to avoid having to discuss China policy in further detail, the governor quickly added, "Why don't we defer to our expert here?" With that, Clinton turned to Zhao Haiqing and yielded the floor.[11]

Zhao was astonished. A leading Democratic presidential candidate seemed to be courting him and deferring to him on China policy. Yet Clinton's behavior was hardly unique. Every single candidate running against George Bush in 1992 attacked his policy of reconciliation with China. Each one criticized the president for extending China's MFN benefits without any conditions.

From within the Republican Party, Patrick J. Buchanan savaged Bush for "playing footsie with Li Peng and Deng Xiaoping. Were these not the gentlemen who sent tanks to roll over the children in Tiananmen Square?" Among the Democrats, Paul Tsongas called for strict conditions on China's MFN status; after the president met Li Peng at the United Nations in January 1992, Tsongas said he was "astounded that President Bush would meet with the architect of the Tiananmen Square massacre." Jerry Brown, too, contended that future American trade with China should be linked to progress on human rights.[12]

Throughout his 1992 campaign, Clinton sounded many of these same themes. He was at least as outspoken in denouncing Bush's China policy as were his Democratic rivals.

Clinton's most remembered words about China during the campaign were those of his acceptance speech to the Democratic National Convention in New York City in July. As one part of his "Covenant with America," he promised "an America that will not coddle dictators from Baghdad to Beijing." [13]

For Clinton, that remark was no momentary lapse, no sudden or impetuous departure from prior statements. Indeed, the broad theme and even the word "coddle" had been part of his campaign from the very start. The line in his acceptance speech was merely the distillation of what he had been saying for many months.

In his first speech on foreign policy, delivered at Georgetown University on December 12, 1991, Clinton asserted, "The [Bush] administration continues to coddle China, despite its continuing crackdown on democratic reform, its brutal subjugation of Tibet, its irresponsible export of nuclear and missile technology, its support for the homicidal Khmer Rouge in Cambodia, and its abusive trade practices."

There was, in this early campaign appearance, a momentary warning, though unheeded, of the economic realities Clinton would confront after taking office. From the audience, a young student in the Georgetown School of Foreign Service named Molly Peterson identified herself as a Student for Clinton, thus assuring the governor she was generally sympathetic to him. Then she said, "There are many industries that depend upon the low tariffs which most-favored-nation status allows, especially the wheat growers and the lumber industries of the Pacific Northwest." How, she asked, would Clinton "balance the moral demands of American foreign policy with the economic needs of these specific groups?"

That was, as it would turn out years later, the multimillion-dollar question. But Clinton brushed it off. "Well, if it were easy, it would be done already," he conceded. However, he went on, "When countries flagrantly violate accepted norms of international conduct, and undermine the interests that we hold dear, and retard the forces of democracy that are plainly welling up, then I think we have to seriously consider whether we should maintain most-favored-nation status." [14]

Clinton's formal position on China during the 1992 campaign was neither novel nor innovative. It followed the positions taken earlier by both the Democratic Party's national leadership and the Democratic majority in Congress.

Specifically, he called for the imposition of a series of conditions China would have to meet for any annual renewals of MFN trade benefits. As a candidate, Clinton was endorsing the approach of Democratic leaders on Capitol Hill like George Mitchell, Richard Gephardt and Nancy Pelosi. During the 1992 campaign, Clinton's staff would call the Democratic leaders in Congress regularly. "What should Governor Clinton say about China?" Nancy Soderberg, a former staff aide to Senator Edward Kennedy who was working for the Clinton campaign, would ask Ed King of Mitchell's staff.[15]

Starting in 1990, the Democratic congressional leadership each year supported legislation attaching conditions to China's MFN renewal. At the time, this was thought to be the moderate position, a compromise between outright revocation of the trade benefits and automatic renewals. In 1991, this legislation—requiring China to change its human rights and arms-sale policies before any extension of MFN benefits—passed both houses of Congress. Bush vetoed the bill; the legislation died when the Senate, in March 1992, voted 60 to 38 for the bill, six votes short of the margin to override the veto.[16]

Over time, Mitchell and Gephardt remained relatively consistent in their approach to China. The same could not be said of other leaders of the Democratic Party, whose attacks on the Bush administration seem, in retrospect, to have reflected merely partisan politics. In 1991, for example, Ron Brown, then chairman of the Democratic National Committee, had excoriated Bush for extending MFN benefits to China without conditions.

"By granting China MFN status, President Bush has aligned himself with China's government instead of standing up for human rights, democracy and social justice," Brown said in a press release at the time.[17] A few years later, as Clinton's commerce secretary, Brown became one of the most vigorous proponents of exactly the same MFN policy he had earlier denounced.

On June 3, 1992, when Bush extended China's MFN benefits for another year without conditions, Clinton (who by then had wrapped up the Democratic nomination) termed the action "unconscionable." The unconditional renewal, Clinton said, marks "another sad chapter in this Administration's history of putting America on the wrong side of human rights and democracy."[18]

At the convention, in order to highlight China as a campaign issue, the Democrats invited two of the most prominent Chinese student leaders of the Tiananmen Square movement, Chai Ling and Li Lu, to appear on the podium. The students introduced Aretha Franklin as she sang "The Star-Spangled Banner."

"Our song of freedom went out all around the world," Li Lu earnestly told the Democrats. "It was heard by many of you tonight who share our dream." In Beijing, the Chinese reacted in a predictable manner, denouncing the Democrats for giving the two student leaders a forum. "The crimes of those persons is beyond refutation," said the Foreign Ministry in a statement.[19]

These student leaders turned out to be, for the Democrats, a passing fashion. They would be noticeably absent from the podium in 1996, when Clinton was renominated for a second term. But in 1992, their appearance was powerful symbolism, embodying the Democratic attack on a China policy they felt had gone astray.

BUSH WAS soon to demonstrate that, in one respect at least, he was not coddling China. While his administration was unwilling to restrict China's trade benefits, Bush was willing to go further than any other president of the previous two decades in arming Taiwan.

Though the United States broke off diplomatic relations with Taiwan in 1979, it continued to serve as Taiwan's principal source of arms and other military hardware. Taiwan obtained these American supplies in a well-established annual ritual. Every winter, its military would come to Washington with a shopping list of American weapons systems. In the spring or early summer, at another Washington meeting, the Taiwan officials would be told which American weapons systems they could buy and which remained forbidden.

Since 1982, when Taiwan's request for advanced combat planes had been rejected by the Reagan administration, Taiwan had tried repeatedly to obtain these jet fighters from the United States. "F-16s had been the number one item on their list every year, bar none," recalled Carl Ford, a senior Pentagon official in the Bush administration.[20]

During the fall of 1991, officials from all the foreign policy agencies in the Bush administration—the Pentagon, CIA, State Department and National Security Council, as well as the office of Vice President Dan Quayle—began meeting once a month to talk in broad terms about the future of American policy toward Asia. The focus was upon what might happen in East Asia during Bush's second term and how the United States might respond. These internal meetings were modeled on similar ones the Bush administration had been conducting to decide what its policy toward Europe should be after the collapse of the Soviet Union and the reunification of Germany.[21]

One of the main issues that arose was the balance of military power between China and Taiwan. The question was whether, because of the deterioration of Taiwan's air force and China's purchase of the Russian Sukhoi-27 jet fighters, the People's Liberation Army was gaining an edge over Taiwan that it hadn't had in the past.

By 1992, quite a few Bush administration officials believed Taiwan had a legitimate case for buying new planes. Its air force was operating with antiquated American F-5E and F-104 jet fighters. Some of these planes crashed in such alarming numbers that they were being called "widow-makers." Taiwan was in the process of producing its own new combat aircraft, but it would not be ready for several more years. Taiwan's "fighter gap," as it was called, worried officials not only in Taipei, but also at the Pentagon and the White House.

"We at Defense were generally of the view that we really had a problem," recalls Paul Wolfowitz, the undersecretary. The situation had become "untenable," says Douglas Paal, who was in charge of Asia policy at the National Security Council. "Taiwan had lost 150 aircraft over the past ten years. It had gone from about 500 planes to 350, and then China goes out and buys Su-27s." [22]

Taiwan's political leaders actively courted the Bush administration. In January 1992, James Soong, the secretary-general of the Nationalist Party, flew to Washington for a private breakfast at the home of Dan Quayle; it was the highest-level political contact between Taiwan and the United States since diplomatic relations had been broken off in 1979. [23]

At the same time, throughout the early months of 1992, Taiwan put additional pressure on the Bush administration to sell the F-16s by flirting publicly with the idea of purchasing French Mirages. France was making a determined attempt to win contracts for new weapons systems in Taiwan; in 1991, it had agreed to sell Taiwan 16 naval frigates in a deal worth more than $4 billion. [24] French arms dealers were courting Taiwan and touting the glory of the Mirage.

Within the administration, the participants at the interagency discussions about Asia began talking in early 1992 about letting Taiwan purchase the F-16s or some other advanced plane. However, these officials reached no conclusion and made no recommendation. Instead, they bucked the issue upward to Bush, Brent Scowcroft, Defense Secretary Dick Cheney and James Baker. [25] These internal deliberations were kept secret.

Meanwhile, Taiwan officials had come to Washington for the annual review of their needs for military equipment. As usual, F-16s were at the top of the list. This time, largely at Lilley's instigation, the Pentagon and State Department took the request seriously, studying the balance of power across the Taiwan Strait. Nevertheless, in June 1992, Taiwan was once again turned down. A State Department official informed the Taiwan officials politely that the F-16s were still off-limits; if they really felt they needed more advanced warplanes, he said, maybe they could try to buy French-made Mirages. [26]

In theory, this formal rejection should have been the end of the process. In fact, it wasn't. Pentagon officials realized that when it came to Taiwan arms sales, nothing was ever final. "In any sort of big, controversial sale to Taiwan, Taiwan was originally told no by the bureaucracy," recalled Carl Ford. "In earlier periods, what that meant was that someone would go to Ronald Reagan and would say, 'We think you ought to do something for Taiwan,' and he would call over or send a message over to the secretary of state saying, 'I want you to do this one.' "[27]

Inside the Pentagon, Lilley continued to argue forcefully that Taiwan needed the new American planes. China's military cooperation with Russia was deepening, and it was obtaining all kinds of new hardware, he said. Lilley pressed his case with Wolfowitz in the Pentagon and Paal at the National Security Council. "I think really this is the time to do it [sell F-16s to Taiwan]," he told them. He also pointed out that politically, the sale would help to offset the idea that Bush was coddling Communist dictators.[28]

"I do recall Jim [Lilley] being an aggressive advocate," recalled Cheney in an interview. "He was strongly in favor of the F-16s."[29] Lilley talked with the defense secretary about Taiwan's need for new planes when Cheney visited Australia in early May and continued to send him memos on the issue over the next two months. Soon, Cheney himself became a staunch proponent of the Taiwan deal. Sometime in June or July, the Pentagon, led by Cheney, began quietly pushing hard for the sale.

This was the state of affairs at the end of July, when the presidential campaign and the faltering domestic economy prompted the Bush administration to break from ten years of American policy. On July 29, 1992, General Dynamics, the manufacturer of the F-16s, suddenly announced that it would lay off 5,800 workers by the end of 1994 at its Fort Worth division.[30]

The layoffs were made public only a day before Bush was to make a campaign appearance in Texas. The state's most prominent Democrats, led by Senator Lloyd Bentsen and Governor Ann Richards, blamed Bush's China policy for holding up a sale of the F-16s to Taiwan. "I don't know what deals have been made between George Bush and Communist China, but when it means the loss of 5,800 workers in Fort Worth, Texas, it is time to wake up and smell the coffee," said Richards.

Bentsen (who, like Ron Brown, would later become one of the Clinton administration's strongest proponents of a more accommodating policy toward China) began a month-long series of attacks on what he, too, called Bush's coddling of the Chinese regime. "We must learn to 'just say no' at least once to Beijing," Bentsen asserted. "What, after all, can Beijing do? Threaten to terminate its $20 billion-a-year trade surplus with us?"[31]

By this time, Bush's reelection campaign was already in serious trouble. Polls showed him running 20 percentage points behind Clinton.

Unemployment was running at well over 7 percent, and economic growth in the second quarter of 1992 was a mere 1.4 percent. And Texas was one of the most important states in the presidential campaign.

On the flight to Texas the day after General Dynamics announced its layoffs, the president told a group of Texas radio reporters that he was "taking a new look" at whether the United States might sell F-16s to Taiwan. By this time, few in America were aware of the history of acrimony, of how the dispute with China over Taiwan's request for F-16 combat planes during the first year of the Reagan administration had led to the 1982 communique restricting American arms sales to Taiwan.

On its face, Bush's talk about a "new look" at the F-16 sale was vague and noncommittal. In fact, however, it represented a decision by Bush and his advisers to make the sale to Taiwan. Lower-level officials at the Pentagon were instructed a few days before Bush flew to Texas that they should start working out the details: exactly what model of F-16s should be sold, how many planes, how the United States might make the sale more palatable to China.[32]

The State Department waged a last-ditch battle against the deal. However, it was operating at a handicap: During those weeks, its leader, Secretary of State Baker, was in the process of stepping down to become Bush's White House chief of staff and, in effect, campaign manager. By contrast, Cheney, at the Defense Department, was a strong proponent of the sale.

Nevertheless, Assistant Secretary of State William Clark drew up a memo for the White House, contending that American approval for Taiwan to buy F-16s would provoke an intense reaction from China. From Beijing, Ambassador Stapleton Roy, Lilley's successor, argued that the sale seemed to violate the 1982 communique signed by the Reagan administration, which limited American arms sales to Taiwan to prior levels.

The United States ought to live up to its agreements, Roy contended.[33] But administration officials supporting the F-16 sale countered (as had Reagan himself) that the 1982 communique was merely supposed to preserve the balance of power across the Taiwan Strait.

In practical terms, the State Department's objections were meaningless. "I think it was already decided in the White House," Clark later reflected. "They were just going through the form."[34] He was right. The department weighed in against the F-16 sale several weeks after the president and his advisers had made up their minds to go ahead with the deal.[35]

One day in early August, Bush had a drink in the residence quarters of the White House with a visitor from Beijing, one of the Chinese officials he had known for years. The official urged the president to halt the Taiwan deal. Sorry, Bush told him, the decision has already been made.[36] On September 2, the president formally announced American approval for the sale of 150 F-16s to Taiwan for an amount estimated at $6 billion.

Several administration officials have said that the pressures of the presidential campaign influenced only the timing of the F-16 sale, not the decision itself. The same action would have been taken later on, they argue, because of the progressive deterioration of Taiwan's air force and China's acquisition of the Russian planes.[37] Such claims seem plausible, given the extent to which the administration's foreign policy team had been talking about the changes in the military balance between China and Taiwan. The decision was not based *exclusively* on political considerations, as China and some of its supporters in the United States subsequently suggested.

Nevertheless, separating the F-16 deal from presidential politics is impossible. Bush's action reflected not only a desire to maintain the military balance in the Taiwan Strait, but also a judgment that selling the planes would help him win votes.

The Taiwan sale was one of two major arms deals announced with considerable fanfare by the Bush administration at the beginning of the fall presidential campaign. A few days after the Taiwan announcement, the White House made public a $9 billion sale of F-15 warplanes to Saudi Arabia. The F-15s were made by McDonnell Douglas in Missouri and California, two more key states in the 1992 campaign. Some Pentagon officials believed the Taiwan and Saudi arms deals were linked: one for California and one for Texas; one each for General Dynamics and for McDonnell Douglas, rival defense contractors. Over the summer, Cheney had asked what the Pentagon might do to help Bush's reelection effort. In an interview, Cheney said he didn't recall any top-level discussion about the political ramifications of the F-16 sale, although he acknowledged that Bush's campaign team "tried to package it for political reasons."[38]

Together, the two transactions with Taiwan and Saudi Arabia added up to $15 billion. To put this figure into perspective: In 1991, the total of all American arms sales to the Third World had been $14.2 billion—and that was more than for any other exporting country.[39]

The president announced the F-16 arrangement in a campaign appearance before General Dynamics workers in Fort Worth. Aides arranged for Bush to stand under a banner that said, "Jobs for America. Thanks Mr. President." Bush declared, "This F-16 is an example of what only America and Americans can do."[40]

·   ·   ·

THE SIGNIFICANCE of the F-16 sale was not well understood at the time. It illustrated, more than any other event of the early 1990s, how the end of the Cold War had altered the relationship between the United States and China. The deal showed the Chinese that America no longer cared what Beijing thought to the extent that it had before the collapse of the Soviet Union.

During the Cold War, the United States would never have sold the same warplanes to Taiwan. Indeed, Taiwan had sought the F-16s for a decade before the 1992 sale, and had been repeatedly turned down. Of course, in that same Cold War period, China would not have been able to buy advanced combat planes from the Soviet Union, either. China's purchase of the Su-27s was another reflection of the changing times.

During the late 1970s and the 1980s, American policy explicitly supported the modernization of the People's Liberation Army. Now, for the first time and in a dramatic way, the United States was taking strong action to counteract China's military modernization. America no longer worried about the PLA's ability to withstand a Soviet invasion or to pin down divisions of the Red Army in Asia. Instead, Washington was more worried about the impact of a more powerful PLA on the rest of East Asia.

To illustrate just how great a change this was for America's dealings with China and Taiwan, it is worth comparing the Bush administration's F-16 sale with another episode involving Taiwan two years earlier. During the late summer of 1990, the administration tried to raise money from other governments to support the costs of its Desert Storm buildup in the Persian Gulf. One official, Richard Armitage, got the idea of asking Taiwan for some quiet help.

After getting tentative approval from Baker and Scowcroft, Armitage approached Taiwan's chief Washington representative, Ding Mou–shih. "We don't want any announcement," Armitage told Ding. "We're just looking for a little contribution." The Taiwan representative quickly called back and offered the impressive sum of $300 million. Armitage arranged a trip to Taipei to pick up the check. But at that point, Undersecretary of State Bob Kimmitt intervened, saying the United States ought to inform China about the arrangement. China objected, and the deal was called off. "They [Chinese officials] said no, so we backed away, and that cost us $300 million," recalled Armitage in an interview.[41]

Kimmitt's reaction was not exceptional. Rather, it reflected the way the United States had dealt with issues concerning Taiwan for years. On anything of consequence, even a financial transaction like Taiwan's $300 million offer, Washington had checked first with Beijing. If China objected, the United States usually gave way. But on the F-16 deal it.

1992, only two years after the Desert Storm episode, the administration was disregarding China on an issue of far greater consequence, a deal Beijing had opposed for years. For the United States and China, and for Taiwan, too, a new era was beginning.

ON THE day that the F-16 sale was announced, Foreign Minister Qian Qichen warned that it was "a very serious incident" and that Washington would be held accountable for "serious consequences."[42]

In fact, however, China didn't react strongly at the time. A few months later, when Taiwan proceeded to buy 60 Mirage jets from France to complement the F-16s, China countered by closing down the French consulate in Guangzhou and by denying French companies any chance to bid on a contract to build Guangzhou's subway. The French protested that China was punishing France much more severely than it had the United States, but Chinese officials brushed off the complaint. France wasn't America, the Chinese said; the United States had a much longer history with Taiwan than France did.[43]

Bush administration officials attributed the mild Chinese reaction to their own diplomatic skill in handling Beijing. Within days after the Taiwan deal was announced, Clark was sent to Beijing with a package of peace offerings. The idea was to make sure that China got some rewards of its own to counterbalance the F-16 sale.

Clark told the Chinese that the administration would send Commerce Secretary Barbara Franklin to Beijing to revive the Joint Commission on Commerce and Trade, which had been suspended under Bush's sanctions of June 1989. Moreover, the United States would deliver some leftover American military equipment, such as torpedoes and radar, which had been bought by China before 1989 but had been held up in storage in the United States after the sanctions were imposed. Clark's delegation included a three-star general, yet another sign that the Tiananmen Square sanctions were being phased out.[44] At the time of Clark's trip in September 1992, all of these blandishments for China were kept secret: Franklin's visit and the release of the military equipment weren't announced until well after election day. Although Bush wanted to keep China happy, he also didn't want the American electorate to know what he was doing.

The Clark mission may have helped assuage China's anger, but there were other reasons for Beijing's subdued reaction to the F-16 sale. The Chinese were so stunned that they probably didn't know how to respond. Moreover, for Beijing the timing could not have been worse. The Taiwan deal was consummated by President Bush, whom Beijing viewed as the preferred candidate in 1992. Any harsh Chinese protest might have hurt Bush's chances for reelection. China did not want to do anything that would help the Democrats, who had been considerably more critical of its human rights practices and more eager to restrict its trade benefits.

China may well have decided to respond to the F-16 sale in its own fashion, indirectly and in secret. In November 1992, in the last weeks of the Bush administration, American intelligence noticed a shipment of parts of China's modern M-11 missiles passing into Pakistan at the port of Karachi. These were precisely the sort of missiles the administration had been trying for four years to stop China from exporting.

Administration officials believed they had obtained an assurance during Baker's 1991 trip to Beijing that would bar China from selling the M-11s. At the time, China had agreed to abide by the Missile Technology Control Regime, and the secretary had told a press conference "we understand" that the agreement covered the M-11 missiles. It turned out that Baker's "we" meant only the Americans. China subsequently argued that the range of the M-11 missiles fell slightly below the MTCR's guidelines, and that therefore it was not violating its agreement with the United States.

When the Chinese missiles were detected in Pakistan in late 1992, Clark asked Baker (who by then was working as White House chief of staff) whether he had won an airtight agreement from Beijing not to sell the M-11 missiles. "I'm not sure I did have that kind of agreement," Baker confessed.[45] In the frenetic negotiations on the last day of his 1991 visit to Beijing, Baker had failed to nail down a Chinese commitment.

Some officials thought the sale of the missiles was not a coincidence. It had come only a few months after the American sale of the F-16 warplanes to Taiwan. The Chinese M-11 transaction could be seen as a tit-for-tat response to the Taiwan deal: China was playing loose with, if not actually breaking, its agreement to abide by the missile-control regime, just as (so Chinese officials claimed) the United States had played loose with the 1982 agreement on arms deliveries to Taiwan.[46] For the next several years, every time the United States asked to talk to China about its missile sales to Pakistan, China countered that it would do so only if the United States agreed to talk about the sale of the F-16s to Taiwan.

Under American law, the M-11 deal, if confirmed, would have required the imposition of new sanctions against China. In its last weeks, the Bush administration decided not to try to cope with such an explosive issue. Instead, it bucked the matter over to the incoming Clinton administration on grounds that there wasn't enough intelligence information to determine conclusively whether China had exported the missiles.

During his final weeks in office, George Bush took one last action that demonstrated how the times were changing: He sent U.S. Trade Representative Carla Hills to Taiwan. The trip attracted little attention, because it seemed such a small and obvious step in pursuit of America's clear economic interests. Taiwan had become the world's 13th-largest trading power; it was in the early stages of a six-year, $300 billion public works program in which American firms were bidding for contracts against European and Japanese competitors. Yet Hills was the first Cabinet member to visit Taiwan since the United States had established diplomatic ties with China.

In the thirteen years since 1979, America had barred all such high-level missions to Taiwan, out of fear of arousing China's ire. At the beginning of the Bush administration, Baker casually told Chinese Ambassador Han Xu he thought the United States should be able to send high-level officials to Taiwan, at least to talk about economic issues. This casual and mild suggestion provoked an intense Chinese response. During Bush's trip to Beijing a few weeks later, Premier Li Peng angrily warned the president not to ease the ban on high-level visits to Taiwan, and the Bush administration hurriedly dropped the idea.[47]

Thus, in sending Hills to Taiwan, too, the Bush administration was venturing onto new ground. The United States was demonstrating that with the end of the Cold War, it was willing to deal with Taiwan in new ways, no longer giving China the veto power it had earlier enjoyed.

BUSH ADMINISTRATION officials claimed that in their last weeks in office, they cleared the way for President Clinton to start fresh with China. The delivery of torpedoes, radar and other military supplies to China had settled one of the grievances left over since Bush's imposition of sanctions in 1989. Franklin's visit had ended another of the Tiananmen sanctions and had opened the way for routine high-level business between the two governments. The slate was being wiped clean for a new administration, White House officials said.[48]

These claims were true, but also incomplete. The administration was cleaning the slate between the United States and China only in certain, selected areas. It was eager to settle the disputes over human rights and the Tiananmen crackdown; officials also wanted to reestablish military ties with China.

On the other hand, when it came to China's exports of missiles, the administration wasn't wiping the slate clean. It was, rather, leaving office with crucial decisions unsettled. Most important of all, on Taiwan, the outgoing Bush administration had during its final year embarked upon new initiatives whose repercussions would be felt for years. When it came to Taiwan, in fact, George Bush was leaving a legacy of bitterness in Beijing.

Thus, the Bush administration left office dealing with China much as it had over the previous four years.

Bush had no appetite to confront China over human rights. He had failed to give voice to America's outrage over the crackdown of 1989 or the nationwide repression that followed it. He dealt comfortably with the Chinese leaders he had known for years. He seemed to have difficulty taking seriously the idea that there might be passionate dissent in China, of the sort that he and other American leaders had long honored in the Soviet Union and Eastern Europe.

Nevertheless, with the end of the Cold War and amid the pressures of his unsuccessful reelection campaign, Bush had opened the way for change between the United States and China. By selling American warplanes to Taiwan and sending a Cabinet member there, he had demonstrated that the United States was willing to defy China in ways that had been unthinkable for more than a decade.

Perhaps Bush was harking back to his first direct experience with China, two decades earlier. When he had served as United Nations ambassador in 1971, it had been his job to try to save Taiwan's seat in the United Nations. "He was indefatigable in lobbying for this policy," recalled Harry Thayer, an aide at the U.N. Mission. "He believed in it."[49] Bush had failed to preserve Taiwan's U.N. seat, in part because Henry Kissinger's visits to Beijing had undercut the American efforts. Two decades later, during his final days in office, Bush was giving a little bit back to Taiwan.

CHAPTER FIFTEEN

Enter President Clinton

A T THE TIME HE was elected president, Bill Clinton had never seen China. His only indirect experience with the world's most populous country had come from his travels as governor of Arkansas. Clinton had visited Taiwan four times, more than anywhere else, enjoying the hospitality the Nationalist government always showered upon American dignitaries, particularly up-and-coming politicians.

On Taiwan's National Day celebration and parade on October 10, 1985, the two principal American guests were the governors of Virginia and Arkansas, Charles Robb and Bill Clinton. Years later, Robb would confess that Clinton had drunk him under the table at one banquet during that trip, keeping up with the endless toasts well after Robb's capacity had been exceeded. Clinton, who liked to tease, had never let Robb forget it.[1]

Clinton's principal work on these Taiwan excursions had been the pursuit of business contracts. He had lobbied hard, for example, for the Arkansas Parking Meter Company, and with apparent success: Some of the parking meters in Taipei were imported from Arkansas.[2]

The new president had little experience in foreign policy. During the 1992 campaign, he had relied heavily on the work of others. Clinton had pounded George Bush repeatedly for coddling China; yet his own policy prescription, to impose conditions on the renewal of China's most-favored-nation trade benefits, had been merely borrowed from the Democratic leadership in Congress.

In any policy area where he felt insecure, Clinton's instinct was to rely on established authority, in order to give himself credibility. If questioned about his defense policies or his own military credentials, for example, Clinton would respond that William Crowe, the former chairman of the Joint Chiefs of Staff, was supporting him. So it had been with China, too: When questioned during the campaign, he would say that he was endorsing the approach of Senate Majority Leader George Mitchell.[3]

On China, Clinton took office believing he could have everything and please everyone. He saw no conflict between American ideals and American commerce, or between his desire to please the Chinese students, whom he had so carefully courted during the campaign, and the business community whose support he had also assiduously cultivated. Those choices would be confronted later. At the beginning of 1993, everything seemed possible. Clinton was about to embark upon a foreign policy that would lead to one of the most remarkable American turnabouts of the modern era, yet he seemed blissfully unaware of what was at stake.

The new president was not focused upon China. At the time he took office, Clinton did not want to devote much of his time and energy to foreign policy of any kind. The central message of his 1992 campaign had been that Bush was too preoccupied with foreign policy and not enough with the domestic economy. Moreover, even within the field of foreign policy, China was not at or even near the top of the list of the president-elect's priorities.

During the interim between Clinton's election and his swearing-in, the CIA set up shop in Little Rock in order to give the president-elect daily intelligence briefings. Agency officials installed secure communications that could produce high-quality maps and imagery, carrying their materials from their motel to the Governor's Mansion. As Clinton prepared for press conferences, the CIA described the problems he would soon confront around the world. The main subjects of conversation at these briefings were Russia, Somalia and Yugoslavia. In the next tier were Iraq, Haiti, Lebanon, Israel and the world trade talks. China wasn't anywhere in these top ranks.[4]

Though some in Washington speculated during this time that Clinton might immediately abandon his campaign position on China's most-favored-nation benefits, his position remained consistent. At the economic conference Clinton chaired in Little Rock in December 1992, one businesswoman tried to talk to the president-elect about China. Jill Barad, the president and chief executive officer of Mattel, the American toy company, warned of the consequences if China's MFN status was withdrawn. Duties on Chinese-made toys would go up from 12 to 70 percent, she said, and American companies like Mattel might lose their market share to foreign competitors. And not just toy companies would be hurt, she went on: American shoe companies obtained 60 percent of their products from China, and American imports of textiles from that country added up to $4 billion a year.

Clinton told Barad he hoped not to have to dislocate any of these industries. He didn't favor the revocation of China's MFN benefits "if we can achieve continued progress" in areas like human rights, Clinton said. He was thus reaffirming his campaign position, the approach of placing conditions upon the renewal of China's benefits. "I don't want to do it economically, I don't want to do it politically," he said. "But I think we've got to stick up for ourselves and for the things we believe in and how these people are treated in that country."[5]

He also sounded another theme about China in Little Rock, one that he would repeat on numerous occasions in the transition and throughout his first year in the White House. China had a $15 billion-a-year trade surplus with the United States, Clinton pointed out. Its stake in trade with the United States was considerably larger than America's.

This statistic that Clinton liked to cite was true but not particularly meaningful in predicting what would happen on MFN. Clinton's suggestion was that in any showdown over trade benefits, China would yield, because its exports to the United States were larger than were America's to China. Yet any such showdown would inevitably boil down to a test of political wills, not merely a dollar-for-dollar calculation of the balance of trade. If Clinton didn't have the ability to withstand opposition from the U.S. business community (which included not only the American firms exporting to China but also those, like Mattel, which imported from it), then these comparative trade figures were irrelevant. Indeed, four years later, China's annual trade surplus with the United States would reach $40 billion, nearly three times the level when he arrived in the White House, yet Clinton had by then abandoned the idea of restricting MFN.

IN PUTTING together his foreign policy team, Clinton turned to well-established names: Warren Christopher as secretary of state, Anthony Lake to be his national security advisor. Both men had served in the State Department during the Carter administration, Christopher as deputy secretary and Lake as director of policy planning. Both had been tangentially involved in the 1979 establishment of diplomatic relations with China; both also had strong commitments to the causes of human rights and democracy.

In his confirmation hearing, Christopher minced no words. "Our policy will be to seek to facilitate a broad, peaceful evolution in China from communism to democracy," he said, "by encouraging the forces of economic and political liberalization in that great and highly important country." [6] If China's hard-line leaders were looking for evidence that America was seeking the end of Communist rule, they could point to Christopher's forthright statement. In response, Foreign Ministry spokesman Wu Jianmin warned that the United States should not try to meddle in China's internal affairs. [7]

In filling out his new administration, Clinton made one other foreign policy appointment, which was, for dealing with China, more important than all the others. For the job of assistant secretary of state for East Asia and the Pacific, the official directly responsible for day-to-day policy toward Beijing, he named Winston Lord.

The former ambassador had been an adviser to the Clinton campaign; during the fall, when the Democratic candidate had a meeting with foreign policy specialists in New Haven to talk about what the United States should do in Asia, Lord had taken the leading role on China. [8] Lord was the sort of person to whom Clinton was often drawn: He was a member of the foreign policy elite, a recognizable name, part of the comfortable world inhabited by other Democratic Party stalwarts like Lake and Richard Holbrooke.

Thus, Lord, the one-time aide to Henry Kissinger and ambassador to China during the Bush administration, was returning to government for a Democratic administration. A few years later, in his self-mocking style, Lord would joke in public that he had worked for both Ronald Reagan and Bill Clinton, "which proves one of two things: either I'm indispensable or I have absolutely no principles." [9] In fact, Lord's work in the Clinton administration showed that he did have a strong point of view and that he was dispensable.

Since 1990, he had not only repeatedly excoriated the Bush administration for being too conciliatory toward China on human rights, but had also sketched out what his own policy prescription would be: Lord had been one of the earliest proponents of the idea of attaching conditions to the renewal of China's MFN trade benefits. Indeed, his endorsement had lent credibility to this approach.

In Washington, personnel appointments do not always determine policy. In Lord's case, however, the appointment was the message. At his Senate confirmation hearing, Lord made it plain that the Clinton administration intended to require improvements in human rights if China wanted renewal of its trade benefits. "We will seek cooperation from China on a range of issues. But Americans cannot forget Tiananmen Square," he testified. [10]

Nevertheless, submerged in Lord's testimony, which gave the first detailed overview of the new Clinton administration's policies toward Asia, there appeared to be the makings of a quiet, unacknowledged trade-off with China. In its crudest terms, it was human rights for Taiwan: That is, if China made the concessions on human rights that the Clinton administration sought, the United States would pull back from the venturesome new Taiwan policies of the final year of the Bush administration and return to the straight and narrow approaches of the previous decade.

Lord had broken with Kissinger over issues of human rights and democracy in China, but not over Taiwan. He was behaving like a son who rebels against his father but embraces many of the father's underlying values. In his testimony, he went out of his way to pay homage to the three communiques with China over Taiwan. America's ties to Taiwan were merely "unofficial," Lord said, leaving unmentioned the Cabinet-level visit in the dying days of the previous administration. He referred to Taiwan and Hong Kong merely as parts of the "greater Chinese communities." Thus, he made clear he saw no need for changes in the one-China policy that had been worked out in the days when he was taking notes for Kissinger.

As it turned out, this implicit bargain was not one that China accepted. Whether the Clinton administration could have carried out such a bargain is an open question. It is clear, however, that after Clinton's MFN policy fell apart, the administration lost control of its position on Taiwan, too. Once Clinton demonstrated on MFN that he would abandon his policies in the face of pressure, supporters of Taiwan saw an opportunity to capitalize on this political weakness.

YEARS LATER, Clinton administration officials would perpetuate a myth about their China policy of 1993. They had been forced to act as they had, they said, because Congress had been on the verge of revoking China's MFN benefits. "We succeeded in not having the revocation of MFN in 1993," asserted Samuel R. "Sandy" Berger, then Clinton's deputy national security advisor, in an interview. Such sentiments were echoed by other officials.[11]

There is, however, no evidence to support this claim and considerable evidence to the contrary. Congress was not moving to revoke MFN in 1993. Over the previous two years, bills to cut off MFN, pushed forward primarily by conservative Republicans such as Representative Gerald Solomon of New York, had failed by large margins. By contrast, votes to impose conditions on the renewal of MFN had easily passed Congress in both 1991 and 1992, only to be vetoed by Bush both times. No major change in Congress had occurred in the 1992 elections. It was still in the hands of Democrats who pushed for conditions on MFN, not the revocation of it.

On Capitol Hill in the early weeks of 1993, the sponsors of the prior years' MFN legislation—Mitchell in the Senate and Pelosi in the House—started to work once again on writing a new bill. They decided it would be like the measures of 1991 and 1992: It would again require China to change its policies on human rights, trade and the proliferation of weapons over a one-year period in order to win MFN renewal the following year. If China failed to meet these conditions, the trade benefits would be cut off specifically for the products of China's state-owned enterprises.[12]

Once the House bill was drafted, Pelosi embarked upon the next legislative task, which was to line up sponsors. Bills have a considerably greater chance for passage if they are sponsored not merely by a single member of Congress but on behalf of scores of members from both political parties.

But she was called by Robert Rubin, the chairman of Clinton's National Economic Council, the top economic policymaker in the new administration.

"I'd like to ask you not to continue to get sponsors," Rubin told her. The White House wanted her to drop the MFN legislation. Instead, the administration would draft its own executive order, to be signed by Clinton, imposing conditions on the renewal on MFN in much the same fashion as the proposed legislation.

"That's impossible," Pelosi replied. "The bill's already out there."[13] Still, Rubin and others in the administration persisted.

In April and May, the administration conducted several rounds of talks with Mitchell and Pelosi on what Clinton's executive order should say. In these negotiations, Lord represented the administration, although Lake sat in on at least one of the sessions. Mitchell, the Senate majority leader, usually handled the talks on his own, rather than leaving them to his staff; he met with Lord at least three times.[14]

The administration's goal was to come up with a unified policy on China's MFN benefits, one that represented both the White House and Congress. It was eager to stop the prolonged skirmishing between the executive branch and Congress that Bush had confronted. This was not a novel approach. In the early months of the Bush administration, James Baker had negotiated the compromise deal with Congress that had successfully ended years of division between the executive branch and Capitol Hill over American policy toward Nicaragua.

Mitchell and Pelosi made several important concessions, watering down the approach taken in their legislation. First, they agreed that Clinton's executive order would require improvements from China only on human rights, and not on trade or arms proliferation. The administration promised that it would handle problems with China on trade and arms control in other ways, separate from MFN.

Other congressmen were unhappy that Clinton was dropping the linkage between MFN and China's arms exports. Pelosi didn't care so much. Three years earlier, her own first bill on MFN had covered only human rights and not these other issues. Back then, she had added language to cover China's export of deadly weapons only after other members of Congress, such as Senator Joe Biden of Delaware, had insisted that this issue was more important than human rights. How could she complain now if Clinton scaled the order back to what she had originally sought? [15]

Second, the administration significantly weakened the human rights language, too. The Chinese students had wanted Clinton's MFN order to include a provision, similar to the one in the congressional legislation, requiring China to release "all political prisoners" held as a result of the Tiananmen crackdown. In the negotiations between Lord and the congressional leaders, the administration succeeded in deleting the word "all," so that Clinton's order vaguely sought the release of some political prisoners. [16]

Still, when the negotiations were finished, Pelosi was relatively content. If George Bush had offered congressional leaders the same deal the Clinton administration was now proposing, she figured, they would certainly have taken it. Among other things, the executive order they had negotiated with Lord said that after a year, the secretary of state should decide whether China had made "overall, significant progress" on releasing and accounting for political prisoners, allowing access to its prisons, protecting Tibetan heritage and allowing international broadcasts into China.

What followed attracted little notice at the time, but it turned out to be the critical step in the entire process. Once the Clinton executive order was completed, administration officials then pressed Mitchell and Pelosi once again to drop their legislation. After all, the officials argued, Clinton was now going to do by executive order what the legislation was proposing: He would require China to meet certain conditions to get a renewal of its trade benefits. That made the legislation superfluous, administration officials said.

If Mitchell and Pelosi had gone forward with their bill at this point, it would surely have passed. The Democratic Congress had already approved versions of the same legislation for the two previous years, only to have it vetoed by Bush. This time, Bush was not in the White House, and a new Democratic president had taken office after repeatedly endorsing the legislation in his campaign. To strengthen their case Mitchell and

Pelosi might even have watered down the conditions in their legislation to match the language of Clinton's executive order. In that way, the same logic that Rubin and others had thrown at Mitchell and Pelosi could have been applied in reverse: How could the administration object to legislation that did what Clinton himself was already promising in his executive order?

Instead, they dropped their legislation, believing that it wasn't necessary because Clinton would carry out the executive order they had just negotiated. "He was our new president. It never occurred to me, and frankly it never occurred to George Mitchell or Richard Gephardt, that he wouldn't keep his word," reflected Pelosi years later. "I was trusting. This [conditioning MFN] was now our policy. We thought it was a great victory." Even the Chinese students decided not to press for the legislation. Doing so would have been an unfriendly act, Zhao Haiqing thought; it would have been taken as a sign that they didn't trust Clinton to enforce his own order.[17]

Berger's assertion that the Clinton administration headed off the revocation of MFN in 1993 was inaccurate. The administration had, however, done something that was more subtle: It had dissuaded Congress from writing into law the very position of MFN conditionality that Clinton had endorsed in the campaign and was enshrining in his executive order. At the time, such congressional action seemed unnecessary. A year later, after Clinton did an about-face, it made all the difference in the world.

ON FRIDAY, May 28, 1993, Clinton signed his MFN executive order in a ceremony in which he was joined by Mitchell, Pelosi and about 40 Chinese student leaders, dissidents and Tibetan activists.

Zhao Haiqing was invited to the White House for the occasion, as were Lodi Gyari, the representative of Tibet's Dalai Lama, and Chai Ling, the Tiananmen leader who had been put on display at the previous year's Democratic convention. The participants had originally been told the ceremony would be outside the White House, for the best possible television coverage, but on the night before, they were informed it had been moved indoors to the Roosevelt Room without any cameras present for the actual signing. The administration evidently had second thoughts about displaying Clinton alongside those who were challenging the Chinese leadership; this was a hint of the underlying unease about what the president was doing.

Nevertheless, everyone proclaimed it to be a glorious day. "For the first time since the events of Tiananmen Square, nearly four years ago, we have a president who is willing to act in order to bring about positive change," said Mitchell. After signing the order, Clinton handed out pens, as presidents often do with historic legislation. One went to Mitchell, who in his role as Senate majority leader had been given more signing pens than he needed; he handed his to Ed King on the way back to the Capitol. Pelosi got a pen, and so did Zhao Haiqing.[18] They didn't know it at the time, but these pens would eventually prove to be embarrassing souvenirs.

The president was as exuberant as his guests. "It is time that a unified American policy recognize both the values of China *and* the values of America," he said. The annual battles that had proved so divisive over China in the Bush years, Clinton claimed, were over. "Starting today, the United States will speak with one voice on China policy," he declared.[19]

As the events of the following year were to show, this last assertion was remarkably optimistic.

CLINTON'S ORDER was above all a compromise. The administration had succeeded through its negotiations in weakening significantly the conditions Congress had imposed in its bills of the prior two years. The initial reviews were overwhelmingly positive. At the time, the result was praised as "statesmanlike" and "creative" by Henry Kissinger. "China must understand that even those of us who have reservations regarding conditionality on MFN believe that the president should not abandon his basic convictions," wrote Kissinger.[20] Indeed, when the order was signed, most of the public criticism of it focused on the claim that it was too soft. The Republican National Committee accused Clinton of "a complete reversal of his campaign rhetoric" by extending MFN for another year with "no strings attached."[21]

Moreover, at the time Clinton issued the order, the American business community showed no sign of the intense opposition it would offer later on. In their public statements in May 1993, companies and business groups registered little if any unhappiness. They were, indeed, mildly approving. After all, the new administration had renewed MFN, loosened the conditions China would have to meet the following year and per-suaded Congress to withdraw its legislation. "We are encouraged," said a spokesman for Boeing. Robert Kapp, then the president of the Washington State Council for International Trade and subsequently the leader of the U.S.-China Business Council, said, "The president has done a great service."[22]

Clinton's action rested upon the notion that China would bargain or negotiate over the human rights conditions rather than simply defy the presidential order. The expectation was that over the following year, there would be a give-and-take between Washington and Beijing.

Based strictly on China's behavior during the previous two years, this was not an implausible assumption. During the final years of the Bush administration, China had indeed demonstrated a willingness to make some well-timed concessions on human rights. Each year, as the congressional vote on MFN drew near, China had released a dissident or two or made other concessions, in order to help the Bush administration to avoid defeat on Capitol Hill. If China had done so before, why wouldn't it do so again?

This logic turned out to be faulty for a number of reasons, not least of them the fact that the good cop/bad cop approach by the Bush administration and its Democratic Congress put far more pressure on China than Clinton's supposedly united front. But in May 1993, there seemed to be at least some grounds in recent history for believing that China might try, in its own way, to satisfy the MFN order rather than flout it.

Indeed, over the next few months, Beijing started down this conciliatory path, publicly suggesting that it might be ready for the first time to let the International Committee of the Red Cross into its prisons. Ultimately, however, China decided to deal with the Clinton administration in a fundamentally different way.

Thus, Clinton's MFN order was hardly as daring or far-reaching as its critics would later characterize it. Indeed, the new president's policy on China at first won a considerable degree of acceptance, or at least tolerance, from those who would later fight it.

Nevertheless, several fundamental defects marred Clinton's MFN order and the manner in which it was produced, and these contributed to the ensuing debacle.

First, Clinton had failed to line up active support for his new China policy from the business community or even the economic wing of his own administration. The focus had been much more upon making peace with Congress than upon building a broader political base for what Clinton was about to do.

The negotiations over the MFN order had been conducted almost exclusively with Mitchell and Pelosi and with human rights groups. Business representatives had not been part of this process. No prominent business leaders were at Clinton's signing ceremony; no executives of Boeing or AT&T stood alongside the Chinese dissidents to show Beijing that they, too, supported the new president. The fact that American companies didn't actively oppose the new president was less significant than it appeared. They were merely being polite and hopeful; there was nothing to stop them from challenging the policy later on.

Second, the bluntness of the penalties was a problem. Neither

Clinton's MFN order nor the bills in Congress on which it had been based devoted enough attention to the question of the punishments that might be imposed upon China if it failed to meet the conditions. Instead, the approach seemed to be all-or-nothing: If China didn't do what America required, it would lose all of its MFN trade benefits—a result with such sweeping economic effects that it frightened American companies as much as it did China. If the penalties had been more subtle and gradual (say, for example, an increase in tariffs of 5 percent on Chinese imports each year that it failed to satisfy the conditions), then the MFN order might conceivably have been one the administration could credibly threaten to enforce.

Finally, and most seriously of all, there was the problem of the president of the United States himself. In issuing his MFN order, Clinton was giving China an ultimatum. Before doing so, he needed to be sure he had the resolve to carry it out. It was the president's responsibility to decide, in advance, whether he was willing to follow through on his threat to cut off China's trade benefits; if not, he should not have issued the order. There is, however, no indication that in May 1993 Clinton confronted these questions. Indeed, not until the following winter and spring did he seem to understand what he had done and what the consequences might be.

IN THE early months of 1993, just after the Chinese New Year, Ambassador J. Stapleton Roy began to notice a remarkable change. Suddenly, the titans of American business were rushing to Beijing.

Every day or two, some new board chairman or chief executive of a leading American corporation would arrive, eager to launch a venture in China. Roy hadn't seen such interest before. When he had first come to Beijing, nearly two years earlier, the American business interest in China had been tepid.[23]

The statistics confirm Roy's impressions. Nineteen ninety-three was the peak year for new investment in China, both from the United States and from the rest of the world. That year, China signed 83,437 new contracts with foreign companies, worth $111 billion in new investment; more than 6,700 of these contracts were with American companies.[24] No other country in the world was attracting such capital. The dramatic increases in new investment started in 1992 and continued throughout the first half of the decade.

In early 1992, Deng Xiaoping had staged what amounted to his last political comeback. On a trip to southern China, Deng had galvanized the leadership to open the way for a new burst of economic growth, overcoming the resistance of those, like Premier Li Peng, who had wanted to maintain the restraints that had been applied in 1989. China's growth rate leaped from little more than 4 percent in 1990 to more than 12 percent in 1992 and nearly 14 percent in the first half of 1993.[25]

In two years, China had thus suddenly become the fastest-growing economy in the world, and businesses everywhere dreamed of capitalizing on the growth. Moreover, China's careful courtship of other Asians at the beginning of the decade, when American and European companies were ignoring China, had begun to produce a snowball effect. By 1992, Japanese firms were rushing to invest in China ahead of their Korean competitors, and Europeans and American companies were trying to gain an edge on the Japanese.

With its new growth, China was, for the first time, perceived as a world economic power, one that might some day rival Japan or even the United States. "The Titan Stirs," proclaimed the *Economist* in late 1992, raising the specter of "a self-confident nuclear-armed China presiding over the biggest economy on earth." In May 1993, the International Monetary Fund released the first study ever to measure the size of China's economy in terms of "purchasing-power parity." The study, published on the front page of the *New York Times,* concluded that China's economy was four times larger than previously estimated; China was, by this new measure, the third-largest economy in the world, slightly smaller than Japan but ahead of Germany.[26]

The implications for Clinton and his new MFN policy were profound. China possessed vastly greater ability to withstand the threat of American sanctions in 1993 than it had had three years earlier. The pressures from American business to keep open trade with China were much more intense.

This was, then, the ultimate irony and tragedy of the entire American effort to use economic pressure to goad China into easing its repressive political system. The timing was all wrong. Clinton's tough approach of 1993 might have had a better chance of success immediately after the Tiananmen crackdown, when the Chinese economy was fragile and American business interest in China was at its nadir. But George Bush was in the White House then, pursuing policies that were, in fact, better suited to the time when Clinton was in office.

One of the clichés about China is that its system moves too slowly. Clinton's MFN order was an example of the American system moving too laboriously, taking three years to adopt a policy that no longer matched the economic conditions in China.

THE FIRST signs of trouble for Clinton's China policy arose in a roundabout way, in an unrelated dispute. On August 25, 1993, the administration announced it would impose sanctions against China for its transfer of M-11 missile parts to Pakistan. These sanctions, unveiled by Undersecretary of State Lynn Davis, prohibited the export of American satellites to China.

The new administration was finally responding to the discovery of the M-11 shipment by American intelligence the previous fall. The Bush administration had left office without deciding what to do about the transfer of the M-11s, saying the intelligence was not yet conclusive [see chapter 14]. By mid-1993, however, the evidence was clear.

American law required the imposition of sanctions for a violation of the Missile Technology Control Regime. Moreover, only a few months earlier, the administration had specifically promised members of Congress that if the nonproliferation conditions were dropped from Clinton's MFN executive order, it would invoke these other laws to curb China's arms exports. "If we determine that China has, in fact, transferred M-11 missiles or related equipment in violation of its commitments, my administration will not hesitate to act," Clinton had pledged on the day he announced his MFN order.[27]

These missile sanctions had nothing to do with MFN. They did, however, hurt some American companies, such as Hughes Aircraft and Martin Marietta, which had signed a series of contracts for communications satellites that were to be launched by Chinese rockets. Sales of these satellites and satellite parts were estimated at about $500 million a year.[28] Their export had been the subject of often-secret negotiations between the United States and China for more than five years; they had been an important element both in the visit of Defense Secretary Frank Carlucci to China in 1988 and the second Scowcroft sojourn of late 1989. The satellites, in other words, had a long history and were worth a lot of money.

Most significantly, the new sanctions harmed precisely those elements of the American business community that had most strongly supported Clinton's 1992 campaign. While Bush remained strong with traditional banking and manufacturing sectors, Clinton had attracted the support of newer, high-technology industries—the computers, software, and electronics industries concentrated in California and along the East Coast.

One of Clinton's early business supporters had been Michael Armstrong, the chairman and chief executive officer of Hughes. During the late summer and fall of 1993, Armstrong launched an intensive campaign, both public and private, to undo the China sanctions. Privately, he went directly to the president, reminding Clinton of his past support and complaining bitterly about the impact of the sanctions at Hughes. He also gave speeches in which he complained that the administration's

China policy was causing Hughes to lose contracts to European competitors.

"It escapes me what effect our laying off 4,000 to 5,000 more people in California and shifting this export business to Europe has on the Chinese," Armstrong said. "I know it doesn't affect missile technology transfer, but I do know it affects American jobs, American families, American business and the American satellite technology base." [29]

For good measure, Armstrong also lined up the support of the California congressional delegation. One prominent member, Senator Dianne Feinstein, needed especially little prompting. Feinstein had cultivated Chinese President Jiang Zemin when she was the mayor of San Francisco and he the mayor of Shanghai; and Feinstein's husband, Richard Blum, was an investor with extensive business interests in Shanghai. As a senator, Feinstein became Congress's leading proponent of a policy of conciliation with China. "I think the prevailing view is that we have to get something for everything we do [with China]," she once explained. "I think that is a mistake." On another occasion, she seemed to plead for understanding of China's Tiananmen Square crackdown, in which many hundreds of people died, by comparing it to the American shootings at Kent State University, in which four students were killed. [30]

Armstrong's campaign on behalf of Hughes put strong political pressure on Clinton. At the time, California's economy was still struggling to emerge from recession. Clinton was traveling to California regularly; his economic team was devoting special attention to the state's problems; yet his sanctions against China were accused of undercutting these efforts.

Over the next few months, with the president taking the lead, the administration slowly backed away from its missile sanctions. On a trip to California in December, Clinton said publicly he was considering a Commerce Department recommendation to open the way for export of the satellites. [31] Soon afterward, the administration began granting waivers from the August sanctions, opening the way for satellites to be sent to China. [32]

Although the furor over these missile sanctions was unrelated to either human rights or China's trade benefits, the impact of the dispute inevitably spilled over onto MFN. The satellite sanctions roused the American business community from its slumber. Executives took their complaints about China policy directly to the administration's senior economic officials, to members of Congress and to Clinton himself. In dealing with China, the administration began to find itself on the defensive.

For the Chinese leadership, this controversy over the satellites carried important lessons. It demonstrated that the Clinton administration, to an extent considerably greater than its predecessors, was subject to commercial pressure. It also demonstrated that the administration sometimes adopted policies it was unable to sustain. These lessons would soon be carried over to the battle over MFN benefits.

BY SEPTEMBER 1993, the administration was confronting more pressures to come up with a less confrontational approach to dealing with China.

The Pentagon was pressing hard for change. The primary reason was the looming crisis over North Korea's nuclear weapons program. In March, two months after Clinton took office, North Korean leader Kim Il Sung had announced that his government would withdraw from the Nuclear Nonproliferation Treaty rather than submit to inspections that would have revealed how much nuclear material it had already produced.

Pentagon officials realized that if unresolved, this showdown could lead to a war on the Korean Peninsula that could conceivably cost American lives. They were eager to settle the problem through negotiations rather than force.[33] The key to any diplomatic solution was China, the only Asian power to maintain any semblance of ties with North Korea. Pentagon officials chafed at the administration's restrictions on dealing with the Chinese leadership.

"When the North Korean issue arose in March of 1993, when [Defense Secretary] Les Aspin, in a meeting in the White House Situation Room, suggested that we talk to the Chinese about the problem, he was brushed aside by Tony Lake on the grounds that China was politically unacceptable and we could not have such a dialogue," recalled Charles W. Freeman Jr., then the assistant secretary of defense for international security affairs. (In interviews, Lake and Daniel Poneman, a National Security Council staff aide dealing with Korean nuclear problems, said they do not recall any such incident.)[34]

The Defense Department had other reasons for wanting a more conciliatory China policy. The Pentagon had been frustrated by the cutoff in military ties with the People's Liberation Army. Talking to the PLA, it argued, was the key to curbing China's arms exports, and the army was an important constituency in determining the country's future political leadership.

Two senior Pentagon officials—William Perry, then the deputy secretary of defense, and Freeman—had been closely involved in the American opening to China in the 1970s, and both had maintained ties in Beijing. "You had this real China grouping of people at the Pentagon, who felt that we somehow had to get a dialogue started again after Tiananmen," recalled another administration official, Stanley Roth.[35]

By July 1993, with Perry in the forefront, the Pentagon was pressing the White House to deal more amicably with China. "Korea was certainly at the top of my list," Perry later explained. "That provided a pretty strong incentive to see if we could go out and reestablish a reasonable relationship with them [China]."[36]

Clinton and his foreign policy team were also being prodded by Henry Kissinger to change their China policy. By this time, Kissinger had been out of government life for 16 years. His consulting firm, Kissinger Associates, earned lucrative fees by helping American corporations to gain entree in China and access to China's top leaders. Kissinger often protested that his views on China were not determined by these business concerns. It is certainly true that even without the fees, he would have been a staunch opponent of change, a champion of preserving the American relationship with China that he helped to create. But such claims did nothing to eliminate the conflict of interest.[37]

One senior White House official recalled that in the summer of 1993, Kissinger was particularly active in urging the new administration to talk to the Chinese more often and at higher levels. Kissinger was working with Maurice R. Greenberg, the chairman of American Insurance Group (AIG), which sold policies in China and was a client of Kissinger Associates. According to this official, Kissinger and Greenberg talked to the Treasury and Commerce Departments, and also dropped by the White House occasionally to meet with Lake.[38]

The official meetings were only part of Kissinger's campaign, which he waged in his newspaper column, too. "Nothing is more grating to the Chinese than U.S. refusal to engage in regular Cabinet-level discussions," Kissinger wrote in June 1993.[39] That was the public version of the views he was pressing more forcefully and in more detail at top levels of the Clinton administration.

DURING ITS first summer, the Clinton administration found itself squabbling with China on several fronts.

Buoyed by its success in regaining international recognition after the Tiananmen massacre, China had promoted Beijing as the site of the Olympic Games for the year 2000. The United States was decidedly unenthusiastic. The House of Representatives passed a resolution against taking the games to China. Officially, the Clinton administration remained neutral, but Warren Christopher acknowledged, "We have provided information [to the International Olympic Committee] on the human rights performance of all possible candidates."[40] After the games were awarded to Sydney, some Chinese blamed the United States for frustrating China's ambitions.

America's arms-control diplomats were upset to find that China was on the verge of resuming nuclear testing. Moreover, throughout July and August, the U.S. intelligence and military had an especially nasty contretemps with China. American intelligence believed that a Chinese ship was transporting to Iran chemicals that could be used to make mustard gas and nerve gas. When American officials asked China to have the ship turn around and return home, the Chinese refused, insisting there were no chemicals on board. After U.S. Navy ships and helicopters began trailing the Chinese vessel on the open seas, China whipped up anti-American sentiments by accusing the United States of "bullying" tactics. Finally, the ship was docked in Saudi Arabia and inspected; the chemicals in question were not found on board.[41]

All of these developments—the business community's unhappiness, the pressure from the Pentagon, Kissinger's efforts and the series of acrimonious public confrontations with Beijing—culminated in the first significant change in the China policy of the new administration.

After a contentious series of internal meetings, the administration launched what would eventually come to be called a policy of engagement with China. The theme was that the Clinton administration would be willing to talk to the Chinese at all levels of government and on a wide range of subjects.

A paper proposing this new approach had been drafted by the State Department and sent to the White House in late July. Two months later, as its disputes with China intensified, the administration finally approved the policy. On September 25, 1993, Lake summoned Ambassador Li Daoyu to the White House to inform the Chinese government of the change. Tensions between the two countries had been so high that Li's hands trembled throughout the meeting.[42]

As one part of the new policy, Clinton would meet for the first time with Chinese President Jiang Zemin at a summit meeting of Asian leaders in Seattle in November; no preconditions would be set for these talks. "There was intense debate," recalls Stanley Roth, an administration official who took part in the policy review. "Do you really want to have a meeting with the Chinese president? Has there been enough progress on human rights to justify a summit?"[43] The administration decided to go forward. After all, proponents reasoned, even at the height of the Cold War, American presidents had talked to Soviet leaders.

The new engagement policy (one bemused official dubbed it "promiscuous engagement") extended far beyond the Clinton-Jiang meeting. The administration also announced that it would lift the ban imposed in 1989 on military contacts; Freeman, the Pentagon's China specialist, would go to Beijing to open a new dialogue with the Chinese military. Moreover, several other Cabinet-level officials would also be dispatched to China, including Treasury Secretary Lloyd Bentsen.

It was a momentous change. This administration's policy review marked the effective end of efforts to ostracize the Chinese leadership and the People's Liberation Army following the Tiananmen crackdown. Over the following years, the Clinton administration would seek to limit where meetings might take place and with how much ceremony. It would still, throughout Clinton's first term in office, avoid presidential visits to Beijing or state ceremonies honoring Jiang Zemin in Washington. But it was no longer opposed to the meetings themselves.

Although President Bush had gradually restored high-level contacts with the Chinese, the Democrats had often criticized him for doing so— not only at the time of the Scowcroft mission of December 1989, but also when Bush met with Premier Li Peng in 1992. Now, a new Democratic president was launching his own top-level talks with the Chinese regime.

The public outrage over Tiananmen Square was subsiding. Leading Democrats in Congress were acknowledging the importance of contacts. Congresswoman Patricia Schroeder of Colorado, a member of the House Armed Services Committee, endorsed the lifting of the ban on military contacts. "We'd like to know where their intentions are, which way their guns are pointed, whether they have their own agenda," Schroeder said. "These are things we don't pick up through [intelligence] satellites."[44]

For China, this American policy change had another meaning, too. It demonstrated that the Clinton administration was not eager for a full-scale confrontation with Beijing, that it had a range of other interests with China beyond human rights. The administration's behavior was beginning to suggest the possibility that if China were to defy Clinton's human rights policy and, in particular, his MFN executive order, the administration might back down.

CHAPTER SIXTEEN

Clinton's Retreat

THE TALKS BETWEEN PRESIDENT Clinton and Chinese President Jiang Zemin in Seattle settled nothing. Both men were new to high-level diplomacy. Jiang was stiff and formal, reading his presentation from papers prepared for him, nervously eyeing Foreign Minister Qian Qichen and other Chinese officials to make sure he was performing adequately. Clinton, mindful of the furor over Scowcroft's friendly toast in Beijing, took care to maintain a stony visage as photographers shot pictures of him with Jiang. He told reporters afterward he had been "as frank and forthright as possible" with the Chinese leader.[1]

The events that accompanied Jiang's visit were, in the end, considerably more significant than his meeting with Clinton. As soon as the Chinese president landed in Seattle, he paid a visit to the Boeing plant in Everett, Washington. Addressing an audience of about 1,000 employees, he spoke of the need for the American business community to "remove all the negative factors and artificially imposed obstacles" between America and China, an obvious reference to the MFN order.

The Chinese leader dined with Boeing executives. Boeing's Chief Executive Officer Frank Shrontz acknowledged that China "is a very important sustaining market for us." America's leading aircraft company even helped Jiang arrange a visit with a model Boeing worker—the sort of stunt that is commonplace on tours of China. At the $93,000 house of Cary Qualls, Jiang handed a stuffed panda and a doll to the children, accepted chocolate-chip cookies from Quall's wife, Melanie, and delivered the weighty conclusion that "every country's families have different characteristics."[2]

If the message of Jiang's Boeing visit wasn't clear enough, the Chinese regime drove it home with another event that weighed heavily upon the Clinton administration. In Beijing, the Chinese gave a lavish welcome to German Chancellor Helmut Kohl and a 40-member entourage of business leaders from companies such as Daimler-Benz and Siemens. Before the Germans landed, Premier Li Peng proclaimed that they would be handsomely rewarded. "Chancellor Kohl is sure to fly back with full suitcases," he said.

Kohl officiated at Beijing ceremonies for the signing of eighteen contracts between China and Germany worth more than $2 billion, including deals for six Airbus planes, railway cars, steel rolling mills, machine tools and power and telecommunications equipment. Kohl said he thought these business deals were only the start of Germany's commercial involvement in China. "This huge country is opening up," he told reporters, adding that China's growth "will naturally have enormous repercussions for Germany as an export nation."[3]

From China's point of view, the timing of Kohl's visit could not have been more perfect. The news stories about Germany's $2 billion in contracts appeared on the front page of the Seattle newspapers on the very day Clinton landed there. All of the top members of the administration's economic team were present in Seattle with Clinton, including Treasury Secretary Lloyd Bentsen, Commerce Secretary Ron Brown, U.S. Trade Representative Mickey Kantor and Robert Rubin, head of the National Economic Council.

The lesson was obvious: America's closest allies were not going to join in its effort to link trade with China to improvements in human rights. Nor, for that matter, were the Europeans even going to remain neutral, holding off with China while America took the lead on human rights. Rather, other countries were going to avidly pursue their own economic interests in China, whether doing so undercut the American policy or not. The Germans were openly seeking advantage from the friction between Washington and Beijing.

The Clinton-Jiang meeting had led to a brief upsurge in activity by Chinese dissidents, aimed primarily at attracting America's attention to their cause. The most noteworthy effort came from Wei Jingsheng, who had served a long prison term in China for his advocacy of democracy. Wei was arrested when Deng Xiaoping cracked down on the Democracy Wall movement in 1979 and had just been freed in September, after serving 14 1/2 years of his 15-year sentence. His release came during the final weeks of China's unsuccessful effort to persuade other countries to support its bid for the Olympic Games.

Writing for the op-ed page of the *New York Times,* Wei called the Clinton administration's policy of engagement "misguided" and attributed it to the pursuit of profits. The Chinese Communist Party, he said, "was right all these years in saying that the American government is controlled by rich capitalists. All you have to do is offer them a chance to make money and anything goes."[4]

But the tide was ebbing for these voices of dissent in China. Within the Clinton administration, the idea of using economic muscle in support of the causes of democracy and human rights was being viewed with disfavor, if not outright disdain. Incidents like Jiang's visit to Boeing or the Kohl visit were only part of the reason. Indeed, the problem was much broader and extended beyond China itself.

By the time of the Seattle meeting, Clinton was beginning to grope toward the outlines of a broad new post–Cold War strategy for dealing with the rest of the world, an approach that would emphasize free trade and commercial diplomacy. By this time, the new administration had already won approval of the North American Free Trade Agreement and was on the verge of another groundbreaking accord setting up the World Trade Organization. The economic focus of Clinton's meeting with Asian leaders in Seattle fit in perfectly with this emerging strategy. Linking trade with China to improvements in human rights did not.

In the past, American presidents from Harry Truman to George Bush had argued that America should remain engaged with the rest of the world for reasons of military security and to counter the power of the Soviet Union. Now, Clinton argued the cause of internationalism primarily on behalf of America's economic interests. He was "recognizing what a lot of private companies have recognized: We're dependent on world trade," Rubin explained to reporters in Seattle.[5]

BY EARLY 1994, Clinton's economic team was virtually in open revolt against his MFN order. In internal meetings within the administration, in background briefings to reporters and sometimes in public as well, Clinton's economic advisers made clear their strong unhappiness with the linkage between trade with China and human rights. "One of the ways to promote human rights is to encourage market reform and trade," Lloyd Bentsen told one Washington audience, thus implicitly challenging the underlying rationale for the president's order.

Ron Brown was particularly active, in a way that illustrated Washington gamesmanship and hypocrisy at its worst. From 1990 to 1992, as Democratic Party chairman, Brown had scathingly criticized President Bush for vetoing bills that would have attached human rights conditions to the renewal of China's trade benefits. "MFN should stand for 'More Failed Notions' on the part of the Bush administration," Brown had said back then. Now, as commerce secretary, he tirelessly pressed for precisely the same MFN policy he had previously denounced, urging that China's trade benefits be preserved without conditions. In public, he spoke of unconditional MFN for China as a matter of "economic security," vital for America's national security.[6]

By this time, members of Clinton's economic team were so worried about a loss of trade with China that they considered the MFN compromises the administration had made in early 1993 to be either irrelevant or wholly inadequate. In drafting the executive order the previous year, the administration had stripped down the conditions Congress was preparing to impose on a renewal of China's MFN benefits, eliminating everything but human rights and also weakening the human rights language. Yet this fact was increasingly forgotten. Rather than uniting behind the relatively modest conditions, the administration's economic officials belatedly criticized the entire concept of linkage.

The internal disagreements over China policy were not confined to the economic agencies. Within the National Security Council, Deputy National Security Advisor Sandy Berger was more sympathetic to the business community's point of view on MFN. His boss, National Security Advisor Anthony Lake, was the strongest proponent among senior administration officials of vigorous policies on behalf of human rights in China.[7]

During the early winter, U.S. Ambassador to China J. Stapleton Roy tried to obtain from Washington an answer to an important question that had not been addressed in the MFN order: If China somehow managed to satisfy the conditions Clinton had laid down in 1993 and thus won an extension of its trade benefits, would the administration impose a new set of human rights conditions in 1994 that would have to be satisfied the following year? In other words, was the linkage between MFN and human rights for one year only, or would it be reestablished each year? This question was of considerable significance for negotiations with China: A promise to end the linkage could be used as a bargaining chip, a possible concession that might give China a stronger incentive to meet Clinton's 1993 conditions.

But Roy couldn't get an answer from Washington. Some administration officials favored ending the MFN linkage after a year, while others wanted to hold out the possibility of imposing new conditions. Nor could the ambassador get a specific, detailed answer on precisely what China needed to do in order to satisfy Clinton's MFN conditions.[8]

In evident frustration, Roy alluded to the administration's internal divisions in one newspaper interview. Asked whether China would meet Clinton's standard of "overall significant progress" on human rights, the ambassador pointedly replied: "I can't answer those questions, because the administration is going to have to define what it views as significant progress." [9]

The responsibility for trying to pull the administration together into a unified and coherent position lay, of course, with Clinton. Other presidents at other times have picked up the telephone and ordered their aides to support a policy, or at least to stop undermining it. Clinton did not, leaving unclear the extent to which he himself stood behind his own executive order.

Needless to say, Chinese officials saw what was happening in Washington, that the administration was both badly divided and also nervous about the consequences of having to revoke China's trade benefits. They could have learned this simply by reading the newspapers, but in addition they were talking regularly to Americans and were gaining insights and advice from the endless stream of former U.S. officials to Beijing. Some in the Clinton administration also believed the American business community was working with China against the MFN order. "They [business executives] were not only not supporting us, but they were undercutting us with the Chinese," Winston Lord later complained. [10]

By early 1994, the Chinese government began openly and unabashedly turning up the commercial pressure in its dealings with the Clinton administration. It had become the linchpin of China's entire strategy for circumventing Clinton's human rights conditions.

On January 28, 1994, while making the rounds in a Washington plagued by ice storms, Vice Foreign Minister Liu Huaqiu, the official with the longest experience in handling Americans, met with Rubin and coolly laid out China's new line. The French used to be with you on human rights, but they have changed their tune, Liu told Rubin. As for the Germans, you saw that Chancellor Kohl was just in Beijing and got several billion dollars' worth of contracts. Even the Canadians, who you Americans always say share the same values as you, just left Beijing with many business contracts, too, Liu said.

His message was clear: Other governments were forgetting about human rights in their desire for contracts in China, and ultimately the United States would, too. Liu's brazen use of commercial pressure was, one American participant said later, "truly offensive"—so much so that Rubin, not ordinarily a proponent of linking trade to human rights, countered with a strong defense of Clinton's MFN policy. [11]

By this time China was moving toward a harder line. Instead of bargaining over the human rights conditions, trying to satisfy some of the MFN requirements and go halfway on others, China was realizing that it could simply defy the administration. It appeared increasingly likely that if Beijing was unyielding, the administration would simply back down.

Originally, it appeared that the Chinese aim had been to persuade Clinton to say at the end of the year that China had met, at least minimally, the standard of "overall significant progress" in his MFN order. Now, the goal was to force a full-scale American retreat.

These were the forces at work as the Clinton administration reached the culmination of its year-long diplomatic campaign to win human rights concessions from China: the visit by Secretary of State Warren Christopher to Beijing.

IF ONE were to make a composite sketch of the sort of American official with whom Chinese leaders least like to do business, he would probably look something like Warren Christopher.

The Chinese prefer an American like Henry Kissinger or Zbigniew Brzezinski, one who places a maximum of importance on global strategy and a minimum on abstract law or rules; Christopher, a lawyer by training, was the reverse. The Chinese like to deal with someone who believes in personal relationships, an American who can be flattered that he alone has the superior wisdom to deal with China; the self-effacing Christopher, unlike Kissinger, always acted as though he was replaceable. China likes a risk-taker, someone who at the climax of negotiations can be persuaded to make a concession or two. Christopher was fanatically cautious. Indeed, his outlook and low-key style seemed roughly comparable to that of President Carter's Secretary of State Cyrus Vance or perhaps to Senator George Mitchell, two other American officials whom the Chinese regime had done their best to circumvent.[12]

Christopher's mission was designed to tell the Chinese precisely what they needed to do in order to satisfy the MFN executive order, and to persuade them to make the changes Clinton had required. By this time, March 1994, less than three months remained before the MFN order would expire. In June, Clinton would have to decide whether China's performance merited a renewal of its trade benefits. Christopher wanted to talk with the Chinese leadership while there was still time for changes to be made before the deadline. "The theory was that we could go, tell them [Chinese officials] what had to be done, and if they did it, we would have made progress," recalled one of those on the trip. "And if not, we would at least have had a face-to-face confrontation with them, and would then have had the basis to revoke [MFN] if we had to."[13]

From China's standpoint, however, the timing was awkward. The National People's Congress, China's parliament, was opening its annual series of meetings on March 10, the day before Christopher was scheduled to arrive in Beijing. These meetings allow China's top leaders to show their mettle to representatives from the provinces, and sometimes serve as a vehicle for China's democracy movement to test how far the leadership is willing to tolerate opposing points of view. Chinese dissidents had become outspoken and active once again in the weeks leading up to the government meeting and Christopher's visit.[14]

It was not long before the Clinton administration became caught up in the maneuvering between the regime and the dissidents.

Christopher had dispatched Assistant Secretary of State for Human Rights John H. Shattuck for exploratory talks in advance of his own trip. Shattuck, who had previously worked with the American Civil Liberties Union and been a Harvard University vice president, was the State Department official in charge of human rights policies around the world. Over the previous year, he had devoted considerable time and energy to China.

On February 27, 1994, the Sunday night before the start of his talks with Chinese officials, Shattuck met with Wei Jingsheng, China's most prominent dissident. Wei was by this time fearlessly criticizing the Chinese regime, hoping that others in China would follow in his path and thus create a newer, more open political climate there.

Wei's young assistant, Tong Yi, had chosen the highly public location: the coffee garden on the first floor of the China World Hotel, a gleaming modern complex in eastern Beijing. It was supposed to be an early dinner, but Shattuck didn't eat. As the two men talked, Wei pointed out the several Chinese security agents nearby who were watching or trying to overhear them.

Shattuck asked Wei for his view on the Clinton administration's MFN policy. Was there, Shattuck wondered, any real impact on China from the administration's relatively tough position? Wei said there was. "Although it [linking MFN to human rights] may not be the best way, at the moment it is an effective way to improve human rights in China," Wei said. "Without international pressure, I would not be sitting here today."

Which was more important, Shattuck asked: Having the United States put direct pressure on the Chinese government, or having it simply voice public support for Chinese dissidents? He seemed to be groping for some way out, some alternative to the MFN policy. But Wei said the pressure on the regime was more important, because without it, statements of public support for the dissidents would never be allowed to enter or be broadcast into China.

Before leaving, Shattuck asked Wei whether he had any message for Clinton. Wei did. "Tell President Clinton that you should be as strong as the Chinese government," he answered. "You should not retreat."

Shattuck departed, telling Wei vaguely, "We should meet again."[15]

In talking to Wei, Shattuck was doing no more than Americans have done elsewhere. In Moscow, officials at levels considerably higher than Shattuck had met with Soviet dissidents. Such meetings were "standard operating procedure for us," asserted Christopher in an interview. "I mean, we meet with dissidents every place." [16]

There were accusations in Washington later on that Shattuck had been operating on his own and had not told other American officials in advance of the meeting. In fact, the American embassy in Beijing had been involved from the start. Although he generally didn't like the idea of such meetings with dissidents, Ambassador Roy knew what was happening and went along with it. Shattuck's intention to see Wei was also included in an embassy cable describing his planned visit, and no one in Washington objected. [17]

"Shattuck came in [to Beijing] and, for reasons I respect, felt that in his position he had to meet with a dissident," explained one senior American embassy official. "We arranged a meeting to take place discreetly, but not clandestinely." The customary procedure, this official explained, is that "if the local dissident is prepared to take the risk, we don't stand in the way." [18]

Neither Shattuck nor any other American official said anything to the press about the meeting with Wei. Some believed mistakenly that Wei would stay quiet, too. Instead, he quickly passed the word to American reporters that he had met with Shattuck, thus enhancing his stature and reputation for fearlessness inside China. [19]

The American embassy later theorized that the Chinese leadership did not know about the session until after Wei made it public. When the Chinese belatedly found out, they were surprised and genuinely outraged, American officials believed. [20] Both conclusions seem questionable. China's security apparatus was watching Wei Jingsheng intensely, and probably Shattuck as well. Moreover, the Chinese had several good reasons to feign outrage: By calling attention to Shattuck's meeting with Wei, they could argue that opposition to the regime was inspired by foreigners, find an excuse for a new crackdown on dissidents and also warn the Clinton administration to keep its distance from the Chinese democracy movement.

In effect, the regime was giving the United States an updated version of the same message it had given when the Bush administration invited Fang Lizhi to dinner in 1989: Do not deal with any forces opposed to the government. Maintain the arrangements of the Nixon-Kissinger years, under which America would deal with China only through or with the permission of its Communist Party leadership.

Over the following week, Chinese security officials arrested Wei

Jingsheng and began rounding up other prominent dissidents as well. At least 15 democracy and labor activists were arrested in Beijing and Shanghai. Most were released after they were questioned for a day or two, but a few were held longer. They were warned not to make trouble, particularly during Christopher's trip. Wang Dan, one of the student organizers of the 1989 Tiananmen Square demonstration, said he was told he would "pay the price" if his public statements had a "bad impact" upon China.[21]

These arrests were made on the very day that Christopher left Washington for Beijing. China's actions amounted to a gesture of defiance, a warning that Beijing would not be receptive to Christopher's message. Indeed, they could also be read as a test of just how far the regime could go in curbing dissent before the United States would do anything about it.

Quite far, it turned out. In Washington, the Clinton administration denounced the arrests but left further action up to Christopher. By the time he arrived in Australia, his first stop, he and his aides realized they ought to reconsider whether he should go to China or not. During a stopover in Canberra, they sat down for long talks about what to do.[22]

Two of Christopher's advisers—Thomas Donilon, his chief of staff, and Michael McCurry, his press secretary, the two men responsible for Christopher's image—argued that he should cancel the visit to China and go home because of the series of arrests. But Winston Lord, who was in charge of the administration's China policy, argued that the trip should go forward, and the secretary agreed. "I hesitated to cancel the visit, because I felt engagement, trying to have a dialogue, was important," recalled Christopher in an interview. He decided that he and his party would proceed with the trip, "but that we would not mute our criticism [of China]."[23]

This was, in retrospect, a mistake. Both Chinese and American officials were swept up in political dynamics that were leading inexorably into a confrontation. In the wake of the Shattuck meeting, the Chinese were eager to show America how tough they could be in dealing with dissent. At the same time, because of the wave of arrests in China, Christopher needed to demonstrate he meant business on human rights. "You can be sure human rights will be right on the top of my agenda when I get to Beijing," he told reporters.[24]

The decision not to cancel the trip underscored the limitations inherent in the Clinton administration's initial policy of engagement, of which both Christopher and Lord were both apostles. The policy seemed to assume that meetings are inherently beneficial, no matter what the context or underlying political dynamics might be. Christopher's visit to

China became an example of a case where engagement didn't work and actually set back the goals the secretary had set for himself.

Christopher's three-day visit to Beijing was, from beginning to end, the most discordant high-level meeting between America and China since the Nixon opening. Both sides were angry. Neither made any pretense of friendship.

Before he landed in Beijing, Christopher announced he would avoid any events other than work-related meetings. He would not have dinner with Chinese officials, and he would not visit the Great Wall or other cultural attractions. This was meant to demonstrate, particularly to American audiences, his seriousness of purpose on human rights. It also showed, however, how steadily relations between the two governments were eroding. When Secretary of State James Baker had visited Beijing three years earlier, he had forsworn attending any public banquet, but nevertheless had dined with Chinese officials, thus preserving the appearance that perhaps the two governments could do business amicably with one another in private. Now, Christopher was avoiding even a private dinner.

As soon as Christopher's plane landed in Beijing, American and Chinese security officials began jostling and pushing one another on the tarmac. "Is this how the visit's going to go?" one of the State Department's aides shouted to a Chinese official who was blocking his way. There was another shoving match between the American and Chinese security details at the China World hotel where the secretary was staying. Christopher decided to dispense with the customary arrival statement about the great tradition of friendship between the two peoples. "He wants to set a tone that is focused on the business he is here to do," explained McCurry.[25]

China was setting a tone of its own. Several prominent dissidents were asked to leave Beijing on the day Christopher arrived. Others had homes surrounded by Public Security Bureau employees. At least two American correspondents in Beijing were held for six hours when they went to the Beijing apartment complex of a labor activist. In order to make sure no American official could meet with Wei Jingsheng, he was forced into exile in the city of Tianjin before and during Christopher's trip.[26]

The talks were equally ugly. On the first day, Premier Li Peng as usual took the lead in heaping vituperation upon the American human rights policy. It was a role Li had cultivated for many years and always seemed to relish. Even by past standards, Li's performance with Christopher was remarkable for his unyielding fervor. "China will never accept the United States's concept of human rights," he said. Noting that China had

100 million people in poverty, he went on, "You have to have humans before you can have human rights."

Li also brashly told the secretary that his views did not represent those of the entire Clinton administration. When Christopher patiently explained what China would need to do on human rights in order to obtain an extension of its trade benefits, Li brushed him off. Our embassy in Washington tells us that MFN is going to be extended in any case, the premier said; we understand that not everybody in the Clinton administration agrees with this executive order.

Li even got personal with the secretary, invoking the 1992 racial unrest in Los Angeles, Christopher's hometown. "You know, you had riots in your own city. You were charged with cleaning things up," Li said, referring to Christopher's role as chairman of a commission assigned to investigate the police beating of Rodney King. "You've got racism and human rights problems in the United States. The Rodney King beating was a human rights problem. So don't come over here and talk to us about our human rights problems." The secretary countered that in the United States, those who were unhappy with government policies could vote and express their points of view. Needless to say, he didn't change Li Peng's rigid mind.[27]

Christopher's talks the first day with Chinese Foreign Minister Qian Qichen were not much better. Qian attacked Shattuck for interfering in China's internal affairs by meeting with Wei, and claimed that Shattuck had violated Chinese law because Wei was a prisoner on parole. After a midday meal of scallops and Peking duck with the foreign minister, Christopher pointedly told Qian, "I wish the meeting had been as good as the lunch." At the end of his first day in China, Christopher talked with aides about breaking off the talks and going home. Instead, he decided to persevere.[28]

The secretary had almost as much trouble with the American business community. On the second day of his trip, he had breakfast with the American Chamber of Commerce in Beijing. The representatives of some of America's leading corporations repeatedly complained about Clinton's MFN order. "United States policy puts U.S. business at a competitive disadvantage," said one executive. Another, from AT&T, warned that if MFN were cut off, America would be removed from the fastest-growing market in the world.

This session was a telling example of how American foreign policy had changed under Clinton. Christopher's confrontation with the business representatives in Beijing was strikingly similar to one that George Shultz, President Reagan's secretary of state, had had in Beijing 11 years earlier. In both sessions, the American executives had protested to the secretary of state that U.S. government policy was hurting their chances for business in China. But Shultz had responded by angrily dismissing the complaints, telling the executives that they weren't responsible for U.S. government policy and that if they didn't like it, they could move to Japan or Europe. Christopher, by contrast, was restrained and defensive. He wouldn't have felt free to tell off the executives in the way Shultz had, even if he had wanted to do so. The business community's influence over America's relations with the rest of the world was vastly greater in 1994 than it had been in 1983; commerce was much closer to the heart of the Clinton administration's foreign policy.

On the final day, there were signs from Qian that China might be willing to make at least a concession or two on human rights. In particular, the foreign minister informed Christopher, in confidence, that China intended to release two dissidents, Wang Juntao and Chen Ziming, who in 1991 had been sentenced to 13 years for sedition for their roles in organizing the Tiananmen Square demonstrations. However, Qian asked that the planned releases be kept secret; in this way, the party leadership could maintain the fiction that China has an independent judicial system. In order to avoid jeopardizing the releases, Christopher kept the secret, even as his trip was being criticized for achieving nothing at all.[29] In April, Wang was allowed to leave for America, and in early May, Chen was set free. These releases fell far short of the administration's hope for the freeing of at least 20 or 30 dissidents.

Despite this limited gesture, China in public did nothing that could be interpreted as positive or even conciliatory toward the United States on human rights. In the final hours, a joint news conference for Christopher and Qian was canceled. Instead, the two men appeared separately.

Qian denounced American policy toward China in general and Shattuck's meeting with Wei Jingsheng in particular. For good measure, a day later the foreign minister told reporters he had been disappointed with the whole trip.

Christopher acknowledged in an interview three years later that, after the seemingly upbeat mood of his last morning in Beijing, he had not expected to be attacked once again as he was departing. "The last day, my meeting with Qian Qichen, I thought was a good meeting, and thus I was surprised at how the Chinese were characterizing me," he said.[30]

FOR PRESIDENT Clinton, this was the fateful moment. Christopher's departure from Beijing marked the point where he was finally forced to confront the choices inherent in his executive order of the previous year, and in fact in his entire policy toward China. The Chinese had treated

Clinton's secretary of state with disdain, making clear their willingness to repress political dissent both before and during his trip. They had rebuffed Christopher's efforts to talk about how China could meet the human rights conditions that Clinton had issued. No longer could Clinton remain detached from his own China policy or leave it in the hands of subordinates.

When the trip ended, State Department officials sought to have the president issue a statement of support for Christopher. They were asking the White House to reiterate that the secretary had been in China not on some quirky mission of his own, but on behalf of the president and his MFN policy. Instead, the White House remained detached. "We were trying to get a White House statement, and it just never came," acknowledged one participant in Christopher's delegation.[31]

It was clear at this point that Clinton was faced with the ultimate decision on MFN. He had to carry through on his 1993 executive order, by cutting off China's trade benefits, or else back down from it. The economic agencies of the U.S. government were adamantly against revocation. By the end of Christopher's trip, the president had finally confronted the issue he had avoided the previous year: whether he was willing to deliver on his threat to China. He was not.

Asked in an interview at what point he realized Clinton's MFN policy of 1993 was not going to work, Christopher replied: "On the way back from my trip."[32]

THE NEXT two months were spent arranging the details of Clinton's retreat on MFN.

Back in Washington, Christopher convened a meeting in the Roosevelt Room of the White House for all agencies of the government involved in China policy. He insisted that the administration needed to speak with one voice. It was a point that should have been made and enforced months earlier. The participants politely nodded and went their own ways.

By now, the State Department was quickly losing its authority over China policy. Before Christopher's trip to Beijing, the interagency meetings within the Clinton administration on China had been run by Lord. After the secretary returned from Beijing, these sessions were run by Berger and an official from the National Economic Council.

Less than two weeks after Christopher's return to Washington, the secretary was making strained efforts to placate the Chinese regime. When South Korean President Kim Young Sam visited Beijing on March 27, Christopher telephoned Foreign Minister Han Sung Joo from Washington and spoke to him at length about his and America's goodwill toward China. Han thought it was a funny conversation, because he knew, and he was sure Christopher knew, that the Chinese must be monitoring the call. In effect, the secretary was talking to the Chinese and smoothing over the frictions from his trip, under the guise of a conversation with the South Korean foreign minister.[33]

There were a few final appeals to China to make more human rights concessions of the sort that might help the Clinton administration to save face. Lake and Rubin secretly met with Chinese Vice Foreign Minister Liu Huaqiu when he flew to California to attend the funeral of Richard Nixon. Not long afterward, a secret emissary, former State Department official Michael Armacost, was sent to Beijing.

By these last weeks, the Clinton administration in its desperation was making China the offer it had been unwilling to make a few months earlier: The administration promised Chinese officials it would drop the linkage between MFN benefits and human rights for the following year if Beijing would take steps to meet the conditions Clinton had already imposed in 1993.

These efforts produced no far-reaching concessions from China. Indeed, in one significant respect, the regime tightened its control over dissent during this period. It did so in a way that it knew would attract the greatest possible attention from the Clinton administration. On April 1, 1994, as he was attempting to return to Beijing from exile in Tianjin, Wei Jingsheng was surrounded by seven vans and pulled from his car by about 20 Chinese security officers.[34] It was Wei's last day of freedom, only six months after his release. He was held without charges for more than a year, then finally sentenced at the end of 1995 to another 14 years in prison for plotting to overthrow China's Communist Party leadership.

As THE deadline approached for the president's decision on China's trade benefits, two internal debates went on within the administration. There was no question that Clinton would extend China's trade benefits. But officials disagreed over exactly how he should do so.

One debate concerned exactly what the Clinton administration should say about China's conduct on human rights over the previous year. Should the administration claim that the small changes China had made amounted to "overall significant progress"? In other words, should it try to declare victory by maintaining that the Beijing government had met the legal standards of Clinton's executive order?

Some officials were in favor of this approach. To be sure, they argued, China had not let the Red Cross into its prisons or stopped the jamming of the Voice of America, but it had at some points during the year suggested it would be willing to discuss these subjects. The regime had not released 20 or 30 dissidents from prison as the administration had hoped, and it had locked up Wei Jingsheng once again, along with some others, but it had nonetheless set free Wang Juntao and Chen Ziming. Maybe this was sufficient for Clinton to say China had made the "overall significant progress" he had required.[35]

In this debate, those within the administration who most strongly supported the cause of human rights won out. They were about to lose the overall battle, since Clinton was in the process of abandoning his 1993 executive order; but they were permitted this smaller victory. In internal meetings at the State Department, Lord argued passionately that no matter what action the administration took on MFN, it should not be put into the position of twisting or covering up the truth about the repressive conditions inside China.

"Win was just adamant that we would not say things were so when they weren't," recalled one participant. Lord's view was based upon his conviction that it would have damaged the Clinton administration's credibility, both with the American public and in Beijing, to pretend the Chinese leadership had made progress on human rights when, in fact, it hadn't.[36]

The second debate was whether the administration should impose some form of limited sanctions, short of an outright revocation of China's MFN benefits, because of China's failure to do what Clinton had required. By imposing some form of economic penalty, the administration would have been able to claim that it had followed through to some extent on Clinton's original MFN policy, instead of capitulating.

One option was to cut off MFN benefits only for products made by state-owned enterprises in China, while retaining the privileges for goods made by private enterprises. By doing this, proponents said, the administration would have overcome the complaint that a revocation of MFN would hit hard on the growing private sector, the part of the Chinese economy most deserving of America support. Another option was for the United States to impose sanctions only on the products of Chinese trading companies owned or controlled by the People's Liberation Army. AFL-CIO Chairman Lane Kirkland formally proposed sanctions aimed at the army in a letter to the secretary of state.[37]

During April and May 1994, the administration studied these options for partial sanctions. The Council of Economic Advisers, headed by Laura Tyson, did computer runs on the impact of various kinds of partial sanctions, both upon China and upon the United States. "We went through them with the president a number of times," recalled Lake.[38]

The studies concluded that partial sanctions would be difficult to enforce, because it would be hard to figure out which Chinese exports came from state enterprises, or People's Liberation Army companies, and which did not. Moreover, Chinese companies could circumvent such sanctions through false labeling—that is, listing the product of a state enterprise or PLA company under the name of a private firm whose exports were not subject to sanctions.

"As we got into it, even those who were in favor of this approach found it so complicated that it really wasn't feasible," recalled Lord. "There were still some [in the administration] toward the end who would still do it, even though it was messy, and say, 'Make your best hit, and maybe you can do it so that you're hitting 80 percent PLA or state enterprise.' There were still some arguing that, but not at the Cabinet level."[39]

Clinton's decision to forsake partial sanctions was influenced by far more than Laura Tyson's computer analyses. The president was also, in these final weeks, being repeatedly urged to make a clean and complete break with the MFN policy he had adopted the previous year, the one he had embraced during his campaign. Representatives of the business community and former American leaders like Henry Kissinger and Jimmy Carter were advising Clinton to drop the MFN linkage once and for all. Clinton's decision was ultimately a political one, and by now the president himself was eager for a sweeping change, not for partial sanctions.

The administration settled on the rationale it would use for its action. It would say that the attempt to link MFN to human rights had run its course; the administration had tried for a year; the policy hadn't worked, and so it was time to move on. There were some gaps and difficulties in this line of argument. The administration hadn't ever followed through with the policy, because it hadn't imposed any penalties for China's failure to improve the human rights climate. This argument also raised obvious questions about why the 1993 order, containing what turned out to be meaningless threats, had been imposed in the first place.

Thursday, May 26, 1994, was designated as the day for Clinton to announce his decision. The last hours were frantic and improvised. White House officials drew up a plan to have Jimmy Carter head up a commission to deal with human rights in China. Carter—whose own administration had championed the cause of human rights elsewhere in the world, but not in China—spurned the idea. The administration also decided to add a ban on importation of Chinese semi-automatic weapons, essentially a gun-control measure, in order to head off the criticism that it was imposing no sanctions against China at all.

Finally, the president appeared in the White House press room to announce his decision. He acknowledged that "not all the requirements of the executive order were met." Nevertheless, he was cutting the linkage between China's MFN benefits and human rights. "We have reached the end of the usefulness of that policy, and it is time to take a new path," he said.[40]

China had, in reality, won not one victory but two. First, the administration was agreeing to extend MFN to China in 1994 and in future years without conditions. Second, it was also backing away from imposing penalties upon China for its unwillingness to meet the conditions Clinton had already imposed for the year 1993–94. Overall, it was a far-reaching reversal by the president who had once accused his predecessor of "coddling dictators" in Beijing.

MORE THAN four years had passed since George Mitchell and Nancy Pelosi first sponsored bills to tie China's MFN benefits to human rights. They had dropped their legislation in 1993 only after President Clinton and his aides promised that his executive order would do the same thing. In the spring of 1994, both of them believed, until the final days, that Clinton would not abandon them.

Mitchell had visited the State Department for a session with Christopher. I want to know in advance where things are heading, he told the secretary; I don't want to get left out on a limb. Yet the administration itself didn't know exactly what it was doing until near the end. During the final week, the Senate majority leader went to the White House to talk to the president. When he returned, he told his aide Ed King to draft two statements, one praising the Clinton administration's action on MFN, another one criticizing it. A day later, he called and told him glumly, "Send up the tough one." Mitchell had favored imposing at least limited sanctions on China, but Clinton turned down his advice.[41]

Pelosi, too, was pushing for partial sanctions. She wanted the president to do at least something. When he didn't, she was bitter and angry. She also felt betrayed. She had been too foolish in 1993, she realized, when administration officials appealed to her to drop her legislation at a time when it was certain to pass; she had been too trusting when she was told that the new president would carry out his own executive order. "It's not that he did something I disagreed with. That happens all the time," she said. "He said he was going to do something, and he walked away, as if he was tossing away a used napkin. We [the United States] should never, never had said we were going to do one thing and then not do it."[42]

Contributing to Mitchell and Pelosi's defeat was not only their tactical blunder (in withdrawing their 1993 legislation), but also an erosion of their political strength. By the spring of 1994, the politics underlying the MFN legislation in Congress was virtually the mirror image of four years earlier. In 1990, the American business community had been weak and politically inactive, while Chinese students and human rights groups were well-organized and vocal.

Each year since 1990, leading U.S. corporations had worked longer and harder in support of MFN status for China. In the weeks before Clinton's 1994 decision, nearly 800 major American companies and trade associations wrote him, urging continuation of China's benefits.[43] By contrast, the Chinese students who had been such a potent political force during the congressional battles of 1989–90 had gradually settled into American life and retreated from politics. The students' computer network still flourished, but it was devoted more to notices of job openings than to the political causes that had galvanized the students in 1989.

Increasingly, the base of political support for restricting China's MFN benefits came not from Chinese students or from American human rights groups, but from organized labor. The AFL-CIO worried more each year about the transfer of American jobs and technology to China. Yet organized labor had failed to muster enough political strength to defeat the Clinton administration on other issues, such as the North American Free Trade Agreement, and it was equally unable to do so on China's trade benefits.

CLINTON AND other officials insisted that in abandoning the MFN linkage, they were not downgrading the cause of human rights in China, but merely shifting tactics.

When he announced his decision, the president said he had a "new and vigorous American program" for promoting human rights and democracy in China. Over the following days, the administration listed a series of measures that supposedly would help ease repression in China.

Under what was called the "new human rights strategy" of May 1994, the White House proclaimed that it would encourage American businesses to develop a series of principles through which companies could advance human rights in China, comparable to ones that had been drafted for American firms dealing with apartheid in South Africa. The administration promised to step up efforts to work with other nations by, for example, seeking to pass a resolution on human rights in China at the United Nations Human Rights Commission. It also said it would increase programming into China by the Voice of America and Radio Free Asia, and increase support for nongovernment groups working on human rights in China.[44]

Over the following years, some of those elements, such as the increased radio programming, were put into effect. However, the code of conduct for American companies in China died a quiet death because of a lack of support from the business community. Morton S. Halperin, the

National Security Council aide in charge of human rights, believed that this effort fell through because Clinton failed to obtain commitments of support for it from U.S. business executives in the final weeks before he decided to do away with the MFN conditions. After the linkage was dropped, Halperin said, the pressure was off, and the business community had no reason to endorse the new approach.[45]

The reality was that despite the administration's claims for it, the new strategy announced in May 1994 did not prove to be a more successful way of improving human rights in China. At the beginning of 1997, the State Department acknowledged in its annual human rights report that the Chinese regime had succeeded (temporarily) in eradicating all vestiges of dissent, forcing those who opposed the regime into jail or exile.[46]

Indeed, senior administration officials would later admit that the package of alternatives to MFN that Clinton announced in May 1994 had little if any impact in easing Chinese repression of dissent. "We didn't achieve what I thought we would achieve through that policy," reflected Lake three years later.[47]

THE CLINTON administration's turnabout on MFN represented an epochal change, both for America's dealings with China and for U.S. foreign policy.

It marked the effective end of the American view of China that Winston Lord had put forward and of which he stood out as the best example: the view that there was nothing inherently incompatible between America's ideals and its interests in China; that the United States could and should push China's Communist Party leadership to gravitate peacefully toward democratic change while, at the same time, pursuing America's own strategic interests there. Although this approach sometimes seemed confrontational, it was also, ironically, remarkably optimistic: It assumed that the Chinese Communist Party was willing and eager to reform itself, and that political change in China could be accomplished without far-reaching or revolutionary upheaval.

Lord reflected the perspective of the mid-to-late 1980s, the time when reformers operated at the top of the party hierarchy and China seemed to be opening up to political change. That ferment had been abruptly stopped by the Tiananmen massacre, and American policies like the MFN linkage were designed to restore the process of reform. Lord's view failed to reckon with the fact that in the Chinese party politics of the early 1990s, even those modest changes the administration sought were viewed by Beijing's post-Tiananmen leadership as a threat. The very ideas of reform and political change were associated with the turmoil of the late 1980s, which had briefly threatened the party's control.

After Clinton's reversal of 1994, an older, darker American view reemerged: that the Chinese regime might be nasty and ruthless, but that one way or another, the United States had to deal with it. This had been a common theme in the 1970s, and it became once again a viewpoint of the 1990s. The only difference was that in the 1970s, America put aside its democratic ideals in order to cultivate China's support against the Soviet Union; in the 1990s, it did so for other reasons, including America's economic interests and the need for stability in Asia.

Winston Lord himself stayed on at the State Department through the end of Clinton's first term. It was not in his nature to quit; he was wealthy enough to leave a job whenever he wanted, but a public resignation would have conflicted with his innate caution. After 1994, he turned his energy to other Asian issues, notably America's reestablishment of diplomatic relations with Vietnam. While he still took part in high-level meetings, Lord never regained his influence over Clinton's China policy.

THE MFN reversal of 1994 had ramifications for America's future dealings not only with China but with other nations. It made other governments more recalcitrant in responding to American appeals. In this respect, Clinton's retreat on human rights made matters worse than if he had never imposed his MFN conditions. China had called the administration's bluff; it had shown that America would back down from the threats it made about human rights and democracy in cases where its commercial and strategic interests were jeopardized.

In China, American officials had hoped that ending the threat to cut off trade benefits would open the way for some improvement on human rights. During the previous year, the Chinese had repeatedly argued that the MFN linkage was counterproductive and that they would never make changes in response to American pressure. But China didn't change after the pressure was off, either. Beijing broke off discussions about letting the Red Cross into its prisons or about ending its jamming of Voice of America broadcasts; China's security apparatus continued or increased arrests of religious, labor and democracy advocates.[48] One administration official who dealt regularly with the Chinese regime and was sometimes sympathetic toward it found that Chinese government officials were "obnoxious" in the summer of 1994. "They were crowing about the fact that they had forced the administration to back down."[49]

Clinton's reversal emboldened other governments, particularly in Asia. In Indonesia, President Suharto's authoritarian regime took a harder line toward its political opposition and the press. A member of Indonesia's Human Rights Commission said authorities had "become more confident that they could do the same thing [as China] if the

United States wanted to make sanctions on Indonesia." Indonesian authorities spread the message that America's rhetoric about human rights should not be taken too seriously, because the reversal on China's MFN benefits showed that in the end, America would give higher priority to its economic interests. "The realists within the Indonesian army found new evidence of the hypocrisy of America," observed Mohtar Massoed, an Indonesian social scientist.[50]

It seems fair to ask whether the Clinton administration was sincere in the first place in linking trade with human rights in China. Was Clinton's 1993 executive order a well-intentioned effort that went astray?

There are other, more Machiavellian interpretations. Was the administration's goal from the outset to perpetuate the Bush administration's policy of unconditional MFN benefits for China? Might the goal of the 1993 executive order have been not to change China's behavior, but primarily to co-opt Congress and pave the way for a reversal of course on MFN a year later?

A number of senior administration officials have insisted that they were not so devious in 1993. Rather, they say, they genuinely believed that China would meet the modest conditions Clinton was imposing. "I thought that we would get more," said Lake.[51] It was only in 1994, after it was clear China would remain intransigent, these officials say, that the administration realized it could not follow through on its threat.

However, Sandy Berger suggested a greater degree of forethought. "As we arrived [in the White House in 1993] . . . we came to the conclusion that we needed to try to break this annual cycle of debate and the rather destructive linkage between MFN and human rights," he said. "Based on the situation that then existed in Congress, we could not do that in one fell swoop. Therefore, we needed to do this perhaps in two bites."[52] Berger seemed to be suggesting that from the outset, the administration realized it wanted to abandon the position that it had taken in the 1992 campaign; Clinton's 1993 order, then, was merely a way station to that end.

Berger's viewpoint may not be quite as different from that of other officials as it may at first appear. He, too, may have believed in 1993 that Clinton had scaled back the MFN conditions to the point where China could meet them. Under this scenario, China would satisfy Clinton's executive order, and at that point, the administration would cut the linkage between trade and human rights. It is important to keep in mind that during this first year, 1993–94, the administration faced two separate, distinct decisions: whether to impose penalties if China did not meet the human rights conditions of 1993, and whether to impose new conditions in 1994. The administration had never endorsed the idea of permanent linkage; it had left the door open to the possibility it would drop human rights conditions for future years if China satisfied the presidential order of 1993.

No administration official has admitted believing that at the time the new president announced his MFN order, China would be able to defy Clinton's human rights conditions and avoid significant penalties for doing so—and that Washington would also agree to drop conditions on the renewal of MFN in future years. In the spring of 1993, any such suggestion would have been dismissed as unthinkable. Yet that is precisely what happened. For China, it was, indeed, a remarkable double victory.

The fault for the MFN debacle lay first with the president. It was Clinton who had strongly endorsed linking MFN to human rights in his presidential campaign. It was Clinton who imposed the MFN conditions in 1993 and then decided a year later to back away from his threats.

Yet others should shoulder some of the blame. The Democratic Party as a whole had found China to be an advantageous issue to invoke against President Bush. However, with a Democratic president in the White House, the idea of MFN linkage, which had been the party's principal alternative to the Bush administration's China policy, no longer seemed so appealing, and it backed away.

While some Democrats can be said to have stuck to the same position on China policy after Clinton took office (such as Mitchell, Pelosi and House Majority Leader Richard Gephardt), many other Democratic members of Congress did not. The conclusion seems inescapable that for these congressional Democrats—as for Clinton himself and Democratic Party leaders like Ron Brown—the MFN disputes of the Bush years had been primarily an issue of partisan politics.

What is one to make, for example, of an exemplary centrist Democrat like Senator Bill Bradley of New Jersey? During the Bush administration, he voted to attach conditions to the renewal of China's MFN benefits. As late as October 1992, he voted to override a Bush veto and link MFN renewals to improvements in human rights. But in the spring of 1994, when President Clinton was nearing action on MFN, Bradley was one of the most fervent opponents of any such linkage. A decision either to revoke or to impose conditions on China's trade benefits, he said in 1994, "would be a blunder of historic proportions." [53]

Perhaps it can be argued that Bradley's about-face was prompted by evolving economic conditions in China. It also reflected a change in what was politically convenient for the Democrats. Clinton was merely the most visible representative of this broader Democratic tergiversation. The president was follower as much as leader.

Its reversal on MFN demonstrated that the new administration could be swayed by pressure and that its China policy was malleable. Lacking a clear sense of what he wanted and how much opposition he was prepared to withstand, Clinton had over the course of a year been turned around on one of the principal elements in his China policy. Politics had driven his early stance on behalf of linking trade to human rights. And politics, in the form of pressure from the business community, had prompted him to reverse himself.

His administration's conduct over the first year showed that the president was not always in control of American policy toward China. Foreign policy, it seemed, was not unlike domestic issues like health care; a well-organized campaign could persuade Clinton to shift course. That lesson was learned by, among others, the government of Taiwan.

CHAPTER SEVENTEEN

Crisis over Taiwan

IN THE SPRING OF 1994, at a time when the Clinton administration was preoccupied with the impending decision of what to do about China's trade benefits, U.S. officials became embroiled in a seemingly minor contretemps involving Taiwan. The incident took place in a remote setting thousands of miles from Washington. It went unreported in most American newspapers. Most officials at top levels of the administration didn't even realize it had happened. The episode was, however, the first step in a slowly building crisis that would eventually overshadow the most-favored-nation dispute and lead to the most serious military confrontation between America and China in a quarter-century.

On May 4, a Boeing 747 owned by the Taiwan government touched down at Hickam Air Force Base in Honolulu. The plane carried Taiwan's President Lee Teng-hui and several of his top advisers, who were on their way both to Central America and to the inauguration of Nelson Mandela as president of South Africa.

The State Department, fearing China's reaction, had denied permission for Taiwan's president to stop over for a night in Honolulu. Lee was told he would not be given a visa to enter the United States even briefly. Instead, he had been invited to a reception in a transit lounge at the American air force base while his airplane was refueling.

But after arriving in Hawaii to prepare for Lee's stopover, Ding Mou-shih, the head of Taiwan's Washington office, had found the arrangements for the reception to be insultingly spartan. There was little security. Lee and his party were supposed to walk anonymously through an airport terminal bustling with American soldiers, into a dingy room furnished with a few old, rickety chairs and a closet-sized toilet. "It was

embarrassing," acknowledged Natale Bellocchi, the lone American official sent out to welcome the Taiwan president.

From Honolulu, Ding quickly telephoned to Lee's plane to tell him
how meager a reception the Americans had planned for him. As a result,
when the plane landed in Hawaii, Taiwan's president refused to disem-
bark. Instead, Bellocchi, who was director of the small Washington office
responsible for American relations with Taiwan,[1] boarded the plane with
his wife.

He found that the president, wearing slippers and a casual sweater,
was fuming. Sitting with Bellocchi at a small table inside the plane, Lee
swore that Taiwan would no longer accept quietly the second-class status
to which it had long been relegated. Things can't be the way they were
before, Lee said; Taiwan is now a democracy, and its leaders are responsible to the people.

As Bellocchi was preparing to leave the aircraft, the Taiwan president
joked about his inability to obtain a visa. "I can't get too close to the door
of the plane," Lee said, his voice dripping with sarcasm. "I might slip and
enter America."[2]

Lee's brief stop in Honolulu was, in fact, part of a concerted diplomatic offensive by Taiwan aimed at challenging Beijing's insistence that
the rest of the world treat the island as a province of China.

Two months earlier, the Taiwan president had barnstormed through
Southeast Asia conducting what was called "vacation diplomacy." Ac-
companied by a delegation of 40 Cabinet members and business execu-
tives, Lee had spent the Chinese New Year in the beach resorts of Bali,
Indonesia, and Phuket, Thailand. He met with President Suharto of
Indonesia, President Fidel Ramos of the Philippines, King Bhumibol
Adulyadej of Thailand and other leading officials of those countries.

China was irritated. All of these Asian governments had established
diplomatic relations with Beijing and had cut off official ties with Taipei.
Lee's vacation diplomacy seemed to be aimed at boosting Taiwan's status.
In New York City, meanwhile, Taiwan launched a new campaign to
return to the United Nations, from which it had been ousted more than
two decades earlier, at the time of Henry Kissinger's Beijing diplomacy of
1971.[3]

Behind Lee's efforts was more than a trace of politics. He was preparing to face, in 1996, the first direct elections for president of Taiwan in
the island's history. In order to be sure of winning, Lee needed to seize
the political initiative from the opposition Democratic Progressive Party,
whose members supported the cause of an independent Taiwan. Lee's
diplomacy demonstrated to the Taiwan electorate that he was making
efforts to gain new international recognition for the island. If by doing

so, he aroused the ire of the People's Republic of China, that didn't hurt his political standing in Taiwan, either.

When Lee had first asked permission to spend a night in Hawaii, the dispute was left in the hands of lower-level American officials, who quickly found themselves caught between Beijing and Taipei.

Chinese Ambassador to Washington Li Daoyu warned that there would be "serious consequences" for the United States if the president of Taiwan were allowed to touch down for even a moment on American soil. Peter Tomsen, a deputy to Assistant Secretary of State Winston Lord, took the Chinese threats seriously and decided that Lee should be prohibited from even landing his plane in Honolulu.

An American official in Taipei was instructed to inform Foreign Minister Frederick Chien that Honolulu was off limits; Lee would have to find some refueling stop outside the United States. Chien vehemently denounced what he called America's cave-in to China. Taiwan should not be forced to suffer the consequences of the Clinton administration's poor relations with Beijing, he argued. He added a few words that went beyond the traditional language of diplomacy. "I had no idea what a bunch of spineless jellyfish you [Americans] were," he told Lynn Pascoe, the head of the American Institute in Taiwan.[4]

Stung by Taiwan's rebuke, Lord and his aides hurriedly reversed course and worked out what they thought was a Solomonic compromise: Lee's plane would be allowed to refuel in Honolulu, but the Taiwan president would not be permitted to leave the airport lounge. Lee was barred from meeting with Honolulu's Chinese community, speaking at the East-West Center, playing golf or even spending the night in a downtown hotel.

"This was a step forward, not a step backward," Lord asserted in an interview two years later. "No Taiwan president had ever landed in the United States, so in effect we did more than any other administration had ever done. We were threading a needle here. We explained to Taiwan, 'Don't push the envelope.' We explained to the Chinese that this was an unofficial stop, it was a matter of courtesy that didn't have huge political significance."[5]

Lord was accurate in his history. Lee was, indeed, the first president of Taiwan ever to land in the United States. Generalissimo Chiang Kai-shek had never ventured from Taiwan to America; he had always left the handling of Americans to his wife, and in any case probably feared the cool reception he would have received in the United States after his defeat on the mainland. By the time his son Chiang Ching-kuo came to power in 1975, American relations with Beijing were far too close for Washington to have permitted a visit.[6]

However, the State Department's grasp of the rules of the past always surpassed its sense of domestic politics in the United States. America's cool treatment of Lee Teng-hui's Honolulu refueling stop did not sit well on Capitol Hill. Several members of Congress denounced the administration. In June, two of Taiwan's supporters in Congress, Senators Frank Murkowski of Alaska and Hank Brown of Colorado, wrote a letter to Lee, inviting him to come back and visit the United States. The following month, the Senate voted 94 to 0 to to approve a resolution calling upon the State Department to grant visas to officials from Taiwan.[7]

American attitudes toward Taiwan had changed. In the 1970s, it had been relatively easy for Congress to dismiss Taiwan as a relic of the Chinese civil war, an authoritarian police state in which Chiang Kai-shek and his aides repressed the native Taiwanese population. By the early 1990s, however, Taiwan was undeniably a thriving democracy. Lee was himself an ethnic Taiwanese, and the island had become America's sixth-largest trading partner. So too, after 1989, American views of China had obviously been transformed: The Tiananmen massacre made clear the nature of the Communist Party's rule over the Chinese people, and the collapse of the Soviet Union called into question the necessity for America to avoid offending Beijing.

Furthermore, the Washington politics concerning Taiwan were quite different from those involving MFN. While the Beijing leadership could count on support from the American business community in its campaign to win an extension of China's trade benefits, it could not rely on U.S. companies in its efforts to constrain Taiwan.

American exports to Taiwan were $16 billion in 1993, more than twice as much as to China. Where China was the dream of the future for American business, Taiwan represented the profits of the present day. American corporations were rushing to Taipei to compete with European firms for the contracts in a $300 billion public works program.[8] U.S. defense contractors were eagerly testing to see whether the Bush administration's approval of F-16s to Taiwan had opened the way for more arms sales. The business interest in Taiwan grew stronger year by year.

In handling Lee's stopover, administration officials ignored these larger changes and the shifting political climate in Congress. They were annoyed that after deciding to let Lee's plane touch down in Honolulu, they had been criticized for not having gone a step further by letting him spend the night. "Lee very cleverly changed the debate by not getting off the plane," said Stanley Roth, who was on Clinton's National Security Council. "He made it look like he'd been a prisoner and had been insulted."[9]

Administration officials didn't realize it, but Lee's Honolulu refueling stop was only the beginning skirmish in a larger battle over Taiwan.

WHEN IT first took office, the Clinton administration had initiated a comprehensive review of American policy toward Taiwan. At the time, that policy had seemed to be in flux. In its last weeks, the lame-duck Bush administration had sent U.S. Trade Representative Carla Hills to Taiwan, the first Cabinet-level official from America to visit the island since the rupture of diplomatic relations in 1979.

According to Bellocchi, a career State Department official who served as head of the Washington office of the American Institute in Taiwan from 1990 to 1995, the administration's motivation in launching the policy review had been to put off any controversy over Taiwan. "It was, 'How can we get Congress off our backs?' " he explained.[10] The administration wanted no distractions during the year in which it was pursuing its unsuccessful policy of MFN linkage.

In the late summer of 1994, the administration finally announced the results of this review. The changes in Taiwan policy were mostly minor, merely redefining the details of the unofficial relationship through which America had done business with the island since 1979.

For example, the administration decreed that officials from Taiwan would still be barred from setting foot in the White House, State Department and Pentagon, but would henceforth be allowed to visit other government buildings in Washington. Senior American officials dealing with economic issues, even Cabinet members, would be permitted to travel to Taiwan, as Hills had for the Bush administration. However, top-level Taiwan officials, such as President Lee Teng-hui, would not be granted visas to travel to the United States. Bowing to Congress, the administration conceded that officials like Lee would be permitted to make "transit" stops on American soil—and thus would be allowed in the future to spend a night in a place like Honolulu.

The review left virtually everyone unhappy. "In retrospect, it might have been wiser not to do it [the Taiwan policy review], since there wasn't enough room to make anyone satisfied," acknowledged Roth. "It came down to an incredible series of nits."[11] China was irritated because the United States was for the first time making explicit the fact that some Cabinet officers could visit Taiwan. Members of Congress were irked because the changes did not go further. At a hearing before the Senate Foreign Relations Committee, Winston Lord was besieged by criticism, as one senator after another complained that the administration should have taken bolder steps that would have showed greater respect for Taiwan.[12]

Above all, Taiwan's President Lee was annoyed because the Clinton administration seemed to have preserved considerably more than it had changed. In its policy review, the administration had reaffirmed America's one-China formulas of the past, and it had gone on record in opposition to Taiwan's campaign for United Nations membership. The president of Taiwan was still prohibited from visiting the United States for anything other than an overnight transit stop.

By the fall of 1994, Lee realized that he had vastly greater support on Capitol Hill than within the administration. He set out to enlist Congress's help to reverse the administration's newly announced Taiwan policy.

JUST BEFORE Lee had launched his vacation diplomacy, a curious new organization was established in Taipei. It was called the Taiwan Research Institute and was headed by Liu Tai-ying, one of Lee's closest advisers. Liu was the head of the Business Management Committee of the ruling Kuomintang, or Nationalist Party, which with more than $3 billion in assets is one of the world's wealthiest political organizations. The Taiwan Research Institute, funded with money from the Kuomintang, seemed to be a vehicle for putting financial power behind Lee's overseas diplomacy. Its first venture was to direct Taiwan investment into Indonesia soon after President Suharto agreed to meet with Lee.[13]

In the summer of 1994, the Taiwan Research Institute ventured into American politics by launching a lobbying organization in the United States. It signed a three-year, $4.5 million contract with a Washington firm, Cassidy & Associates, whose members had strong ties to the Democratic Party; its staff included Jody Powell, President Carter's press secretary.

With the help of this lobbying firm, Taiwan went to work in Congress on behalf of President Lee. Taiwan got an additional boost in the congressional elections of November 1994, which returned control of Congress to the Republican Party and brought to Washington scores of new members who had no connection to the China policies of the previous two decades.

At the beginning of 1995, the new House Speaker Newt Gingrich endorsed the idea of a visit to the United States by the president of Taiwan, as well as the readmission of Taiwan to the United Nations. "Frankly, Taiwan does deserve to be treated with respect," declared Gingrich after a meeting with a delegation of Kuomintang officials from Taipei. "It has certainly deserved it."[14]

The administration should have been paying attention to what was happening on Capitol Hill and trying to devise a strategy that would take account of Taiwan's growing support. It wasn't, and it didn't.

Lee Teng-hui and his supporters had gradually settled upon the right pretext for a trip to the United States by the Taiwan president. Lee was an alumnus of Cornell University, where he had obtained a doctorate in agricultural economics in 1968. In the early months of 1995, Taiwan officials began seeking permission in Washington for Lee to make a private visit to the United States to attend his Cornell reunion. The university itself was eager to have Lee come; he was the only Cornell alumnus who was a head of state. In 1994, Taiwan donors, whom the university officially described as "Lee's friends," had contributed $2.5 million to the university to endow a Lee Teng-hui Professorship of World Affairs.[15]

Some of the State Department's China specialists felt that with a bit of forethought and finesse, the administration could have approved Lee's trip in a way that would not have provoked an intense reaction in Beijing. These career professionals believed the administration should have recognized early on Taiwan had so much support in Congress that any efforts to keep Lee out of the United States would fail. Then Washington might have slowly and carefully prepared the Chinese leadership for the idea of a trip by Taiwan's president—while at the same time offering Beijing some rewards or incentives as unacknowledged compensation for Lee's visit. At the time, for example, Chinese President Jiang Zemin was looking for an invitation to visit Washington on his own.

"On Lee Teng-hui, my feeling was that we couldn't hold the line," one senior State Department official said in an interview. "I felt that trying to maintain a justification for not letting Lee come on a clearly private visit was going to be a political problem in this country, and that it would be difficult to sustain. Instead, I would have set out to create the conditions [with China] that would have enabled him to come without paying a big cost. That would have required a lot of advance work [with Beijing]."[16]

Instead, the administration for months adamantly rejected any suggestion of a visit by Lee. Responding to questions on Capitol Hill in late 1994, Lord had said unequivocally that the administration's Taiwan policy would not permit Lee to attend his reunion.[17] On February 15, 1995, Secretary of State Warren Christopher was asked during congressional testimony whether the administration would let Lee visit the United States, and he, too, dismissed the idea. It would be "inconsistent with the unofficial character of our relationship" with Taiwan, he testified.[18]

Taiwan refused to accept this rejection as final. Throughout the early months of 1995, its officials and their lobbyists intensified their campaign on Capitol Hill. "They [Taiwan officials] decided to go to Congress and stir things up," Lord complained bitterly.[19]

Two months later, the secretary of state took matters one final step further. In a meeting at the United Nations on April 17, Christopher told Chinese Foreign Minister Qian Qichen that the administration would deny a visa to the Taiwan president. That assurance would come back to haunt the Clinton administration, giving China grounds to claim that the secretary had made false promises. Christopher subsequently explained that he had also warned Qian about the pressures building up in Congress and had suggested the administration might not be able to withstand them. These qualifications, however, seem to have been dropped before they reached Beijing.[20]

In early May 1995, the administration was finally forced to confront political reality. The House of Representatives approved, 396 to 0, a nonbinding resolution calling upon the administration to permit Lee Teng-hui to make a private visit to Cornell. One week later, despite last-minute efforts of administration officials to line up support for its Taiwan policy, the Senate followed suit, voting 97 to 1 in favor of Lee's visit. (The lone opponent was Senator Bennett Johnston of Louisiana, a strong supporter of the Chinese regime, who was preparing to retire and would later, in private life, seek to profit from business ventures in China.)[21]

By this time, many of the nation's newspapers carried editorials in favor of Lee's visit. "When you have all but one member of Congress, in both houses, voting in one way, plus the entire media establishment, plus local political leaders around the country, it was enormous pressure," said Roth, who was in charge of Asia policy for the National Security Council at the time. Moreover, recalled Roth, Taiwan's lobbying firm, Cassidy & Associates, was skillfully lining up support for Lee's visit from President Clinton's domestic advisers, thus neutralizing the State Department's opposition.[22]

In retreat, State Department officials desperately offered Lee alternatives to the Cornell visit of precisely the sort that they had turned down the previous year. Perhaps the president of Taiwan might want to visit Honolulu for a time, they suggested; he could not only play golf there, but take part in private academic exchanges. By now, however, the department was becoming marginalized. Lee's supporters were focused upon the president of the United States.

THERE WAS never any doubt what President Clinton himself wanted to do about Lee Teng-hui's request.

Clinton had, as governor of Arkansas, been a frequent visitor to Taiwan. In the days when he had been a struggling state official little recognized among Washington's elite, Clinton had been greeted in Taipei as an honored dignitary. Moreover, as an astute politician, Clinton realized Taiwan's power in America: Supporters of Taiwan could provide campaign contributions and other help for a person seeking public office.

From a foreign policy perspective, too, Clinton had reasons to support Lee's visit. His administration had already welcomed Palestinian leader Yasir Arafat, Israel's longtime adversary, to the White House; it had also permitted Gerry Adams, the Irish leader of the Sinn Fein, to visit the United States, despite determined opposition from Britain. Amid these actions, the prohibition of a visit by Lee to take part in a college reunion in upstate New York seemed indefensible.

Indeed, Clinton subsequently defended his decision by suggesting that to turn Lee down even would have been a violation of fundamental rights. "In our country, we have the constitutional right to travel," the president later argued. "It is very difficult in America to justify not allowing a citizen of the world . . . to come to his college reunion and to travel around our country." [23]

The only conceivable rationale for denying Lee a visa, of course, was the fact that China was so determinedly opposed to it. To Beijing, the mere fact of permitting Lee to enter the United States, even on a private trip, conveyed a greater degree of official recognition of Taiwan than the United States had displayed since 1979.

But in the spring of 1995, Clinton was in no mood to yield once again to China's wishes. The president had, a year earlier, given way to Beijing by dropping the linkage between trade benefits and human rights. Since then, China had remained as repressive toward political dissent as it had been beforehand, disappointing those in Washington who had hoped Beijing would ease up on human rights after its trade benefits were renewed.

Indeed, Clinton himself seemed during this period to be tiring of lectures and admonitions from the Chinese. "Just as the Chinese demand to be respected in their way, they have to respect our way," Clinton said at one of the White House discussions about Lee Teng-hui's visit. "Just as we're supposed to be sensitive to their [Chinese] traditions and history and their way, they need to be sensitive to ours. And our values with respect to Lee Teng-hui coming here were reflected in the congressional majorities." [24]

Thus, for the second time in four years, a president was breaking new ground in American policy toward Taiwan as a means of demonstrating that he was willing to stand up to the Chinese leadership. President Bush had sold F-16 jet fighters to Taiwan after he was accused of coddling dictators in Beijing. So too, President Clinton decided to support an unprecedented visit by the president of Taiwan after he had been embarrassed by China into backing away from his MFN executive order.

American human rights groups and Chinese student organizations had only intermittent success in Washington. Taiwan, by contrast, had enough support, resources, experience and political skill to capitalize on America's disenchantment with China.

Clinton did not make his decision all at once. Instead, he held a round of talks with congressional leaders and his foreign policy team.

On May 18, he discussed the U.S. budget with a small group of senators allied with the Democratic Leadership Council, the organization of moderate Democrats with which Clinton had long been identified. They included Senators Charles Robb, Sam Nunn, Joseph Lieberman and John Breaux. Before this session started, Robb raised the subject of Taiwan and the State Department's continuing refusal to permit Lee Teng-hui to attend his reunion. Clinton assured the senators he was leaning toward granting Lee a visa.[25]

By the time the senior members of the administration's foreign policy team gathered together to make the formal recommendation to Clinton concerning Lee's visa, they realized they had little choice but to approve Lee's trip. "At a breakfast, we agreed that a) we don't have much choice, and b) we just can't be absolutely steamrollered by Beijing or let Beijing's sensitivities totally dominate us as we make these decisions," said Anthony Lake.

The participants—Lake, Christopher and Defense Secretary William Perry—all realized the president himself felt strongly that Lee should have the right to travel to Cornell. They also feared that if the administration continued to deny the visa to the Taiwan president, Congress would likely take the final step by enacting binding legislation requiring it to permit Lee's trip. Such action would have made the administration look even weaker and more driven by congressional pressure than it already was. Moreover, there was always the risk that Congress would go further and enact still broader legislation in support of Taiwan, perhaps strengthening the Taiwan Relations Act of 1979.

"Christopher and Tony [Lake] and Perry thought that this was the lesser of two evils," said another official. "If the president decided not to allow entrance into the United States and attendance at the Cornell reunion, then the Congress would act legislatively. So they decided to go with the lesser of two evils, and try to manage it."

There were a handful of dissenting voices. At the State Department, James Steinberg, the head of the policy planning staff, and an aide, Alan Romberg, argued to Christopher that the administration should turn down Lee's request because the potential harm to American relations with China would be too severe. Christopher rejected these pleas on grounds that the consequences of turning Lee down could be even worse.[26]

In the end, Clinton's top advisers gave the president the recommendation they knew he wanted. "I think Clinton was relieved when we all recommended to him that he do this," observed one of them. Within hours, the president approved. Lee's visa was to be granted.

Before the decision was made public, the administration made some last-minute efforts to minimize the damage. Taiwan officials were informed that Lee could travel to the United States, but that his visit was to be a strictly private affair, with no press conferences or other political activity. Officials made clear that no one from the U.S. government would meet with Taiwan's president. Lee was permitted to stop over for a night in Los Angeles, a natural resting point between Taipei and Ithaca, New York. But when Taiwan officials asked if Lee could travel to Cornell by way of New York City, they were turned down. State Department officials decreed that the Taiwan president would have to fly into the smaller airport of Syracuse, far removed from the press hordes and the Chinese communities in America's largest city.[27]

On Saturday, May 20, one day after Taiwan was notified that Lee could come to America and two days before the decision was to be made public, Lake and Undersecretary of State Peter Tarnoff called in Chinese Ambassador Li Daoyu to deliver the bad news; they explained that the president of Taiwan would be making a private trip to the United States, one with no broader implications for American relations with China. The embittered Chinese ambassador inquired sarcastically whether the Clinton administration planned to let Fidel Castro visit the United States, too: Did the leader of Cuba, he inquired, enjoy the same freedom to travel to America that the Clinton administration had just granted Lee Teng-hui?[28]

The ambassador had suspected that, despite Christopher's earlier assurances to the Chinese foreign minister, the administration might back down and grant Lee the visa. "We are not blind, and we are not deaf," Li had said afterward, making clear that he had seen that the growing congressional pressure might force the administration to reverse itself.[29] Still, knowing what was about to happen did not soften the blow. China clearly did not carry the same weight in Washington as it had in the past. The Chinese realized that the United States had managed its China policy in such a way that the president of Taiwan had missed his Cornell reunions year after year until 1995.

Ultimately, the Chinese were given a day's notice, over a weekend, of the news that a president of Taiwan would for the first time in history visit America. "The reality is that a decision is done within two to three hours," acknowledged Stanley Roth. "You don't have the opportunity to manage the flip-flop. The flip-flop is instantaneous. That led to some sense of betrayal [by the Chinese leadership]."[30]

Even if the administration had taken months to prepare China for the bad news, its decision would not have gone down well in Beijing. The wavering conduct made the situation considerably worse and the reaction more intense.

WHEN LEE landed in Los Angeles on June 7, 1995, hundreds of supporters, waving Taiwan flags, gathered outside of his hotel. "I am excited about this development and hope that it will lead to an official recognition of Taiwan as a sovereign country," one Taiwanese-American banker told reporters. Lee met leaders of the Chinese-American community, with Los Angeles Mayor Richard Riordan and with a representative of California Governor Pete Wilson—although, in order to satisfy the administration, a spokesman for the Taiwan president solemnly assured reporters that these meetings were private rather than official.[31]

In Syracuse, the welcoming party at the airport included the mayor, the president of Cornell, a motorcade of stretch limousines, four state police cruisers and three Republican members of the U.S. Senate. One of them, Senate Foreign Relations Committee Chairman Jesse Helms, told Lee, "Mr. President: today, Syracuse; very soon, I hope, the capital of the U.S. in Washington, D.C."[32]

At Cornell, the Taiwan president spoke in a field house with hundreds of demonstrators outside—some waving the Republic of China flags of Taiwan's government, others with flags from the People's Republic of China, and still others with the flags of Taiwan's independence movement. His address amounted to a plea for the people of Taiwan and the cause of democratic change:

> Today, we are entering a new post–Cold War era, where the world is full of many uncertainties. Communism is dead or dying, and the peoples of many nations are anxious to try new methods of governing their societies. . . . Democracy is thriving in my country. No speech or act allowed by law will be subject to any restriction or interference. Different and opposing views are heard every day in the news media, including harsh criticism of the president.[33]

Lee added, "The people of the Republic of China on Taiwan are determined to play a peaceful and constructive role among the family of nations. . . . We are here to stay." These words were not what the Beijing leadership wanted to hear.

AFTERWARD, A myth about Lee Teng-hui's trip would take hold within the Clinton administration. It was the sort of fantasy that sustains members of an administration in the belief that a policy would have worked well if only some malefactors from outside their ranks hadn't sabotaged it at the last minute.

The myth went like this: China might have been willing to tolerate Lee Teng-hui's trip to America were it not for the speech he gave at Cornell. If Lee's remarks had not been so inflammatory, the Chinese reaction would have been subdued.

"The single biggest problem with the visit was the speech itself at Cornell," Lord maintained afterward. "We told Taiwan in advance this should be a nonpolitical speech. They said it would be. They in fact said it would be reminiscences about Cornell days and about economic reform in Taiwan. . . . But the speech itself clearly was political, and clearly we were blindsided by it. We kept trying to get advance copies, and they didn't play straight with us. . . . When the Chinese looked at that speech, they went bananas." Virtually identical explanations were offered by other administration officials.[34]

Although this analysis was widely accepted within the administration, it does not hold up to critical scrutiny. One problem is that the argument exposes some of the internal contradictions in Clinton's position concerning Lee Teng-hui's trip. The president claimed Lee had a constitutional right to travel to Cornell. But if Lee was to be treated like a private American citizen, rather than the president of a government the United States does not recognize, why didn't he have the right to freedom of speech as well? The administration was trying to have it both ways: It wanted to claim Lee had the freedom to travel to his reunion, but it also wanted to decide what he could say and censor his speech.

More fundamentally, Beijing's objection was not to Lee Teng-hui's reunion speech but to the trip itself. Even if Lee had talked at Cornell exclusively about football and fraternities, China would have found some cause for complaint, such as his meetings with mayors and U.S. senators or his presence in Los Angeles. No previous administration had permitted the president of Taiwan to visit the United States. Clinton had relaxed American policy, and the Chinese were not going to let this action pass quietly.

At this juncture, China was reacting to the cumulative impact of the past few years of friction with the United States, much as America was with China. In granting the visa to Lee, Clinton had been influenced by the legacy of his earlier dispute with Beijing over human rights; he was determined not to yield to the Chinese once again. In China's case, the leftover grievance was the Bush administration's sale of F-16 warplanes to Taiwan. In its desire not to hurt Bush's chances for reelection, the Chinese had let that groundbreaking transaction go forward without much complaint. This time, Chinese leaders did not intend to compound their earlier mistake.

China began its retaliatory campaign with a series of diplomatic pinpricks. It postponed a series of high-level meetings, such as a trip to the United States by Defense Minister Chi Haotian and a visit to Beijing by John Holum, the director of the U.S. Arms Control and Disarmament Agency. Scheduled talks between the two governments concerning nuclear energy and the control of missile technology were put off. A Chinese air force delegation visiting Washington was ordered to come home.

On June 17, China stepped up the pressure by recalling its ambassador from Washington. The Chinese also delayed giving the formal acceptance necessary for President Clinton's appointee, former U.S. Senator James Sasser, to take his post as the next American ambassador to China. As a result, for the first time since the establishment of relations in 1979, America and China found themselves in the summer of 1995 with no ambassadorial representation on each other's territory.[35]

These Chinese measures were merely the warm-up for the main event—which the Clinton administration, at least at senior levels, had failed to anticipate.

During the weeks when the administration had been weighing what to do about Lee Teng-hui's visa request, the State Department drafted a paper for the White House that sketched out the actions China might take in retaliation for Lee's visit. One of the possibilities was military action by China's People's Liberation Army. Lord instructed his subordinates to take this section out of the memo. There was no need to scare the White House with military scenarios, he had explained.[36]

Nevertheless, on July 19, the Chinese army announced that it planned to conduct a week-long series of military exercises in the East China Sea north of Taiwan. The exercises were to include not only naval warships and warplanes, but also live fire, including the launching of Chinese missiles into the waters off Taiwan's coastline.

As promised, over the following days, the army fired four M-9 missiles into the East China Sea north of Taiwan. Taiwan's stock market plunged by more than 4 percent in a day and by 33 percent over the following weeks. Its currency fell to a four-year low. Fishermen, understandably fearful, kept their boats in port during the missile firings.

Taiwan's airlines hurriedly changed the routes of scheduled flights. One public opinion poll found that support among Taiwan's population for the cause of independence dropped by 7 percent in less than a month.[37]

THE PLA exercises and the launchings of missiles represented a significant turning point in China's relations with the United States. The military actions were aimed primarily at intimidating the population of Taiwan, but they also had a profound impact in Washington, both upon officials of the Clinton administration and upon military leaders in the Pentagon.

Within the administration, the events of the summer of 1995 ushered in a new era. Over the previous two and a half years, its foreign policy team had been preoccupied with Russia and Bosnia and with the Third World crises in Somalia and Haiti. China had been accorded intermittent high-level attention, such as during the last weeks of the decision on its most-favored-nation benefits. More often, however, as in the case of Lee Teng-hui's Honolulu stopover, decisions about China had been relegated to lower-level officials.

In mid-1995, for the first time, China began to be treated as one of the principal problems confronting American foreign policy. Lake, Christopher and Perry, the three Cabinet-level officials dealing with foreign policy, began gathering for occasional breakfasts or lunches to talk about China, even at times when there was no pending crisis, in the same fashion as they met regularly to discuss Russia.

During Clinton's first two and a half years in office, the administration had been obliged to retreat from its policies on China not once but twice. Both of these reversals—one on China's MFN benefits and the second on Lee's visit to Cornell—had been embarrassingly public. In both instances, the administration had failed to foresee how great would be the resistance to its original policies.

By this time, in the summer of 1995, China was threatening the use of military force in a way that could unsettle U.S. allies in East Asia. Beyond the frictions over Taiwan, the United States faced a growing series of problems with China in other areas, too. That summer, Harry Wu—the Chinese-American émigré who had exposed China's practice of exporting goods manufactured with prison labor—had been detained by Chinese authorities as he tried to sneak into China in a remote northwestern border town.

Once again, China's supposedly independent judiciary worked in miraculously timely ways, just as it had in releasing Wei Jingsheng in 1993 on the eve of the vote on the Olympics Games or in freeing Wang Juntao and Chen Ziming before Clinton's 1994 decision on MFN. Harry Wu got out just in time for the United States to agree to send First Lady Hillary Clinton to the International Conference on Women in Beijing.

The Cabinet-level sessions were one demonstration of the administration's belated determination to pay closer attention to China. Washington took other steps as well. In the months after Lee Teng-hui's visit, officials quietly worked out a new understanding with Taiwan. If you have any complaints, Taiwan officials were told, bring them directly to us first instead of trying to defeat the administration in Congress.[38] The White House did not want to be embarrassed again.

At the same time, the administration secretly offered new concessions to China. In August, Christopher held an amicable meeting with the Chinese foreign minister in Brunei and handed him a letter from Clinton to President Jiang Zemin. In it, the administration for the first time said that Jiang would be welcome to visit Washington—a possibility that, if offered several months earlier, might have been used to counterbalance Lee Teng-hui's visit to Cornell.

Even more significantly, in Clinton's letter, the text of which has never been made public, a series of promises were made to China about Taiwan. The president told Jiang that the United States 1) would oppose or resist efforts by Taiwan to gain independence; 2) would not support the creation of "two Chinas," or one China and a separate Taiwan; and 3) would not support Taiwan's admission to the United Nations. These assurances were the first formulation of what would later come to be called the "three noes."

In many respects, Clinton's commitments were similar to the secret promises about Taiwan that Henry Kissinger and Richard Nixon had given to Chou Enlai during their visits of 1971 and 1972. However, Clinton's pledges were in their own way more important. The "three noes" had never been packaged together in this fashion before. They were made in writing at a time whan Taiwan was about to hold its first presidential election, and in an era when the possibility of Taiwan declaring independence seemed far less remote than it had been in the early 1970s. In addition, one of Clinton's secret promises to Jiang, that the United States would *oppose* Taiwan's independence, seemed to go beyond what had been said in the past. (In later years, the Clinton administration would back away from this language, and say merely that the United States *does not support* an independent Taiwan.)[39]

Soon, China returned Ambassador Li Daoyu to Washington, and it agreed to accept Sasser as the new American ambassador in Beijing. In the early fall, the political tensions between the two countries seemed to ebb. Nevertheless, the military consequences of Lee Teng-hui's visit were far from over.

. . .

UNDER CLINTON, the Pentagon's approach to China had been subject to a series of overlapping and sometimes conflicting pressures.

Perry had emerged as a strong proponent of developing strong relations with the Chinese leadership. Many years earlier, during the Carter administration, he had been instrumental in opening the way for American defense cooperation with China against the Soviet Union. During the 1980s, he had visited China at least four times while working for a Stanford University center on arms control.

Perry had come to know and like some of China's military leaders. He sometimes referred to Liu Huaqing, China's top-ranking soldier and a member of the Politburo Standing Committee, as "my old friend." During his trips for Stanford, Perry had also gotten to know some of China's leading politicians. One of them had been Jiang Zemin, then the government minister in charge of the electronics industry, who would later rise to become the leader of the Communist Party. In Jiang's Beijing office, filled with modern gadgets, the two men had talked mostly about microelectronics, a subject on which Perry found that Jiang was well-informed.[40]

In 1994, not long after becoming secretary of defense, Perry had volunteered to visit Beijing for talks with China's military and civilian leaders. Perry's idea was, in its way, remarkable for the rapidity of change it represented: Only two years earlier, the United States had still been operating under the Bush administration's Tiananmen Square sanctions prohibiting any contact between American and Chinese military leaders. Nevertheless, Clinton gave his approval.

When Perry returned to Beijing that October, he renewed his friendship with Liu Huaqing and met with other Chinese military leaders as well. He set up a new U.S.-China Defense Conversion Commission, through which American firms were supposed to work with Chinese military enterprises to produce and sell products for civilian use.

Perry felt that the days when America had sold weapons and provided military technology to the People's Liberation Army were past. The world was considerably different in 1994 than it had been during his last official visit to China in 1980, he conceded. But he argued that joint efforts on defense conversion could be a small step toward new cooperation between the United States and the Chinese military. The idea of helping the People's Liberation Army, even on commercial ventures, was soon criticized in Congress, and Perry's commission was abolished two years later.[41]

Perry's top priority in Beijing was obtaining China's assistance in dealing with North Korea. He and other administration officials believed that China could help stop the North Korean nuclear weapons program. The evidence was sketchy, but there were signs that China, North Korea's principal source of energy and food, was quietly using its leverage to influence Pyongyang.

The Chinese may also have been making use of the North Korean nuclear dispute as a way of demonstrating their importance to the United States. The timing of their efforts in Pyongyang was remarkable. In early June 1994, just two weeks after Clinton announced he would extend China's most-favored-nation benefits, the Chinese for the first time told North Korea that China might go along with a United Nations resolution imposing sanctions against Pyongyang. Within only a few days, President Kim Il Sung agreed to freeze his country's nuclear program.[42] China had first obtained what it wanted from the Clinton administration concerning MFN, and had then rewarded the United States by applying some tough pressure against North Korea.

At the time of Perry's visit to China in October, North Korea was still balking at signing a written agreement to close down its nuclear installations. In Beijing, Perry asked Chinese officials to convey a message from the United States to North Korea. The message, as Perry later described it, was "that we were prepared to take very strong sanctions [against North Korea], that we were prepared to send more troops to [South] Korea and that we were prepared to risk a war" to prevent North Korea from making weapons-grade plutonium. In short, Perry was warning that the United States might use force against North Korea if it didn't conclude the nuclear deal.[43]

Neither Perry nor any other administration official knew for sure whether China passed on this tough message, or what impact it may have had in Pyongyang. But within days, the impasse was broken and North Korea finally agreed, in writing, to dismantle its existing nuclear installations.

WITHIN THE Defense Department, however, another, darker perspective on China was emerging—one at some variance with the views of Perry and others who saw the Chinese as benign and potentially helpful to the United States. From this different outlook, China seemed like a possible long-term rival, a future threat to American interests.

U.S. military commanders working in the Persian Gulf complained about the harmful impact of China's sales of advanced weaponry to Iran.[44] In Asia, the Pentagon worried about whether China might intimidate its neighbors. So, too, those strategists responsible for long-range planning worried about the cumulative impact of China's growing economy and its rising defense budgets. Virtually no one in the Pentagon viewed China as a threat to the United States in the 1990s; yet few were willing or able to make predictions about the capability of the PLA in 20 or 30 years.

Among the Pentagon officials warning of China's future military capabilities was Michael Pillsbury. During the 1970s, Pillsbury had been the first to propose American military help for China to offset the Soviet Union. However, during the 1990s, following the Soviet collapse, Pillsbury—working in the Pentagon's Office of Net Assessment, which is responsible for the analysis of long-range trends—sounded alarms about China's advances in military technology.[45] Judged strictly from the standpoint of how to deal with China, it was a remarkable turnabout. There seemed to be, however, a larger underlying consistency: Pillsbury always favored a hawkish approach of seeking to constrain any nation that might some day challenge the United States.

The Pentagon's formal policy statements, while cautiously worded, began to reflect this new, warier view of China. An East Asia Strategy Report released in February 1995 observed, "Although China's leaders insist their military buildup is defensive and commensurate with China's overall economic growth, others in the region cannot be sure of China's intentions." Without a better understanding of China's intentions, the Defense Department report said, "other Asian nations may feel a need to respond to China's growing military power."[46]

In the autumn of 1994, a brief military encounter demonstrated the increasing potential for conflict between the United States and China. The American aircraft carrier *Kitty Hawk* had been cruising in international waters in the Yellow Sea off China's coastline when its antisubmarine aircraft detected a Chinese nuclear submarine about 200 miles away. American planes tracked the Chinese submarine, using sonar devices to do so; in response, the Chinese air force sent its own jet fighters toward the American jet fighters. Eventually, the submarine returned to its port of Qingdao and the *Kitty Hawk* sailed off toward South Korea.

This episode was the sort of cat-and-mouse game that had been commonplace between the American and Soviet navies during the Cold War. For the United States and China, however, it was a new sort of confrontation. Not long afterward, at a dinner in Beijing, a Chinese official told an American military attaché that the next time such an incident occurred so close to China's coastline, the PLA would have orders to shoot.[47]

TAIWAN'S first direct presidential election was scheduled for March 23, 1996, with Lee running as the ruling Nationalist Party candidate against challenges from the Democratic Progressive Party and from the New

Party, which favored reunification with China. The Chinese military operations in the summer of 1995 appeared to be aimed at influencing the elections; they served to remind the people of Taiwan that a vote for independence could provoke military intervention from the Chinese mainland. The actions may also have been designed to keep Lee and his party from trying to co-opt their political opposition by flirting with the cause of independence.

In the months after the military exercises started, Clinton sent several private letters directly to President Jiang Zemin, and Christopher dispatched similar messages to Foreign Minister Qian Qichen, complaining about the PLA exercises and the missile launches.[48]

These communications from Washington had little effect in Beijing. The Chinese were sending their own messages back to Washington, more indirect but also considerably more bellicose in nature. They warned that if the United States intervened to defend Taiwan against China, America's action could lead to war. China was, in effect, testing the administration, trying to assess just how much it cared about Taiwan and how far it might go in protecting the island.

These efforts reached a climax in the late fall and early winter of 1995, when the Chinese began to suggest vaguely the possibility that a conflict between the United States and China over Taiwan could lead to a nuclear exchange. During one visit to Beijing in October 1995, Charles W. Freeman Jr.—the former State and Defense Department specialist on China who was, by this time, retired from the government—was told by one PLA leader that China was prepared to sacrifice millions of people, even entire cities, in a nuclear exchange to defend its interests in preventing Taiwan's independence. "You will not sacrifice Los Angeles to protect Taiwan," Freeman was told.[49]

Although Freeman did not disclose who made this threat, others identified the Chinese official as Xiong Guangkai, the deputy chief of general staff of the PLA and its chief of military intelligence. Freeman received similar though less specific warnings from other military leaders.

Freeman was not alone. There appears to have been a broader effort during this period to caution the United States against defending Taiwan. Two months later, an American scholar with close ties to the Chinese leadership met with Qiao Shi, the head of China's National People's Congress; he later told associates Qiao had warned that if China were attacked with nuclear weapons, it could respond by hitting New York City.[50]

Freeman believed that these Chinese nuclear warnings were "deterrent, not aggressive" in nature. During the confrontations between the United States and China over Taiwan in the mid-1950s, the Eisenhower administration threatened to use nuclear weapons. Indeed, these American threats prompted Mao Tsetung to launch the Chinese nuclear weapons program.[51] Freeman thought PLA leaders were trying to say they were no longer so intimidated by American nuclear power as they had been four decades earlier. "The context was, 'We can retaliate, so you do not have the strategic superiority you once had. If you hit our homeland, we can hit yours,' " Freeman explained.[52]

The nuances and the diplomatic history were understandably lost in Washington. Whatever the background, China was threatening to use nuclear weapons against America if it came to Taiwan's defense in a military conflict.

By the end of 1995, the administration was taking small steps to counteract this Chinese campaign of threats and intimidation. In December, the American aircraft carrier *Nimitz* sailed through the Taiwan Strait, accompanied by a cruiser, a destroyer, a frigate and two support ships. Officially, the Pentagon explained that bad weather had forced the American warships to sail through the strait. Nevertheless, it was the first time any American aircraft carrier had appeared in the Taiwan Strait since the United States and China established diplomatic relations in 1979.[53]

When a Chinese Foreign Ministry official, Li Zhaoxing, visited Washington a few weeks later, the Clinton administration told him that the United States had a clear interest in protecting peace across the Taiwan Strait. This message was, once again, a warning that the administration wanted China's military threats against Taiwan to stop.

However, officials once again coupled this warning with a private assurance aimed at pleasing Beijing: Li Zhaoxing was told that the administration did not "expect" Lee or any other leading Taiwan officials to be visiting the United States in 1996.[54] With that quiet promise, the supposed constitutional right to travel in America that President Clinton had once extended to the president of Taiwan vanished almost as quickly as it had been discovered the previous spring.

ONCE AGAIN, the Clinton administration's polite messages and low-key warnings had little impact upon Beijing's military operations.

In February 1996, a month before Taiwan's elections, the PLA massed about 150,000 troops along China's southeastern coast for another round of military exercises, still larger than the ones of the previous year. On March 8, China once again fired missiles into waters off Taiwan. This time, the modern, accurate, solid-fuel M-9s, of the sort that several American administrations had tried to keep China from exporting to the Middle East, landed considerably closer to Taiwan than had the missiles of the previous year. The target areas in the ocean reached within 30 miles of Kaohsiung and Keelung, the island's two leading ports, which handle about 70 percent of the trade to and from Taiwan.[55]

Taiwan's stock market began to fall again, and people on the island lined up at banks to change their money into dollars. Foreign-exchange reserves began dropping at the rate of $300 million to $500 million per day. China's message was unmistakable: Its missiles could devastate the economy of Taiwan.[56]

With these new Chinese exercises and missile firings, the Clinton administration decided that the time for private messages and subtle signals had passed.

On March 7, 1996, a Chinese delegation headed by Vice Foreign Minister Liu Huaqiu arrived in Washington. At dinner that night, Perry and National Security Advisor Anthony Lake warned that any military action against Taiwan would have "grave consequences" for China. The language was vague, but carefully chosen and unprecedented: U.S. officials, ordered by Lake to search the record of American diplomacy with China, could not find that any such warning had been delivered in the quarter-century since the Nixon opening.[57]

Still, on March 8 China began a new round of missile firings. On Saturday, March 9, the administration's foreign policy team gathered in Perry's office at the Pentagon. Christopher, Lake and CIA Director John M. Deutch were at the session, along with General John M. Shalikashvili, the chairman of the Joint Chiefs of Staff, and Lord, the assistant secretary of state for East Asia. Everyone at the meeting agreed that the United States should counteract China with a show of force, one that would reassure both Taiwan and American allies in Asia.

The State Department had expected that the administration would send an aircraft carrier to the waters near Taiwan.[58] But Perry laid out a proposal for considerably stronger action: He suggested that the United States should dispatch not just one aircraft carrier, but two. "I don't recall anyone saying we should only do one [aircraft carrier]," Lord said. "Shali[kashvili] thought it was an option, but Perry clearly thought we should do both."[59]

Shalikashvili and Perry had been discussing what the United States should do. "We wanted the egregious actions [by China] to stop," Perry later explained. "We did not want this to escalate. We considered sending one carrier, but decided that wasn't strong enough. We considered sending two carriers and docking them by Taipei. We decided that was provocative." By several accounts, it was Perry, ordinarily the most forceful advocate within the administration of strong relations with Beijing, who took the lead in presenting China with an overwhelming display of U.S. military force during the confrontation over Taiwan.[60]

The other policy question was whether to sail either of the American aircraft carriers through the Taiwan Strait. On that issue, the U.S. had gotten a bit of cautionary advice from an unusual source: Some Taiwan officials had privately urged the administration not to put a carrier in the strait.[61]

Thus, the Pentagon's decision, approved at the Saturday cabinet-level meeting, was to send two aircraft carriers to the waters near Taiwan, though not directly into the strait between the island and the mainland. Within hours Clinton authorized the deployment of the two carriers.

The result was that the United States deployed its largest armada in Southeast Asia since the end of the Vietnam War. Within days, the aircraft carrier *Independence* was patrolling near the island along with the missile cruiser *Bunker Hill* and a frigate, two destroyers and two submarines. The second carrier, the *Nimitz,* sailed from the Persian Gulf with seven more warships, arriving the following week.[62]

Three months earlier, the administration had sought to explain away its dispatch of the *Nimitz* through the Taiwan Strait by claiming it was the accidental result of bad weather. This time, by contrast, Washington went out of its way to flaunt the dispatch of the aircraft carriers, openly proclaiming it to be a display of American military might.

"Beijing should know, and this U.S. fleet will remind them, that while they are a great military power, the strongest, the premier military power in the Western Pacific is the United States," Perry said to one gathering on Capitol Hill.[63] American news correspondents were flown onto the *Independence* for special tours, so that the carrier's deployment would be given the widest possible coverage.

One reporter aboard the *Independence* found jumpsuited U.S. fighter pilots using model airplanes to study how to engage in dogfights with an unnamed enemy: The American jet fighters were pitted against model Sukhoi-27 warplanes precisely like those that China had recently obtained from Russia. American helicopter pilots on the aircraft carrier were supposed to talk in nondescript language about "blue versus orange" teams, so that no countries were named. Sometimes, however, they dropped the pretense and spoke openly about "pursuing Chinese subs."[64]

THE PASSIONS soon subsided. On March 23, the people of Taiwan voted in overwhelming numbers for Lee to remain on the job as president. He obtained nearly 55 percent of the vote, more than twice the

percentage of any of his opponents. It was a clear mandate for the Taiwanese leader who had so openly defied Beijing's wishes. Meanwhile,
having demonstrated what the People's Liberation Army could do, China
phased out its military exercises soon after the Taiwan election. In
response, the Clinton administration redirected the two aircraft carriers
away from Taiwan.

Nevertheless, the Taiwan crisis of March 1996 had a longer-term
impact, both upon U.S. foreign policy in Asia and upon America's
domestic politics. In April 1996, Clinton visited Tokyo and signed a new
agreement with Japanese Prime Minister Ryutaro Hashimoto, extending
and broadening the security treaty between the United States and Japan
even though its original Cold War rationale had disappeared. Thus,
China's military exercises and missile firings had helped to solidify the
alliance between the United States and Japan.

Before departing from Japan, Clinton boarded the *Independence* as it
was docked in Tokyo Bay. Standing aboard the flight deck, before nearly
5,000 American sailors, Marines and their families, the president alluded
to the carrier's duty near Taiwan. "Without firing a single shot, you reassured nations all around the Pacific," he told them. "You gave the world
another example of America's power and America's character." The presence of the aircraft carrier near Taiwan had helped to "calm a rising
storm," he declared.[65]

Within American politics, too, the confrontation over Taiwan had
lasting consequences. At least for a few days, China had again loomed as
America's adversary in a way that it had not for the previous 25 years.
That fact helped make China a ripe target for aspiring political candidates and members of Congress.

America was on the verge of another about-face on China, a shift in
the positions taken by the country's two main political parties. The stage
was thus set for the election of 1996.

CHAPTER EIGHTEEN

The 1996 Campaign
and Its Aftermath

BY EARLY MARCH 1996, Bob Dole had wrapped up the Republican presidential nomination. Many of the other Republican candidates, such as Phil Gramm and Lamar Alexander, had fallen early. Patrick Buchanan's fiery campaign against immigration and free trade lingered a bit longer, as did Steve Forbes's appeals for a flat tax. But the outcome was never really in doubt, and when Dole swept the primaries of "super Tuesday," the campaign for the nomination was over.[1]

Over the next few weeks, Dole and his advisers turned their attention to the task of staking out positions for the fall campaign against Clinton. On foreign policy, the candidate and his staff decided that he should give a major speech describing Dole's views on Asia in general and China in particular.

There was a natural venue for such a speech, some of Dole's aides felt. He had been invited to give the keynote address for a dinner April 22 at the Richard Nixon Library in Yorba Linda, California. In 1996, the 25th anniversary of Henry Kissinger's first trip to Beijing, the library was giving an award to Kissinger as an "architect of peace" and as "America's statesman nonpareil." Randy Scheunemann, Dole's Senate aide, was put in charge of drafting his speech.[2]

But Dole's team of advisers couldn't agree on what he should say about China. The campaign was divided. One group of Republicans felt Dole should follow the tradition of Nixon and Kissinger by emphasizing China's strategic importance to the United States and should criticize Clinton for an overemphasis on human rights. Another group, including leading Republican members of Congress, argued that Dole should take a much tougher, more confrontational approach, broadly challenging the president's China's policy in much the same fashion as Clinton had

against George Bush in 1992. In addition, the Republicans strongly disagreed on what Dole should say about Taiwan. Some conservative
Republicans argued that the very concept of giving a speech on China at
an event in honor of Nixon and Kissinger was misguided.

As a result, Dole's speech was put off. The candidate declined the
Nixon Library's invitation, claiming it would be difficult to fit into his
schedule. The symbolism was striking: Instead of seeking to identify himself with Nixon's and Kissinger's approach to China, Dole felt compelled
to distance himself from their policies.

Dole delivered his Asia speech the following month in the safer con-
fines of a Washington think tank. Briefly echoing the themes of Nixon
and Kissinger, he accused Clinton and the Democrats of lacking a "strategic policy" toward China. However, Dole also strongly endorsed the concept of establishing new ballistic missile defense systems for China's
neighbors in East Asia, including Taiwan, an idea to which he gave the
grandiose name "Pacific Democracy Defense Program." Furthermore, he
called for a stronger American defense commitment to Taiwan and suggested that the United States should supply Taiwan with several new
defensive weapons systems, including air-to-air missiles and submarines.[3]

These positions, which by themselves were unsettling to the Chinese
leadership, were made doubly worrisome by Dole's own long record in
the Senate.

Over the years, Dole had displayed little interest in China except
insofar as it purchased wheat, the main export from his home state of
Kansas. He had traveled to China only once, as Senate majority leader in
1985, and typically used that occasion to push for grain sales. "We have
plenty of good product to sell, and such purchases would benefit us
both," he said. Dole had regularly supported China's most-favored-
nation trade status, but on one occasion, in 1992, he had threatened to
withdraw his support for MFN unless Chinese Ambassador to Washington Zhu Qizhen guaranteed that his government would continue purchasing American grain.[4]

By contrast, Dole had for a quarter-century been one of Taiwan's
most reliable supporters in Congress. At the time of the Carter
administration's recognition of Beijing in 1978, Dole had helped lead the
efforts on Capitol Hill to preserve U.S. defense ties to Taiwan. In July
1995, just as his presidential campaign was getting under way, Dole had
sponsored a warm Capitol Hill reception for Madame Chiang Kai-shek,
the aged, long-forgotten symbol of American ties to Nationalist China.
In March 1996, Dole had said he would favor giving Taiwan a seat in the
United Nations.[5]

.   .   .

WHEN IT comes to America's quadrennial presidential elections, the governments of the world can be divided into two categories: those who fear second-term presidents and those who favor them.

Some countries enjoy a strong base of support in Congress. Israel falls into this category, and so does Taiwan. Such governments tend to worry that they will lose their leverage over a president after he no longer faces the need to run for office again. Such a president may look to his role in history by seeking far-reaching changes, even ones that are unpopular. A lame-duck president has particular strength in the field of foreign policy, because he has greater latitude there than in domestic affairs to take actions that do not require congressional approval.

By contrast, other governments tend to prefer a lame-duck president in Washington, because they have little grassroots support in America and do better when it matters less. The former Soviet Union was one such government; the Palestinians are another.

China falls into this latter category. Sometimes, to be sure, as in the 1970s, good relations with China have enjoyed strong popular support. But on the whole, over the past quarter-century, China's strongest political ties have been with American foreign policy elites, not with the public. As a result, in presidential elections, China has tended to prefer dealing with an incumbent, calculating that it is better to do business with a president who has been in office for four years than with one who is worried about facing the electorate in his next campaign. China helped Nixon's reelection campaign in 1972 with its warm hospitality on his historic trip. Since then, the Chinese have in one way or another favored Jimmy Carter over Ronald Reagan, Reagan over Walter Mondale, and Bush over Clinton. In 1988, Bush, then Reagan's vice president and virtually an incumbent, even won a public endorsement from Deng Xiaoping in his campaign against Michael Dukakis.

Given all of these factors—Dole's speech, his extensive record of support for Taiwan and China's longstanding preference for incumbent presidents—the leadership in Beijing had plenty of grounds to support Clinton's reelection.

Yet it also had reasons to hesitate. Clinton was, after all, still the same politician who had promised in 1992 to stop "coddling dictators" in Beijing; he was the same president who had attempted to impose conditions on the renewal of China's trade benefits. Only a short time earlier, in March 1996, he had sent two aircraft carriers to help protect Taiwan, a use of American force that Clinton and Vice President Al Gore had begun to emphasize in the presidential campaign as a demonstration of their toughness.[6]

So China proceeded carefully. In the late spring and early summer of

1996, Chinese officials quietly conducted a series of high-level talks that might be viewed in retrospect as interviews of the two presidential campaigns.

In the late spring, Robert F. Ellsworth went to Beijing twice for meetings with Chinese leaders. Ellsworth had been, like Dole, a Kansas congressman, had served as Nixon's ambassador to NATO and had become a private businessman. He hadn't visited China since his service in the navy at the end of World War II. Ostensibly, he was traveling as a representative of a Washington think tank, the Atlantic Council, and for his own interest in energy issues. Yet Ellsworth was no ordinary visitor. He was the Republican presidential candidate's oldest friend and most trusted campaign adviser; he had stood with Dole against George Bush in the 1988 primaries. His stature in the 1996 campaign was demonstrated by the fact that, at the time of his two visits to China, he was in charge of selecting Dole's running mate. Ellsworth said in a later interview that Chinese officials believed he had come to Beijing for Dole.

Ellsworth's trips went unreported in any news media, either in the United States or in China. On the first visit, he met with Vice Foreign Minister Liu Huaqiu, the government's leading America-handler; on the other, he talked with Xiong Guangkai, the chief of intelligence for the People's Liberation Army, the PLA's own America-handler and the man who had, in late 1995, warned of China's ability to hit Los Angeles with nuclear weapons.

Liu Huaqiu, in particular, complained bitterly about Dole's Asia speech. "Why is Dole proposing theater-missile defenses for Taiwan?" he asked. At a dinner in the state guest house at Diaoyutai, Ellsworth pulled out a copy of Dole's speech, patiently explaining it, going over the fine print. All Dole had really done is say that theater-missiles defense should be *considered,* Ellsworth said. And what about Dole's proposals for more arms sales to Taiwan? Liu persisted.

Ellsworth departed with the feeling that China couldn't really figure out what was going on in American politics. The Chinese drew their own conclusions. They were left unsatisfied with Dole's speech and his campaign positions.[7]

Within a few weeks, in early July, Anthony Lake made his first and only visit to China as Clinton's national security advisor. Lake was not traveling to China as an official representative of Clinton's political campaign, any more than Ellsworth was formally representing Dole. Nevertheless, his trip did have political implications; he was the most senior adviser to Clinton to visit Beijing during the presidential election year, or indeed at any time since Warren Christopher's conflict-laden sojourn of 1994.

What Lake had to say was especially reassuring to Chinese leaders. His message—repeated in meeting after meeting with Liu Huaqiu, Foreign Minister Qian Qichen, Premier Li Peng and President Jiang Zemin—was as flattering as it could possibly be. Lake and his delegation had a name for it: They called it the "strat rap," the rap about strategy. China is a great nation, Lake kept saying. America respects China. America wants China to be part of the system governing the world in the 21st century; indeed, America wants China to help design that system. The United States plans to maintain its strong military presence in Asia and the Pacific, but only to preserve stability and not to contain China.[8]

Lake had written out the "strat rap" himself during the plane ride over the Pacific. Before leaving Washington, he had asked the bureaucracy to prepare talking points for his trip. When the papers came in, he found that they addressed specific policy issues but lacked broad overview. He called in the CIA's China specialists and outside experts to ask what the Chinese regime thought and worried about. He concluded that, above all, Chinese leaders were like the old Aretha Franklin song: They wanted respect. Lake intended to give it to them.

Lake's approach represented the completion of the Clinton administration's transformation on China policy. The national security advisor was repudiating the policies of Clinton's first two years, not just on trade benefits, but more broadly. In contrast to the administration's earlier way of doing business with China, Lake now asserted that the administration was seeking to avoid confrontation on human rights or arms proliferation. "You can do it better when not every issue becomes, in itself, so confrontational that in effect they (Chinese leaders) cannot afford to make a compromise, because then we'll look as if we have steamrollered them," he explained.[9]

Lake also offered the Chinese one concrete, important policy change. For the first time, the administration announced that it would be ready to receive President Jiang Zemin on a state visit to Washington, and for Clinton to make his own state visit to China. "Because of our recent progress, I would expect that there will be an exchange of state visits," Lake told reporters in Beijing.

The previous year, in his letter to Jiang during the Taiwan crisis, Clinton had secretly thrown out the vague possibility that Jiang could visit Washington sometime. However, two months later, the president had turned down a specific Chinese request for a full state visit.[10] He did not want to give Jiang full honors, with a red carpet, 21-gun salute, state dinner and flags along Pennsylvania Avenue, at a time in late 1995 when he was preparing to run for reelection. But during Lake's 1996 visit to

Beijing, Clinton was promising to bestow such honors after election day—thus giving Beijing another incentive to hope for his reelection.[11]

Lake's message to the Chinese contained a strong political component as well. Like it or not, Clinton's going to win the 1996 elections, he indicated: Lake didn't want Chinese leaders to exploit the campaign for diplomatic advantage. This was, in a sense, a made-for-export version of one of the oldest lines in American politics: You'd better get on the bandwagon, because the train is leaving the station.

On the day he returned to Washington, Lake said he had made it clear to the Chinese that "I was speaking for the president." And the Chinese realized, he said, that there was a "good chance" Clinton would be reelected in November.[12]

Indeed, they did. As the 1996 campaign progressed, a curious thing happened: The Chinese government and the Clinton administration, erstwhile adversaries, began to do business. Each side began to get deals and concessions from the other.

China has considerable ability to help or hurt any president running for reelection. It can behave in a way so that everything between the two countries goes smoothly, at least in public. Or alternatively, Beijing can create or emphasize conflict. Any nasty public conflict (short of war) tends to harm the incumbent president—because, no matter how it started, the operating assumption of the American public, not entirely rational, is that the president should have been able to prevent it.

Throughout 1996, the administration and China bent over backwards to avoid conflict with one another. In May, the United States settled an acrimonious arms proliferation dispute that had arisen when American intelligence discovered that China had secretly sold ring magnets, which are used to refine bomb-grade uranium, to a state-run nuclear weapons laboratory in Pakistan. Under the law, Washington could have imposed economic sanctions upon China for the sale. Instead, Secretary of State Warren Christopher announced that the administration had decided to waive the sanctions, after obtaining private assurances from China that it would not sell such nuclear equipment again.[13]

A month later, China handed the Clinton administration a well-publicized deal of importance to the American business community. After negotiations with American trade officials, the Chinese agreed to crack down on the piracy of compact disks, laser discs, movies, videos and computer software within its borders. Days before the agreement was announced, Chinese authorities closed more than a dozen factories that had been churning out pirated CDs.[14]

In reality, this arrangement on piracy was hardly groundbreaking. China was merely agreeing to do what it had earlier promised. In early

1995, the United States and China signed a far-reaching Intellectual Property Rights Enforcement Agreement. Washington had proclaimed that earlier deal to be a major advance, too. But China had failed to carry out this accord until the administration threatened to impose trade sanctions. Finally, in June 1996, China agreed to enforce the previous agreement.

That summer, Lake was able to offer China one additional peace offering. After extensive lobbying by the White House, the House of Representatives voted 286 to 141 to go along with Clinton's decision to extend China's most-favored-nation trade benefits for another year. During his meetings in Beijing, Lake emphasized the importance of this MFN vote. The overwhelming margin showed, he said, that the administration was building a consensus for its China policy.[15]

After the national security advisor left Beijing and while he was still in Asia, a Clinton administration official called the *Los Angeles Times* to offer a White House interview with Lake about his China trip as soon as he returned home. The Los Angeles newspaper was being offered the first interview, the official said, because America's leading Asian-American banks and businesses are located in California.[16] The significance of that cryptic remark would become clear only many months later. Lake was not raising funds from Asian-Americans for the Clinton campaign. But others were.

FOLLOWING THE Lake and Ellsworth visits, Clinton had no trouble from Beijing during his reelection campaign. The Chinese could see that the administration had been chastened by its earlier difficulties in dealing with China, and that Clinton did not intend to challenge Beijing again as he had with his MFN policy of 1993–94 and with the visa to the president of Taiwan. Lake had made clear that after Clinton's reelection, Jiang Zemin would get the state visit he had earlier been denied.

After election day, when Clinton easily defeated Dole, China had every reason to believe its ties with the United States were about to improve, and that after Clinton's second inauguration, the regime would finally get the respect from Washington it had been seeking since 1989.

Clinton had already begun to lay the groundwork for post-election changes. During the fall of 1996, in the midst of the campaign, he quietly dispatched a new team of U.S. trade negotiators to Beijing with instructions to explore the possibility of a deal for China's entry into the World Trade Organization. Membership in the organization, which helps govern international trade, would not only boost China's prestige, but would be a tangible symbol of the administration's new policy of integrating China into the world's rule-making elite. Within a week after the election, Washington indicated it wanted to speed up the talks on getting China into the organization. Perhaps, officials suggested, such a trade agreement could be concluded within a year and be used as the center-piece of a state visit by Jiang Zemin.[17]

THERE WERE other signs, too, of a change in climate in Washington, a determination by the Clinton administration to show a much friendlier face to Beijing.

On the evening of December 8, 1996, a convoy of cars from the Chinese embassy rolled into Fort McNair, an aging army base along the Potomac River that houses the National War College, the Pentagon's military think tank. In front of the War College's main building, the convoy stopped, and out stepped General Chi Haotian, China's defense minister, who seven years earlier had carried out the orders of the Chinese leadership to bring troops into Beijing and to use force against the demonstrators there.

Chi had been invited to Washington by Defense Secretary William Perry two years earlier. The trip had already been put off twice because of the continuing acrimony over Taiwan. In May 1995, China had post-poned Chi's visit to protest Clinton's visa for Lee Teng-hui. Chi was scheduled to come again in the spring of 1996, but Perry called off the trip after China's missile firings and military exercises near Taiwan.[18]

Now, with the presidential election safely past, the Pentagon was giving Chi a warm welcome. The military had a number of practical reasons for wanting to improve relations with China. Hong Kong was to be returned to Chinese sovereignty the following July, and the U.S. Navy wanted to make sure it could get Chinese approval to keep making port calls in Hong Kong. The Pentagon continued to seek Chinese help and support in dealing with North Korea, too.[19]

In the interior, column-ringed courtyard of Roosevelt Hall, a War College building bedecked with red banners proclaiming "50 Years of Strategic Thinking in Peace and War," a U.S. Army band serenaded the Chinese general and his delegation. Perry's American guests included General John Shalikashvili, chairman of the Joint Chiefs of Staff, and Alexander Haig and Brent Scowcroft, former officials who embodied the Nixon-Kissinger era of cooperation.

Chi's entourage included not only the ubiquitous Xiong Guangkai, the PLA leader who had threatened Los Angeles, but also some of China's leading arms dealers. At one table sat He Pengfei—officially the vice commander of the Chinese navy, but better known as the first head of Poly Technologies, the company set up by the Chinese regime in the 1980s to sell weapons and missiles around the world. "This is the first time I've been in the United States since 1988," He Pengfei, the son of a famous Chinese marshal, explained. "Before that, I was here four or five times." [20]

Indeed, his return to Washington epitomized the up-and-down relationship between the Pentagon and the Chinese military. In the mid-1980s, during the Cold War partnership against the Soviet Union, He Pengfei had visited Washington as an honored guest of Secretary of Defense Caspar Weinberger, studying what American military technology China might buy. [21] In the decade since then, he had been closely involved in some of the Chinese arms sales in the Middle East that so annoyed the Pentagon. [22] After June 1989, he had been barred from visiting the Pentagon for several years because of the ban on U.S. military contacts with China imposed after the Tiananmen Square massacre. He Pengfei carefully explained to an American at the dinner that he himself had not been involved in the PLA's Tiananmen operations. But no matter: Now the American sanctions had been removed and He Pengfei had come back.

Near the end of the dinner, the secretary of defense lifted his glass for a toast. There had been tensions between the American and Chinese militaries, noted Perry, who only ten months earlier had taken the lead in sending two aircraft carriers to help prevent China from intimidating Taiwan. Nevertheless, he went on, such differences must be set aside and overcome. It was a relatively judicious speech. Not everyone at the dinner was so restrained. Douglas Bereuter, the Nebraska congressman who was chairman of the House of Representatives subcommittee on Asia, rose to welcome the Chinese leaders with a brief toast in which he sought to please Chi and his delegation by denouncing China's critics in the United States.

Over the following days, Chi met with Pentagon officials, had a brief audience with Clinton, and then traveled through the United States for more than a week visiting several American military facilities. The Chinese defense minister and his delegation were also given a tour of Sandia National Laboratories, the U.S. government facilities in New Mexico for research on nuclear weapons and arms control.

The purpose was somewhat different than it had been when PLA officers like He Pengfei had been taken on tours of America in the 1980s. Back then, the Pentagon had been eager to see what kinds of military hardware or technology China might want to buy. This time, the Pentagon's aim was to flaunt America's advanced military technology: The purpose was not so much to sell arms as to deter competition. Some in the Defense Department thought the Chinese military leaders became increasingly uneasy and even bitter as they saw that it would take China at least two decades to catch up with the levels of technology the United States already had.[23]

Chi Haotian's visit symbolized the administration's eagerness to restore relations with China to a more normal footing during Clinton's second term. Yet as things turned out, Chi's visit also illustrated that Congress and the American public were not nearly as eager as the administration to forget about the past.

Two days after the welcoming dinner, the Chinese defense minister returned to Fort McNair to speak to a group of students from the National War College. One U.S. Navy officer asked Chi what had happened at Tiananmen Square in 1989. "I can tell you in a responsible and serious manner that at that time, not a single person lost his life in Tiananmen Square," answered Chi, who had been the PLA's chief of staff. He said that "the problem occurred" in areas surrounding Tiananmen Square, where "there was some pushing."[24]

Astonishing as it sounded to an American audience, Chi probably didn't believe he was saying anything new or controversial. The line that no one had died in Tiananmen Square in 1989 was boilerplate for the regime; it had been used and repeated since the days after the massacre.[25] The claim was based upon an essentially meaningless geographical distinction—the fact that most of the killing took place not in Tiananmen Square itself, but just outside it, in the streets to the west. Even then, the assertion was false: Witnesses had also seen incidents where Chinese were killed in the square itself, and there is photographic evidence that a person was crushed under an armed personnel carrier as it rolled over a tent in the square.[26]

This evasive Chinese line about Tiananmen Square had originally been designed primarily for use inside China, where it could not be challenged. When Chi repeated it in the United States, the reaction was swift. At the State Department, spokesman Nicholas Burns contradicted the defense minister. "It is simply not true that no one died at Tiananmen. It's just not true," Burns said. "History cannot be rewritten." The House of Representatives's international relations subcommittee on human rights held a hearing at which witnesses described what they had seen in Tiananmen Square. Representative Chris Smith (R-N.J.), the subcommittee chairman, accused the Clinton administration of "aggressive appeasement" of China.[27]

China blithely dismissed the criticism. "This question is so far in the past," said Foreign Ministry spokesman Shen Guofang. The issue of Tiananmen came up, he said, only because some Americans "don't want to see an improvement and development in Sino-U.S. ties."[28]

For the Clinton administration, the flap over Chi's remark was a harbinger, the first sign of the intense public reaction, press scrutiny and political attacks to which its China policy would be subjected over the next few months.

BILL CLINTON was about to suffer the consequences of his reelection campaign, which had been tarnished by scandal. Over the previous two years, he had devoted more time and effort to fund-raising than any of his predecessors. He had rushed through 237 fund-raising events in 1996 alone, including coffees, lunches, receptions and dinners—sometimes canceling regular presidential appointments and briefings in the process, and sometimes taking in two banquets back-to-back in the same Washington hotel the same night.[29] In this relentless pursuit of campaign money, the Clinton campaign had not been careful or scrupulous about the people from whom it sought donations.

The scandal had broken loose during the two months before the election with revelations that some of Clinton's campaign money had come from foreign sources, in violation of the requirement that contributions must be donated by American citizens or legal residents. The Democrats had especially sought to mine the Asian-American community as a rich new vein of campaign funds, without asking many questions about the origins of the money. Following a series of press inquiries, the Democratic National Committee began returning hundreds of thousands of dollars in donations, and the Republicans quickly set up formal investigations and public hearings in the Congress they still controlled.

At the heart of the affair were the activities of Clinton's Asian-American fund-raisers. One of them was Charlie Trie, originally the owner of a Chinese restaurant in Little Rock. Another was John Huang, once the American representative of the Lippo Group, an Indonesian banking conglomerate run by a wealthy businessman named Mochtar Riady and his sons James and Stephen. Clinton had known the Riadys since the 1970s, when James Riady lived in Little Rock overseeing Lippo's interests in an American banking venture.

Of the $3.4 million raised by Huang for Clinton's campaign, about 47 percent eventually had to be returned. All of the $645,000 collected by Trie was sent back. Press investigations showed that Clinton had given Huang and the Riadys extraordinary access to the White House and had listened to their views and recommendations on American policy toward Asia. The Riadys appeared to have reciprocated by doing some extraordinary favors for Clinton. In 1994, when Clinton's Little Rock friend Webster Hubbell was forced to resign from the Justice Department in the Whitewater investigation, James Riady met with Clinton at the White

House and, a few days later, hired Hubbell and arranged to have him paid $100,000.[30]

The unfolding scandal at first seemed to have little direct connection to China or to the administration's policy toward Beijing. The Riadys' close ties to Clinton had been established long before they or their company had even begun to do business in China. The single element of Clinton's China policy that the Riadys had clearly sought to discuss with him was his 1994 turnabout on China's most-favored-nation benefits. Yet the administration had been lobbied on MFN so intensively by America's Fortune 500 companies, such as Boeing and AT&T, that it seems unlikely that the Riadys made any difference in Clinton's decision.

Moreover, the campaign fund-raising operations appeared at the outset to have quite a few links to Taiwan—although these were investigated more aggressively by the press than by Republicans in Congress, many of whom enjoyed longstanding connections to Taiwan that they were not eager to disturb.[31]

Huang had been raised in Taiwan, Trie had been born there and both men had gone on Clinton fund-raising missions to Taiwan for the 1996 campaign. The Buddhist temple in California from which Trie had helped raised phony contributions for the campaign and Clinton's legal defense fund represented a sect based in Taiwan. James C. Wood, whom the administration had appointed as the Washington director of the American Institute in Taiwan, had resigned amid charges that he solicited Taiwan businessmen to contribute to Clinton's reelection. Liu Taiying, the shadowy figure in charge of handling more than $3 billion in assets for Taiwan's ruling Nationalist Party, had flown to the United States in the fall of 1995 for a brief meeting with Clinton that Trie helped to arrange.[32]

Nevertheless, as the scandal unfolded, some sketchy but tantalizing links to China began to emerge. Among those participating in a small fund-raising coffee klatsch hosted by the president had been Wang Jun, the son of one of the leading figures of the Chinese Communist Party and the chairman of Poly Technologies, China's arms-trading corporation. He had been brought into the White House by Trie. Clinton quickly acknowledged that it had been "clearly inappropriate" for him to meet with Wang.[33]

In early 1997, the *Washington Post* reported that Justice Department investigators had turned up evidence, based in part on electronic surveillance, that Chinese officials had tried to steer some contributions to the Democratic National Committee before the 1996 campaign, and that the FBI had also warned members of Congress they had been targeted by China to receive illegal contributions.[34] Trie, meanwhile, fled to China, beyond the reach of American subpoenas.[35]

Increasingly, China was brought onto center stage in the fund-raising affair. The elements of the affair relating to China were pursued with admirable vigor; the Taiwan connections were mostly dropped. When the Senate Committee investigating the fund-raising opened its hearings in July 1997, Senator Fred Thompson, the committee chairman, charged that China had tried to "pour illegal money into American political campaigns" and to "subvert our electoral process. . . . Our investigations suggest that it [the Chinese plan] affected the 1996 presidential race." [36]

During the 1997 hearings, neither Thompson nor his investigative committee produced evidence to substantiate these allegations. [37] The first clear indication of Chinese government involvement did not come to light until the following year, when Johnny Chung, another of the Asian-American fund-raisers for the Clinton campaign, said that he had received more than $100,000 from the daughter of Liu Huaqing, China's top military commander. Chung said he had been told that this money came from the People's Liberation Army. [38]

Nevertheless, in 1997 the swirl of accusations and news stories about the scandal had an impact. They put Clinton on the defensive concerning China and prompted the administration to hold temporarily in abeyance its plans for a far-reaching improvement in American relations with Beijing.

Efforts to work out a deal for China's entry into the World Trade Organization faltered. China didn't seem willing to make as many trade concessions as the administration sought, and the political climate in Washington in the early months of the new administration made it questionable that any such deal would win congressional support. In April, the U.S. trade negotiators who had been assigned to try to reach an agreement with China resigned. [39]

That spring, Vice President Gore made the highest-level visit to China by any American official since the Tiananmen crackdown. Once again, as with Chi Haotian's visit to Washington four months earlier, the press and public reactions were largely critical.

Chinese Premier Li Peng caught Gore off guard by exchanging toasts with him at a ceremony to commemorate new American business deals with China—thus evoking memories of Brent Scowcroft's banquet toast in honor of Chinese leaders six months after the 1989 massacre. An American embassy official told reporters the vice president had assured Li that the fund-raising scandal would not affect the administration's overall policy of engagement with China. Within hours, Gore himself awkwardly summoned reporters to add the qualification that there would be "very serious" repercussions if allegations about the Chinese regime's involvement were true. [40] Newspaper editorials spoke of Gore's "embarrassment" in China and said he "seemed hobbled by the White House fund-raising mess." [41]

The Clinton administration was falling into the same political traps into which the Bush administration had stumbled in 1989. Clinton was dealing with Beijing in ways that lacked public support at home. He was seeking to improve relations with the Chinese regime while it continued to repress political dissent and imprison its leading critics. The administration tried to justify its approach by exaggerating the degree of political change in China—thus attracting further criticism at home. "Mr. Gore seemed to go out of his way last week to praise 'a significant advance in the process of democracy' in China that few others have been able to detect," observed the *New York Times* in an editorial after Gore's trip. [42]

Washington, in short, was beginning to reestablish an approach to China in which a small number of U.S. and Chinese officials tended to view one another as partners, and to view American public opinion as an obstacle or an adversary. The White House was modeling its China policy upon a distorted view of the Nixon administration—failing to recognize that the opening to China had rested implicitly upon public support and that Richard Nixon himself had worked carefully, if secretly, to bring along and co-opt potential opponents in Congress.

Clinton had left ample room for the Republicans to turn China into a political issue, and they quickly seized the opportunity. Within the Republican Party, two powerful groups were, by 1997, increasingly interested in China. One faction was composed of neo-conservatives—those Republicans who believed American policy was overly influenced by trade and business interests and felt the United States should combat Communism in China much as it had in the Soviet Union. The other faction consisted of religious activists, who were beginning to focus intensively upon China's longstanding repression of religious freedom. The neo-conservatives had strong connections in Washington, while the religious groups had the support of grassroots activists who provide crucial help in Republican primary campaigns.

It was not surprising, then, that House Speaker Newt Gingrich quickly staked out a position on China more critical than that of Gore. Arriving in Asia with a congressional delegation only a few days after the vice president's departure, Gingrich vowed that he would not "remain silent about the lack of basic freedom—speech, religion, assembly, the press—in China." [43] Gingrich was not ordinarily so critical of the Chinese regime; his well-publicized remarks reflected the growing salience of China as an issue among the Republican majority in Congress.

.   .   .

ON FEBRUARY 19, 1997, Deng Xiaoping died at age 92. From the perspective either of American foreign policy or of China's domestic politics, his death was curiously anticlimactic. Deng had not been seen in public for three years, and his influence over the leadership had gradually faded with his failing health. The era had long since passed when Washington had looked to Deng as a strongman and savior who could settle all problems between the United States and China. Jiang Zemin and Li Peng, the two men who had increasingly run China's affairs in the aftermath of the Tiananmen crackdown, had had the time to establish control over the leadership of the Communist Party.

Jiang headed a carefully controlled funeral in Beijing for Deng. Four months later, at midnight on June 30, it was again Jiang who presided over the ceremonies in which Britain relinquished sovereignty over Hong Kong. Stiffly, he welcomed the 6.3 million residents of the former British colony to "the embrace of the motherland," and swore in Tung Chee-hwa as Hong Kong's Beijing-selected chief executive.

By this time, the Clinton administration was beginning to make plans for Jiang's state visit to Washington. In the spring of 1997, Secretary of State Madeleine Albright had told Chinese Foreign Minister Qian Qichen that a trip by Jiang in the fall would work well, and in July, at the time of the Hong Kong ceremonies, Albright and Qian set up teams of Chinese officials to work out what business might be conducted at the summit.[44]

On August 10, 1997, Samuel D. (Sandy) Berger, who had taken Lake's place as national security advisor for Clinton's second term, flew to China to prepare for the summit meeting. Jiang's trip to America was to be the first state visit by a Chinese leader in more than a decade and by far the most important such mission since Deng Xiaoping toured the United States in 1979.[45]

In the summer of 1997, the United States was in an unusually advantageous position in dealing with China. The American economy was strong. China had just recovered Hong Kong, but its leaders were increasingly worried about their own economy; state enterprises were losing ever more money, yet reforming them meant running the risk of greater unemployment. In order to concentrate on economic changes at home, the regime needed a stable environment overseas, particularly with the United States.

Berger was carrying a pointed message with him. There are three broad possibilities for this summit, he told the Chinese. The meeting between Jiang and Clinton can be historic, dramatically transforming American relations with China—such as, for example, the Nixon visit of 1972. The summit can be substantive, making progress on some of the policy disputes dividing America and China. Or, thirdly, it can be strictly ceremonial, without any policy changes at all. But if the summit turns out to be strictly ceremonial, Berger warned, relations between America and China will over the long run get worse, rather than better.[46]

The American delegation flew to the seaside town of Beidaihe, the resort where, each summer, China's top leaders gather for informal meetings. There, Berger and his aides saw Qian Qichen, Li Peng and Jiang Zemin.

As usual, Li Peng was the toughest and nastiest of the three. He treated the Americans primarily as supplicants in search of business deals. U.S. companies might want to enter the market to sell nuclear power equipment in China, yet the time to do so was running out, Li said. You Americans want China to buy your Boeing planes instead of the European Airbus, but you behave differently from the French: The French openly ask us for commercial contracts without bothering us about other issues like human rights. Berger countered that the United States didn't view China as a purse, but wanted a strategic dialogue. We'd be pleased if you bought some Boeings, Berger said, but that's not what we're here for.

Jiang was considerably more amicable. He said he was prepared to take some risks in order to improve China's relations with America. It was a hopeful sign, suggesting to the visitors that the summit might not turn out to be a disaster.

Carefully, Berger laid out what were Clinton's top priorities: China should stop helping Iran's nuclear program and to discontinue selling it missiles and other arms. And Clinton wanted the Chinese regime to release some of its imprisoned dissidents.

The Chinese laid out their own objectives. They urged the Americans to prevent Congress from passing legislation aimed at China and to lift some of the remaining sanctions that had been legislated after the Tiananmen massacre. Above all, Taiwan was at issue: The Chinese sought new promises or assurances from the administration that would restrict American support for the island.[47]

Jiang was, meanwhile, consolidating his power in Beijing. On September 18, a Communist Party Congress—the gathering held every five years to set the party's direction and to name its leaders—removed Jiang's principal rival, Qiao Shi, from the Politburo. Qiao, for many years the party's intelligence chief and later the head of China's legislature, had become increasingly the patron of those within the party who favored political reform and a revision of the condemnation of the Tiananmen Square protests of 1989. The Chinese Communist Party was not ready for political change.[48]

Jiang was now ready to deal with the United States. Five days after the Party Congress ended, at a meeting between Qian and Albright in New York City, the Chinese served notice for the first time that they were thinking seriously of releasing political dissidents. Qian specifically dangled the possibility that Wei Jingsheng, imprisoned since his meeting with Assistant Secretary of State John Shattuck in 1994, might be set free. Qian also suggested China would be willing to promise it would not sell cruise missiles to Iran. These promises were not made public, but they provoked a sense of anticipation inside the administration. The haggling over what would happen at the summit now proceeded in earnest.

However, over the following weeks, as the administration sought to work out the details, China proved elusive. In early October, the White House learned that the Chinese had decided not to release Wei Jingsheng before or during the summit. Clinton made a personal appeal on Wei's behalf a few days later to Chinese Vice Foreign Minister Liu Huaqiu, but to no avail.[49]

Administration officials found that China was willing to give a written promise that it would end all new programs for nuclear cooperation with Iran.[50] That concession was made only the week before Jiang left for the United States, after a flurry of negotiations. However, the Chinese refused to put in writing or give any specifics about their earlier, vague suggestion they would stop selling cruise missiles to Iran. Moreover, China's promise concerning Iran was linked to a long-sought change in American policy: The administration needed to lift the restrictions first imposed 12 years earlier upon the sale of civilian nuclear technology to China.

There was one little drama just before the summit, which the administration kept well hidden. In the final two weeks before Jiang left for Washington, a battle erupted over Taiwan.

The White House dispatched a team of administration officials, headed by Sandra J. Kristoff of the National Security Council, to China to negotiate the wording of a joint statement Clinton and Jiang were supposed to issue after their meeting. In Beijing, officials pressed determinedly for new American commitments concerning Taiwan. China wanted the Clinton administration to put into writing for the first time the package of promises Clinton had made in his private letter to Jiang Zemin in the summer of 1995: that the United States would not support Taiwan's independence, the creation of two Chinas or Taiwan's admission to the United Nations. These "three noes," Chinese officials argued, should be made public in the two governments' statement at the summit.

Kristoff and her delegation, who were checking back regularly with Washington, refused to go along. The Chinese warned that the success of the summit would be in jeopardy, but the ploy didn't work. In the end, the Americans effectively walked out: They got on a plane and left China without any agreement.

The Chinese, it turned out, were testing Washington to see just how much ground it was willing to give on Taiwan. Within a few hours after Kristoff's delegation left Beijing, a Chinese embassy official in Washington called the White House to say China hoped the talks that had just been broken off could be resumed when Jiang and his delegation reached the United States.[51]

When Jiang arrived in Williamsburg, Virginia, on October 28, the day before he was supposed to visit Clinton, Kristoff was there for more secret talks. Finally, the language for the public statement was worked out on the afternoon of October 29, scarcely two hours before Jiang and Clinton were scheduled to appear at a televised news conference at which the statement was to be released. In it, the administration clung to the past and said nothing new, merely reaffirming America's past agreements with China about Taiwan.[52]

Thus, though few people realized so at the time, both Clinton and Jiang went into the summit after having failed to obtain the policy concessions they most wanted from one another. The administration had been unable to win the releases of Wei or other dissidents, and China had failed to obtain new commitments concerning Taiwan. Other negotiations had bogged down, too. About ten days before the summit, talks about a partial trade deal that would have represented progress toward China's entry into the World Trade Organization broke down when the Chinese refused to ease their restrictions on American exports of citrus fruit.[53]

Nevertheless, Clinton and Jiang made the best of what they had. The nuclear deal became the centerpiece of the summit: After getting China's written promise about ceasing nuclear cooperation with Iran, the administration agreed to open the way for American companies to sell nuclear-power equipment and technology to China—thus reviving, after more than a decade, an agreement that had first been reached by the Reagan administration. Clinton breezily told reporters the deal was a "win-win-win. . . . It serves America's national security, environmental and economic interests."[54]

China offered Clinton other blandishments on behalf of America's economic interests, too. Despite Berger's earlier claim that the administration cared more about strategic cooperation with China than selling Boeing airplanes, the White House got its Boeing contract. Clinton announced that China had agreed to buy 50 Boeing jets, a sale valued at $3 billion.[55]

For Washington, the touchiest problem by far was how to address the issue of human rights. Wei Jingsheng was still in jail, and the White House had nothing to show yet for its secret campaign throughout the fall to win his release. Administration officials didn't want to be placed in the position Vice President Gore had been forced into on his trip to Beijing by appearing to tolerate and explain away continuing Chinese repression.

In the absence of tangible results, the White House decided rhetoric would have to suffice. In preparation sessions before the summit, Clinton was encouraged to challenge Jiang in public concerning China's positions on human rights.

Clinton was not, by nature, confrontational in style. Indeed, both in public and in private, his inclination was to please, conciliate and win over his opponents, smoothing over differences rather than emphasizing them. But in dealing with China, he now realized he needed to ensure greater American support for his endeavors by making clear he would not make apologies for repression of dissent.

At the press conference, Clinton said that the United States and China had "profound disagreements" about human rights. Then he launched into what amounted to a prolonged debate with the Chinese president about political freedom. When Jiang sought to justify China's policies, Clinton jumped in with his punch line: On democracy and human rights, he said, the Chinese government was "on the wrong side of history." [56]

It was a stinging rebuke, particularly for the leader of China, a country where history is taken seriously. Clinton's performance was reminiscent of Nixon's kitchen debate with Nikita Khrushchev in 1959; it was a noteworthy change from the soft-edged manner in which American presidents had dealt with Chinese leaders over the previous quarter-century.

Clinton's remarks were, of course, only words. He was not proposing any specific action to combat Chinese repression. Indeed, he seemed to be implying that the United States did not need to do much, because the impersonal force of history would ensure China would eventually democratize.

Nevertheless, his performance at the press conference served to deflect public criticism of the summit. Clinton "showed plenty of spine," editorialized the *New York Times.* "In their sweep and moral certitude, Clinton's words will surely stand among the most memorable of his presidency," wrote columnist Ronald Brownstein. [57]

Overall, the summit carried a broader significance: China's Communist Party leadership had managed not only to survive the Tiananmen massacre but to resume normal relations with the United States. For the first time since 1989, the leader of China had been received with full honors at the White House.

At the beginning of the decade, many Americans, both inside and outside the U.S. government, believed that China's post-Tiananmen leadership was only temporary in nature. They had been wrong. In 1995, Clinton was unwilling to receive Jiang Zemin for a state visit. Now, he had reversed himself.

The ties between the Clinton administration and China were certainly not back to those of the Nixon-Kissinger era. America was much warier of Beijing and certainly far more willing to voice public criticisms of it. Still, with Jiang's state visit, China had clearly passed an important milestone. Clinton, who had taken office denouncing the dictators of Beijing, was treating the regime with respect.

As it turned out, Jiang's and Clinton's summit was merely the catalyst for the broader diplomacy between the Clinton administration and China.

On Friday, October 31, the day after the Chinese president left Washington, the administration took a little-noticed step toward satisfying China's demands concerning Taiwan. During a routine daily news briefing, State Department spokesman James P. Rubin casually volunteered a version of the ritual "three noes" that China had sought to obtain in writing. "We don't support a two-China policy, we don't support Taiwan independence, and we don't support membership in organizations that require you to be a member state," Rubin said.[58]

It was the first time anyone in the administration had uttered these words in public. China had failed to persuade the administration to commit them to writing in a joint statement at the summit; administration officials did not want to be seen as teaming up with China to determine the future of democratic Taiwan. But Beijing had at least persuaded the Clinton administration to take the first step toward such a commitment.

Now, China was ready to reciprocate Clinton's hospitality.

On Tuesday, November 11, less than two weeks after the end of the summit, a Chinese foreign ministry official in Beijing delivered a message to Ambassador James Sasser. China was ready to free Wei Jingsheng from prison for medical treatment, the official said, so long as he would go to the United States rather than remaining inside China. Would America be willing to accept Wei?

Absolutely, said the White House, so long as American officials can first talk directly with Wei and make sure he is leaving China voluntarily. In the past, Wei had refused to accept any deal that required him to quit his country, explaining that he wanted to work for democracy inside China.[59]

Wei still languished at China's Nanpu New Life Salt Farm, the labor camp about 200 miles east of Beijing where he had been held for most of the previous eight years. By this time, he was virtually the personification of America's past failures on behalf of human rights and democracy in China. He had been in custody for nearly 18 years, except for a few brief months at the time of China's bid for the Olympics. Wei's imprisonment spanned four U.S. presidents, four congresses of the Chinese Communist Party and five Soviet or Russian leaders.

Five days after China's message to Sasser, Wei was escorted to a tense Beijing airport ringed by Chinese security guards. There, he met with American embassy officials and confirmed that he was indeed willing to leave China. He was put aboard a Northwest Airlines flight to Detroit.

The Clinton administration understandably rejoiced at the success of its efforts. It was "a very happy day," Berger announced on a Sunday television talk show in Washington soon after Wei was airborne. "Hopefully, this will be an indication of a new direction toward greater freedom of speech and freedom of religion inside China," asserted John Shattuck.[60]

Yet from a longer-term perspective, the release of Wei did not necessarily represent any dramatic change in China's handling of dissent. The regime was merely restoring the situation to what it had been in 1993, when Wei had previously been freed. By incarcerating him again the following year, China had retrogressed; it had set a much lower standard against which its human rights policies would be judged, so that when Wei was finally released, China's action would be perceived as a step forward. It was hard to escape the conclusion that after his second arrest in 1994, Wei was held as a bargaining chip that China could use in its dealings with the United States.

Furthermore, the regime succeeded in releasing Wei in a fashion that did not entirely restore the status quo of 1993, either. Wei was freed, but was also required to leave China; he would not be permitted to live, work and proselytize for democracy in his own country, as he had four years earlier. This was a significant change: The Chinese were forcing their critics and opponents to go abroad, where they could more easily be accused of being tools of foreign governments or criticized for not understanding the conditions inside China. Wei was specifically informed before leaving Beijing that if he returned, he could be imprisoned again. "Nobody would like to go back there [to China] to go to jail," he admitted.[61]

.   .   .

AFTER RESTING in a hospital for four days, Wei Jingsheng emerged from seclusion for his first press conference in America. "I have waited for decades for this chance to exercise my right to free speech, but the Chinese people have been waiting for centuries," he told reporters. "Loving China is not the same thing as loving the Chinese Communist Party. The Chinese Communist Party asks the Chinese people to love it and asks people to equate this with patriotism, but these are two separate things."[62]

Wei was speaking in a spacious room on the ground floor of the New York Public Library. Standing among the many reporters and human rights activists at the news conference was a figure whose background was different from the others: It was Winston Lord, the veteran of President Nixon's opening to China, the only present or former American official at the press conference. He and his wife, Bette Bao Lord, had come to see Wei Jingsheng and to honor the ideals of democracy and the right to dissent that America had set aside when Lord first flew to China with Henry Kissinger in 1971 and when he himself arrived as ambassador in Beijing in 1985.

Lord had stepped down from the Clinton administration in January 1997. His influence over American policy toward China had slipped away after Clinton abandoned the MFN policy that Lord had drafted.

In his many years dealing with China, Lord had never met Wei Jingsheng. "I now see why Chinese leaders are so scared of this guy," Lord told reporters after the news conference. "This guy is a very powerful political figure, as well as a great humanitarian. . . . He's so humane. And so human."

In the secret talks between the two governments, China had won a promise that the United States would not exploit Wei for "anti-China" purposes. This language was unclear—deliberately so, from the perspective of the Americans.[63]

As soon as Wei had left China, administration officials announced that President Clinton hoped to meet Wei in the White House. The Chinese claimed to be outraged. Such a meeting would violate the agreement they had reached, they protested. Not so, countered the Americans: A meeting with the president did not amount to exploitation and did not have any "anti-China" purpose. China protested, but without success.

Explaining the decision to grant Wei a presidential audience, administration officials said they were being careful to protect themselves from political attack. They did not want Clinton to face the criticism to which President Ford had been subjected when he refused to invite Alexander Solzhenitsyn to the White House in 1975.[64]

It was a revealing analogy, a comparison between China and the former Soviet Union, one that Americans would not likely have made two decades earlier.

WHEN WHITE HOUSE aides first sketched out a list of foreign trips to be made by Clinton in 1998, they set down China for mid-November. That timing seemed to fit: It would be roughly a year after the Washington summit with Jiang. The mid-term congressional elections, requiring the president's energy at home, would be over. The annual gathering of Asian heads of state was always held in November; Clinton could attend that meeting and visit China on the same cross-Pacific trip.[65]

However, at the beginning of 1998, U.S. Ambassador to China James Sasser arrived in Washington urging that Clinton go to Beijing much earlier. If the administration waited a full year between summits, he argued, American relations with China would drift, be battered by the annual debate over China's MFN benefits and ultimately deteriorate. Sasser, who had talked to Chinese officials, suggested that Clinton should make a "stand-alone" visit to China in which he visited no other Asian country. "He actually argued for an April meeting," Berger later recalled. That was too soon, but White House officials began to consider a visit in June.[66]

Clinton had other reasons to welcome the idea of foreign travel at this time. In personal terms, January and February 1998, was the low point of his presidency. During the course of the unsuccessful sexual-harassment suit against him by Paula Jones, private lawyers and Special Prosecutor Kenneth Starr had uncovered his relationship with Monica Lewinsky, the former White House intern. Inside the United States, political debate and news coverage were consumed by this scandal. Clinton was in any case becoming ever more interested in foreign policy and ever less so in domestic issues, where his power was hamstrung by a Republican Congress. Why not go to China sooner rather than later?

Once again, the administration's China specialists began crisscrossing the Pacific to see what could be arranged. The talks were kept secret. On the weekend of March 7-8, Kristoff and two aides, Jeffrey Bader of the National Security Council and Deputy Assistant Secretary of State Susan Shirk, all of whom had already been in China a few weeks earlier, arrived in Beijing on a clandestine mission, ready to make a deal on behalf of the administration.[67]

Clinton would be prepared to move up his trip to China, the Americans told their Chinese counterparts. Moreover, they said, sweetening the offer, the president might be willing to take another step of even more immediate importance to Beijing: He was willing to drop America's eight-year-old campaign to obtain a formal United Nations condemnation of China's human rights record.

Throughout the 1990s, the United States had regularly endorsed a resolution condemning China at the U.N. Commission on Human Rights, which meets in Geneva each spring. The resolution had never passed, but in 1995 it fell short by a single vote; defeating it had required intensive diplomacy by China. By March 1998, the international support for such a resolution had waned, and the European Union had already announced it would no longer go along with the idea. Now Clinton was suggesting that the United States would abandon the effort, too.

However, before making these plans final, the U.S. officials said, the Clinton administration needed some help from China on human-rights issues. In particular, the administration was looking for two things from China. The first was an agreement to sign the United Nations Covenant on Civil and Political Rights, a document which would, in theory, commit China to abide by a series of international rules concerning human rights. The second was the release of some additional Chinese dissidents —such as Wang Dan, the student leader from the 1989 Tiananmen Square demonstrations. Wang, in a fashion similar to Wei Jingsheng, had been released while China's bid for the Olympics was pending in 1993 and then subsequently arrested and jailed once again.

Chinese officials at first refused to make promises. Eventually, Kristoff met alone with Chinese Vice Premier Qian Qichen, making clear that before the United States dropped the Geneva resolution, Clinton needed to know for sure what steps China would take afterward.

You can have confidence we will reciprocate, Qian told her.[68] The deal was set. Within days, on March 12, the administration made public the fact that Clinton would be visiting China in late June. A day later, the White House also announced that it was dropping its longstanding support of the U.N. resolution. Finally, on the weekend of April 18-19, Wang Dan was taken from a Chinese prison and shipped off into exile in the United States, flying the same Northwest Airlines flight that Wei Jingsheng had been herded onto five months earlier.[69]

The administration's package deal permanently altered the dynamics on human rights issues between America and China in several ways. No other jailed Chinese dissidents were as well known as Wei Jingsheng or Wang Dan. Their release seemed to bring an end to the hostage diplomacy of the previous few years; no longer would America and China bargain so intensively over the fate of individual prisoners.[70] China's decision to free these two men to go to the United States represented a calculated gamble that China's dissident movement would have far less impact from abroad than from inside China.

At the same time, the abandonment of the campaign at the United Nations meant that another approach once touted as promising by the Clinton administration had ended in failure. Several years earlier, when Clinton had sought to use China's MFN benefits as a lever to win human rights concessions, critics had complained that the United States shouldn't be acting on its own against Beijing, but rather should work in concert with other governments. In 1994, when Clinton had dropped his MFN order, he and other administration officials had said one of the cornerstones of future American policy would be the international effort to obtain a U.N. resolution condemning China.

"The administration will . . . step up its efforts, in cooperation with other states, to insist that the U.N. Human Rights Commission pass a resolution dealing with the serious human rights abuses in China," announced the White House on May 27, 1994, on the day of Clinton's MFN decision.[71] But the United States had never obtained as much help from other countries as it had wanted. Beijing had, once again, frustrated and outlasted the administration.

AT THE time Clinton decided upon his trip, it seemed as though China might be fading as a political issue on Capitol Hill. The congressional investigations of Clinton's fund-raising were winding down. In the spring of 1998, however, the furor erupted once again with a new series of disclosures involving Clinton's help for American satellite companies doing business in China.

Since the last years of the Reagan administration, the U.S. government had been allowing American companies to export satellites to China for launch on Chinese Long March rockets. Clearing the way for the export of these satellites had often been at the heart of the top-level diplomacy between the two governments. Satellite exports were one of the hidden factors prompting the secret visit to Beijing by National Security Advisor Brent Scowcroft in December 1989. Limits on satellite exports had been the first issue to galvanize the American business community against President Clinton's China policy during his first year in the White House. [See chapters 8, 11 and 15].

In February 1996, a Chinese rocket exploded near its launch site, carrying a satellite from the American firm Loral. Experts from Loral and Hughes Electronics were called in to help Chinese officials investigate the reason for the failure. Without obtaining advance approval from the U.S. government, some of the experts provided data to China that could have helped improve the guidance systems of its ballistic missiles. A federal grand jury was called to investigate what had happened.[72]

In February 1998, Loral applied to the White House to clear the way for the export of still another satellite to China. This time, Justice Department officials warned the White House that if Clinton gave his approval, his action could jeopardize the chances of prosecuting the 1996 case.

However, Loral officials were lobbying the White House to clear the way for the export. Loral's chairman, Bernard L. Schwartz, had been the largest single contributor to the Democratic Party the previous year. Schwartz went to a White House state dinner in February 1998, hoping to lobby National Security Advisor Sandy Berger for the satellite export; Schwartz failed to find Berger in the crowd, but his lobbyist contacted the White House a few days later. Before the end of the month, Clinton overrode the Justice Department objections and gave his authorization for Loral to export another satellite, arguing that his decision was made solely on the basis of the national interest.[73]

The Republicans seized upon this transaction, arguing that Clinton was jeopardizing national security. The congressional leadership initiated a series of new investigations. Even established Republican foreign policy officials like Brent Scowcroft argued that the relationship between Schwartz's campaign contributions and Clinton's decisionmaking was "of profound significance and should be pursued."[74]

Congressional leaders began recommending that Clinton cancel his trip to China. "I do not believe this president can go to China unless he clears up, in public, everything about Chinese illegal campaign funds and everything about national missile secrets going to China," said Gingrich.[75]

Many others lamented the fact that Clinton would take part in formal ceremonies at Tiananmen Square in Beijing, where state visits to China customarily start. By doing so, critics said, he was giving new legitimacy to the regime and suggesting that America was willing to forget the events of 1989. More than 160 Republican members of Congress signed a letter urging Clinton to postpone his trip. Not only conservative Republicans, but moderates such as Senator Richard Lugar (R-Ind.) joined in the chorus saying that it was inappropriate for Clinton to go to Tiananmen Square.[76]

CLINTON IGNORED the criticism. On June 25, 1998, he landed in the city of Xi'an, carrying along with him throngs of White House aides, Cabinet officials and members of Congress. Clinton thus became the first American president since the Tiananmen massacre to set foot in China. He was greeted in a lavish arrival ceremony that included Chinese men dressed as ancient warriors, women in flowing white gowns and children bearing flowers.

The Chinese government served notice at the very beginning of the trip that it had no intention of relinquishing its controls. Three reporters originally included in the White House press entourage were denied visas to enter China on grounds that they came from Radio Free Asia, the station Clinton had helped create to spread democratic values. While the president was in Xi'an, several dissidents were rounded up, both in that city and in others Clinton was preparing to visit. That caused Berger to jibe at a press conference that "people are not debris to be swept up. . . . I think China's human rights record is terrible." [77]

Nevertheless, the president and his aides stuck with the scenario that had been laid out before the trip. In Beijing, Clinton proceeded quietly through the 15-minute state welcome at Tiananmen Square, saying nothing, his face solemn, as Chinese troops marched past him. In doing so, he gave the Chinese leadership the formal show of respect and recognition for which it had been waiting for nine years.

Meanwhile, in the hours before, during and after this event, the Clinton administration moved to dilute the press coverage of it. White House aides distributed copies of an agreement reached between the United States and China, under which each government would stop targeting each other's territory with nuclear missiles. Clinton had pressed for this accord as a way to show that China and the United States did not view one another as adversaries. [78] It was largely a symbolic step, since missiles can be retargetted within a matter of minutes, but it also served the purpose of diverting public attention away from Clinton's presence at Tiananmen Square.

Clinton then acted quickly on his own to put the Tiananmen ceremony behind him. After a round of private talks, Clinton and Jiang held a joint news conference at the Great Hall of the People alongside Tiananmen Square. The American president, acting according to the script worked out in advance with his aides, unequivocally condemned the Chinese Communist Party's suppression of the 1989 Tiananmen Square demonstrations. "I believe, and the American people believe, that the use of force and the tragic loss of life was wrong," he told Jiang. [79]

The press conference blossomed into a lively debate. Jiang defended the regime's conduct in 1989. "Had the Chinese government not taken the resolute measures, then we could not have enjoyed the stability that we are enjoying today," he argued. [80] The two presidents swapped views about dissidents, democracy and Tibet. As soon as the event ended, White House spokesman Michael McCurry announced triumphantly that the press conference had been televised live and in its entirety on Chinese television. It was the first time Chinese authorities had permitted open public discussion of the Tiananmen massacre. It was also the first occasion in which Chinese television had shown a direct challenge to one of the nation's top leaders since student leader Wu'er Kaixi had upbraided Premier Li Peng at the peak of the 1989 demonstrations.

Clinton administration officials had been preparing for this press conference for weeks. During talks in Beijing in early June to prepare for the summit, Berger had told Chinese officials that Clinton's participation in the welcoming ceremonies at Tiananmen Square would subject the president to intense political criticism in the United States. He didn't specifically ask the Chinese to move the event, and Chinese officials showed no willingness to do so.[81]

Realizing that there was no way around the Tiananmen ceremony, administration officials then decided they had to do something dramatic to counterbalance it. The press conference seemed like the logical setting. There had been an extensive debate within the administration over exactly what the president should say about the Tiananmen massacre: Some argued for a stronger, more ringing condemnation than Clinton delivered, while others felt he should say nothing at all. Administration officials had earlier won a promise from the Chinese that a Clinton speech at Beijing University could be televised, but no one knew the press conference would also be on live television in China until Jiang informed Clinton after their private talks.

The Clinton-Jiang press conference was modeled upon the one the two men had held in Washington the previous October, during which the American president had said China's Communist regime was on "the wrong side of history." Those earlier remarks had attracted editorial praise for Clinton in the United States and thus turned the summit into a success.

Now, the Beijing press conference was even more successful. As soon as the president publicly denounced the Tiananmen crackdown, the press coverage of his trip turned almost instantaneously from negative to positive. Network news shows, which had been concentrating almost exclusively on China's arrests of a handful of dissidents, switched direction and began emphasizing the theme that China was opening up once again. As at the October press conference, Clinton's words didn't change anything; they had no policy implications; but his rhetoric itself seemed to suffice in defusing criticism in America of the summit meeting.

Three days after the Tiananmen ceremony, the president offered China another reward, an acknowledgment about Taiwan that the Chinese leadership had eagerly sought. In Shanghai, Clinton for the first time publicly embraced the so-called three noes, promising that the United States would not support Taiwan's independence, its admission to the United Nations or the creation of two Chinas.[82]

These promises matched what his aides had been saying in public for nine months, and what Clinton himself had privately promised Jiang in writing after Lee Teng-hui's 1995 visit to the United States. Indeed, the agreement not to support Taiwan's independence or the creation of two Chinas also echoed the words that John Holdridge had written and Henry Kissinger had uttered at the very start of Kissinger's secret visit 27 years earlier [see chapter 2]. Still, no president had ever given this package of assurances about Taiwan in public before. Moreover, Clinton did so in a new political context: Taiwan had emerged as a full-blown democracy and its government no longer claimed to represent the Chinese mainland. China gave prominent display to Clinton's new commitment; it called Taiwan to "face realities" and begin negotiations toward eventual reunification with China.[83]

With Clinton's trip, America completed another remarkable about-face in dealing with China. The American president who had campaigned against the "coddling" of Chinese dictators was now showing them respect. The Republicans, the party of Richard Nixon and George Bush, had reemerged as the proponents of a more confrontational approach toward Beijing.

More broadly, the United States had reversed itself, too. After shunning the world's most populous country for two decades, America embraced it during the Nixon administration and came to treat it as a partner against the Soviet Union. With the end of the Cold War, the United States distanced itself from China. By the late 1990s, the Clinton administration was beginning to embrace China once again, to treat it as a partner in dealing with the rest of Asia.

This was, however, a new form of partnership. Nixon and Kissinger had told Mao Tsetung and Chou Enlai that China's domestic politics was its own internal affair; the United States would not ask questions about how the Chinese leadership treated its own people. Clinton was now openly espousing American political values of democracy and free speech, both to Chinese leaders and directly to the people of China. This was, in its way, the biggest about-face of all.

IN HONG KONG, at a press conference on the final stop of his China trip, Bill Clinton pressed one last time the theme he had put forward on several occasions during the previous week: that democracy and free debate can help any country to achieve greater stability. This time, however, the American president added a new thought, one that applied specifically to China.

"Look at just the last 50 years of history in China, the swings back and forth," Clinton said. He referred to China's series of political campaigns: the encouragement and then repression of dissenting views in the late 1950s, the Cultural Revolution and the reaction against it, the Tiananmen Square protests of 1989 and the subsequent crackdown. Allowing dissent, Clinton said, is a way for China to "avoid these wild swings." [84]

Clinton did not mention it, but in dealing with China, America had gone through some wild swings of its own.

Conclusion

NONFICTION BOOKS SOMETIMES END with grandiose predictions. I will resist the temptation. Anyone, American or Chinese, who claims to be able to say with certainty what will happen in China, or between the United States and China, can be accused of hubris. The Cultural Revolution, Richard Nixon's opening to Beijing, the ascent of Deng Xiaoping and the Tiananmen massacre—all in turn took many of the experts in Washington and Beijing by surprise. This book was designed not to forecast the future, but to understand the past: to probe what happened between the United States and China over three decades, as America first aligned itself with the Chinese leadership and then, changing course, sought to distance itself.

America's seemingly disparate policies toward China before and after 1989 cannot be viewed in isolation from one another. It is impossible to comprehend the dynamics of U.S. relations with China in the 1990s without knowing what transpired during the last two decades of the Cold War, from the time of Nixon's opening until the Tiananmen crackdown and the fall of the Berlin Wall. Conversely, one cannot fully understand the Nixon opening without looking at some of its long-term consequences that became all too evident after 1989.

During the two decades before 1989, America increasingly cultivated China, wooed its leaders and secretly helped China to get the arms and technology that would make it more powerful. At the same time, the United States largely ignored evidence of the darker side of the Chinese regime. It did so in the cause of enlisting China's help against the Soviet Union.

The Cold War relationship forged with China was secretive in nature. Richard Nixon was careful to make sure his steps toward China had political support in Washington; the archives demonstrate that as early as 1969, he was bringing old friends from the Republican right wing in on his venture. Yet the relationship forged largely by Kissinger was so personalized that often even other senior officials within the executive branch of the U.S. government had little idea what was happening, and Congress and the public knew still less. Successors, notably Zbigniew Brzezinski, fell into the same pattern. It should not have been surprising that after 1989, the Bush administration found itself without sufficient public and congressional support to continue a relationship about which the public had been told little and from which Congress had often been excluded.

In the 1970s and 1980s, American policy toward China took on a life of its own. What began as an improvised but subtle approach to Beijing soon became a blunt policy of uncritical favoritism. Originally, Nixon and Kissinger envisioned a strategic effort to balance China and the Soviet Union against one another in hopes of producing more moderate behavior by each of them. Nevertheless, from the outset, the preference for China was clear; by early 1973, the archives show, Kissinger offered Nixon the startling suggestion that in its view of the world, the United States was closer to China than to any other nation except Britain. By the end of the 1970s, the United States had formally abandoned any pretense of equivalence in its treatment of Beijing and Moscow.

The history of most-favored-nation trade benefits illustrates well how American policy evolved. Originally, the Nixon administration offered MFN benefits to China as an afterthought, because it was already preparing to tender the same privileges to the Soviet Union. For most of the 1970s, American leaders planned to extend MFN to the Soviet Union and China at the same time. By the end of that decade, China had gotten MFN and the Soviet Union hadn't. Years later, in 1990, a bewildered and infuriated Mikhail Gorbachev wondered how China could have kept its MFN benefits in the wake of the Tiananmen massacre, while the Soviet Union was still waiting and confronting new American human rights requirements.

Nixon and Kissinger displayed little interest in how China was treating its people during what we now know were the last years of the Cultural Revolution. However, they were also relatively straightforward about the fact that their policies were motivated by strategy, not human rights. The same could not be said of the Carter administration, which professed a strong commitment to human rights, and yet, when faced with Chinese repression of dissent, looked the other way.

After 1989, American policy toward China was in flux. As a result of the revolutions in Eastern Europe, the Cold War basis for the relationship vanished, and the Bush administration struggled to come up with some new rationale for preserving the ties constructed over the previous two decades. Bush's effort was often stymied by congressional, Democratic Party and public opposition.

Within only a few years, however, America was once again eager for a close working relationship with China. By the mid-1990s, the United States was once again courting the leadership in Beijing. To some extent, this effort reflected Washington's desire for China's help in dealing with new, post–Cold War foreign policy problems; American leaders sought China's help in stopping North Korea's nuclear weapons program and restricting exports of ballistic-missile technology. However, the new American policy toward China was driven largely by commercial interests.

During the Cold War, American business had taken a back seat to strategic concerns. Secretary of State George Shultz had told American executives that if they didn't like the U.S. government's policy toward China, they could move somewhere else. Under Clinton, commerce became the dominant motivating force behind American policy. This transformation was a reflection of changing economic realities: The unprecedented upsurge in foreign investment in China in the early 1990s gave Beijing vastly greater commercial power and leverage than it had ever had in the past.

While Clinton and his administration were the prime movers behind this new emphasis on American business, Congress was almost equally responsible. Many legislators who had regularly voted against the Bush administration on China switched position and by 1994 were beseeching the White House to give greater weight to America's commercial interests in China.

Thus, a relationship between America and China originally aimed at the Soviet Union managed to survive the collapse of the Soviet empire. America's preoccupation in dealing with China switched from Cold War strategy to business, yet some of the underlying dynamics were the same. In the 1970s the Chinese had tried to exert their will over America by suggesting that Beijing might restore its ties to Moscow. In the 1990s they instead threatened to award business contracts to other countries.

Indirectly, at least, this new, 1990s basis of the U.S. relationship with China also had its origins in the Cold War. The United States had opened its markets to Chinese goods, encouraged American firms to invest in China and granted the country most-favored-nation status, thus developing commercial ties broader than with any other Communist country. These efforts were carried out with the hope of strengthening China as a partner against the Soviet Union. The economic infrastructure developed in the last years of the Cold War, especially the opening of America's market to Chinese exports, helped China to become in the 1990s a much more prosperous and powerful nation, with which American firms were much more eager to do business.

In some ways, American attitudes toward China before and after 1989 can be seen as mirror images of one another. Beforehand, American leaders had repeatedly made clear that they had no particular interest in how the Chinese regime treated its people. By contrast, after 1989, every American president and secretary of state, even those who were reluctant, became deeply involved in human rights questions. Indeed, on human rights, American attitudes changed far more than did China's practices, which had, after all, been repressive before 1989.

American perspectives concerning China's military power changed, too. Those who in the 1990s voiced concern about the Chinese People's Liberation Army sometimes seemed unaware of the extent to which the United States had tried regularly, if secretly, to help and strengthen the PLA in the years before 1989. When it suited the Pentagon's interest in the early 1980s to give arms to China, it did so; when the interest in combating Soviet military power vanished in the 1990s, the United States became more wary of the capabilities of the PLA. Once again, American attitudes changed more than the realities in China.

Finally, the process by which U.S. policy toward China was carried out also did an about-face after 1989. Beforehand, members of Congress had played a relatively submissive role. After the Tiananmen crackdown, Congress became much more assertive and was often the dominant factor in determining policy.

A FEW LESSONS from the past three decades may provide at least some help for the future.

How America deals with the world's most populous country remains subject to vast swings in mood and attitude.[1] This is an old lesson, one that applied as well to the vicissitudes of U.S. policy toward Nationalist China earlier in this century. Many years ago, this phenomenon was thought to be largely the result of China's distance from America and the relatively little information available. Yet the American susceptibility to romance and then disenchantment with China is just as pronounced in an era of air travel, satellite television and the Internet.

During the 1980s, visiting American television crews landed at the Beijing airport with requests to be taken immediately to a disco, a golf course or some other supposed symbol of China's Westernization. In the early 1990s, they arrived with instructions to be escorted to the scene of the Tiananmen massacre or to get shots of a death-penalty placard or some other visual sign of repression. In both cases, the images sent back were superficial. Those who complained about the overly negative American television coverage of China after 1989 often overlooked the too-flattering coverage before that time.

The history of the past three decades shows that China requires sustained attention at the highest levels of the U.S. government. When presidents and their top advisers tried to deal with Beijing irregularly—every few months, for example, or only on trips—they often ran into trouble. The Clinton administration's early rejection and subsequent granting of a visa for Taiwan's President Lee Teng-hui serves as a classic illustration of the problem. The Bush administration's clumsy mishandling of the Pelosi legislation protecting Chinese students is another example.

The past three decades should also teach some important lessons about China and the American political system.

One of the great shibboleths of Washington in the 1990s is that China doesn't understand Washington or American politics. The historical record shows that nothing could be further from the truth. Over the past three decades, the Chinese have succeeded in playing off Richard Nixon against his Democratic opponents, Henry Kissinger against the State Department, James Schlesinger against Kissinger, Zbigniew Brzezinski against Cyrus Vance, Alexander Haig against Richard Allen and Clinton's economic advisers against his foreign policy aides.

Whenever an American president has begun to move in a direction China didn't like, Beijing has opened its arms to ex-presidents as a way of undercutting the effort: Consider the trips to Beijing by Nixon in 1976 or Carter in 1981. The Chinese have learned, too, the importance of treating former Cabinet members well, letting them know that once they leave the U.S. government, these officials can profit from good relations with Beijing. As a result, many former officials have elected to do business in or with China after returning to private life.

Sometimes, it appeared that the Chinese understood U.S. politics better than the Americans did. Those in the United States who deal with China, either in public or private life, could certainly have been more attuned to the ways in which Beijing was using them for essentially political purposes.

Above all, history shows that American leaders need to understand the degree to which U.S. policy toward China relies upon public support. Policy cannot be hidden from the public and carried out exclusively by elites, because in the long run, it won't survive. Kissinger set a pattern in which diplomacy with China was conducted secretively and in a personalized manner; this was too narrow a political base to survive the upheavals of 1989. So, too, the Carter administration's downplaying of human rights issues and Ronald Reagan's effort to portray China as a "so-called Communist country" all helped contribute to the sense of shock when China crushed the Tiananmen democracy movement.

This is not to suggest that American leaders must always follow public opinion. They can try to lead it, figuring that American attitudes will change. But if they miscalculate, the result is usually disastrous. When President Bush sent Brent Scowcroft to Beijing in 1989, their hope was that the mission would spur Americans to the realization that it was time to restore a more normal relationship with China. Their judgment about American public opinion was wrong, and it served to make the opposition to their efforts far more intense. For years afterward, American leaders tried to recover from that mistake.

IN THE 1990s, it was virtually impossible for Americans to escape the legacy of the Cold War in dealing with China. This was true for all sides of the debate in the United States—hard-liners and soft-liners, hawks and doves, those in favor of "engagement" with China and those for containment.

One of the most frequent accusations made about American attitudes toward China in the 1990s is that they reflected a "Cold War mentality." The United States needed an enemy, and China fit this purpose, said those who advanced this argument; America in the 1990s was said to be trying to treat China in the adversarial fashion in which it had once treated the Soviet Union.

There was some truth to this claim. Yet the American supporters of the Chinese regime in the 1990s were also displaying a "Cold War mentality" just as much as China's critics were. They were reflecting the American mentality of the last two decades of the Cold War, not toward the Soviet Union but toward China itself. The reflexively positive view of the Chinese regime, the apologies for its repressive practices, the studied disinterest in democracy in China, the instinctive tendency to minimize conflict with China at all costs, the notion that Communism should be opposed in Eastern Europe but not China—this cluster of attitudes was a legacy of the Cold War relationship America had developed with China in the 1970s and 1980s.

America's behavior during the Cold War left an imprint upon the Chinese, too. Because of the way America had treated China in the 1970s and 1980s, the Chinese had every reason to believe that the U.S. response even to the Tiananmen crackdown would be short-lived.

Indeed, the Bush administration behaved as China thought it might: Through Scowcroft's missions, it sought to restore the earlier American relationship with Beijing within six months. Nevertheless, the overall

American policy toward China after 1989, driven largely by Congress and by public opinion, was considerably tougher than Chinese leaders had come to expect in the halcyon years.

The effect of America's Cold War behavior was that the Chinese could plausibly feel that they had been used. The United States had enlisted China's support against the Soviets, suggesting along the way that America didn't care too much about Chinese repression of dissent. After the Berlin Wall came down and the Soviet Union collapsed, America changed the rules by which it dealt with China.

There is another subtle but important way in which the legacy of the Cold War affected the thinking of the Chinese leadership. Watching from up close how the United States dealt with the Soviet Union may have made Beijing all the more suspicious of American policy in the 1990s.

During the 1970s and 1980s, America's highest-ranking officials brought their Chinese counterparts into their secret strategy sessions for how to conduct the Cold War. Presidents and secretaries of defense, CIA directors, uniformed military leaders and their underlings in the Pentagon and CIA sat down with Chinese counterparts to talk about how to combat, counteract, undermine, perhaps even bring down the Soviet Union. Through these talks, the Chinese gained insights into how American officials thought and operated, not just in public.

Once the Soviet Union fell, the Chinese naturally feared that they might be next. As American foreign policy began to shift in the early 1990s, the Chinese wondered if the United States might now be trying to overthrow them. American leaders regularly protested that they did not seek to weaken China, but such formal public statements could always be viewed with skepticism in Beijing. After all, hadn't the Americans often denied in public during the Cold War that they were trying to bring down the Soviet Union?

The Chinese realized, too, that during the 1970s, congressional and political pressure had often blocked attempts at detente with the Soviet Union. As a result, in the 1990s, even when U.S. presidents and secretaries of state promised Beijing they were not seeking to contain China, Beijing could not be sure that these leaders could make their policies stick in Congress.

In Washington, Americans who dealt with China often perceived their policies as a chaotic amalgamation of many disparate influences— various U.S. government agencies, Congress, the business community, human rights groups, arms controllers, Taiwan. But to China, the net effect sometimes looked like a concerted policy aimed at bringing down Chinese Communism. This perception, too, was engendered by America's anti-Soviet partnership with China during the Cold War.

After the collapse of the Soviet Union, China's leadership saw itself as threatened not just by its adversaries in the United States, but also by its American friends. This was a point not always grasped.

It was commonplace in the 1990s for Washington to defend the maintenance of a good relationship with Beijing by making either or both of two arguments: One claim was that democracy will inexorably come to China someday. The other argument was that conciliatory U.S. policies toward Beijing—such as trade, education and cultural contacts— would in the long run help serve the causes of liberty and democracy in China.

These two arguments were put forward primarily for an American audience. They were designed to counteract those who called for some sort of action, such as trade sanctions, against China. However, these arguments had an impact on China's leaders, and not a particularly comforting one. The American defenders of good relations were asserting that they, too, were looking forward to, or even trying to bring about, the collapse of Chinese Communism. Once again, Americans on all sides of the debate were unable to escape the undeniable history of the end of the Cold War.

In their historic overture to China, Richard Nixon and Henry Kissinger had set aside troubling questions about the nature of China's political system. Understandably, they did not want their initiative to be stillborn. However, in the years that followed, as the new relationship developed, and as the United States sought ever harder to enlist Beijing's support against Moscow, American leaders continued to leave these questions unaddressed. Did America care about freedom and democracy in China? What was the justification, moral or otherwise, for opposing Communism in Eastern Europe while seeming to accept it in China?

The events of 1989 shattered this uneasy accommodation. These questions could no longer be submerged. The Tiananmen massacre reminded Americans of the basis on which the Chinese regime held power. The revolutions in Eastern Europe also demonstrated that Communist regimes do not necessarily last forever—a fact received with considerably different emotions in the United States and within the Chinese leadership. We are still grappling today with this history, and we will continue to do so for some time.

Afterword to the Vintage Edition

A FEW MONTHS BEFORE this book was first published, I mentioned its title to a journalist. She responded with the world-weary cynicism suitable to the profession. "What do you mean, *About Face*?" she asked. "What's changed?"

At that juncture, in the fall of 1998, President Clinton had just completed his visit to China. In the glow of tranquil, even friendly relations that immediately followed that trip, it was at least conceivable for cynics to argue (and for some others to hope) that not much had changed over the past thirty years, because after a brief aberration, the Clinton administration had restored American China policy to the traditions of the Nixon-Kissinger era.

The events of the year that followed, however, made it clear that there can be no such restoration. The Clinton trip ended a nine-year hiatus on presidential visits to China that began with the Tiananmen Square crackdown. Yet it did not and could not bring about larger, more fundamental changes in the relationship between the two countries.

In the early months of 1999, the United States and its NATO allies launched their three-month military campaign to protect the ethnic Albanians of Kosovo from human rights abuses by Yugoslavia's Serbian government. From the start, China reacted angrily. Beijing complained that there should be no such military intervention without the authorization of the United Nations Security Council, and seemed to worry that the action could set a precedent that might be used to justify outside military intervention to protect the people of Tibet, Xinjiang or Taiwan.

In May 1999, China erupted in fury when American warplanes carrying out the Yugoslavia campaign hit the Chinese embassy in Belgrade, killing three Chinese inside, in what the Clinton administration called a terrible mistake. With the encouragement of the leadership, throngs of Chinese in Beijing and other cities took to the streets. The American ambassador to Beijing, James Sasser, was trapped inside the U.S. embassy for several days as it was pelted by rocks; in Chengdu, Chinese demonstrators set fire to the residence of the American consul general. Never since the time of the Nixon opening had there been such an outpouring of anti-American demonstrations in China.

In Washington during these same months of 1999, the Republican-led Congress was swept up with a melange of investigations and allegations concerning China. A special bipartisan committee headed by Congressman Christopher Cox reported that China had carried out espionage at U.S. nuclear laboratories and had stolen or illegally acquired American missile and space technology. Critics quickly denounced this report as sloppy, biased or exaggerated; yet its release was itself a political event, leaving no doubt that on Capitol Hill, many elected legislators had come to view China as an adversary.

As the furor over the Chinese embassy bombing and the Cox report were beginning to subside, America and China found themselves facing a new crisis over Taiwan. President Lee Teng-hui, nearing the end of his presidency, suddenly announced in July 1999 that the ties between Taiwan and China should henceforth be considered to be "special state to state" relations, and Lee's aides suggested he no longer subscribed to the "one-China" formulas of the past.

These events demonstrated once again that, much as this book has argued, the end of the Cold War and the Tiananmen Square crackdown had an enduring impact on America's relations with China. Any efforts to go back to the Nixon-Kissinger approach cannot last, because the underlying dynamics between the two countries have changed. In the United States, even when an administration, such as Clinton's, seeks to revive the amicable ties of the past, the Congress will not permit it to do so. In China, the United States is now often portrayed as an hegemonist power seeking to limit China's ambitions. In such an atmosphere, the best the two governments can expect is to limit the extent of strategic competition between the two countries. The idea of America and China teaming up together to try to work their will on the rest of the nations of Asia no longer seems feasible.

When I wrote this book, I fully intended the phrase "About Face" to apply not only to the succession of turnabouts on China policy by individual American presidents and political parties, but also to the entire era from 1969 to 1999. American policy has turned from courting China as an anti-Soviet ally in the Cold War to trying to cope with it in the post–Cold War world. So, too, the United States has abandoned the

Nixon-era policy of refusing to challenge China's Communist political system; instead, America now openly espouses and encourages the cause of democracy in China.

Despite the cynicism expressed by my journalist friend, there has, indeed, been a remarkable "About Face" in American policy toward China.

SINCE THIS book came out, there has been one other development of some historical interest. The transcripts of President Nixon's secret conversations with Chou Enlai during Nixon's 1972 trip were finally made public. These transcripts were obtained by the National Security Archive, the non-profit Washington organization which seeks to obtain U.S. government documents under the Freedom of Information Act.

The Nixon-Chou transcripts further confirm the accuracy of the account of the secret diplomacy in Chapter Two of this book. That account was based to a considerable extent on Nixon's handwritten notes of what he planned to tell Chinese leaders in Beijing. He had jotted down the points and themes he wanted to convey about American policy concerning Taiwan, Vietnam, the Soviet Union, India and Japan. The new transcripts demonstrate that Nixon did, in fact, proceed to deliver to Chou Enlai the ideas he had written down for himself in advance of their meetings.

Concerning Taiwan, Nixon laid out precisely the five points listed on page 46 of this book. On Japan, the American president presented to Chou Enlai the ideas described on page 44: that the American security treaty with Japan and American nuclear protection for Japan would serve China's interests because they would limit Japan's influence in Asia and keep Japan from building its own nuclear arsenal. Concerning the Soviet Union, Nixon promised Chou that he would inform China of all deals between Washington and Moscow and would offer China similar deals. On Vietnam, Nixon emphasized the importance of what he called an honorable settlement. In all of these policy areas, Nixon not unexpectedly carried through with his plans.

The transcripts provide additional information about the extraordinary extent to which Nixon sought to control and limit the access of rival American political leaders to China, as described on pages 29 and 30 in this book.

In their secret talks in Beijing, Chou pointedly reminded Nixon that "we have abided by our promise to Dr. Kissinger" not to invite any rival politicians to China before the visit by the American president. Nixon suggested that China should follow up his trip by inviting two congressional leaders, Republican Senator Hugh Scott of Pennsylvania and

Democratic Senator Mike Mansfield of Montana, on a bipartisan delegation to China. Although he was a Democrat, Mansfield was not running
for president and was not considered a political threat by Nixon.

"This avoids having political candidates," Nixon told the Chinese
premier. "A candidate does not act sometimes with the same responsibility as someone who is not a candidate." At the time, of course, Nixon was
just starting his own 1972 political campaign for reelection to the White
House.

Finally, the Nixon-Chou transcripts show how much China viewed
Kissinger as the embodiment of its new relationship with Washington
and as its interlocutor and supporter in Washington. The Chinese premier
said China hoped Nixon would be reelected. "It is also our hope that Dr.
Kissinger, too, will remain with you to help, Mr. President, in your work,"
the Chinese premier boldly told the American president on February 24,
1972.

A few moments later, Chou broached to Nixon the subject of what
China really wanted. "It is our hope, it would be good if the liberation of
Taiwan could be realized in your next term of office," he said.

Yet this was, of course, not the end of the story.

Note on the Spelling of Chinese Names

The pinyin system of romanizing Chinese, introduced in 1979, has been used throughout this book for personal and geographical names, as well as for other terms current in the People's Republic of China. Exceptions have been made for names that are universally known in their old Wade-Giles spelling, such as Mao Tsetung and Chou Enlai. The Wade-Giles system has been used for Taiwanese names, such as Lee Teng-hui.

Pinyin is generally considered to be an improvement over the Wade-Giles system, which is still in use in Taiwan. For the most part, the pinyin system is pronounced as it looks, although native speakers of English should take note of the following exceptions:

PINYIN	ENGLISH	EXAMPLE	PRONUNCIATION
c	ts	cang	tsang
q	ch'	qiao	ch'iao
x	sh	xi	she
z	dz	zang	dzang
zh	j	zhong	jong

The "i" is sometimes pronounced like the "er" in New Jersey.

In Chinese names, the family name comes first, e.g., President Jiang Zemin is not Mr. Zemin, but Mr. Jiang. Chinese who come into daily contact with Westerners often choose a Western first name, such as Joe Zhang. Chinese living in the West who do not use a Western first name often put their Chinese given names first.

Notes

PROLOGUE

1. Interview with Winston Lord, Dec. 11, 1996.
2. See Maurice Meisner, *The Deng Xiaoping Era* (Hill and Wang, 1996), pp. 162–83.
3. Reagan made his remarks in Fairbanks, Alaska, on his way home from China. See Lou Cannon, "Finding Capitalism in China Provides an Out on Old Stances," *Washington Post,* May 7, 1984, p. 2.
4. A. Doak Barnett, "A Peek at China's Foreign Policy Process," *New York Times,* Aug. 13, 1984, p. 23.
5. Testimony of Morton I. Abramowitz, National Security Archives.
6. Notes of H. R. Haldeman, June 16, 1971, Nixon papers, National Archives.
7. See, for example, Harry Harding, *A Fragile Relationship: The United States and China Since 1972* (Brookings Institution, 1992); and Robert S. Ross, *Negotiating Cooperation: The United States and China, 1969–1989* (Stanford University Press, 1995).
8. The CIA attempted for five years to keep this study secret. It was declassified and released, in sanitized form, after the *Los Angeles Times* filed suit in U.S. District Court in Washington in 1994. The study has since been published: Richard H. Solomon, *Chinese Political Negotiating Behavior, 1967–1984* (Rand Corporation, 1995). The 125-page chronology attached to the CIA study, perhaps more important for historical purposes than the study itself, was not published.
9. See Solomon, *Chinese Political Negotiating Behavior,* pp. 44–47.

CHAPTER ONE

1. President Nixon's daily diary, Feb. 18, 1972, National Archives. On Nixon's unhappiness with the residence, see Henry Kissinger, *White House Years* (Little, Brown and Company, 1979), p. 1053.
2. The question mark is Nixon's. He apparently wasn't sure exactly how much the United States wanted or could expect from China concerning Indochina.
3. See President's personal files, Box 7, Nixon papers, National Archives.

4. Bundy memorandum for the record, Sept. 15, 1964, National Security Archives. See also Gordon H. Chang, *Friends and Enemies: The United States, China and the Soviet Union, 1948–1972* (Stanford University Press, 1990), p. 250.

5. China sent the protest note after a Chinese diplomat defected to the West. Declassified telegram, "U.S.-Chicom Talks," Feb. 20, 1969, in collection of declassified cables concerning Warsaw Talks, National Security Archives.

6. Richard M. Nixon, "Asia After Vietnam," *Foreign Affairs,* vol. 46, October 1967, p. 121.

7. Interview with Roger Sullivan, Oct. 9, 1996. Singapore's longtime leader and former Prime Minister Lee Kuan Yew also recalls talking with Nixon in Singapore in 1967. "We discussed the Vietnam War. But his main interest was China . . . what should U.S. policy be?" Speech to Nixon Center for Peace and Freedom, Washington, D.C., Nov. 11, 1996.

8. Interview with Arthur W. Hummel Jr., Apr. 22, 1994. Hummel's conversation with Nixon was first reported in Nancy Bernkopf Tucker, *Taiwan, Hong Kong and the United States, 1945–1992* (Twayne Publishers, 1994), p. 272, fn. 29.

9. Chang, *Friends and Enemies,* p. 283.

10. Recounted in Charles W. Freeman Jr., "The Process of Rapprochement," in Gene T. Hsiao and Michael Witunsky, eds., *Sino-American Normalization and Its Policy Implications* (Praeger, 1983), p. 2.

11. Vernon A. Walters, *Silent Missions* (Doubleday & Company, 1978), p. 525.

12. Richard M. Nixon, *The Memoirs of Richard Nixon* (Touchstone [Simon & Schuster], 1978), p. 257. Hereafter cited as Nixon, *RN*.

13. Alexander M. Haig Jr., *Inner Circles* (Warner Books, 1992), p. 257.

14. Kissinger, *White House Years,* p. 1086.

15. See declassified cable, Stoessel to Washington, Feb. 20, 1969, in Warsaw talks papers, National Security Archives.

16. Kissinger, *White House Years,* p. 169.

17. Bundy memorandum for the record, Sept. 15, 1964, at National Security Archives. See also Chang, *Friends and Enemies,* p. 250.

18. Kissinger, *White House Years,* pp. 172–73; Robert M. Gates, *From the Shadows* (Simon & Schuster, 1996), p. 36.

19. Anatoly Dobrynin, *In Confidence* (Time Books, 1995), p. 207.

20. See Allen S. Whiting, "Sino-American Detente," in *China Quarterly,* June 1980, p. 336; John H. Holdridge, *Crossing the Divide* (Rowman & Littlefield, 1997), p. 35.

21. Nixon papers, White House Central Files, Confidential Files 1969–71, Box 6 CO34,6, CO 34, National Archives.

22. Cable, Stoessel to Secretary of State, Dec. 3, 1969, in Warsaw talks files, National Security Archives.

23. Stoessel-Lei Talks, Report of 135th Meeting, Jan. 20, 1970; and Memorandum for the President, Guidance for Sino-U.S. Ambassadorial Meeting, National Security Archives.

24. Stoessel-Lei Talks, Feb. 20, 1970, in National Security Archives.

25. Department of State memorandum, March 5, 1990, Warsaw talks files, National Security Archives.

26. See John H. Holdridge, *War and Peace with China* (Dacor-Bacon House, 1994), p. 113.

27. Interview with James Lilley, Dec. 30, 1996.

28. CIA Study, "US–PRC Political Negotiations, 1967–84, An Annotated Chronology," p. 10, released to author under Freedom of Information Act.

CHAPTER TWO

1. This and the following paragraphs are taken from author's interview with Sultan Muhammed Khan, Nov. 13, 1996.

2. CIA Chronology, p. 11.

3. National Security Study Memoranda 106, 107, National Security Archives.

4. Interview with James Lilley, Dec. 30, 1996; interview with Roger Sullivan, Oct. 9, 1996.

5. Kissinger, *White House Years,* p. 270.

6. Rosemary Foot, *The Practice of Power* (Oxford University Press, 1995), pp. 17–18.

7. Memo, Harlow to Nixon, June 23, 1969, National Archives; Chang, *Friends and Enemies,* p. 280.

8. Whiting, "Sino-American Detente," p. 339.

9. Nixon, *RN,* p. 552; Haldeman, *The Haldeman Diaries* (G. F. Putnam's Sons, 1994), p. 307.

10. CIA Chronology, pp. 13–17.

11. Sultan Muhammed Khan interview.

12. Nixon papers, National Archives; Haldeman notes, June–July 1971. (See also *Haldeman Diaries,* p. 316.)

13. Kissinger, *White House Years,* p. 734.

14. Interview with William Smyser, May 7, 1997.

15. Sultan Muhammed Khan interview; *White House Years,* pp. 738–40.

16. Holdridge, "Through China's Back Door," in *War and Peace with China*, p. 122.

17. Kissinger, *White House Years,* p. 745.

18. CIA Chronology, pp. 14–15.

19. Kissinger, *White House Years,* p. 749.

20. CIA Chronology, p. 14.

21. Holdridge, "Through China's Back Door," in *War and Peace With China,* p. 124.

22. CIA Chronology, p. 15.

23. Smyser interview, May 7, 1997.

24. Seymour M. Hersh, *The Price of Power* (Summit Books, 1983), pp. 375–76.

25. Kissinger, *White House Years,* p. 765.

26. Walters, *Silent Missions,* p. 532.

27. CIA Chronology, p. 18; Raymond Garthoff, *Detente and Confrontation* (Brookings Institution, 1985), pp. 261–62; Hersh, *Price of Power,* p. 376; Robert C. McFarlane, *Special Trust* (Cadell & Davies, 1994), p. 150.

28. Conversation with Dennis Kux, October 1996.

29. The best account is in Hersh, *Price of Power,* pp. 468–69.

30. Garthoff, *Detente and Confrontation,* p. 265, quoting Lee Lescaze, "Lin Piao Attempt Seen to Give Russia Secrets," *Washington Post,* March 15, 1972.
31. U. Alexis Johnson, *The Right Hand of Power* (Prentice-Hall, 1984), pp. 553–54.
32. Memo, Charles Colson to Nixon, July 20, 1971, White House Central Files, TR-24, China 1971–74, Nixon papers, National Archives.
33. Interview with Richard Allen, Nov. 12, 1996.
34. See George Bush, *Looking Forward* (Doubleday, 1987), pp. 112–13; Whiting, "Sino-American Detente," in *China Quarterly,* June 1980, p. 340; Kissinger, *White House Years,* pp. 770–74 and 784–87; Haldeman, *Haldeman Diaries,* p. 369.
35. Kissinger, *White House Years,* p. 865.
36. Haldeman, *Haldeman Diaries,* p. 364.
37. CIA Chronology, p. 19.
38. The failed effort to bring Le Duc Tho to Beijing is mentioned briefly in the memoirs of Vernon Walters. "They [Chinese officials] said it was none of their business, and they would not arrange the meeting," Walters says in *Silent Missions,* p. 546.
39. Nixon's notes, Feb. 15, 1972, Nixon papers, National Archives.
40. Haldeman, *Haldeman Diaries,* pp. 367, 413.
41. Kissinger, *White House Years,* p. 1071.
42. Interview with Charles Freeman, Nov. 4, 1996.
43. Nixon's notes, "First Private Meeting," Feb. 22, 1972.
44. CIA Chronology, p. 20; Nixon's notes, "First Private Meeting."
45. Nixon's notes, "First Private Meeting." Nixon and Chou Enlai had held on the previous day one "plenary" session, which Rogers and other State Department officials were permitted to attend. The private sessions included Kissinger, but not the State Department.
46. Nixon's notes, Feb. 18, 1972.
47. Memo of conversation, Nixon and Prime Minister Heath, Dec. 20, 1971, Japan collection, National Security Archives.
48. Nixon's notes, Feb. 18, 1972.
49. Nixon's notes, "First Private Meeting."
50. Hersh, *Price of Power,* p. 380.
51. Nixon's notes, "First Private Meeting."
52. Nixon, *RN,* p. 568.
53. President's personal files, Box 72, Nixon papers, National Archives.
54. Solomon, *Chinese Political Negotiating Behavior,* p. 47 (quoting from transcript of Kissinger-Qiao meeting, Feb. 24, 1972).
55. Nixon's notes, "First Private Meeting."
56. On Walters and the planes, see *Silent Missions,* p. 538. For China's threat to drop the trade language, see CIA Chronology, p. 21.
57. Among several scholarly accounts of the negotiations over the Shanghai Communique, the best is in Ross, *Negotiating Cooperation,* ch. 2, pp. 45–50. Kissinger's version is in *White House Years,* pp. 1074–87.
58. See Paul Kreisberg, Georgetown University Oral History Project, p. 14, Lauinger Library, Georgetown University.

59. In addition to Kissinger's and Ross's accounts, see CIA Chronology, pp. 21–22, and Marshall Green essay in *War and Peace with China*, pp. 161–65.
60. Haldeman, *Haldeman Diaries*, p. 422; Kissinger, *White House Years*, p. 1069.
61. Nixon's notes, "Last Meeting-Chou."
62. Nixon's notes, "First Private Meeting." In his memoirs, Nixon revived a version of this thought but changed the setting and circumstances: "As I put it in a diary dictation shortly after returning home [from China] . . . I have only ten months to live (politically)—or at most four years and ten months, and I must get results now" (*RN*, p. 575). This served the purpose of separating the idea that his administration had limited duration from the secret promise to normalize relations with China.
63. McFarlane, *Special Trust*, pp. 92–93.
64. Solomon, *Chinese Political Negotiating Behavior*, p. 47.

CHAPTER THREE

1. William F. Buckley Jr., "Nixon Diplomacy Won't Work," *Washington Star*, Feb. 23, 1972.
2. Memo, H. R. Haldeman to Mrs. Nixon, and Buchanan, "Memorandum for the First Lady," March 28, 1972, Nixon papers, National Archives; Kissinger, *White House Years*, p. 1093; Haldeman, *Haldeman Diaries*, p. 424.
3. Nixon, *RN*, p. 571.
4. Haldeman, *Haldeman Diaries*, p. 424.
5. Kissinger, *Years of Upheaval* (Little, Brown and Company, 1982), p. 70.
6. Memo of conversation, Henry Kissinger and Deng Xiaoping, Nov. 25, 1974, Gerald R. Ford Presidential Library.
7. Memo of conversation, Henry A. Kissinger and Deng Xiaoping, Oct. 19, 1975, Ford Library.
8. Memo, Brent Scowcroft to the president, Nov. 26, 1974, and memo, Brent Scowcroft to the president, Nov. 28, 1974, Ford Library.
9. The following account is based on an interview with Michael Pillsbury, Feb. 9, 1997, and upon groundbreaking research by Banning N. Garrett, "The 'China Card' and Its Origins," unpublished doctoral dissertation, Brandeis University, 1983.
10. Michael Pillsbury, "U.S.-Chinese Military Ties?" in *Foreign Policy*, no. 20, Fall 1975, pp. 50–64.
11. Memos, Kissinger to Nixon, "My Trip to China," March 2, 1973, p. 3, and "My Asian Trip," Feb. 27, 1973, p. 5, Nixon papers, National Archives.
12. See Kissinger memo, "My Asian Trip," p. 6.
13. Kissinger memo, "My Trip to China," p. 19.
14. Memo, Kissinger to Nixon, "My Meeting with Chairman Mao," Feb. 24, 1973, Nixon papers, National Archives.
15. Kissinger says he was first offered this interpretation by Bette Bao Lord, the wife of his aide Winston Lord, *Years of Upheaval*, p. 68.
16. Kissinger memo, "My Meeting with Chairman Mao."
17. Ibid.

18. Kissinger memo, "My Asian Trip," p. 8.
19. Kissinger memo, "My Meeting with Chairman Mao," highlights, p. 3.
20. Kissinger memo, "My Trip to China," p. 2.
21. For a description of the early days of the liaison office, see Holdridge, *Crossing the Divide,* chs. 7–9.
22. Donald Anderson, Georgetown University Oral History Project, p. 7.
23. Interview with U.S. government official.
24. Interview with James Lilley, Dec. 30, 1996.
25. Transcript of hearing of the Commission on the Roles and Capabilities of the United States Intelligence Community, Jan. 19, 1996.
26. McFarlane, *Special Trust,* p. 150.
27. CIA Chronology, page 32.
28. CIA Chronology, page 43.
29. Interview with Richard Cheney, Dec. 6, 1996.
30. "Meeting With George Bush, Tuesday, Oct. 14, 1974, From: Henry A. Kissinger," Ford Library.
31. Memo, Henry A. Kissinger to President Gerald Ford, Oct. 15, 1974, Ford Library.
32. Holdridge, *Crossing the Divide,* pp. 157–58.
33. Memo, Russ Rourke to Jack Marsh, March 20, 1975, Ford Library.
34. See National Security Decision Memorandum 248, "Changes in U.S. Force Levels on Taiwan," National Security Archives.
35. Memo, George Bush to the president, May 23, 1975, Ford Library.
36. Memo of conversation, Henry A. Kissinger, Assistant Secretary Habib, Winston Lord, Deputy Assistant Secretary Gleysteen, Richard Solomon, Jerry Bremer, July 6, 1975, Ford Library.
37. CIA Chronology, p. 52.
38. Lilley Interview, Dec. 30, 1996.
39. CIA Chronology, p. 52.
40. Memo of conversation, President Gerald Ford, Henry A. Kissinger and Brent Scowcroft, Oct. 17, 1975, Ford Library.
41. CIA Chronology, pp. 52–54; Solomon, *Chinese Political Negotiating Behavior,* pp. 49–50.
42. Memo, Hartmann to Ford, Oct. 25, 1975, and memo of conversation, Oct. 31, 1975, Ford Library.
43. See Gerald Ford, *A Time to Heal* (Harper & Row, 1979), p. 335.
44. Conversation with a former State Department official who participated in the Ford visit.
45. Harry E. T. Thayer, Georgetown University Oral History Project, p. 60.
46. For an account of Nixon's trip, see Stephen E. Ambrose, *Ruin and Recovery* (Simon & Schuster, 1941), pp. 481–93.
47. Letter, Goldwater to Kissinger, May 28, 1976, Ford Library.
48. See CIA Chronology, p. 59.
49. Lilley interview, Dec. 30, 1996.
50. See Garrett, "China Card," pp. 65–66.
51. Lilley interview, Dec. 30, 1996.

52. Solomon, *Chinese Political Negotiating Behavior*, p. 79.

53. Lilley interview, Dec. 30, 1996; Solomon, ibid.

54. Interviews with Charles H. Freeman, Feb. 23, 1996, and Lilley, ibid.; Ross, *Negotiating Cooperation*, p. 89.

55. "Jackson on China," *National Review*, Aug. 16, 1974, pp. 907–8.

56. Letter to Madame Mao Tsetung, Sept. 9, 1976, Ford Library.

57. Garrett, "China Card," pp. 80–82; Harding, *Fragile Relationship*, p. 54.

58. CIA Chronology, p. 60.

CHAPTER FOUR

1. Interview with State Department official present at the meeting with Woodcock in Beijing.

2. Zbigniew Brzezinski, *Power and Principle* (Farrar, Straus & Giroux, 1983), p. 200.

3. See Cyrus Vance, *Hard Choices* (Simon & Schuster, 1983), p. 118.

4. Interview with Roger Sullivan, Oct. 9, 1996.

5. CIA Chronology, p. 61.

6. See Jimmy Carter, *Keeping Faith* (Bantam Books, 1982), p. 192.

7. See Vance, *Hard Choices*, p. 79. Some Carter administration officials later speculated that Chinese leaders weren't ready for normalization at the time of Vance's trip in 1977, either, because of their own internal divisions. See Michel Oksenberg, "A Decade of Sino-American Relations," in *Foreign Affairs*, Fall 1982, p. 175.

8. Kreisberg, Georgetown University Oral History Project, p. 17.

9. Kissinger memo, "My Trip to China," p. 19.

10. See Vance, *Hard Choices*, p. 82.

11. CIA Chronology, p. 62.

12. George Bush, "Inside the New Tibet," *Newsweek*, Nov. 8, 1977.

13. Carter, *Keeping Faith*, p. 194.

14. Brzezinski, *Power and Principle*, p. 196.

15. Memo, Vance to Carter, April 15, 1977, quoted in *Hard Choices*, p. 76.

16. The account of Brzezinski's efforts is taken from his memoir, *Power and Principle*, pp. 202–209, and Vance's memoir, *Hard Choices*, pp. 113–15.

17. Brzezinski, *Power and Principle*, p. 209.

18. Ross, *Negotiating Cooperation*, p. 130.

19. Notes of background briefing by Alexander Haig, August 1981, given to author by a Washington journalist.

20. CIA Chronology, p. 65; Nayan Chanda, *Brother Enemy* (Harcourt Brace Jovanovitch, 1986), p. 280.

21. Holgar Jensen, "Polar Bear Tamer," *Newsweek*, June 5, 1978. Brzezinski recounts the episode in his memoirs, but says he joked about Soviet-backed Cuban forces, not Russians themselves, *Power and Principle*, p. 210.

22. Interview with U.S. official who served at American embassy in Beijing during Brzezinski's trip. Woodcock's trip to Tokyo is also described in Chanda, *Brother Enemy*, pp. 278–79.

23. Brzezinski, *Power and Principle,* p. 208, and Annex I, p. 4.
24. Excerpts of transcripts for Brzezinski's meeting with Huang Hua, May 20, 1978, and with Deng Xiaoping, May 21, 1978, quoted in Solomon, *Chinese Political Negotiating Behavior,* pp. 26–27.
25. Ibid., pp. 26–27.
26. See Brzezinski, *Power and Principle,* p. 224.
27. Ibid., p. 230.
28. Sullivan interview, Oct. 9, 1996; Ross, *Negotiating Cooperation,* p. 138.
29. Brzezinski, *Power and Principle,* pp. 230–32; Oksenberg, "A Decade of Sino-American Relations."
30. CIA Chronology, pp. 71–73.
31. See Vance, *Hard Choices,* pp. 110–12 and 117–19; see also Dobrynin, *In Confidence,* p. 419.
32. Vance, *Hard Choices,* p. 118.
33. George Bush, "Our Deal with Peking: All Cost, No Benefit," *Washington Post,* Dec. 24, 1978.
34. Interview with Leonard Unger, March 25, 1997.
35. James Shen, *The U.S. and Free China* (Acropolis Books, 1983), pp. 235–60.
36. Interview with Warren Christopher, Jan. 16, 1997.
37. Ibid.
38. See Nancy Bernkopf Tucker, *Taiwan, Hong Kong* (Twayne Publishers, 1994), pp. 132–34 and p. 277, fn. 31.

CHAPTER FIVE

1. Interview with James Schlesinger, March 26, 1997.
2. This account is based on interviews with two senior U.S. intelligence officials directly involved in the agreement on the monitoring stations, and on the account by former CIA Director Robert M. Gates in his book, *From the Shadows* (Simon & Schuster, 1996), pp. 122–23. The quote from *Defense Electronics* is in Chanda, *Brother Enemy,* p. 444, fn. 23.
3. Interview with James Lilley, Sept. 10, 1996.
4. These Vietnam paragraphs are based on Chanda, *Brother Enemy,* pp. 322–25 and 350–54; Carter, *Keeping Faith,* pp. 206–209; Brzezinski, *Power and Principle,* pp. 405–13.
5. Gates, *From the Shadows,* p. 121.
6. Brzezinski, *Power and Principle,* p. 25 and pp. 410–11.
7. See Daniel Tretiak, "China's Vietnam War and Its Consequences," *China Quarterly,* no. 80, December 1979, pp. 740–67; Maurice Meisner, *The Deng Xiaoping Era,* pp. 108–9.
8. Interview with senior U.S. intelligence official. See also Gates, *From the Shadows,* p. 122.
9. Jay Mathews, "Rights Campaign Spreads in China," *Washington Post,* Dec. 11, 1978.
10. Roger Garside, *Coming Alive: China After Mao* (McGraw-Hill, 1981), pp. 277–28.

11. Ibid., pp. 256–62.
12. Jay Mathews, "Crackdown in China," *Washington Post,* Oct. 17, 1978.
13. Interview with Steven Cohen, March 13, 1997; Roberta Cohen, "People's Republic of China: The Human Rights Exception," *Human Rights Quarterly,* vol. 9 (1987), pp. 478–79.
14. See Roberta Cohen, ibid., p. 450.
15. United Press International, June 30, 1987; *Los Angeles Times,* Nov. 23, 1987, p. 1.
16. Pierre M. Perolle, "Long-Term Educational Exchange with China," in Hsiao and Witunsky, eds., *Sino-American Normalization and Its Policy Implications,* pp. 128–43.
17. Letter, Frank Press to Richard Holbrooke, Oct. 11, 1978, in National Security Archives.
18. "China on Campus," *Newsweek,* Nov. 20, 1978.
19. Jay Mathews, "Peking to Wellesley: Student Is First of Hundreds," *Washington Post,* Oct. 24, 1978, page 12.
20. Jim Mann, "China's Lost Generation," *Los Angeles Times Magazine,* March 1990.
21. "China Tries to Cut Loss of Students Staying Abroad," *Los Angeles Times,* April 1, 1986, p. 1.
22. Nixon's notes, Feb. 23, 1972, Nixon papers, National Archives.
23. CIA Chronology, pp. 39, 54.
24. Carter, *Keeping Faith,* pp. 201–2.
25. Carter, *Keeping Faith,* p. 209; interview with senior Bush administration official.
26. CIA Chronology, p. 76.
27. Brzezinski, *Power and Principle,* p. 414.
28. "Hearing on U.S.-China Trade Agreement," Nov. 1, 2, 29, 1979; Report, U.S. House of Representatives, Committee on Ways and Means, Subcommittee on Trade, p. 212.
29. Barnett testimony, July 22, 1980, in congressional hearings, "The United States and the People's Republic of China, Issues for the 1980s," House of Representatives, Subcommittee on Asian and Pacific Affairs, GPO, 1980, p. 37. See also Barnett, "Military-Security Relations Between China and the United States," *Foreign Affairs,* April 1977, pp. 584–97.
30. See Vance, *Hard Choices,* pp. 388–91; Brzezinski, *Power and Principle,* p. 423.
31. Edward N. Luttwak, "Against the China Card," *Commentary,* October 1978, p. 43.
32. Toon testimony to Congress, Aug. 26, 1980, in "The United States and the People's Republic of China," p. 116.
33. Garthoff, *Detente and Confrontation,* p. 821.
34. Dobrynin, *In Confidence,* pp. 445, 449.
35. Brzezinski, *Power and Principle,* p. 431.
36. Interview with Roger Sullivan, Oct. 10, 1996; Brzezinski, *Power and Principle,* p. 424.
37. Jonathan D. Pollack, "The Lessons of Coalition Politics: Sino-American Security Relations" (Rand Corporation, February 1984).

38. The account of Perry's trip is taken from an interview with William Perry, Jan. 30, 1997.

39. Ibid.

40. Ibid.

41. Sullivan interview, Oct. 9, 1996.

42. U.S. Department of Defense, "Trip Report: Visit of the United States Military Technology Delegation to the People's Republic of China, September 6–19, 1980," p. iii.

43. Ibid., pp. iii, 1.

44. Interview with Robert Gates, Feb. 7, 1997; see also Gates, *From the Shadows,* p. 123.

45. Interview with William Webster, Nov. 20, 1997.

46. Interview with Carl Ford, Oct. 3, 1996, and with another former U.S. intelligence official.

47. Gates interview, Feb. 7, 1997.

CHAPTER SIX

1. Associated Press, April 21, 1978.

2. Interview with Richard Allen, Nov. 12, 1996.

3. Don Oberdorfer, "Two Top Reagan Advisers Are on Taiwan's Payroll," *Washington Post,* June 6, 1980, p. 1.

4. Allen interview, Nov. 12, 1996.

5. Interview with James Lilley, Dec. 30, 1996.

6. The account of the meeting with Reagan in Los Angeles is based upon interviews with Allen and Lilley.

7. Alexander Haig, *Caveat* (Macmillan, 1984), p. 194.

8. See *Caveat,* p. 195; Ronald Reagan, *An American Life* (Simon & Schuster, 1990), p. 361.

9. Interviews with Richard Armitage, Oct. 4, 1996, and William Rope, April 3, 1997.

10. CIA Chronology, p. 85.

11. Rope interview, April 3, 1997.

12. Holdridge, *Crossing the Divide,* pp. 203–6.

13. Interviews with Allen, Nov. 12, 1996, and Armitage, Oct. 4, 1996.

14. Reagan's quote is taken from Gene T. Hsiao, "A Renewed Crisis over Taiwan," in Hsiao and Witunsky, eds., *Sino-American Normalization and Its Policy Implications,* p. 94.

15. Interviews with Armitage, Oct. 4, 1996, and Lilley, Dec. 30, 1996. For Haig's airport conversation, see Haig, *Caveat,* p. 208.

16. Haig remark recalled by William Rope in interview, April 3, 1997.

17. Huang Hua, William Rope interview, ibid. Chinese press commentary quoted in Ross, *Negotiating Cooperation,* p. 181.

18. See Michael Weisskopf, "Peking a Popular Destination for Past and Present U.S. Officials," *Washington Post,* Aug. 15, 1981; and Don Oberdorfer and

Michael Weisskopf, "Carter: No Time Limit on Taiwan Arms Sales," Aug. 28, 1981.

19. CIA Chronology, p. 89.
20. Rope interview, April 3, 1997.
21. Tad Szulc, "The Reagan Administration's Push Toward China Came from Warsaw," *Los Angeles Times,* Jan. 17, 1982.
22. Interviews with Rope, April 3, 1997, Lilley, Dec. 30, 1996, and Armitage, Oct. 4, 1996.
23. Rope interview, ibid.
24. Interview with Donald Gregg, April 4, 1997; Rope interview, ibid.
25. Ronald Reagan, *An American Life,* p. 362.
26. Interviews with Mark Mohr, Sept. 16, 1996, and Rope, April 3, 1997.
27. Lilley interview, Dec. 30, 1996.
28. Interviews with Rope, April 3, 1997, Lilley, ibid., Mohr, Sept. 16, 1996, and David Gries, Nov. 11, 1996.
29. Lilley interviews, ibid.
30. Interviews with Armitage, Oct. 4, 1996, and Lilley ibid.; interview with Carl Ford, Oct. 3, 1996.
31. This section comes from an interview with Paul Wolfowitz, Oct. 31, 1996.
32. Interview with a former State Department official involved in the 1982 negotiations; interview with Wolfowitz, ibid.
33. George Shultz, *Turmoil and Triumph* (Scribner's, 1993), p. 382.
34. Ibid.
35. Richard Nations, "A Tilt Towards Tokyo," *Far Eastern Economic Review,* April 21, 1983, p. 36.
36. See Leslie H. Gelb, "U.S.-China Ties: Lower Expectations," *New York Times,* Feb. 2, 1983.
37. Shultz, *Turmoil and Triumph,* p. 390; Oberdorfer, "Shultz Scolds U.S. Group for Trade Gripes," *Washington Post,* Feb. 4, 1983, p. 1.
38. Interview with former State Department official.
39. Interviews with Armitage, Oct. 4, 1996, and Ford, Oct. 3, 1996.
40. Interviews with Rope, April 3, 1997, and Mohr, Sept. 16, 1996.
41. Interview with Lawrence Korb, Sept. 23, 1996.

CHAPTER SEVEN

1. See Solomon, *Chinese Political Negotiating Behavior,* pp. 87–88.
2. "The Talkative Hu Yaobang May at Last Have Tripped Over His Own Tongue," *Los Angeles Times,* Jan. 17, 1987, p. 8.
3. Interviews with former CIA Director William H. Webster and with another senior U.S. intelligence official; Gates, *From the Shadows,* pp. 348–49; Mohammed Yousaf and Mark Adkin, *The Bear Trap* (Leo Cooper, 1992), pp. 84, 109.
4. Yousaf and Adkin, *The Bear Trap,* pp. 83–84.

5. Ibid., pp. 71, 83. See also Steve Coll, "CIA in Afghanistan," *Washington Post,*
   July 19 and 20, 1992, p. 1.
6. See William Safire, "The Madison Group," *New York Times,* Dec. 4, 1980, p. 31.
7. Diego Cordovez and Selig Harrison, *Out of Afghanistan* (Oxford University
   Press, 1995), p. 197.
8. This account of the Stinger decision is based upon Cordovez and Harrison,
   Out of Afghanistan, pp. 194–98, and Coll, "CIA in Afghanistan," *Washington
   Post,* July 20, 1992.
9. Robin Wright and John M. Broder, "U.S. Bidding to Regain Missiles Sent to
   Afghanistan," *Los Angeles Times,* July 23, 1993, p. 1.
10. Interview with former U.S. intelligence official who took part in top-level
    discussions of the covert program in Afghanistan.
11. Declassified State Department memo, "U.S. Export Controls and Technology
    Transfer to China," National Security Archives; Caspar Weinberger, *Fighting
    for Peace* (Warner Books, 1990), p. 255.
12. Weinberger, *Fighting for Peace,* pp. 255, 269.
13. Pollack, *The Lesson of Coalition Politics,* Rand report R-3133-AF (Rand
    Corporation, 1984), p. 117.
14. John Burns, "Vessey in China: A Dual Symbolism," *New York Times,* Jan. 20,
    1985, p. 3.
15. Interview with Lawrence Korb, Sept. 23, 1996.
16. Interview with senior Pentagon official, May 28, 1991.
17. See Weinberger, *Fighting for Peace,* pp. 281–82.
18. Eden Y. Woon, "Chinese Arms Sales and U.S.-China Military Relations,"
    Asian Survey, vol. 29, no. 6, June 1989, pp. 602–3.
19. "U.S. Helicopters Delivered; Haig Says Chinese-U.S. Ties Vital," Associated
    Press, Nov. 15, 1984; Howard Kurtz, "Critics Claim Haig's Influence Boosted
    Copter Maker Unfairly," *Washington Post,* Feb. 12, 1984, p. A4.
20. Kerry B. Dumbaugh and Richard F. Grimmett, "Arms Sales to China,"
    Washington Quarterly, Summer 1986, pp. 91–92.
21. Interview with Richard Armitage, Oct. 4, 1996.
22. "Taiwan to Lobby Against U.S. Naval Aid to China," *Los Angeles Times,* Jan.
    23, 1985, p. 5.
23. Interview with Carl Ford, Oct. 7, 1986.
24. Interview with Paul Wolfowitz, Jan. 22, 1997; Lou Cannon, *President Reagan:
    The Role of a Lifetime* (Simon & Schuster, 1991), pp. 478–79.
25. Ronald Reagan, *An American Life,* pp. 368–69; Goldwater remark from
    interview with James Schlesinger, March 26, 1997.
26. For meeting between Reagan and Hu Yaobang, see CIA Chronology,
    p. III.
27. White House pool reports; Cannon, *President Reagan,* pp. 480–81; Christopher
    S. Wren, "China Again Censors Reagan TV Talk," *New York Times,* April 29,
    1984, p. 10.
28. Interviews with Wolfowitz, Oct. 31, 1996, and Charles Freeman, Nov. 4, 1996.
29. "Reagan Ends Trip with a 'Dream' of Friendship," *Washington Post,* May 1,
    1984, p. 1; Cannon, *President Reagan,* p. 481.

30. Cannon, ibid., p. 482; James Mann, *Beijing Jeep* (Simon & Schuster, 1989), p. 109.
31. Reagan, *An American Life*, p. 369.
32. Shultz, *Turmoil and Triumph*, pp. 388–89; see also Weinberger, *Fighting for Peace*, p. 273.
33. Ibid.; interview with a former CIA official.
34. Interview with a former senior U.S. intelligence official.
35. Interview with a former Pentagon official.
36. Michael Wines, "Chinese Defector Reportedly Named Spy," *Los Angeles Times*, Sept. 5, 1986. See also Roger Faligot and Remi Kauffer, *The Chinese Secret Service* (Morrow, 1989).
37. Stephen Engelberg, "Spy for China," *New York Times*, Feb. 22, 1986, p. 1.
38. Interview with James Lilley, Dec. 30, 1996.
39. Ibid.
40. The British point of view is taken from Margaret Thatcher, *The Downing Street Years* (HarperCollins, 1993), pp. 259–62 and 488–95; and from Geoffrey Howe, *Conflict of Loyalty* (St. Martin's Press, 1994), pp. 361–82.
41. Howe, *Conflict of Loyalty*, p. 376.
42. Solomon, *Chinese Political Negotiating Behavior*, pp. 132–33.
43. Howe, *Conflict of Loyalty*, p. 368; Thatcher, *Downing Street Years*, pp. 488–98.
44. Jan. 26, 1983, "Memo to the Secretary from East Asia/Paul Wolfowitz. Subject: Your January-February Trip to East Asia," National Security Archives.
45. Freeman interview, Feb. 23, 1996; conversation with Jonathan Mirsky, Mar. 20, 1996.
46. Interviews with Wolfowitz, Jan. 22, 1997, and Freeman, ibid.
47. Ford interview, April 20, 1997; interview with a State Department official.
48. Wolfowitz interview, Jan. 22, 1997.
49. Interviews with Wolfowitz, ibid., and Freeman, Feb. 23, 1996.

CHAPTER EIGHT

1. "Peking Campus Scene of Rare Protests," *Los Angeles Times*, Dec. 17, 1984; "Peking Students Protest Effect of Economic Reform," *Los Angeles Times*, Jan. 12, 1985.
2. See "China Radically Alters Economy," *Los Angeles Times*, Oct. 21, 1984, p. 1; "Chinese Grapple with Uncertainties," *International Herald Tribune*, Nov. 27, 1984.
3. "Student Protests Challenge Deng's Policies in China," *Los Angeles Times*, Dec. 5, 1985, p. 1; "Chinese Students Urged to Shun Dissent," *Los Angeles Times*, Dec. 9, 1985, p. 6.
4. Quoted in Richard Baum, *Burying Mao* (Princeton University Press, 1994), p. 200.
5. "Thousands Stage Rally in Shanghai Demanding Rights," *New York Times*, Dec. 21, 1986, p. 1; "20,000 Students Protest in Shanghai," *Washington Post*, Dec. 21, 1986, p. 1; Baum, ibid., p. 202.

6. "Shultz Visit May Help U.S. Assess China's Power Shift," *Los Angeles Times*, Feb. 25, 1987, p. 1.

7. "U.S. Ambassador to Peking Winston Lord Describes a Transformation," *U.S. News and World Report*, Sept. 8, 1986, p. 33.

8. "China Critic Takes Leaders to Task," *Los Angeles Times*, Sept. 24, 1985.

9. Interview with a State Department official.

10. Interview with Winston Lord, Feb. 24, 1997.

11. Kissinger, *White House Years*, p. 721.

12. Kissinger, *Years of Upheaval*, p. 68.

13. Shultz, *Turmoil and Triumph*, p. 396.

14. Interview with a State Department official who served in the American embassy in Beijing.

15. William Safire, "The New-Boy Network," *New York Times*, March 31, 1988, p. 27.

16. See Edward Gargan, *China's Fate* (Doubleday, 1990), p. 20.

17. For the background of the Grass Salon, see Jane Macartney, "U.S. Ambassador's Visit Results in Student Expulsions," United Press International, July 22, 1988.

18. Interview with Winston Lord, Dec. 11, 1996. Lord would not identify the Chinese intermediary. One warning reportedly was delivered in Beijing by Hu Qili, then a young reform-minded leader with close connections to Beijing University. State Department officials also say a warning about Lord's activities was delivered in Washington by Chinese Ambassador Han Xu. Interview with Jeffrey Bader, June 16, 1997.

19. Lord interview, Dec. 11, 1996.

20. Interview with Richard Armitage, Oct. 4, 1996.

21. Lord interview, Dec. 11, 1996.

22. David Remnick, "Reagan, Refuseniks Meet in 'Moment of Hope,' " *Washington Post*, May 30, 1988.

23. Interviews in mid-1980s with American diplomats in Beijing.

24. For a detailed account of China's domestic upheavals in this period, see Baum, *Burying Mao*, pp. 227–29, and Meisner, *Deng Xiaoping Era*, pp. 384–92.

25. See Woon, "Chinese Arms Sales," pp. 603–607.

26. "U.S. Policy in the Persian Gulf," *Department of State Bulletin*, October 1987; Don Oberdorfer, "U.S. Warns Tehran on Missile Menace," *Washington Post*, March 20, 1987; Don Oberdorfer and Molly Moore, "New Accord to Let Kuwaiti Tankers Fly U.S. Flag," *Washington Post*, May 20, 1987.

27. Edward A. Gargan, "Major Deals Cited in China-Iran Arms," *New York Times*, June 10, 1987, p. 8; Clyde H. Farnsworth, "U.S. Will Penalize China on Missiles," *New York Times*, Oct. 23, 1987, p. 1.

28. Woon, "Chinese Arms Sales," pp. 611–12.

29. Don Oberdorfer, "U.S. Agrees to Lift Sanctions Against Beijing," *Washington Post*, March 10, 1988, p. A41.

30. See Congressional Research Service, "Chinese Missile and Nuclear Proliferation," July 19, 1993.

31. The details of the Saudi purchase are taken from HRH General Khaled bin Sultan, *Desert Warrior* (HarperCollins, 1995), pp. 138–42.

32. Interview with Richard Armitage, Oct. 4, 1996.

33. Shultz meeting with and letter to Wu Xueqian: declassified March 28, 1988, letter from Secretary of State to Chinese Foreign Minister, National Security Archives.

34. See *Beijing Review,* Nov. 10, 1986, p. 30.

35. See "U.S. Opposes Chinese Missile Sale to Syria," *Los Angeles Times,* June 23, 1988, p. 1, and "China-Syria Missile Deal Concluded," *Los Angeles Times,* July 14, 1988, p. 1; see also Woon, "Chinese Arms Sales," and Congressional Research Service, "Chinese Missile."

36. Press conference, Secretary of State George Shultz at Shangri-La Hotel, Beijing, July 15, 1988.

37. David Holley, "China to Limit Arms Sales, Carlucci Says," *Los Angeles Times,* Sept. 8, 1988, p. 9; interview with Stapleton Roy, June 18, 1997.

38. "U.S. Approval of Chinese Launches Determined by Value of Satellites," *Aviation Week and Space Technology,* Oct. 3, 1988, p. 25.

39. Ibid.

40. Interview with William Webster, Nov. 20, 1996.

41. Interview with Karl Jackson, Sept. 25, 1996; see also "Chinese Government Delegation Arrives in Washington," New China News Service, May 17, 1987.

42. Jackson interview, ibid.

CHAPTER NINE

1. *Los Angeles Times,* Sept. 8, 1988, p. 9.

2. For the Han Xu gathering, see David Broder, "Bush's China Agony," *Washington Post,* June 28, 1989.

3. Interview with James Lilley, Sept. 10, 1996; Betty Cuniberti, "Bush's Dash Across Asia," *Los Angeles Times,* Feb. 20, 1989, View section, p. 1.

4. Fang Lizhi, "China's Despair and China's Hope," *New York Review of Books,* Feb. 2, 1989, pp. 3–4.

5. Interview with State Department official who served in the American embassy in Beijing in 1989.

6. Interview with Winston Lord, Dec. 11, 1996.

7. Ibid.; interview with James Kelly, Nov. 6, 1996; interview with Jeffrey Bader, Dec. 2, 1996.

8. "Bush, on China Trip, to See Key Dissident," *Los Angeles Times,* Feb. 21, 1989; see also "U.S. Thought It Had Deal on Inviting Dissident," *Los Angeles Times,* March 4, 1989.

9. Lord interview, Dec. 11, 1996.

10. Lilley interview, Sept. 10, 1996, and with a State Department official.

11. This account of the negotiations is taken from interviews with Lord, Kelley and two State Department officials.

12. Interview with a senior State Department official who took part in the Bush trip; Lord interview, Dec. 11, 1996.

13. Written memo of events of Feb. 26, 1989, by Perry Link; see also David Holley and James Gerstenzang, "Chinese Bar Dissident from President's Farewell Banquet," *Los Angeles Times,* Feb. 27, 1989, p. 1.

14. Interview with a former U.S. diplomat who served in 1989 at the American embassy in Beijing.

15. Lilley interview, Sept. 10, 1996.

16. R.W. Apple Jr., " 'Blunder' at Beijing Dinner: U.S. Chides Embassy," *New York Times,* March 3, 1989, p. 3.

17. Department of State cable 03662 and cable 04485, Beijing Embassy to State Department and White House, released to author under Freedom of Information Act.

18. Lord interview, Dec. 11, 1996.

19. "U.S. Thought It Had Deal on Inviting Dissident," *Los Angeles Times,* March 4, 1989, p. 8.

20. Lord interview, Dec. 11, 1996.

21. "Warming Sino-Soviet Ties Stir U.S. Concerns," *Los Angeles Times,* Dec. 18, 1988, p. 1.

22. Interview with Mark Mohr, Sept. 18, 1996.

23. "China Welcomes Appointment of Lilley," Associated Press, March 18, 1989.

24. Story told by a participant in the meeting.

25. Lilley interview, Sept. 10, 1996. During this time period, Lord also complained in a similar fashion to other senior Bush administration officials; interview with Richard Armitage, Oct. 4, 1996.

26. Lilley interview, Sept. 10, 1996.

27. Memo, State Department to White House, March 30, 1989, regarding presidential aircraft; memo, State Department to White House, April 6, 1989, regarding tennis game; memo, State Department to White House, May 13, 1989, regarding talking points, National Security Archives.

28. Declassified State Department cable 10518, National Security Archives.

29. See Daniel Southerland, "Navy Ships to Visit China After Gorbachev Summit," *Washington Post,* May 11, 1989, p. 25; Thomas L. Friedman, "Unfazed by Soviet-Chinese Thaw, U.S. Sees Both Nations as Needing the West More than Each Other," *New York Times,* May 16, 1989, p. 8.

30. "U.S. Navy Calls on Shanghai," Reuters, May 19, 1989; "U.S. Warships Arrive in Shanghai," Associated Press, May 20, 1989.

31. This section based upon Lilley interview, Sept. 10, 1996.

32. "Students' Patriotic Enthusiasm to Be Protected, Wan Says," Xinhua News Service, May 21, 1989.

33. For a cogent account of these events, see Baum, *Burying Mao,* pp. 267–72.

34. The events inside the Chinese embassy are based on the account of a former Chinese official who was serving in the embassy in 1989.

35. Daniel Southerland, "Students Call Rallies in China," *Washington Post,* May 28, 1989, p. 1.

36. Mohr interview, Sept. 18, 1996.

37. Lilley interview, Sept. 10, 1996.

38. Interview with a State Department official who saw Lilley's cable.

39. Interview with Thomas Fingar, Nov. 19, 1996; interview with Douglas Paal, Sept. 19, 1996.

40. "Secretary's Morning Summary," June 2, 1989, National Security Archives.

41. Bush press conference, June 5, 1989, transcript of Federal News Service.

42. Lilley interview, Sept. 10, 1996.

43. The Chinese Red Cross originally estimated the death toll at 2,600, based on hospital reports. The Swiss ambassador to Beijing, representing the International Red Cross, visited hospitals and estimated 2,700. The Chinese government denied the figure, and the International Red Cross was obliged to disavow the figure because of a lack of documentation. See Timothy Brook, *Quelling the People* (Oxford University Press, 1992), p. 155. According to Lilley, the U.S. government estimated that at least 700 people were killed.

44. "Lack of Tear Gas Led Troops to Use Guns, Li Tells Visitors," *Chicago Tribune,* July 3, 1989.

45. Henry A. Kissinger, "Turmoil on Top," *Los Angeles Times,* July 30, 1989, Opinion section, p. 1.

CHAPTER TEN

1. Interview with Bob Kimmitt, Oct. 4, 1996.

2. "Bush Declines Comment on China Crisis," Reuters, June 4, 1989.

3. Interview with Carl Ford, Oct. 7, 1996.

4. Interview with Richard Schifter, Nov. 5, 1996.

5. "China Taps Into World Coffers," *Los Angeles Times,* Oct. 20, 1992, p. 1.

6. Interviews with Kimmitt, Oct. 4, 1996, and Schifter, Nov. 5, 1996; interview with Douglas Paal, Sept. 19, 1996; interview with Jeffrey Bader, Dec. 2, 1996.

7. Transcript of Summit Declaration on China, July 15, 1989, Federal News Service; Edward Cody, "Eastern Europe Is U.S. Priority at Summit," *Washington Post,* July 14, 1989, p. 1.

8. This section on Mitchell is based upon an interview with Ed King, Oct. 3, 1996.

9. Tom Raum, untitled, Associated Press, June 5, 1989.

10. King interview, Oct. 3, 1996.

11. Interview with James Lilley, Sept. 10, 1996.

12. See David Alan Grier, "Politics, Control and Computer Networks: The Chinese Student Lobby of 1989," *Communications of the ACM,* vol. 41, no. 13 (February 1998).

13. This section is based on interviews with Bader and Lilley and upon the account of Perry Link contained in a special section of *Los Angeles Times,* June 25, 1989.

14. Interview with Fang Lizhi, June 25, 1997.

15. Ibid.

16. Lilley interview, Sept. 10, 1996; "China Protests Over U.S. Sheltering of Dissident," Associated Press, June 8, 1989.

17. Presidential press conference, June 8, 1989.

18. James A. Baker III, *The Politics of Diplomacy* (G. P. Putnam's Sons, 1995), p. 107.

19. See James Gerstenzang, "Bush Orders a Cut in China Contacts, Will Oppose Loans," *Los Angeles Times,* June 21, 1989, p. 1; David B. Ottaway, "Bush Bars High-Level Contacts with Beijing," *Washington Post,* June 21, 1989, p. 1.
20. Paal interview, Sept. 19, 1996.
21. Michael Gelb, "Bush Cuts Off High-Level Contacts," Reuters, June 20, 1989.
22. For the details of the Scowcroft mission, see Baker, *Politics of Diplomacy,* pp. 108–10.
23. Interviews with Bader, Dec. 2, 1996, and Kimmitt, Oct. 4, 1996.
24. "Themes," State Department memo prepared for Lawrence Eagleburger, June 29, 1989, released (with deletions) to author under Freedom of Information Act.
25. Lilley interview, Sept. 10, 1996.
26. Paal interview, Sept. 19, 1996
27. Lilley interview, Sept. 10, 1996.
28. Ibid.
29. Ibid.
30. Baker, *Politics of Diplomacy,* p. 109; Lilley interview, ibid.
31. Interview with a senior State Department official who served in the Bush administration, Sept. 20, 1996.

CHAPTER ELEVEN

1. Interview with Zhao Haiqing, Dec. 30, 1996.
2. Transcript, ABC *Nightline* interview with Wu'er Kaixi, July 28, 1989.
3. See, for example, "The Roll Call 50," *Roll Call,* Jan. 23, 1995.
4. Jim Drinkard, "House Panel Approves Bills to Help Chinese Students," Associated Press, July 21, 1989.
5. Zhao interview, Nov. 27, 1996.
6. Interview with Jeffrey Bader, Dec. 2, 1996.
7. These arguments were made by senior Bush administration officials in private conversations with the author in 1989.
8. "House Votes to Override Bush on Chinese Students," *Los Angeles Times,* Jan. 25, 1990, p. 1.
9. Secret State Department cable, "PRC Suspends Post Graduate Student Exchange," Dec. 3, 1989, National Security Archives.
10. "Bush Rejects Extension for China Students," *Los Angeles Times,* Dec. 1, 1989, p. 1.
11. Presidential veto message, Nov. 30, 1989.
12. Tina Daunt, "Whatever It Takes: Millionaire Throws His Money Behind Bid to Unseat Lagomarsino," *Los Angeles Times,* May 25, 1992, p. B1.
13. Interview with a senior State Department official who served during the Bush administration.
14. Interview with James Lilley, Sept. 10, 1996.
15. Interview with Douglas Paal, Sept. 19, 1996.
16. "China Officers Again Work in U.S. on Arms," *Los Angeles Times,* Oct. 27, 1989, p. 1.

17. See "U.S. to Loosen China Sanctions: Bush Is Expected to Clear the Way for the Chinese to Launch American-Made Satellites," *Los Angeles Times,* Dec. 12, 1989, p. 1.

18. George Gedda, "Chinese Jam VOA First Time in at Least 10 Years," Associated Press, May 22, 1989.

19. Halloween incident from interview with U.S. embassy official; Baker, *Politics of Diplomacy,* p. 107.

20. Interview with Fang Lizhi, June 25, 1997.

21. Thomas Friedman, "China Trip Seeks to Alter Americans' Perceptions," *New York Times,* Dec. 10, 1989, p. 23.

22. Lilley interview, Sept. 10, 1996.

23. Text of banquet toast, Dec. 10, 1989.

24. Lilley interview, Sept. 10, 1996.

25. Interview with U.S. government official who worked on the Scowcroft mission.

26. Elaine Sciolino, "President Defends Aides' China Visit," *New York Times,* Dec. 12, 1989, p. 9; Jim Mann, "U.S. to Loosen China Sanctions," *Los Angeles Times,* Dec. 12, 1989, p. 1.

27. "The China Mission," *Washington Post* editorial, Dec. 11, 1989, p. 14; "Betting on What in China?" *New York Times* editorial, Dec. 15, 1989, p. 42.

28. Winston Lord, "Misguided Mission," *Washington Post,* Dec. 19, 1989.

29. Prepared testimony of Winston Lord to Senate Judiciary Committee hearing on HR 2712, the Emergency Chinese Immigration Relief Act, Jan. 23, 1990.

30. "U.S. China Envoy Leave for Uncertain Future," United Press International, April 16, 1989.

31. Lord conversation with author at Johns Hopkins University in 1990; Lord, "Misguided Mission," *Washington Post,* Dec. 19, 1989, p. 23.

CHAPTER TWELVE

1. Henry A. Kissinger, "A World of Changing Leaders, Struggling Governments and Strange Bedfellows," *Los Angeles Times,* July 30, 1989, Opinion section, p. 1.

2. White House press conference, Jan. 24, 1990; Kissinger, ibid.; Robert S. Greenberger, "Bush Finds It Harder to Defend China Policy," *Wall Street Journal,* May 17, 1990, p. A20.

3. Testimony of Lawrence Eagleburger, "U.S. Policy Toward China," hearing of the Committee on Foreign Relations of the United States Senate, Feb. 7, 1990; GPO, Washington, 1990, pp. 13, 24–25.

4. Ibid., pp. 13–14.

5. Interview with Douglas Paal, Sept. 19, 1996.

6. Author interview with senior Bush administration official in 1990; "U.S. Sours on Beijing, Takes Tougher Stance," *Los Angeles Times,* Oct. 1, 1991, p. 1.

7. Winston Lord, "China and America: Beyond the Big Chill," *Foreign Affairs,* Fall 1989, vol. 68, no. 4, pp. 1–26; Winston Lord, prepared testimony before Senate Judiciary Committee, Jan. 23, 1990.

8. Interview with Zhao Haiqing, Dec. 30, 1996.

9. Ibid.

10. See Igor Korchilov, *Translating History* (Scribner, 1997), p. 255.

11. "Bush Wins Battle on China Students," *Los Angeles Times,* Jan. 26, 1990, p. 1.

12. See Jim Mann, "America and China's MFN Benefits: 1989–94," paper for American Assembly conference on China in 1995.

13. Zhao interview, Dec. 30, 1996.

14. "Most-Favored-Nation Status for the People's Republic of China," Hearings of the Committee on Foreign Affairs, May 16 and May 24, 1990, GPO 1990; "China Buys More Subsidized Wheat," Associated Press, May 22, 1990.

15. Zhao interview, Dec. 30, 1996; interview with Nancy Pelosi, May 21, 1996.

16. See Eagleburger testimony, pp. 10–11; Jim Mann, "U.S. to Loosen China Sanctions," *Los Angeles Times,* Dec. 12, 1989, p. 1; Andrew Rosenthal, "President to Waive Some China Curbs," *New York Times,* Dec. 20, 1989, p. 1; Clyde H. Farnsworth, "Ex-Im Bank Resumes Aid to China," *New York Times,* Feb. 6, 1980, p. D1.

17. Daniel Southerland, "Large Security Force Maintains Tight Control," *Washington Post,* Jan. 12, 1990, p. 25.

18. China also said on Jan. 18, 1990, that it was releasing 573 detainees from the Tiananmen demonstrations. Bush administration officials soon found, however, that they were unable to obtain specific or detailed information about these cases, and by the time of Eagleburger's testimony Feb. 7, the administration was treating these purported releases with considerable skepticism. See Eagleburger testimony, Feb. 7, 1990, GPO, p. 10.

19. Conversation with Robert Strauss, 1990; Jim Mann, "U.S.-China Relations Reach an Unhappy Upcoming Anniversary," *Los Angeles Times,* March 18, 1990, Opinion section, p. 1.

20. Mann, ibid.

21. Kissinger, *White House Years,* p. 750; Nixon, *RN,* p. 562.

22. Text of presidential news conference, Federal News Service, Jan. 28, 1997.

23. This account of the negotiations is based upon interviews with Jeffrey Bader, June 16, 1997; James Lilley, Sept. 10, 1996; and Fang Lizhi, June 25, 1997.

24. Bader interview, ibid.

25. Lilley interview, Sept. 10, 1996; Jay Mathews, "Jiang Meets With American Businessman," *Washington Post,* July 30, 1989, p. 20.

26. Interviews with Lilley, Sept 10, 1996, and Fang, June 25, 1997.

27. Interviews with Lilley, ibid., and Bader, June 16, 1997. Eventually, Chinese officials permitted Fang Lizhi's wife to leave the country; she, too, was escorted to the Beijing airport by an American embassy official.

28. Jim Abrams, "Dissident Fang Lizhi and Wife Allowed to Leave China," Associated Press, June 25, 1990.

29. Political declaration of Houston Summit, July 10, 1990.

30. See "China Taps Into World Coffers," *Los Angeles Times,* Oct. 30, 1992, p. 1.

31. Peter Norman, "U.S. Signals Easier Stand Over China," *Financial Times,* July 9, 1990, p. 6.

32. See "The Chinese Economy in 1991 and 1992," CIA paper submitted to the Joint Economic Committee, July 27, 1992.

33. Wendy Benjaminson, "White House Says Fang's Release 'Significant' for U.S-China Relations," Associated Press, June 25, 1990.
34. Interview with William S. Triplett II, Nov. 13, 1997.
35. Author conversations with Triplett.
36. Triplett interview, Nov. 13, 1997.

CHAPTER THIRTEEN

1. See "Crackdown Leaves China Isolated on World Scene," *Los Angeles Times,* Dec. 11, 1989, p. 1.
2. Andrew Higgins, "Major Fails to Loosen China's Straitjacket," *Independent,* Sept. 4, 1991, p. 9.
3. Baker, *Politics of Diplomacy,* pp. 308–309, 321–24.
4. Interview with Bob Kimmitt, Oct. 4, 1996; Baker, ibid., p. 324; "Bush, Chinese Foreign Minister Confer," *Los Angeles Times,* Dec. 1, 1990, p. 14.
5. See Baker, *Politics of Diplomacy,* pp. 588–89; James Gerstenzang and David Lauter, "Bush Bars Export to China of Satellite Parts," *Los Angeles Times,* May 1, 1991, p. 1; "U.S. Lifts Ban on High-Tech Sales to China," *Los Angeles Times,* Dec. 20, 1991, p. 3.
6. Interview with a senior State Department official directly involved in the diplomacy concerning the Chinese missiles.
7. Baker, *Politics of Diplomacy,* p. 590.
8. "Baker Plans to Get Right Down to Business in Beijing," *Los Angeles Times,* Nov. 14, 1991, p. 6.
9. Baker, *Politics of Diplomacy,* p. 592.
10. Ibid., pp. 591–92.
11. Interview with Dai Qing, Nov. 6, 1997; Lena Sun, "Chinese Freed After 4-Day Ordeal," *Washington Post,* Nov. 21, 1991, p. 46.
12. Baker, *Politics of Diplomacy,* p. 593.
13. Shirley A. Kan, "Chinese Missile and Nuclear Proliferation: Issues for Congress," Congressional Research Service, July 19, 1993, pp. 4–5, 9–10.
14. Baker, *Politics of Diplomacy,* p. 594; Elaine Sciolino, "U.S. Lifts Its Sanctions on China Over High-Technology Transfers," *New York Times,* Feb. 22, 1992, p. 1.
15. Department of State, transcript of press conference by Secretary of State James A. Baker III at Shangri-La Hotel, Beijing, Nov. 17, 1991.
16. Conversation aboard secretary of state's airplane, Nov. 18, 1991.

CHAPTER FOURTEEN

1. See chapter 7.
2. Interview with Eden Y Woon, Oct. 21, 1996; "China Cancels U.S. Deal for Modernizing F-8 Jet," *Los Angeles Times,* May 15, 1990, p. 1.
3. Interview with James Lilley, Sept. 10, 1996.
4. "Israeli Arms Technology Aids China," *Los Angeles Times,* June 13, 1990, p. 1.
5. "China Seeks Russian Weapons," *Los Angeles Times,* July 12, 1992, p. 1; Michael R. Gordon, "Moscow Is Selling Weapons to China," *New York Times,* Oct. 18, 1992, p. 1.

6. Lilley interview, Sept. 10, 1996.

7. See "U.S. Sours on Beijing," *Los Angeles Times,* Oct. 1, 1991, p. 1.

8. The quotes are from Lilley's Penn State speech. See *Los Angeles Times,* ibid.

9. James Lilley, "A Formula for China-Taiwan Relations," *Asian Wall Street Journal,* Sept. 6, 1991, p. 10.

10. Interview with Zhao Haiqing, Dec. 30, 1996.

11. Interviews with Zhao, ibid., and Lilley, Sept. 10, 1996.

12. See Norman A. Kempster, "Briefing Book: U.S. Candidates' Stand on Foreign Issues," *Los Angeles Times,* March 17, 1992, World Report, p. 6.

13. Text of Bill Clinton speech to Democratic National Convention, July 16, 1992.

14. Federal News Service transcript of speech, Bill Clinton, "A New Covenant for American Security," speech at Georgetown University, Dec. 12, 1991.

15. Interview with Ed King, Oct. 3, 1996.

16. Helen Dewar, "Bush Wins on Chinese Trade Status," *Washington Post,* March 19, 1992.

17. Press release, Democratic National Committee, May 28, 1991.

18. Press release, "Clinton Criticizes Bush Decision to Renew China's Most Favored Nation Status," June 3, 1992.

19. "Political News," Associated Press, July 15, 1992; "China Criticizes Dissidents' Talk at Democratic Convention," United Press International, July 16, 1992.

20. Interview with Carl Ford, Oct. 7, 1996.

21. Interviews with Karl Jackson, Sept. 25, 1996, and Douglas Paal, Sept. 19, 1996.

22. Interview with senior Defense Department official, December 1991; interview with Paul Wolfowitz, Jan. 22, 1997; phone conversation with Arnold Kanter, July 24, 1997; Paal interview, Sept. 19, 1996.

23. "Taiwan to U.S.—We're Back," *Los Angeles Times,* July 28, 1992.

24. "France Backs Sale of Fighters and Missiles to Taiwan," Agence France Presse, June 18, 1992.

25. Jackson interview, Sept. 25, 1996.

26. Woon interview, Oct. 21, 1996; Ford interview, Oct. 7, 1996.

27. Ford interview, ibid.

28. Lilley interview, Sept. 10, 1996.

29. Interview with Dick Cheney, Dec. 6, 1996.

30. Michelle Mittelstadt, "General Dynamics Says It Will Lay Off 5,800 Workers," Associated Press, July 29, 1992.

31. "Bentsen Raps Bush's China Policy," United Press International, Aug. 10, 1992.

32. Interview with Eden Y Woon, Dec. 6, 1997. Bush's Undersecretary of State, Arnold Kanter, also said in a separate interview that he was told, at the time of Bush's July trip to Texas, that the decision had already been made to sell the F-16s.

33. Interview with senior State Department official.

34. Interview with William Clark, June 19, 1997.

35. Interviews with Lilley, Sept. 10, 1996; Ford, Oct. 7, 1996; and Kanter, July 24, 1997.

36. Paal interview, Oct. 7, 1996.

37. Interviews with Jackson, Sept. 25, 1996, and Paal, ibid.

38. Andrew Rosenthal, "Jet Sale to Saudis Approved by Bush, Saving Jobs in U.S.," *New York Times,* Sept. 12, 1992; interview with senior Bush administration official; Cheney interview, Dec. 6, 1996.

39. Robert Pear, "U.S. Sales of Arms to the Third World Declined by 22% Last Year," *New York Times,* July 20, 1992.

40. Michael Wines, "The Republicans: $8 Million Directed to Wheat Farmers and Arms Makers," *New York Times,* Sept. 3, 1992, p. 1.

41. Interview with Richard Armitage, Oct. 4, 1996.

42. Associated Press story in *New York Times,* Sept. 3, 1992, p. A20.

43. Bernard Edinger, "China Warns France Over Sale of Fighters to Taiwan," Reuters Business Report, Jan. 6, 1993.

44. Interviews with Clark, June 19, 1997, and Paal, Oct. 7, 1996; see also "Bush OKs Shipment of Arms to China," *Los Angeles Times,* Dec. 23, 1992, p. 4.

45. Clark interview, June 19, 1997.

46. Roy's argument was described in detail by a senior U.S. official with access to his cables from the U.S. embassy in Beijing.

47. Interview with James Kelley, Dec. 6, 1996.

48. Paal interview, Oct. 7, 1996.

49. Harry Thayer, Georgetown University Oral History Project.

CHAPTER FIFTEEN

1. "How Taipei Outwitted U.S. Policy," *Los Angeles Times,* June 8, 1995, p. 1.

2. "Arkansas News Briefs," United Press International, Oct. 12, 1985; "CCNAA Official Congratulates Re-Elected Arkansas Governor," Taiwan Central News Agency, Jan. 14, 1987.

3. Federal News Service transcript of speech, Bill Clinton, "A New Covenant for American Security," speech at Georgetown University, Dec. 12, 1991.

4. John L. Helgerson, *CIA Briefings of the Presidential Candidates, 1952–1992,* pamphlet published by Center for the Study of Intelligence, 1996, pp. 5–23.

5. CNN Transcript of Little Rock Economic Conference, Dec. 14, 1993.

6. Warren Christopher testimony to Senate Foreign Relations Committee, Jan. 13, 1993.

7. "China Issue: Early Test for Clinton," *Los Angeles Times,* Jan. 25, 1993, p. D1.

8. Interview with Anthony Lake, July 22, 1997.

9. Winston Lord speech to Asia Society, Oct. 28, 1994.

10. Testimony of Winston Lord to Senate Foreign Relations Committee, March 31, 1993.

11. Interview with Samuel R. Berger, May 17, 1996; interview with former Clinton administration official, July 30, 1997.

12. George Mitchell, "Dear Colleague" letter to members of the Senate, April 6, 1993.

13. Interview with Nancy Pelosi, May 21, 1996.

14. Interviews with Pelosi, ibid., Winston Lord, June 25, 1996, and Ed King, Oct. 3, 1996.

15. Pelosi interview, ibid.

16. Interview with Zhao Haiqing, Dec. 30, 1996.

17. Interviews with Pelosi, May 21, 1996, and Zhao Haiqing, Oct. 27, 1996.

18. Interviews with King, Oct. 3, 1996, and Zhao Haiqing, Nov. 27, 1996; George Mitchell press statement of May 28, 1993.

19. President Clinton statement on Most Favored Nation Status for China, Office of the White House Press Secretary, May 28, 1993.

20. Henry A. Kissinger, "Why We Can't Withdraw From Asia," *Washington Post,* June 15, 1993, p. 21.

21. Thomas W. Lippman, "U.S. Gives China Renewal of Favored Status in Trade," *Washington Post,* May 29, 1993, p. 21.

22. "Boeing 'Encouraged' on China-U.S. Trade Status," Reuters Financial Service, May 28, 1993; Carol Giacomo, "Clinton Steers Mid-Course on China," Reuters, May 28, 1993.

23. Interview with Stapleton Roy, Nov. 27, 1995.

24. Statistics provided by U.S.-China Business Council, based on figures by China's Ministry of Foreign Trade and Economic Cooperation.

25. Central Intelligence Agency, "China's Economy in 1992 and 1993," paper submitted to the Joint Economic Committee, July 30, 1993.

26. Jim Rohwer, "The Titan Stirs," *Economist,* Nov. 28, 1992; Steven Greenhouse, "New Tally of World's Economies Catapults China Into Third Place," *New York Times,* May 20, 1993, p. 1.

27. President Clinton, statement on Most Favored Nation Status for China, Office of the White House Press Secretary, May 28, 1993.

28. Daniel Williams, "U.S. Punishes China Over Missile Sales," *Washington Post,* Aug. 26, 1993.

29. C. Michael Armstrong speech to U.S. Army Missile Command at Redstone Arsenal, Alabama, Nov. 9, 1993, text supplied by Hughes Aircraft Co.; "Executives Press Clinton to Smooth U.S.-China Ties," *Los Angeles Times,* Nov. 19, 1993.

30. Glenn Bunting and Dwight Morris, "Husband's Business Ties Pose Dilemma for Feinstein," *Los Angeles Times,* Oct. 28, 1994, p. 1; Glenn Bunting, "Feinstein, Husband Hold Strong China Connections," *Los Angeles Times,* March 28, 1997; Geoffrey Crothall, "Senators in Bid to Treat Beijing As Equal," *South China Morning Post,* Jan. 18, 1996, p. 10.

31. Douglas Jehl, "Once Again, President Finds Time to Visit a Troubled State," *New York Times,* Dec. 5, 1993, p. 42.

32. The administration granted the waivers after obtaining assurances that the satellites were being reconfigured in ways so that China would not have access to the technology. See "U.S. to Allow Hughes Satellite Deal for China," *Los Angeles Times,* March 8, 1994.

33. For a definitive account of the North Korean crisis, see Don Oberdorfer, *The Two Koreas: A Contemporary History* (Addison-Wesley, 1997), ch. 13.

34. Charles W. Freeman Jr., 1996 interview for Georgetown University Oral History Project, p. 298; interviews with Anthony Lake and Daniel Poneman, Dec. 18, 1997.

35. Interview with Stanley Roth, May 15, 1996.

36. Interview with William Perry, Jan. 30, 1997.

37. For a thorough discussion of Kissinger associates, see Walter Isaacson, *Kissinger* (Simon & Schuster, 1992), ch. 23 and especially pp. 747–52.

38. Interview with senior official in the Clinton administration, July 21, 1997.

39. Kissinger, "Why We Can't Withdraw from Asia," p. 21.

40. "U.S. Would Accept Any Olympic Choice," Reuters, Sept. 23, 1993.

41. "No Chemicals on Chinese Vessel, State Department Says," *Los Angeles Times,* Sept. 5, 1993, p. 1.

42. Interview with senior Clinton administration official; interview with State Department official. See also "U.S. Prepares Steps to Improve Ties with Beijing," *Los Angeles Times,* Sept. 30, 1993, p. 9.

43. Roth interview, May 15, 1996.

44. "U.S. Prepares Steps to Improve Ties with China," *Los Angeles Times,* Sept. 30, 1993, p. 9.

CHAPTER SIXTEEN

1. Description of Jiang from interview with senior administration official who took part in the meeting, July 22, 1997; "Clinton Presses China on Rights," *Los Angeles Times,* Nov. 20, 1993, p. 1.

2. "Chinese President Sees U.S. Family," Reuters, Nov. 19, 1993; "Executives Press Clinton to Smooth U.S.-China Ties," Nov. 19, 1993.

3. "China, Germany Sign 18 Business Agreements Worth $2 Billion," Associated Press, Nov. 16, 1993; Rone Tempest, "Kohl Seeks China Contracts With No Tie to Rights Issue," *Los Angeles Times,* Nov. 16, 1993, p. 14; "German Chancellor 'Very Satisfied' With China Visit," BBC transcript of Nachrichten-TV interview, Nov. 22, 1993.

4. Wei Jingsheng, "The Wolf and the Lamb," *New York Times,* Nov. 18, 1993. p.27.

5. "New Preference for Asia Meshes with Clinton's Style," *Los Angeles Times,* Nov. 22, 1993, p. 1.

6. Clay Chandler, "Bentsen to Push China on Economic Reforms," *Washington Post,* Jan. 6, 1994, p. D10; Cable News Network interview with Ron Brown, March 14, 1994; Elaine Sciolino, "Christopher Is Drawing Fire in Washington and on China Visit," *New York Times,* March 18, 1994, p. 1.

7. The difference in emphasis between Lake and Berger was acknowledged in an interview for this book by a senior administration official directly familiar with the National Security Council's handling of MFN.

8. This description of the internal discussions between Roy and the State Department are based upon an interview with a senior administration official.

9. Patrick Tyler, "Rights in China Improve, Envoy Says," *New York Times,* Jan. 1, 1994, p. 5.

10. Interview with Winston Lord, June 25, 1996.

11. Interview with U.S. official who took part in Liu Huaqing's discussions with Rubin.

12. The views concerning Christopher are the author's. The analysis of China's negotiating style are based upon Solomon, *Chinese Political Negotiating Behavior.*

13. Interview with senior administration official, July 30, 1997.

14. See Patrick E. Tyler, "With Democratic Stirrings Among Chinese, U.S. Is Pressing Beijing on Crucial Choices," *New York Times,* Jan. 29, 1994, p. 1; Human Rights Watch/Asia, "New Arrests Linked to Worker Rights," March 11, 1994.

15. Interview with Tong Yi, Sept. 17, 1997; interview with John Shattuck, June 26, 1996. See also Charlene L. Fu, "U.S. Human Rights Envoy Meets China's Most Famous Dissident," Associated Press, Feb. 28, 1994.

16. Interview with Warren Christopher, Jan. 16, 1997.

17. Interview with State Department official familiar with the cable.

18. Interview with U.S. embassy official with direct knowledge of the Shattuck-Wei meeting.

19. Tong interview, Sept. 17, 1997. See also Charlene Fu, "U.S. Human Rights Envoy," and Patrick Tyler, "U.S. Human Rights Envoy Meets China's Most Famous Dissident," *New York Times,* Feb. 28, 1994, p. 2.

20. Interview with senior U.S. embassy official.

21. Lena H. Sun, "As U.S., China Trade Barbs, Beijing Gives Dissident Stern Warning," *Washington Post,* March 9, 1994, p. 13; Human Rights Watch/Asia, "New Arrests."

22. Christopher interview, ibid.

23. Interview with senior Clinton administration official, July 30, 1997; Christopher interview, Jan. 16, 1997.

24. Donald M. Rothberg, "Christopher Begins Asia Trip Colored by Chinese Crackdown on Dissidents," Associated Press, March 5, 1994.

25. "Christopher in Beijing; Mood Tense," *Los Angeles Times,* March 12, 1994, p. 1.

26. Human Rights Watch/Asia, report on Wei Jingsheng, July 13, 1994.

27. Li Peng remarks from interviews with two administration officials present in the talks; see also Jim Mann and Rone Tempest, "U.S., China Trade Embittered Words on Human Rights," *Los Angeles Times,* March 13, 1994, p. 1.

28. Interview with senior State Department official who was on the Christopher trip.

29. Interview with senior Clinton administration official, July 30, 1997.

30. Christopher interview, Jan. 16, 1997; Elaine Sciolino, "Sourly, Christopher's Talks in Beijing Come to an End," *New York Times,* March 15, 1994, p. 3; Lena Sun, "China Blames U.S. for Failed Mission," *Washington Post,* March 17, 1994, p. 31.

31. Interview with senior State Department official.

32. Christopher interview, Jan. 16, 1997.

33. Interview with Han Sung Joo, Dec. 8, 1997.

34. Human Rights Watch/Asia, report on Wei Jingsheng, July 13, 1994; Rone Tempest, "Chinese Dissident Is Back in Custody," *Los Angeles Times,* April 6, 1994, p. 7.

35. The account of this internal debate was provided by two separate senior administration officials, both of whom spoke in background interviews.

36. Interview with senior State Department official; Lord interview, June 25, 1996.

37. Letter, Lane Kirkland to Christopher, April 12, 1994; letter, Christopher to Kirkland, May 21, 1994.

38. Interview with Anthony Lake, July 22, 1997.

39. Lord interview, June 25, 1996.

40. Transcript of President Clinton announcement of MFN decision, White House, May 26, 1994.

41. Interview with Ed King, Oct. 3, 1996.

42. Interview with Nancy Pelosi, May 21, 1996.

43. Peter Behr, "Major U.S. Companies Lobbying Clinton to Renew China's Trade Privileges," *Washington Post,* May 6, 1994, p. 19.

44. "Fact Sheet, China MFN Decision," issued by White House Press Office, May 26, 1994.

45. Interview with Morton S. Halperin, Oct. 7, 1996.

46. State Department Human Rights Report for 1996 issued January 1997; Steven Erlanger, "U.S. Report Rebukes China Over Rights," *New York Times,* Jan. 28, 1997, p. 7.

47. Interview with Anthony Lake, Dec. 18, 1997.

48. Patrick E. Tyler, "Abuses of Rights Persist in China Despite U.S. Pleas," *New York Times,* Aug. 29, 1994, p. 1; Human Rights Watch/Asia statement submitted to House of Representatives Ways and Means Committee, July 28, 1994.

49. Interview with senior U.S. official.

50. See "China Called Clinton's Bluff on Human Rights," *Los Angeles Times,* Sept. 11, 1996, p. 1.

51. Lake interview, Dec. 18, 1997.

52. "China Called Clinton's Bluff on Human Rights," *Los Angeles Times.*

53. "Senate Votes to Restrict Trade With China," *Bergen Record,* July 24, 1991, p. 7; "Senate Vote on China MFN Bill Override," Reuter, Oct. 1, 1992; Jim Abrams, "Congress Draws Battle Lines As China Trade Deadline Approaches," Associated Press, May 19, 1994.

CHAPTER SEVENTEEN

1. After the United States broke off diplomatic relations with Taiwan's Nationalist government in 1979, it established offices of the American Institute in Taiwan (AIT) both in Taipei and in Washington to handle the functions that had previously been handled by American diplomats. While the AIT offices have no formal diplomatic status, they are in fact staffed by

Foreign Service officers on temporary leaves of absence from the State Department.

2. Interview with Nat Bellocchi, June 13, 1996.

3. See William Branigan, "Diplomacy by Taiwan Upsets China," *Washington Post,* Feb. 19, 1994, p. 24; Edward A. Gargan, "Taiwan Pushes to Rebuild Its Position in Global Community," *New York Times,* June 26, 1994, p. 8.

4. Interview with State Department official.

5. Interview with Winston Lord, June 25, 1996.

6. Chiang Ching-kuo had visited the United States in 1970, but he was not Taiwan's president at the time.

7. A. B. Stoddard, "Senators Invite President of Taiwan to Visit U.S.," States News Service, June 13, 1994; "Senate Votes to Grant Visas to Taiwan Officials," Reuters, Aug. 5, 1994.

8. See "Taiwan's Wealth Is Forcing the White House to Re-evaluate Its Once-Shunned Ally," *Los Angeles Times,* July 28, 1992.

9. Interview with Stanley Roth, May 15, 1996.

10. Bellocchi interview, June 13, 1996.

11. Roth interview, May 15, 1996.

12. Hearing of the Senate Foreign Relations Committee, Subcommittee on East Asia and the Pacific, Sept. 27, 1994.

13. For the Kuomintang's $3 billion in assets, see *Taiwan Economic Daily News,* Jan. 10, 1997, and "Taiwan Nationalists worth $3 billion," Reuters, Jan. 10, 1997. For investments in Indonesia, see "Taiwan, Indonesia to Co-Produce Cement," Central News Agency, Aug. 27, 1994.

14. Slobodan Lekic, "House Speaker Calls for Taiwan to Be Readmitted to UN," Associated Press, Feb. 3, 1995.

15. Cornell University news release, "Cornell President to Visit East Asia in April," issued March 27, 1995.

16. Interview with senior State Department official, June 18, 1997.

17. Lord testimony to Senate Foreign Relations Committee, Sept. 27, 1994.

18. George Gedda, "Christopher Favors Closer Links With Taiwan," Associated Press, Feb. 15, 1995.

19. Lord interview, June 25, 1996.

20. See Xinhua news agency report on Qian Qichen meeting with Christopher, published in BBC Summary of World Broadcasts, April 20, 1995; "Christopher Aims to Smooth Ties with Chinese Official," *Los Angeles Times,* July 31, 1995, p. 4.

21. Jim Abrams, "House Supports Visit by Taiwan's President," Associated Press, May 2, 1995; Jim Abrams, "Senate Supports Private Visit by Taiwan's President," Associated Press, May 9, 1995. On Bennett Johnston, see Jock Friendly, "Ex-Sen. Johnston Plies Business With China," *The Hill,* Nov. 5, 1997.

22. Roth interview, May 15, 1996.

23. Transcript of interview of the president by newspaper columnists, Sept. 27, 1995.

24. Interview with senior Clinton administration official, July 30, 1997.

25. "How Taipei Outwitted U.S. Policy," *Los Angeles Times,* June 8, 1995.

26. This account of the deliberations is based upon interviews with two senior Clinton administration officials, on July 22 and 30, 1997.

27. "U.S. Spars with Taiwanese to Keep Visit Low-Profile," *Los Angeles Times,* June 2, 1995, p. 1.

28. Interview with State Department official.

29. Li Daoyu remark in 1995 to a private American visitor at the Chinese embassy in Washington.

30. Roth interview, May 15, 1996.

31. K. Connie Kang, "Supporters Greet Leader of Taiwan," *Los Angeles Times,* June 8, 1995, p. B1.

32. Daniel Southerland, "Lee Visit Turns Into a Balancing Act," *Washington Post,* June 10, 1995, p. 8.

33. "Always in My Heart," address of Lee Teng-hui at Cornell University, June 9, 1995.

34. Lord interview, June 25, 1996; Roth interview, May 15, 1996; interview with senior White House official, July 22, 1997.

35. See Elaine Sciolino, "Angered Over Taiwan, China Recalls Its Ambassador in U.S.," *New York Times,* June 17, 1995, p. 5; Steven Mufson, "China Recalls Its Ambassador to U.S. to Protest Visa to Taiwan Leader," *Washington Post,* June 17, 1995, p. 14.

36. Interview with State Department official, Aug. 14, 1997.

37. See Patricia Kuo, "China Tensions, Financial Frauds Batter Taiwanese Markets," Associated Press, Aug. 15, 1995; Kevin Chen, "Taiwan Braces for China Missile Test," Reuters, July 21, 1995; "Taiwanese Pro-Independence Mood Dropped During Chinese Missile Drill," Agence France Press, Aug. 3, 1995.

38. Lord interview, June 25, 1996.

39. The information about Clinton's secret letter of August 1995 was provided to the author both by a senior White House official and by a State Department official with first-hand knowledge of the contents. A version of this letter was also published in a Communist Party newspaper in Hong Kong and is discussed in John W. Garver, *Face Off* (University of Washington Press, 1997), pp. 79–80.

40. Interviews with William Perry, Oct. 7, 1994, and Jan. 30, 1997.

41. Barbara Opall, "Congress Forces Harder U.S. Line toward Beijing," *Defense News,* Sept. 29, 1996, p. 1; Perry interview, Oct. 7, 1994.

42. "China Assisted U.S Efforts on N. Korea, Officials Say," *Los Angeles Times,* June 29, 1994, p. 1; Don Oberdorfer, *The Two Koreas,* pp. 320–21.

43. Perry interview, Jan. 30, 1997.

44. See Robert Burns, "U.S. Gulf Commander Says Iran Tested New Chinese Anti-Ship Missile," Associated Press, Jan. 30, 1996.

45. See, for example, Pillsbury remarks in Bill Gertz, "The Chinese Buildup Rolls On," *Air Force,* Sept. 1977, p. 77.

46. U.S. Department of Defense, East Asia Strategy Report, issued February 1995; "U.S. Starting to View China as Potential Enemy," *Los Angeles Times,* April 16, 1995.

47. Jim Mann and Art Pine, "Faceoff Between U.S. Ship, Chinese Sub Is Revealed," *Los Angeles Times,* Dec. 14, 1994, p. 1; Barbara Starr, "Han Incident Proof of China's Naval Ambition," *Jane's Defense Weekly,* Jan. 7, 1995, p. 5.

48. The information about the letters was provided by a senior State Department official and a senior White House official.

49. Interview with Charles Freeman, May 29, 1996. See also Patrick E. Tyler, "As China Threatens Taiwan, It Makes Sure U.S. Listens," *New York Times,* Jan. 24, 1996, p. 3.

50. See "Chinese Scholar Says China May Use Force Against Taiwan," Kyodo News Service, Jan 13, 1996. After Qiao's threat was made public, the scholar attempted to disavow it by saying that he was misquoted or that a confidence had been broken. "Beijing Threat to Use Force on Taiwan," *Singapore Straits Times,* Jan. 17, 1996; "Account of Qiao Shi's Conversation Was Accurate, Says Writer," *Singapore Straits Times,* Jan. 19, 1996.

51. See Gordon Chang, "To the Nuclear Brink," in *Friends and Enemies: the United States, China, and the Soviet Union, 1948–1972* (Stanford University Press, 1990), pp. 116–42.

52. Freeman interview, May 29, 1996.

53. "U.S. Carrier Group Sails Near China As Tensions Over Taiwan Mount," *Los Angeles Times,* Jan. 27, 1996, p. 5.

54. Account of the meeting between State Department officials and Chinese Vice Foreign Minister Li Zhaoxing provided by a State Department official.

55. For a detailed account of these Chinese exercises, see Garver, *Face Off,* pp. 99–103. See also Michael Richardson, "Defense Specialists Worry Chinese Missiles May Misfire," *International Herald Tribune,* March 9, 1996, p. 1; "Taiwan Port Shrugs Off Missiles," *Los Angeles Times,* March 15, 1996, p. 16.

56. "Beijing's Action and Taipei's Reaction," *Issues & Studies,* March 1996, p. 121.

57. Interview with Anthony Lake, Dec. 18, 1997.

58. Interview with Jeffrey Bader, Dec. 2, 1996.

59. Interview with Winston Lord, Feb. 24, 1997.

60. Perry interview, Jan. 30, 1997.

61. Interview with Pentagon official.

62. Steven Mufson, "Beijing Warns U.S. on Naval Display: Two Carrier Groups to Monitor Chinese Maneuvers in Taiwan Strait," *Washington Post,* March 18, 1996, p. 13.

63. Art Pine, "U.S. Faces Choice on Sending Ships to Taiwan Strait," *Los Angeles Times,* March 20, 1996, p. 8.

64. Maggie Farley, "U.S. Carrier Off Taiwan Trails Analysts' Worries in Its Wake," *Los Angeles Times,* March 19, 1996, p. 8.

65. John M. Broder, "Clinton Defends U.S. Military Presence in Asia," *Los Angeles Times,* April 18, 1996, p. 1.

CHAPTER EIGHTEEN

1. Dan Balz, "Dole Nomination Gets 7-State 'Super' Push," *Washington Post,* March 13, 1996, p. 1.

2. Interview with Robert Ellsworth, Nov. 13, 1997; Jim Mann, "Dole Struggling to Shape His Stand on China," *Los Angeles Times,* April 12, 1996, p. 1; Elaine Sciolino, "Facing Split Over China, Dole Delays Asia Policy Speech," *New York Times,* April 13, 1997, p. 16.

3. "America and Asia: Restoring U.S. Leadership in the Pacific," speech by Bob Dole to the Center for Strategic and International Studies, May 8, 1996.

4. "Dole Urges China to Buy More Grain," United Press International, Aug. 25, 1985; "Dole Riled, Could Sink U.S. China Policy," *Los Angeles Times,* Sept. 23, 1992, p. 8.

5. "Capitol Tribute to Mme. Chiang a Sign of Change," *Los Angeles Times,* July 19, 1995, p. 1; "Dole Supports UN Seat for Taiwan" Associated Press, March 3, 1996. After his losing presidential campaign, Dole became a registered foreign agent working for Taiwan. See "Dole Registers as Taiwan Foreign Agent," *Washington Post,* Jan. 13, 1998, p. 5.

6. See, for example, Gore's remarks in "Dole, Administration Fall Short in Articulating a Creative Asian Policy," *Los Angeles Times,* May 13, 1996, p. 5. Clinton made similar comments during the campaign.

7. Interviews with Ellsworth and with an American official familiar with his 1996 trips.

8. This account is based upon an interview with a Clinton administration official who was part of Lake's delegation, and also upon an interview with Lake on the day he arrived back in Washington from Beijing. See Jim Mann and Doyle McManus, "Official Says U.S. Taking Softer Approach to China," *Los Angeles Times,* July 18, 1996, p. 18.

9. Mann and McManus, ibid.

10. See, for example, Elaine Sciolino, "No Appetite in Washington for a State Dinner Now," *New York Times,* Oct. 1, 1995, p. 10.

11. Interview with senior Clinton administration official, Jan. 2, 1998. See Sciolino, ibid; Keith R. Richburg, "U.S., China, Optimistic After Talks in Beijing," *Washington Post,* July 11, 1996.

12. Mann and McManus, "Official Says U.S. Taking Softer Approach to China."

13. See Tim Weiner, "China Sold Parts for Nuclear Arms," *New York Times,* Feb. 8, 1996, p. 1; Steven Erlanger, "U.S. Won't Punish China Over Sale of Nuclear Gear," *New York Times,* May 11, 1996, p. 1.

14. Rone Tempest, "China Averts U.S. Sanctions By Going After CD Pirates," *Los Angeles Times,* June 18, 1996, p. 1; Seth Faison, "U.S. and China Agree on Pact to Fight Piracy," *New York Times,* June 18, 1996, p. 1.

15. "Top U.S. Security Advisor Upbeat on Ties With Beijing," Agence France Presse, July 6, 1996.

16. Author conversation with Clinton administration official, July 1996.

17. See, for example, David E. Sanger, "U.S. to Spur Beijing and Trade Group Entry," *New York Times,* Nov. 13, 1996, p. 2.

18. "Piqued By Taiwan President's Visit, China Cancels Defense Minister's Trip," Associated Press, May 26, 1995; Bradley Graham and Steven Mufson, "Perry Postpones Visit by Chinese Military Leader," *Washington Post,* March 23, 1996, p. 18.

19. Interview with William Perry, Jan. 30, 1997.

20. He Pengfei, conversation with author.

21. Weinberger, *Fighting for Peace,* pp. 280–81.

22. See, for example, Daniel Southerland, "China Boosts Arms Sales in Mideast," *Washington Post,* April 4, 1988.

23. Interviews with two Defense Department officials involved in Chi Haotian's visit.

24. John Diamond, "Chinese Defense Chief Minimizes Death Toll of Tiananmen," Associated Press, Dec. 10, 1996.

25. See, for example, "Li Peng's Assistant Says No Deaths on Tiananmen Square," June 16, 1989.

26. Jan Wong, *Red China Blues* (Anchor Books, 1997), pp. 256–57; John Diamond, "Witnesses Deny China's Version of Nonfatal Tiananmen Square," Associated Press, Dec. 18, 1996; Baum, *Burying Mao,* p. 288.

27. Transcript of State Department regular briefing, Dec. 12, 1996; Diamond, "Witnesses Deny China's Version."

28. "China Says 1989 Crackdown Raised to Hurt U.S. Ties," Reuters, Dec. 19, 1996.

29. For the best study of how Clinton spent his time in 1996, see Glenn Bunting, "A Hard and Fast Ride on Donation Trail," *Los Angeles Times,* Dec. 22, 1997, p. 1.

30. See David Willman, Alan C. Miller and Glenn F. Bunting, "What Clinton Knew," *Los Angeles Times,* Dec 22, 1997, p. 1.

31. In late 1997, when Taiwan sent a new representative to Washington, he paid calls on Republican leaders and friends of Taiwan in Congress. One of those he visited first was Dan Burton, chairman of the House of Representatives committee investigating campaign fund-raising. See "Taipei Representative Meets with U.S. Congressmen," Taiwan Central News Agency, Oct. 25, 1997.

32. See, for example, Alan C. Miller and David Willman, "Tracing Trails of Donors Leads Inquiry to New Level," *Los Angeles Times,* Feb. 17, 1997, p. 1; Sara Fritz, "Probe of Donors Said to Include Taiwan Envoy," *Los Angeles Times,* Oct. 29, 1996, p. 1; Michael Weisskopf, "Accounts Differ on Role of Ex-White House Aide," *Washington Post,* Nov. 4, 1996, p. 10.

33. Michael Weisskopf and Lena H. Sun, "Trie Gained Entree for Chinese Officials," *Washington Post,* Dec. 20, 1996, p. 1; Susan Schmidt and Lena H. Sun, Clinton Calls Wang Meeting 'Inappropriate,' " *Washington Post,* Dec. 21, 1996, p. 1.

34. Bob Woodward and Brian Duffy, "Chinese Embassy Role in Contributions Probed," *Washington Post,* Feb. 13, 1997, p. 1; Brian Duffy and Bob Woodward,

"FBI Warned 6 on Hill About China Money," *Washington Post,* March 9, 1997, p. 1.

35. See Don Van Atta Jr., "A Tip, but Figure in Inquiry Got Away," *New York Times,* Aug. 15, 1997, p. 28.

36. Opening statement of Fred Thompson at hearing of Senate Governmental Affairs Committee, July 8, 1996.

37. David E. Rosenbaum, "One Phase of Fund-Raising Hearings Ends, with a Shortage of Evidence," *New York Times,* Sept. 7, 1997, p. 28.

38. Jeff Gerth, "Democrat Fund-Raiser Said to Detail China Tie," *New York Times,* May 15, 1998, p. 1.

39. Paul Blustein, "Top U.S. Negotiators to Leave China Talks," *Washington Post,* April 15, 1997, p. E1.

40. Elizabeth Shogren, "Gore, in China, Downplays Funding Flap," *Los Angeles Times,* March 26, 1997, p. 1. The unnamed senior official who gave the revised account was later identified as the vice president himself.

41. "Back from Beijing," *Washington Post,* March 28, 1997, p. 29; "Newt Gingrich on China," *New York Times,* April 1, 1997, p. 22.

42. "Newt Gingrich on China," *New York Times,* April 1, 1997, p. 22.

43. See Rone Tempest, "As Polite Gore Bows Out, Gingrich Enters the Ring in China," *Los Angeles Times,* March 28, 1997, p. 4.

44. This account of the plans for Jiang's visit is based upon interviews with two senior Clinton administration officials.

45. In 1985, Chinese President Li Xiannian had made a state visit to Washington. But at the time, although he held the title of president, Li was not China's top leader; that role was played by Deng, then the chairman of the Chinese Military Commission.

46. This account of Berger's private message was first supplied by a Chinese official and was subsequently confirmed by a Clinton administration official.

47. Interview with a Clinton administration official who took part in Berger's meetings in China.

48. Steven Mufson, "Chinese Shake Up Leadership; Rival to President Ousted from Politburo," *Washington Post,* Sept. 19, 1997, p. 1.

49. This account of the pre-summit diplomacy comes from an interview with a Clinton administration official.

50. According to administration officials, the written assurance was eventually given in a private letter from Qian to Albright.

51. Interview with a Clinton administration official.

52. At his press conference with Jiang Zemin, Clinton seemed to add one potentially important new element to the American position on Taiwan by saying he hoped that China and Taiwan would work out their differences "as soon as possible. Sooner is better than later." Before that time, no American president had sought to put such time pressure on the need for reunification of China and Taiwan. White House officials later insisted that Clinton's remark was extemporaneous and was not intended to change U.S. policy.

53. See "East and West Still Divided Despite Summit," *Los Angeles Times,* Nov. 1, 1997, p. 1.

54. Transcript of Press Conference by President Clinton and President Jiang Zemin, Office of the White House Press Secretary, Oct. 29, 1997.

55. Ibid.

56. Ibid.

57. "The China Summit," *New York Times,* Oct. 30, 1997, p. 30; Ronald Brownstein, "Summit Was Sometimes Blunt, but China Kept Its Edge on Key Points," *Los Angeles Times,* Nov. 3, 1997, p. 5.

58. State Department daily briefing, Federal News Service, Oct. 31, 1997.

59. See "U.S. Effort Led China to Release Dissident," *Los Angeles Times,* Nov. 17, 1997, p. 1.

60. "Meet the Press," Federal News Service transcript, Nov. 16, 1997; "U.S. Effort Led China to Release Dissident," *Los Angeles Times,* Nov. 17, 1997, p. 1.

61. Wei Jingsheng comments at New York news conference, Nov. 21, 1997.

62. Ibid.

63. This account is based upon an interview with a Clinton administration official, Jan. 2, 1998.

64. Interview with a Clinton administration official. On the Ford administration: After intense public controversy, Ford finally gave in and invited Solzhenitsyn to drop by the White House, but by that time the writer was no longer interested. See Walter Isaacson, *Kissinger,* pp. 657–58.

65. Interview with a senior Clinton administration official, March 18, 1997.

66. Interview with President Clinton, June 19, 1998; interview with Samuel D. Berger, May 29, 1998.

67. Jim Mann, "Deal Security Activist's Release," *Los Angeles Times,* April 20, 1998, p. 1.

68. Ibid.

69. James Bennett with Seth Faison, "Clinton Moves Up His Trip to China to Late in June," *New York Times,* March 12, 1998, p. 1; Jim Mann, "China Alters Rights Policy Toward China," *Los Angeles Times,* March 14, 1998, p. 1; Rone Tempest and Anthony Kuhn, "Dissident Set Free by China Flies to U.S." *Los Angeles Times,* April 19, 1998, p. 1.

70. Clinton and Berger both said publicly in the summer of 1998 that while the releases of individual Chinese dissidents like Wei Jingsheng and Wang Dan had been important, they would look in the future for releases of "whole categories" of Chinese prisoners, such as those convicted of counter-revolutionary crimes. See transcript of Clinton press conference in Hong Kong, July 3, 1998.

71. "Fact Sheet: China MFN Decision," White House, May 27, 1994.

72. Jeff Gerth and Raymond Bonner, "Companies Are Investigated for Aid to China on Rockets," *New York Times,* April 4, 1998, p. 1.

73. Jeff Gerth and John M. Broder, "Papers Show White House Staff Favored a China Satellite Permit," *New York Times,* May 23, 1998.

74. Brent Scowcroft and Arnold Kanter, "What Technology Went Where and Why," *Washington Times,* June 5, 1998, p. 19.

75. John Diamond, "Gingrich Urges Clinton to Postpone China Trip," Associated Press, May 19, 1998.

76. Jim Mann, "GOP Shift Curbs Clinton's Goals for China Trip," *Los Angeles Times,* June 8, 1998; Paul Wellstone letter to President Clinton, June 10, 1998.

77. Press conference of Samuel D. Berger in Xi'an, June 26, 1998.

78. Fact Sheet, Agreements of U.S.-China Summit, Office of the White House Press Secretary, June 27, 1998; interviews with two Clinton administration officials during and after the trip to China.

79. Transcript of Press Availability by President Clinton and President Jiang, Office of the White House Press Secretary, June 27, 1998.

80. Ibid.

81. This account of plans for Clinton's trip is based upon interviews with three separate administration officials who took part in the discussions.

82. Transcript of Remarks by the President and the First Lady in Discussion of Shaping China for the 21st Century, Office of the White House Press Secretary, June 30, 1998.

83. "Chinese Spokesman Urges Taiwan to Respond," Xinhua news agency, July 9, 1998.

84. Transcript of Press Conference by the president in Hong Kong, July 3, 1998.

CONCLUSION

1. See Harold Isaacs, *Scratches on Our Minds* (John Day, 1958), pp. 63–238.

Acknowledgments

Two remarkable institutions provided me with the support I needed to write this book. One of them is the *Los Angeles Times,* the newspaper for which I worked as a reporter and columnist during much of the period covered in the narrative. The other is the Woodrow Wilson International Center for Scholars, where I was a guest scholar in 1996–97 as I was putting together the manuscript.

I am particularly grateful to those editors at the *Times* who supported my work and tolerated my book leave, especially Washington bureau chief Doyle McManus and editors Shelby Coffey and Michael Parks. Several reporters shared information or insights, including Rone Tempest, Norman Kempster and Alan Miller. Librarian Robin Cochran was unfailingly helpful to me and to all others in the *Times* Washington bureau.

I am indebted to those at the Wilson Center in the Asia Program who assisted me during my fellowship year, including Warren Cohen, Li Zhao, Beth Brimmer and Mary Lea Cox. Samuel F. Wells Jr. and Ann Sheffield were of great help in arranging the fellowship. Two research assistants, Kameka Sweeney and David Abruzzino, deserve special thanks for the work they did in helping me to track down information and transcribe interviews. Ben Amini, in turn, supported me in finding the right research assistants.

My interest in exploring the history of relations between the United States and China began with a five-year effort, culminating in a lawsuit, to obtain the release of a lengthy, classified CIA study on the negotiations between China and the United States that began during the Nixon administration. That study, "Chinese Political Negotiating Behavior, 1967–84," was conducted by the Rand Corporation for the CIA. At the *Times,* Jack Nelson, then the Washington bureau chief, supported this protracted FOIA effort, and attorney Patrick J. Carome of Wilmer, Cutler & Pickering did the legal work that finally sprung loose the document.

Most of the other documentary material in this book was obtained through the Freedom of Information Act, from the National Archives, from presidential libraries and from the National Security Archives. At the Gerald R. Ford Library,

Karen B. Holzhausen helped me to obtain declassification of documents. At the National Security Archives, Thomas Blanton, Jeffrey Richelson and Robert Wampler deserve thanks for guiding me through the available files on China and Japan. Charles Stuart Kennedy deserves special credit for leading me to the interviews in the Georgetown University Oral History Project.

Many others helped, either by providing information in interviews or by sharing insights and other materials. In some cases, individuals were willing to sit through two, three or four interviews so that I could better understand the history. The following is an alphabetical list of most of them: Richard Allen, Richard Armitage, Jeffrey Bader, Caroline Bartholomew, Nat Bellocchi, Samuel Berger, Dick Cheney, Warren Christopher, William Clark, Patt Derian, Thomas Donilon, Karl Eikenberry, Robert Ellsworth, Thomas Fingar, Carl Ford, Chas Freeman, Banning Garrett, Robert Gates, Donald Gregg, David Gries, Morton Halperin, Han Sung-Joo, Selig Harrison, Karl Jackson, Mike Jendrzejczyk, Arnold Kanter, James Kelly, Donald Keyser, Sultan Muhammed Khan, Robert Kimmitt, Ed King, Lawrence Korb, Paul Kreisberg, Dennis Kux, Anthony Lake, Debra Lehr, James Lilley, Fang Lizhi, Winston Lord, Jay Mathews, Jonathan Mirsky, Mark Mohr, Don Oberdorfer, Douglas Paal, Nancy Pelosi, William Perry, Michael Pillsbury, Jonathan Pollack, Ted Price, Peter Rodman, William Rope, Stanley Roth, Stapleton Roy, Lee Sands, James Schlesinger, Richard Schifter, John Shattuck, Richard Smyser, Richard Solomon, Roger Sullivan, Tong Yi, William Triplett, Leonard Ungar, William Webster, Wei Jingsheng, Alan Wolfe, Paul Wolfowitz, James Woolsey, Eden Woon and Zhao Haiqing. There are a couple of others who cannot be mentioned, but to whom I am equally grateful.

Two outstanding scholars of American diplomacy with China read the manuscript and supplied invaluable commentary on it: Warren I. Cohen and Nancy Bernkopf Tucker. They, of course, cannot be said to subscribe to the book's conclusions or interpretations—an impossibility in any event, since they don't even agree with each other. Lee Sands kindly shared his thoughts on several chapters of the manuscript.

I am grateful to Ashbel Green at Alfred A. Knopf for his encouragement to me in writing this book and for his help in crafting the manuscript. Leyla Aker also deserves gratitude for helping in many ways to make the book a reality. My agents, Lynn Chu and Glen Hartley, assisted in countless ways. Above all, my wife, Caroline Dexter, my daughter, Elizabeth, and my son, Ted, made this book happen by giving meaning to my life.

Index

CHINA WAKES

The Struggle for the Soul of a Rising Power

by Nicholas D. Kristof and Sheryl WuDunn

In this heroically researched book, husband-and-wife reporters Kristof and WuDunn travel from the highlands of Tibet to the bloody environs of Tiananmen Square to produce a canvas that takes in peasants and real estate speculators, dissidents and corrupt officials. Insightful, affecting, and bursting with color on every page, *China Wakes* gives us the rough and rich texture of a peasant empire transforming itself into a world power.

Nonfiction/Asian Studies/0-679-76393-7

CHINA, HONG KONG, TAIWAN, INC.

The Dynamics of a New Empire

by Willem van Kemenade

On July 1, 1997, Great Britain officially returned Hong Kong to China after ninety-nine years of British rule. This event was the beginning of an increasingly problematic reintegration of the old Chinese empire into a new world superpower. The combination of Hong Kong and Taiwan's management and financial expertise with China's geographic vastness and inexhaustible pool of cheap labor has enabled China to develop into a major international trading power. Willem van Kemenade analyzes the power structures of the three Chinas, offering the first comprehensive view of the world's fastest-rising empire.

Business/Current Affairs/0-679-77756-3

HONG KONG

by Jan Morris

Combining firsthand reportage with exemplary research, Morris takes us from Hong Kong's clamorous back alleys to the luxurious Happy Valley racecourse, where taipans place their bets between sips of champagne and bird's nest soup. Morris chronicles the exploits of opium traders and pirates, colonists and financiers, and shows how their descendants view reunification with the Chinese mainland.

East Asian Studies/Travel/0-679-77648-6